MENTAL HEALTH
OF
ETHNIC
MINORITIES

MENTAL HEALTH
OF
ETHNIC
MINORITIES

EDITED BY

Felicisima C. Serafica

Andrew I. Schwebel

Richard K. Russell

Paul D. Isaac

and

Linda B. Myers

New York
Westport, Connecticut
London

Copyright Acknowledgments

Table 10.1 from Bernal, M. E., and A. M. Padilla (1982).
Status of minority curricula and training in clinical psychology,
American Psychologist, 37, No. 7, p. 783. Copyright 1982 by
the American Psychological Association. Adapted by permission
of the publisher.

Library of Congress Cataloging-in-Publication Data

Mental health of ethnic minorities / edited by Felicisima C. Serafica
    . . . [et al.].
       p.   cm.
      Includes bibliographical references.
      ISBN 0–275–93111–0 (alk. paper)
      1. Minorities—Mental health—United States.   I. Serafica,
Felicisima C.
    RC451.5.A2M47   1990
    362.2′0422′08693—dc20   89–26597

British Library Cataloguing-in-Publication Data is available.

Library of Congress Catalog Card Number: 89–26597
ISBN: 0–275–93111–0

First published in 1990

Praeger Publishers, One Madison Avenue, New York, NY 10010
An imprint of Greenwood Publishing Group, Inc.

Printed in the United States of America

The paper used in this book complies with the
Permanent Paper Standard issued by the National
Information Standards Organization (Z39.48–1984).

10 9 8 7 6 5 4 3 2 1

Contents

Contents

Figures and Tables

Figures

Preface

By the year 2000, ethnic minorities will comprise an estimated 30 percent of the total U.S. population (American Council on Education, 1983). In addition to the stressors common to all groups, other factors such as racism, poverty, and the process of acculturation often compound the stress experienced by ethnic minorities. The mental health of ethnic minorities is a growing concern of mental health providers, particularly those who are members of such groups.

This volume is an attempt to contribute to an understanding of the unique mental health needs of ethnic minorities. It is based on papers presented at a conference held at Ohio State University (OSU) on April 7–8, 1986, entitled "Minority Mental Health: A Multicultural Knowledge Base for Psychological Service Providers." The speakers, leading scholars in the field, clearly made this point: Minority mental health, as a field of study, has great promise for producing the kinds of rigorous research that will promote the welfare of ethnic minorities and contribute to an understanding of nonminorities as well. In this volume, they expand on the conference themes.

The goals of the conference and of this volume are the same: to focus attention on cutting-edge research concerning mental health perspectives, psychopathology, assessment, and treatment of ethnic minorities. More specifically, they are: (1) to review the current state of theoretical and empirical knowledge about ethnic minorities, focusing on mental health problems, assessment, and treatment; (2) to articulate some promising new directions for both basic and applied research on the mental health of ethnic minorities; (3) to facilitate the dissemination of minority mental health research findings to service providers; and (4) to provide a vehicle for the integration of new knowledge about ethnic minorities into graduate and professional training curricula.

The book is written at a level such that it can be used as a textbook for an upper-division undergraduate course or a graduate course on ethnic minority mental health. It is also intended as a reference source for researchers, professionals, and graduate or professional students, particularly in psychology, psychiatry, social work, guidance and counseling, education, nursing, behavioral pediatrics, family medicine, and preventive medicine.

Four distinct yet interrelated parts comprise this volume. Part 1 contains essays dealing with psychopathology. Part 2 presents reviews of research on assessment. Part 3 deals with models of therapy for ethnic minorities based upon specific cultural values, practices, and issues. Part 4 offers a comprehensive background of information about what has been happening in the area of minority mental health on a national level. It describes the status of minority mental health curricula in psychology, a professional association's attempts to deal with ethnic minority issues, and the initiatives of a federal government agency in promoting ethnic minority mental health.

To achieve a balanced presentation, each chapter is state of the art. In addition, each part, except the last, has a chapter dealing with the section theme as it pertains to blacks, Hispanics, or Asian-Americans, who were the largest and most visible ethnic minority groups in Ohio in the late 1980s. Each chapter includes a review of theory and research on particular topics, a delineation of conceptual and methodological issues, and recommendations for directions for future research. While striving for balance, the editors were also mindful that strict comparability could not be maintained because research on the three ethnic groups is at different phases in their history. Since the contemporary salient issues are not the same for all groups, the editors chose to identify within an area (e.g., assessment) a critical mass of innovative studies or program of research whose synthesis would be of enormous benefit to mental health professionals. Whenever possible, the choice favored research questions that had been investigated in all target ethnic groups so that group similarities and differences could be identified.

Finally, a distinguishing feature of the volume is its developmental as well as clinical orientation. The emergence of psychopathology can be understood fully only when viewed from the perspective of normal development and its context. Therefore, a deliberate attempt was made to include developmental psychology research with implications for the mental health of ethnic minority children, adolescents, and families. This volume contributes to the continued growth of the ethnic minority mental health field and our fuller understanding and appreciation of cultural and ethnic diversity.

In closing, we acknowledge the funding provided for the conference by the

Affirmative Action Grants Program, one of several initiatives put forward by President Edward H. Jennings to promote affirmative action at Ohio State University. We also thank the former and current chairpersons of the OSU Department of Psychology, Professors Samuel H. Osipow and James C. Naylor, for their support of the conference and the preparation of this volume. We are grateful to all who provided clerical assistance, particularly Cindy Greer and Chris Oakes. Finally, we wish to express our deep appreciation to the contributors and to the Praeger editorial staff for their excellent collaboration and for their sharing in our commitment to this project.

Part I

Mental Health Problems and Perspectives of Ethnic Minorities

Introduction

Linda B. Myers

This section contains chapters dealing with some mental health problems and the related beliefs, attitudes, and practices of Hispanic-, African-, and Asian-Americans. The experiences of these ethnic groups are treated separately by different authors, making possible independent insights into each ethnic group.

In the first chapter Deborah L. Coates integrates and extends three areas of research on adolescents, particularly black adolescents: stress and coping, mental health intervention, and social networks. Reviewing the research literature on stress and coping, she makes the point that black adolescents and their families are particularly at risk for experiencing negative psychological and physical health outcomes associated with stress. Her review of behavioral and cognitive approaches to intervention leads to a consideration of special issues in intervention with black adolescents and a discussion of social networks as an emerging research and intervention paradigm. Research on the social network characteristics of black adolescents is presented. Then, a conceptual model for social network intervention is proposed. In this model, social structure is viewed as a class of predictor variables that influence a set of outcomes that are observable social, interpersonal, and/or academic skills underlying social competence. The relevance of social network schema to theories of adolescent development and mental health is also discussed.

In the next chapter, Luis M. Laosa reviews existing theories and research on psychosocial stress and coping in order to examine their relevance to understanding the processes involved in the adaptation and adjustment of Hispanic immigrant children to their new environment. A conceptual model regarding the factors that account for success in immigrant children's adaptation to their role as students is elaborated and testable hypotheses are derived. Variables that have an impact on adaptation are discussed. These include the characteristics of the sending community, family and child premigration characteristics and life-styles, life changes surrounding migration, characteristics of the receiving community, the "pile up" of life changes, the school context, and the child's and family's cognitive appraisal of their situation. The approach emphasizes examination of psychosocial stressors as they occur over time and the importance of considering the immigrant as a developing organism interacting reciprocally with the environment.

The last chapter in this section, a review of the utilization of mental health services by Asian/Pacific Islander Americans, presents psychiatric epidemiological data in terms of treated prevalence and estimated true prevalence. Research findings are reported for the three disorders that have received the greatest attention thus far: depression, alcoholism, and suicide. The question of mental health resource utilization is explored, as well as the issue of what type of organization structure is optimal for providing services to this population. Ways of increasing utilization rates and directions for future research are delineated.

Taken together, these three chapters provide an overview of the state of research on mental health problems and perspectives of blacks, Hispanics, and Asian-Americans. They also reflect differential rates of progress in ethnic minority mental health research. Mental health studies on blacks and Hispanics have started to go beyond the descriptive phase in research. Besides documenting prevalence of disorders, researchers are beginning to address questions pertaining to explanation and prediction. The conceptual models proposed by Coates and Laosa indicate an interest in theory building. Finally, research on blacks and Hispanics is no longer restricted to adult populations but now encompasses children and youths. Research on Asian-American mental health is, however, just beginning. Available studies are mostly descriptive and focus mainly on adults. Still, the advances in research on blacks and Hispanics instill some optimism about continuing progress of research on Asian-American mental health.

1

Social Network Analysis as Mental Health Intervention with African-American Adolescents

Deborah L. Coates

The purpose of this review is to examine the social network construct as an intervention paradigm for high-risk African-American adolescents. A brief review of the literature on stress, coping, and adjustment and on cognitive intervention in childhood and adolescence is presented. In addition, the unique stressors often experienced by African-American adolescents are discussed. The social network is a research construct. It also is an emerging intervention paradigm. Data are presented for a sample of African-American adolescents to illustrate the clinical potential of social network assessment. A conceptual model is also presented that outlines the usefulness of social system analysis as a cognitive intervention for adolescents. The mental health implications of this approach as well as research, assessment, and evaluation needs are discussed.

STRESS ADAPTABILITY AND COPING

Definitions and Assumptions

A major function of individual adjustment is responding to situational events. Adjustment and its relation to health is well documented in adults (Hamberg, Coelho & Adams, 1974) and in childhood and adolescence (Compas, 1987). Stress is a psychological or physical reaction to life events or chronic life dif-

ficulties (Holmes & Rahe, 1967; Thoits, 1986). The way individuals cope with
stress is a focus of numerous theories of psychological adjustment. The stressful impact of specific and frequent life circumstances has been identified empirically in a number of studies (see Compas, 1987; Thoits, 1986; Tolsdorf,
1976; Walker & Greene, 1987 for discussions of this literature). Theorists describe coping as the continually changing cognitive and other behavior that
individuals exhibit in response to environmental demands (Cohen & Lazarus,
1979; Lazarus & Folkman, 1984). These theorists have also identified several
distinct styles of coping including problem-focused, emotional-focused, and
perception-focused coping (Thoits, 1986).

The role of social relationships in coping with stress is discussed often but
without clarity. Thoits (1986, p.417) has proposed a model that casts social
support as assistance with coping, or "the active participation of significant
others in an individual's stress-management efforts." The model focuses on
cognitively altering situations to seem less threatening to the self through supportive feedback focused on problems or distressing feelings. This model offers
useful conceptualizations of the coping functions of social support for the design of mental health interventions.

Stress and health outcomes. Numerous studies of adults show that the experience of a highly stressed environment is related to a high degree of psychological and physical distress and disorder (Brown & Gary, 1987). Two hypotheses have been suggested that describe how stress and social support relate
to health outcomes. A major viewpoint suggests that social support mediates
stress by providing resources the individual uses to solve problems posed by
the stressful circumstances (Brownell & Shumaker, 1984a). Another view suggests that being embedded in a supportive social network helps individuals to
reduce their negative perception of stress (Lin, 1985). Perception of social support influences social support effects in both instances (Cohen & Wills, 1985).

It is not clear how this psychological buffering process takes place. The
incidence of stressors and the availability of social support may interact with
the personal characteristics of the individual to affect the individual's well-
being. Kaplan, Cassel, and Gore's feedback process model (1977) offers the
best explanation of this effect. In this model stressful life events can prevent
obtaining meaningful information about whether personal action is having a
desired effect. Social support provides information about psychological reality
and the interpretation of events. This feedback is a biological and psychosocial
necessity. Susceptibility to ill health may increase when it is absent. Brownell
and Shumaker (1984a) described the health-sustaining functions of social support: (1) gratifying affiliative needs, (2) maintaining identity, and (3) enhancing
self esteem. Social support is social exchanges that promote well being. This
feedback is often provided by small networks of supportive persons. Negative,
extremely limited, or excessive social contact can result in negative adjustment
outcomes. Mechanic (1974) suggests other distinct functions of support including being a reference point or serving to support, encourage, or relieve con-

cerns. He stresses also that social support can have both negative and positive effects. This implies that some interventions could promote dysfunctional, rather than supportive, feedback.

Empirical Studies of Stress and Coping in Adolescence

Compas (1987), in an extensive review of child and adolescent stress, coping, and adaptation, suggests that while some consensus in theoretical and measurement issues in adult coping has developed, this is not the case for studies of coping during childhood and adolescence. There are fewer studies available of coping that focus on adolescents than there are studies involving adults or children. Compas (1987) suggests that most studies of coping and stress during adolescence have focused on interpersonal problem solving or social support as a mediator of stress and on coping in achievement contexts.

Other studies associate stressful adolescent life events with a variety of self-reported negative health outcomes. Walker and Greene (1987) identify the major negative outcomes associated with stress as: personal adjustment problems; delinquent behavior; poorer health status in the chronically ill; poor school performance; functional disorder; conduct disorder; and bulimia and suicide risk. Studies on the mediating effects of social environment or of social support factors on adjustment are of particular relevance to health intervention and prevention efforts. From these studies we may determine the nature of social support during adolescence and the relevance of specific components to normative adjustment and to maladjustment.

Recent studies of social support and adjustment in adolescence focus on: (1) specific components of the social environment, of the social network, or of social support, (e.g., Felner, Aber, Primavera & Cauce, 1985; Coates, 1985; Compas, Slavin, Wagner & Vannatta, 1986; Shulman, Seiffge-Krenge & Sameat, 1987; Simmons, Burgeson, Carlton-Ford & Blyth, 1988; Walker & Greene, 1987); (2) the relationship between life events or the social environment and health symptoms (e.g., Block, Block & Keyes, 1988; Compas et al., 1986; Walker & Greene, 1987; Windle, 1987); (3) the relationship of social environment to normative adjustment (e.g., Coates, 1985; Dornbusch, Ritter, Leiderman, Roberts & Fraleigh, 1988; Hirsch & Rapkin, 1988; Tolor & Fehon, 1987; Stevens, 1988); (4) gender and race effects (e.g., Block et al., 1988; Blyth & Foster-Clark, 1987; Compas et al., 1986; Walker & Greene, 1987; Windle, 1987) and (5) the social environment-adolescent fit (Lerner, Hertzog, Hooker, Hassibi & Thomas, 1988; Windle, 1987). Most of these are based on early or middle adolescent samples. Few have examined the social relationships of older adolescents or young adults. Compas et al. (1986) and Dean and Ensel (1983) are exceptions and present results based on older adolescent samples.

Characteristics of the social environment. The social environment includes functional and structural characteristics of social relationships and the social organizations in which each social relationship is embedded for an adolescent.

Social support can be considered a component feature of the social environment. Some studies have described several characteristic features of the adolescent's social environment. Felner et al. (1985) and Cauce, Felner, and Primavera (1982) have described features of the general social environment and of social support for samples of low-income ninth to eleventh graders who are predominantly nonwhite and from low-income backgrounds. Their series of studies suggest that the structural dimensions of social support include perceived helpfulness of family support, support received from adults found in institutional settings, and support of friends and adults found in other settings. They also have identified several salient features of the school and home environments of these adolescents. Primary school environment factors, based on factor analyses of self-report rating scales, include Teacher Support, Teacher Control, Rules Clarity, Order and Organization, and Competition. Family factors, based on the 1974 Moos *Family Environment Scale,* include Cohesion, Expression, Conflict, Independence, Achievement Orientation, Intellectual-Cultural Orientation, Active-Recreational Orientation, Moral-Religious Emphasis, and Personal Growth. Shulman et al. (1987) reports similar results for upper-middle-income Israeli adolescents. Walker and Greene (1987) identify cohesion and adaptability as major features of adolescents' family environments. They describe supportive adolescent families as those who are high in cohesion and in adaptability. Dornbush et al. (1988) reports relationships between Baumrind's parenting style variable and school grades for a very large sample of urban high school students of unspecified income and gender but representing several major ethnic groups and family types (e.g., two-parent, single-parent). Compas et al. (1986), Walker and Greene (1987), and Gad and Johnson (1980) describe very specific aspects of social support for adolescents. These studies ask adolescents to rate how useful or helpful they perceive peers, parents and others to be as helpers when faced with material, emotional or informational resources needs. While the specific structure of social support and how support functions are usually not examined simultaneously in one study, these studies have all examined at least one aspect of social support.

Few studies have examined the overall features of the immediate social context in which an adolescent is embedded. Two exceptions, Coates (1985; 1987) and Blyth, Hill, and Thiel (1982), have provided detailed portraits of the variety of dimensions characterizing the organizational and structural features of adolescent social networks and their functional or supportive feature. These studies provide the initial description of the typical adolescent personal social environment as they vary by gender, age, and ethnicity.

Adjustment, health, and social support. There are few detailed studies that describe the relationship of social relationships to normative adolescent adjustment. Although the developmental picture here is sketchy, some recent studies show how social relationships and nonclinical adolescent and early adulthood behaviors are related. An understanding of the relationship between adolescent social relationships and adjustment in later early adulthood is essential for implementing valid and reasoned intervention efforts with adolescents at risk for achieving normative life goals. Coates (1985) has related social network characteristics to self-concept in African-American middle-income adolescents. Stevens (1988) has related aspects of social support to parenting and personality constructs for adolescents from several populations. Hirsch and Rapkin (1987) explored self-esteem, peer social support, and quality of school life, longitudinally in sixth- and seventh-graders from unspecified income groups of African-American and white families. African-American students reported higher satisfaction with school life than white students and highly competent African-American students studied were the only group to report increased social support with age. In general, social support tends to be positively related to aspects of social and academic competence.

Numerous studies in the adult literature on adjustment and coping suggest a strong relationship between low social support in the face of stress and poor adjustment outcomes. A more limited array of studies has explored this relationship for adolescents. Compas (1987), in his review of stress and adjustment in childhood and adolescence, reports that most studies find moderate relationships between daily stressors in the social environment and somatic and behavioral disorders. Results are unclear regarding the mediating effect of social support on adjustment outcomes. Gad and Johnson (1980) find a relationship between stress and health adjustment and that these vary as a function of social support. Rosen (1982), however, reports that psychiatrically disturbed adolescent boys have what they perceive as deficient support networks. These disturbed adolescent boys view their networks as significantly less available, nonsupportive, and more affectively unpleasant than do nondisturbed boys. They also report that they do not rely on these networks for help. The quality of relationships and the availability of network members were strongly related to how often the adolescents used the network members for support. This was true for disturbed and nondisturbed adolescents.

The distinction between perceived and actual support has important clinical implications. Compas et al. (1986) report a significant relationship between stress and psychological disorder in adolescents. They, on the other hand, report that a low level of satisfaction with social support is significantly related to several clinical symptoms of disorder. The results of Cauce et al. (1982) also support this relationship and they report negative associations between various aspects of perceived helpfulness of social support and adjustment. They find that high levels of informal support among an inner-city sample are associated with poorer academic achievement and with better peer self-concept. Inclusion of negative and positive outcomes when considering the impact of social support on emerging competence is important in designing interventions. Felner et al. (1985) also report positive relationships between academic grades and perceived family and teacher support. Hansell (1985) also reports several significant relationships between blood pressure, psychosomatic stress reactions, and peer support for adolescents. Walker and Greene (1987) refer to social support as "use of psychological resources," and they provide additional data supporting the notion that negative, stress-producing life events are related to adjustment disorders. Their results further indicate that social support moderates the impact of stressful life events on some specific psychophysiological symptoms. Tolor and Fehon (1987), in a related study of coping style in adolescent boys, provide further evidence that distinct differences in availability of social resources and ability to manage those resources exist between high-stress and low-stress adolescent boys. Windle (1987) reports similar findings for adolescent females using a measure of general mental health. These studies show that some types of high stress are associated with poor general mental health. Dean and Ensel (1983) have explored classic depression symptoms in young adults, aged eighteen to twenty-four years of age, and social support. Their data indicate that disturbed primary relationships are the best predictors of depression. This pattern of results linking stress and poor adjustment outcomes can be positively changed by influencing actual or perceived social support.

Gender and race differences. Gender and ethnicity differences in the characteristics of social support and in the pattern of relationships between social support and health indicators are described to some extent (Block et al., 1988; Cauce, 1982; Compas et al., 1986; Dean & Ensel, 1983; Feiring & Coates, 1987; Coates 1987; Gad & Johnson, 1980; Walker & Greene, 1987). Most of these studies report consistent differences in favor of women in the level of negative health indicators, in the characteristics of social support, and in the number and nature of significant relationships between social support and health. For example, Walker and Greene (1987) report that peer support seems to buffer stress for male adolescents but not for females. However, some studies find no differences in the relationship between social support and negative health symptoms for males and females (Compas et al., 1986). These differences are useful to psychological theory building but also may have important implications for clinical diagnosis and intervention. No consistent ethnic trends emerge. Group, gender, and ethnicity differences, when found, may not apply across the board to individuals of like gender or ethnicity. They are important, however, as they provide details on the social expectation context in which these individuals must often function. These social expectations may influence perceptions and consequently behavior.

Stress Etiology in African-American Adolescents

African-American adolescents and their families are particularly at risk for experiencing stress associated with negative psychological and physical health outcomes. Adolescents are expected to gradually assume adult roles and responsibilities. The skills and competencies required for achieving adult status are fairly well-delineated in the literature (see review by Kinney, 1988; Greenberger & Sorensen, 1974). The process of acquiring these skills, however, is unclear for adolescents in general although we can clearly see when someone fails to achieve maturity since the goals of adult maturity are well articulated (Kinney, 1989). For African-American adolescents the ill-defined process of acquiring adult skills is further complicated because of overt and subtle racism. Indicators of racism's effects on African-American adolescents' social context include: (a) differential occupational prestige of African-American adults, compared to their non–African-American counterparts; (b) high unemployment and underemployment rates among African-American adults and youth; (c) low health-care utilization and correspondingly high rates of disease, death, and disorder for African-Americans compared to other major ethnic groups. The high incidence of African-American single parents and dual job-families among African-American families are also stressors that affect many adolescents. In addition racism focuses particular negative attention, for nonwhite adolescents, on issues of identity and self-esteem that represent core developmental issues during adolescence.

The socialization experiences of most African-American adolescents are different from those of white adolescents or of adolescents from migrant families. These differences may be a function of family socioeconomic status and inherent differences between the social experiences of African-American and white adolescents. Racism is deeply embedded in American society. It creates socioeconomic and family process variation often associated with negative adjustment outcomes for all adolescents and this occurs at a higher rate for African-Americans than for other groups. Despite these differential stress-occurrence rates for African-Americans many African-American families effectively cope with these stressors. We know little, however, about how the specific coping mechanisms function within African-American families or how they are transmitted to individuals during adolescence. Understanding these socialization processes may provide an important basis for effective mental health and educational program planning for adolescents.

A primary coping mechanism for many African-American individuals is the use of extensive social support systems and flexible family roles for kin and nonkin (Ball, 1983; Martin & Martin, 1978; McAdoo, 1981; Stevens, 1988). African-American adolescents must learn how to cope with the normative life events which occur during adolescence and to achieve the goals expected during and at the end of adolescence within the context of an extremely stressed environment. If they are unable to marshall well-functioning social support systems, using extant and potential social resources, they may be at risk for experiencing physical and psychological stress reactions. In the general population early adolescence is a particularly vulnerable time due to major and dramatic physical changes and changes in self-concept that occur during this period (Hamberg, 1974). The negative associations and stereotypes often associated with ethnic minority status may further exacerbate the difficulties experienced by young African-American adolescents. Despite additional stressors faced by African-American adolescents it is important to note that African-American adolescents vary greatly in how they react to these stressful life circumstances.

Variations in perceptions of social opportunity may hold some potential for positively influencing African-American adolescent adjustment. Banks, Mc-Quarter, and Hubbard (1979) have shown that the African-American adolescent's perceptions of the opportunities for social interaction available to him are related to his view of himself and his motivation to achieve certain goals.

MENTAL HEALTH INTERVENTION IN ADOLESCENCE

Major Traditional Intervention Approaches

In this section the major approaches to intervention that are most applicable to social systems analysis as an intervention approach are reviewed. Cognitive procedures, self-management procedures, and social skill building as intervention are discussed briefly as they provide a theoretical framework, intervention goals, and a set of procedures applicable to a social system intervention approach. These procedures, based on social learning theory (Bandura, 1977), have been used in a number of interventions. Gesten and Jason (1987) have discussed many recent efforts focusing on primary prevention efforts to improve well-being through social support, empowerment, competence building, and mutual help strategies with children, families, and adults. They conclude, based on limited meta-analyses of data on prevention effectiveness that these methods usually show 66 to 71 percent greater improvement rates for treated groups as compared to untreated groups.

Cognitive and self-control procedures. A number of studies provide evidence that perceptions and cognitions influence learned behavior in predictable ways (Ollendick & Cerny, 1981). Some treatment programs for adolescents are based on an approach which aims to change behavior or feelings by influencing thought processes. This involves changing beliefs, attitudes, images, and other cognitive activity through direct interventions that attempt to restructure cognitions associated with maladaptive behavior. Self-management procedures, based primarily on social learning theory, use specific methods for encouraging an individual to master self-control or the conscious manipulation of a mental set of self-imposed rewards and punishments that are immediate or delayed. It is assumed that these conditions can be internalized and replace external agents that impose standards of behavior. Ollendick and Cerny (1981) reviewed nonadult cognitive and self-management intervention efficacy. They concluded that while many approaches have been proposed, few systematic investigations demonstrate effectiveness. Single case-studies, and small-sample, nonreplicated studies, however, provide evidence of potential efficacy.

Social skill building. Problem-solving and coping-skills therapies are also based on cognitive intervention and social learning theory (Mahoney & Arnkoff, 1978). These approaches suggest it may be possible to teach adolescents how to use network information to design self-imposed stress management methods. The coping-skills approach uses a cognitive restructuring method.

That is, the purpose of intervention is to replace old perceptions of reality and/ or self with new ones. The problem-solving and coping-skills approaches attempt to re-educate a client to identify problems and information needed to solve them. These approaches also focus on helping to examine and eliminate options, to compare solutions and situational information, and to revise ideas or plans in accordance with that information. This focus also includes considering alternative courses of action and the advantages and disadvantages of these possible courses of action. Other problem-solving and skill-building approaches have involved physical, emotional, and intellectual tasks as well as peer-focus (see review by Gesten & Jason, 1987; Seltzer, 1982).

Empirical Studies of Cognitive and Skill-building Interventions

Cognitive intervention techniques have been shown to be effective with some types of adolescent social adjustment and behavioral problems. For example, contingency contracting has been used to improve the classroom performance of disadvantaged youths (Kelley & Stokes, 1982). Schinke and colleagues have explored cognitive intervention with adolescents in a number of intervention situations (Barth & Schinke, 1984; Gilchrist & Schinke, 1983; Schinke, Barth, Gilchrist & Maxwell, 1986; Schinke, Schilling & Snow, 1987). Their work presumes the advantages of social support and communications skills for psychosocial maturity. These intervention researchers have conducted several short-term (e.g., two weeks or two month) interventions. About 22 percent of the participants in these interventions are defined as ethnic minorities. They find that group interventions consisting of relaxation exercises, role playing, didactic lectures, and problem-solving and communication exercises result in several positive adjustment outcomes for these adolescents. Newton and Barbaree (1987) have used thought-sampling procedures to control headache symptomatology with older adolescents.

Spivack, Platt, and Shure (1976) find the cognitive problem-solving abilities of psychiatric and delinquent adolescents to be deficient when compared to those of nondisturbed adolescents. Little and Kendall (1979) review the applications of problem solving, role taking, and self-control cognitive-behavioral interventions with delinquents. They conclude that successful adaptation and coping with difficult situations requires interpersonal problem-solving skills that, within the normal range of ability, are distinct from cognitive or intellectual ability. They further conclude that at-risk adolescents (e.g., delinquent, emotionally disturbed) are more likely to be deficient in this skill. However, while a number of promising treatment programs to remediate problem-solving deficiencies have been devised, few have been applied to adolescents. When they have, the results have been successful, as Little and Kendall (1979) report. An important feature of successful programs these authors reviewed is that they involved family units.

Several reviews of studies that explore the effectiveness of cognitive learning approaches conclude that the efficacy of self-regulation procedures is relatively consistent across a wide range of subjects and behaviors (Goldfried, 1979; Hollon & Kendall, 1979; Turk & Genest, 1979). Coping and problem-solving therapies are also effective, according to these reviews. These approaches show some promise for assisting adolescents, yet they have not been shown to have long-term impact or to be generalized to adolescents with serious adjustment problems. Social network information, however, is a rich source of content that could be used as the building blocks of these clinical efforts.

Special Issues in Intervention with African-American Adolescents

As indicated earlier, the socialization experiences of African-American children and the consequent development of these children differ in many ways from those of other American children. Many early analyses of the socialization of African-American children and their families suggest that they were aberrant in their family behavior because they did not conform to prevailing norms with respect to family constellation, disciplinary style, and social accommodation (Slaughter & McWorter, 1985). Socialization differences between major culturally or ethnically distinct groups do not necessarily define one group as superior and the other as aberrant. These differences must figure, however, in explanations of adult outcomes and in helping strategies for persons from different cultural backgrounds (Harrison, Serafica & McAdoo, 1984.)

It can be argued that African-American adolescents need to be viewed differently in clinical and intervention settings. Ogbu (1985) has described a "cultural ecology of competence among inner-city African-Americans" that differs greatly from mainstream developmental models. His model reinterprets the developmental environment to include subsistence and survival strategies such as collective struggle and hustling that are associated more with poverty and caste status than with majority experience. Semaj (1985) suggests African-American children and adolescents are often treated on the basis of color and their identity or self-development is affected negatively by this. He suggests that the experience as a person of color makes the development of an extended self-identity or group identity necessary for psychological survival. This collective identity is thought to be more uniquely an experience of African-American children than of others. These differences create special conditions that may require the use of culture-specific behavioral interventions (Groves, 1982).

Assumptions underlying the importance of social experiences for expression of self are based on a perspective of symbolic interaction. This view suggests that the development of self is inseparable from social interactions and develops from perceptions of how others respond to us (Shrauger & Schoeneman, 1979). The need for special considerations in mental health interventions with African-American adolescents is also based on this assumption. Some of the major factors influencing psychosocial development in African-American adolescents and children are: socioeconomic status of immediate and other family members; family constellation; family support; family interaction style; and perception of how caste status influences experiences. Because of the unique social realities of these adolescents and their families these youth may develop self-concepts and related psychological disorders that are different from those of mainstream adolescents. Such different self-concepts must be dealt with by using appropriate clinical interventions. Brown and Gary (1987) provide an example of these differences in their analysis of stressors, social support, and health in 451 African-American adults. Most of these adults had an income of $25,000 or less. This study describes relationships among these variables that may be predominant in the lives of some African-American families. They suggest that African-American males in declining physical health had an increased number of confidants. However, no social support characteristics were related to the mental health of African-American males. For African-American females, being embedded in a large social support network of nearby relatives did reduce stress; but religiosity was related positively to declining physical health. These authors point out the findings were expected, in light of previous research, but only for females. The findings, for the African-American males in the sample, were not consistent with findings for other populations. These differential ethnic- and gender-based results suggest that special considerations are necessary when designing mental health interventions for African-Americans.

The Social Network: Emerging Research and Intervention Paradigm

Definitions and assumptions. The concept of social network provides a useful analytic tool for exploring the social milieu in which adult competence is achieved. While several definitions of social networks exist, the most general reference is to the linkages between all social units, both groups and persons, with which an individual has contact (Bott, 1955; Boissevain, 1974). These contacts include relationships based on kinship, sentiment, and exchange of material and other resources as well as contacts that have no apparent or less well-defined functions. The structure and functioning of an individual's social network is crucial to solving problems and attaining daily and long-term life goals (Fischer, Jackson, Stueve, Gerson, Jones & Baldassare, 1977; Laumann, 1973; McAdoo, 1981; Wellman, 1979). The social network may be especially critical in understanding the emergence of competence for African-American youths. These youths and their families are often excluded from easy access to desired adult goals because of social inequality and racial discrimination. They often have to work especially hard to create a supportive social environment to protect and aid one another (see, for example, Martin & Martin, 1978).

Symbolic interaction theory assumes that both the structural and interactive content or the function of the network are important for individual functioning. Structure refers to the discernible, persistent organization of formal and informal roles with the network. Interaction or function refers to the nature of relations that exist within the network and especially to the type of material and emotional resources exchanged as an individual solves life problems. This exchange of resources and the person's feelings about how freely these exchanges take place is often referred to as social support (Compas, 1987; d'Abbs, 1982; Heller, Swindle & Dusenbury, 1986; Thoits, 1986). Structure provides opportunities for interaction and may influence the quality of interactions. Therefore both structure and perceptions of support are crucial network characteristics. Network structure provides a social map that identifies the location of an individual within a specific social world. A symbolic interactionist perspective assumes that this structure dictates with whom social exchanges are possible and which social interactions may be supportive (Feiring & Coates, 1987).

The family is a critical component of the network and the role of family and in adolescence, of peers, as influences on development is widely documented. Few studies, however, examine how family relationships are embedded and related to a broad array of social contacts that include peers, extended family, and nonfamilial adults. Research on the families of African-American adolescents is particularly scarce in the literature. Allen (1978a, 1978b) in reviews on African-American families concludes that much of this literature is characterized by a focus on low-income families with little attention to the family in a social context or to diversity among these families. One exception is a study of the social networks of middle-income African-American adolescents (Coates, 1985). This study highlights the differential significance of family and peer subnetwork characteristics for different aspects of self-concept in low- and high-income African-American adolescents. Lindblad-Goldberg and Dukes (1985) document many differences in African-American low-income single-parent families from both clinical and normative populations. Results from both studies support the speculation that examining the quality of support in the network may provide a powerful diagnostic information. This may serve as the basis for clinical intervention that focuses on relationships.

Social systems analysis as cognitive intervention. The social network, and the stress buffering model, have been used to explore the relationship between social structure, social support, and well being. The social network construct has also been used by social workers, "network therapists," and behavior modification specialists as a service delivery and therapeutic aid (Brownell & Shumaker, 1984b; Garbarino, 1983; Shumaker & Brownell, 1984). d'Abbs (1982) describes the way in which natural networks have been used to deliver services. His review suggests that a network delivery system is especially effective, as compared with a community action model, for older, middle-income populations.

Rueveni (1979) has pioneered some aspects of networking or network therapy. In this ecological system intervention a therapist helps a client enlarge, construct, or reconstruct personal networks with the capacity to heal, nurture, or challenge. Rueveni described his technique in 1969. It can involve bringing many members of the network together. It has not been studied widely or with adolescents. Bedrosian (1981) and Sacco (1981) discuss the specific application of network analysis in cognitive therapy, and provide a framework for therapists using significant others, such as primarily family members, in therapy. In Reuveni's and Bedrosian's techniques the therapist interviews significant others and observes the interaction of the client with them. The therapist can then use this dynamic exchange to evaluate dysfunctional communication and help the client devise strategies to promote satisfying interactions. As described earlier these social exchanges can provide health-sustaining feedback. Speck and Speck (1985) provide limited adolescent case studies of this approach.

The content of relationships and interactions is key in the use of social systems analysis as a cognitive intervention. In this approach reciprocity and complementarity are important constructs which explain the quality of social relations. Reciprocity characterizes exchanges that are mutually similar (e.g., sharing confidences) and complementarity occurs in exchanges that are different but together form a whole because each part provides something lacking in the other (e.g., two adolescents with different abilities pooling their efforts in a project to achieve a common goal). The significance of both types of exchanges for social development is described by Youniss (1980). Both are necessary to competent adult functioning. However, it has not yet been demonstrated clearly in the literature whether an individual can be taught to promote these functions in interpersonal relations.

The importance of using a social system rather than an individually focused model in designing behavioral interventions has been stressed by Wahler, Berland, Coe, and Leske (1976) and Wahler, Leske, and Rogers (1979). They argue that the behaviors of a target child are likely to be differently related to several aspects of a complex ecological system which includes family and community. Wahler (1980) has also demonstrated the negative impact of an isolated family network on child behavior and that parents can be retrained to be less insular. The quality of interactions and the number of interaction opportunities available to the mother were related to her ability to manage child behavior. Wahler (1980) suggests that self-regulation of social exchanges, if taught, might be clinically useful. Stress reduction might be enhanced by an expanded and supportive rather than a restricted network. Variation in the supportiveness of even isolated networks may also influence the efficacy of the intervention approach.

Social Network Characteristics of African-American Adolescents

A recent study conducted by the author compared the network characteristics of adolescents who reported having many day-to-day problems (e.g., high degrees of stress) to those of adolescents who reported having few problems (e.g., low stress). Also the network characteristics of adolescents who reported having no network resources to solve a recent problem were compared to the network characteristics of adolescents who reported at least one network resource who could help with a recent problem. These data illustrate a way of generating social system analyses that could be the basis for problem-solving interventions with adolescents.

Sample. The African-American adolescents in this study participated in a larger study of relationships between social network characteristics and social competence. The original sample included 589 adolescents with a mean age of 16.3. The present sample of young adolescents includes 190 adolescents with a mean age of 14.8 and a range of 12–15. About 57 percent of these adolescents are female. All are from middle-income families with a mean Siegel Hodge Rossi prestige rank of 56.3 (see Coates, 1985, 1987 for a further description).

Procedures and measures. Information about the social network was obtained with the *Social Network Record* [SNR] (Coates, 1981). The SNR is a multi-dimensional, two-and-one-half-hour paper and pencil inventory consisting of a graphic, checklist grid, and questionnaire stimulus materials that allow the respondents to describe both the structural and functional support characteristics of their social contacts (see Figure 1.1). Seven major subscores are derived that describe the overall network and also for two network groups: (1) family and (2) friends. Scale definitions are based on previous network literature (Boissevain, 1974; d'Abbs, 1982). In the SNR respondents list network members and for each describe: who they are by gender, age, relation, and so on; how close they live (proximity); how often they see them (frequency of contact); if they know other members in the network (density); how long they have known them (durability); and if they are seen in one or many settings (multiplicity). These scales and their psychometric properties are described further in Coates (1985, 1987).

Several additional subscales are derived from the SNR that measure some of the social support characteristics of the network. Some of the social support scales used here are:

1. *Quality of closeness*—the adolescent's definition of what it means to be close is coded for reciprocity (e.g., Youniss, 1980); that is, mutual exchange of friendship activities and level of closeness that can range from simply sharing mutual activity to communication that includes confiding and trust:

2. *Closeness resource*—number of persons identified as "persons I feel especially close to," using the adolescent's definition of closeness;

3. *Emotional resource*—number and perception of availability of persons identified as sources of help with the hypothetical problem of needing someone to talk with about a personal problem;

4. *Material resource*—number and perception of availability of sources of help with problem of needing money badly;

5. *Support satisfaction*—adolescents' indication of the degree to which they found the help they received for a problem they identified, which occurred within the last

Figure 1.1
Sample Network Assessment Grid

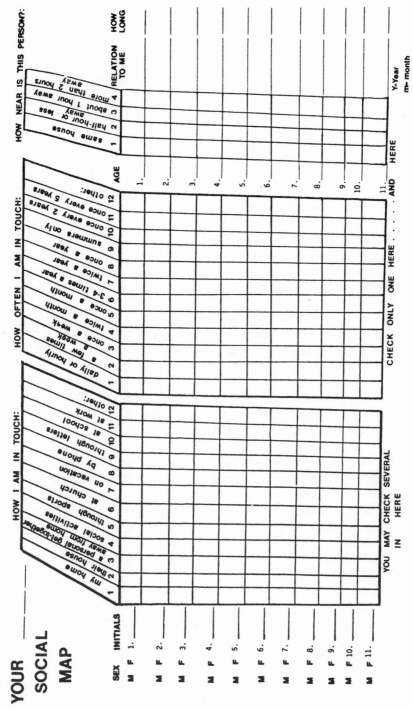

Source: From D. L. Coates (1981). The Social Network Record (Washington, DC: Catholic University, Center for the Study of Youth Development).

week, helpful. A high score indicates satisfaction with the adequacy of the help for resolving the problem.

The problem-solving resources and the number of problems experienced were also measured and were derived from a standard problem checklist constructed by the author. Self-esteem was also assessed using the Coopersmith Self-esteem Inventory.

Results: Network characteristics. Log-linear analyses and *t* tests were used to compare contingency tables and means in order to address these questions:

1. Are the social network characteristics of adolescents who cannot identify a source of help for a recent problem they experienced different from those of adolescents who can identify a helper for this problem?
2. Are the social network characteristics of adolescents who identify many problems occurring recently different from adolescents who experienced few problems in this same period?
3. Are the network characteristics of low-esteem adolescents different from those of high-esteem adolescents?

In Table 1.1 mean comparisons are presented for adolescents who listed 'no one' or 'self' as a helper, with those who listed a helper for the largest problem they had in the past two weeks. The type of helper identified within the overall 'helper' category was also examined for these two groups. This analysis revealed that adolescents with no one to help them had smaller total family and friend networks than those listing a helper. These adolescents, with no helpers and smaller family and friend networks, also saw network members in fewer places.

Subgroup comparisons, based on whom the adolescent identified as a helper, revealed that adolescents who listed a parent had larger friend networks than adolescents with no identified helper. Adolescents who reported parents as the helper also listed more people in their home who might be used as a support resource than adolescents with no helper. Adolescents who relied on peer help were more likely than the no help identified adolescents to have large families and chum groups, to have many school resources, and to see friends in a variety of settings.

Network characteristics of high- and low self-esteem adolescents were also compared. High self-esteem adolescents were more likely to have high frequency of contact with peers and low contact with family while the opposite was true for the low self-esteem group. The high-esteem adolescents were also more likely to identify a greater number of emotional and material resources than the low-esteem group. Table 1.2 shows mean percentages for the relationships chosen by adolescents, with high and with low esteem, as an emotional or material resource. Log linear comparisons of these mean frequencies indicate

Table 1.1
Network Characteristic Means for Adolescents Listing a Type of Help and for Those Who Said No Help Was Available to Solve a Recent Problem

Network Characteristic	Help Factor		
	Type of Help	No Help	p
Parent			
Family Resources	14.1	1.5	.05
Friend Size	13.6	8.8	.02
Non-Family Adult			
Friend Size	12.9	9.87	N.S.
Family Size	16.1	12.4	.04
Friend Multiplicity	11.15	7.3	.02
Peer			
Family Size	14.35	10.78	.03
Friend Multiplicity	10.6	7.8	.03
Chum Group Size (Special Friends)	5.0	2.0	.01
School Resources	10.3	2.1	.002

Notes: N = 300; *p* is for *t* statistic.

several differences for these two groups of adolescents. For example, "father" is the relational choice selected most often as a material resource by the high-esteem group while "mother" was chosen most often by the low-esteem group. Both groups prefer peers as emotional resources and choose "mother" as an emotional resource equally often. However, high-esteem adolescents tend to nominate family and low-esteem adolescents tend to nominate peers or nonfamily resources as potential helpers with emotional problems.

These high- and low-esteem groups were also compared to determine whether or not they differed in some of the characteristics of their peer groups or role models. Low-esteem adolescents were more likely to have smaller peer groups and high-esteem adolescents larger peer groups. Low-esteem youngsters were also more likely to have none or nonfamily role models, while family role models were more often identified by high-esteem youngsters.

Summary. The method and results described indicate the potential for devel-

Problems & Perspectives

Table 1.2
Percentages of Relationships and Relation Types Nominated by Adolescents to Help with Resource Problems for High and Low Self-esteem

Nominations Category	Resource Situation			
	Need Money (Material)		Fight with Friend (Emotional)	
	High	Low	High	Low
Relation				
Father	53.3	33.3	6.0	5.3
Mother	25.3	31.3	18.7	10.0
Brother	5.3	11.5	8.0	2.0
Sister	3.0	2.7	10.0	3.0
Male Family	5.3	4.0	2.0	2.0
Female Family	2.0	—	4.0	2.0
Male Peer	3.0	16.0	25.3	40.0
Female Peer	.6	—	24.0	28.0
Male Adult	1.3	1.2	1.3	4.0
Female Adult	—	—	.7	—
Relation with Type				
No One	.6	8.0	2.1	6.0
Family Only	30.0	10.0	16.1	15.3
Peer Only	5.3	28.0	14.8	27.3

Note: $N = 300$.

oping assessment and intervention tools to assist in social network analysis as an intervention approach with adolescents. Several groups of adolescents have used the Social Network Record and statistical analysis of these adolescents' responses indicated the existence of individual differences in network characteristics. These individual differences vary as a function of preexisting high-risk conditions. Adolescents at risk for problems in social and emotional development and for social inadequacy may differ in the kinds of social relationships they have available. They also may differ in how they perceive and use these social relationships. Identification of these differences offers the possibility of intervening to minimize important differences, both in reality and in the perception of the adolescent.

A CONCEPTUAL MODEL FOR SOCIAL NETWORK INTERVENTION

The Model and Its Assumptions

Prevention and therapeutic interventions have focused most often on key dyadic relationships and family systems. Rarely have mental health services focused on the quality of a person's overall social network. A model is proposed conceptualizing mental health intervention as cognitive restructuring to improve use of social network resources. Several social support theorists argue that consideration of family and dyadic relationships alone is not adequate to explain healthy functioning (Garbarino, 1983; Schinke, Barth, Gilchrist, Whittaker, Kirkham, Senechal, Snow & Maxwell, 1986; Thoits, 1986). Social support, or the purposeful use of social relationships, is important because it provides an individual with opportunities to reduce stress and to enhance self-esteem (Heller et al., 1986). These interactions may solve material problems or may help an individual to understand and/or control reactions to difficult situations. These interactions have been described by some as help-seeking behaviors.

Reisman (1985) suggests that friendship, and particularly its absence during adolescence, is the critical predictor of social incompetence in adolescence and further maladjustment in adulthood. Adolescence is a critical developmental stage during which friendships and the influence of selected peers play a major role in promoting competence. Most adolescents are keenly interested in peer relationships and this interest could be extended to include nonpeer relationships and more direct consideration of how to make adequate use of social relationships that exist.

In the proposed intervention model social structure is conceptualized as predictor variables that influence social competence outcomes. These outcomes include observable social, interpersonal and/or academic skills. This model is presented schematically in Figure 1.2. It is assumed that adolescence represents a critical developmental period for the acquisition of social competence. It is also assumed, from a symbolic interactionist perspective, that important self-understanding and self-conceptions come from social interactions in the context of available social relationships.

Structure, in the proposed intervention model, is the discernible organizational characteristics of the network. Structure is presumed to indirectly influence outcome variables. Structural characteristics directly influence the quality of social support available to an individual. Network support mediates the effects of social structure on adolescent social skills. Perceived self-efficacy also mediates the effects of network structure on adolescent behavioral outcomes.

Figure 1.2
A Network Intervention Model

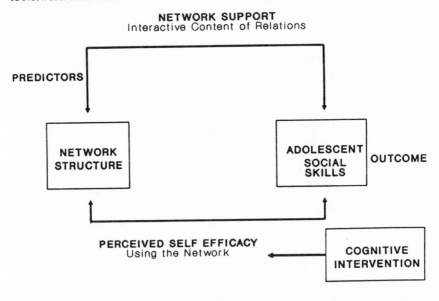

Personal effectiveness, in many circumstances, depends on perceptions of personal adequacy. The proposed intervention model suggests that acting on the social structure can help to promote the kind of social support that fosters social competence. This intervention would allow an individual to explore alternatives to existing network structures that will result in the achievement of desired social skill goals. Self-efficacy may determine how effectively social support is used to achieve goals and is an important related skill in considering adolescent social competence. An important feature of this model is that a portion of it is a continual feedback loop. Self-efficacy and network support are the continually present filters through which social structure influences adolescent skills. The model assumes that interventions that aim to improve effective use of the network are likely to result in significant positive outcomes, such as high self-esteem and social problem solving. The model also assumes that social competence influences the availability of support and the structure of a network as well as perceived self-efficacy although this is not the primary direction of influence. This may affect current as well as future adjustment.

Relationship of a Social Network Intervention Model to Theories of Adolescent Development

Early theories of adolescent development suggested that adolescence is characterized by internal turmoil and crisis. These theories also conceptualized maturation, particularly the expression of identity, as a normative and progressive unfolding of internal stages and events (Conger, 1978). More recent views of adolescent development have focused on the relevance of social context, the specific characteristics of social relationships, and the internal content of social interactions for development (Cooper, 1987; Greenberger & Sorenson, 1974; Peterson, 1987). Identity is still considered a primary developmental challenge during adolescence. However, the relevance of role transitions and role identities, which must be considered in the context of a range of social relationships, has received greater prominence in discussions of adolescent adjustment. Numerous studies have supported these theoretical considerations and underscore the developmental significance of social relationships for cognitive and moral reasoning skills, development of self-concept, expression of sexuality and sexual knowledge, vocational choice, and overall adjustment (Garbarino, 1985).

This development in adolescent theory was accompanied by a similar development in mental health services in the early 1970s. The climate of that time and the current climate suggest that mental illness and adjustment problems are, in many instances, not merely intrapsychic phenomena but are problems generated by external social relations that can be influenced by social interventions (Gesten & Jason, 1987). Mental health intervention models, given this assumption, must also take an expanded perspective so that social factors that ameliorate difficult adjustment and prevent adjustment difficulties during adolescence can be understood. Effective intervention models can not exclusively focus on internal maturation resulting from internal state changes. Social action approaches may be better suited to more socially relevant outcomes for the adolescent. They may also be more easily achieved in both short-term and long-term settings.

Social network intervention may be especially relevant for adolescents since they often experience the stress of individuating from parents and from childhood social relationships. During early adolescence tension between emerging biological development and lagging social skill development produce a number of support needs for this group (Price, 1988). A key developmental task during this period is the development of self-esteem. This requires the availability of close and mutually self-disclosing relationships that can provide stable and sustaining support. This focus on social relationships may be particularly difficult for adolescents from dysfunctional families or who experience diluted social opportunity. These groups may require social intervention to create appropriate systems of support (Speck & Speck, 1985). The Carnegie Council on Adolescent Development (Price, 1988) has suggested that current demographic trends indicate a pressing need for considering how to use social network support to address many problems facing adolescents today. The Council has suggested that many adolescents lack meaningful social relationships within and/or outside of their immediate families and feel unconnected to traditional American values and life goals. In addition some adolescents must cope with difficult school and work transitions, blended families, and living in environments where the risk of substance abuse is high.

Implications for Mental Health Intervention

Intervention goals. The purpose of a social network intervention should be: (1) to help an adolescent identify existing and potential helping relationships available to promote growth and reduce negative stress; and (2) to teach an adolescent the skills required to maintain mutually satisfying reciprocal relationships with network members. These goals represent the major tasks to be implemented through a series of multistep tasks or sessions that solve initially simple but progressively complex social problems.

The goal of this type of intervention is to give the adolescent the skills to cognitively restructure perceptions of how their social world functions so that they maximize the benefits they gain from social interactions relative to their needs and personal goals. This intervention approach focuses on the adolescent's most intimate ties and also on less close ties. The goal is to empower the adolescent to solve problems with naturally occurring social aids. This approach fosters the development of alliances between the adolescent and significant family members and other persons in the adolescent's life (for examples see Baptiste, 1986; Barth, 1983; Ward, 1986).

Implementing an intervention model. At the outset of the intervention it is necessary to make some determinations that will direct the focus of the efforts. For example, is the intervention to prevent adjustment problems or to intervene in correcting existing ones? Can family members play a major role in the implementation of the intervention or must they be a focus of the intervention? It is probably not advisable to focus intervention efforts on nonemancipated adolescents in isolation of family. If these adolescents are members of a family group, it is necessary to find out if engaging family members in the intervention process will be helpful. It is also important, at the outset of the intervention to identify the appropriate strategic setting in which the intervention should occur (Gottlieb, 1988). School, work, the home, a church group, or other naturally occurring formal or informal affiliation groups, such as mentorships, are possible settings in which adolescents can learn from peers, from adults, or from a service provider. Finally, it should be determined whether the network intervention is best offered individually or in a group.

Once these issues are determined an adolescent or a group of adolescents and a service provider could engage in one to two initial assessment sessions. The nature of these sessions would vary according to whether the network intervention is to be preventive or therapeutic and according to the potential role of the family in the intervention. Following this assessment, network data would be analyzed and an intervention strategy would be devised. This specific strategy could be planned with the adolescent. Typically the number of sessions would range from three to twenty for solving short-term crisis situations or preventing crisis. Or they may last over a period of months or years like traditional mental health interventions. This depends on the severity of the problem, ability to pay for services, willingness to invest time in the services plan, and other factors that affect any mental intervention. Prevention of immediate developmental crises may require fewer sessions than major intervention sessions.

The content of network intervention efforts. Several implementation strategies are possible in offering this intervention. First, members of a network are identified. It then is important to focus on teaching the adolescent about the significant emotional function and other functions of social support. The focus of some discussions will be on the match between these functions and the abilities and characteristics of each member of the network. The goal of this is to help the adolescent become fully capable of assessing others' talents and skills and identifying areas where their networks are deficient in particular important functions. In network therapy this requires a cognitive behavioral approach focused on the match between network functions and network member characteristics. Bibliographic and video materials might provide useful vehicles for discussing the specific character of support functions with adolescents. After the adolescents are fully acquainted with the scope and impact of this match or mismatch, they need to be led to develop specific self-management techniques. These techniques would teach them how to purposefully use their available social network resources and to minimize the negative impact of dysfunctional members. These techniques are fairly well known and could involve a commitment to alter behaviors and situations, as well as self-rewards and self-punishments (Ollendick & Cerny, 1981).

Gottlieb (1988) has identified several action-oriented interaction processes that often occur in peer support groups and might help to promote positive responses to risks faced by the adolescent. These processes include normalizing feelings and experiences; describing frustrations, problems, and the feelings associated with them; problem solving, reducing the uncertainty in one's life; and gaining a sense of control and personal efficacy from assuming the role of helper. In order to normalize the experience of support, it is important to give the adolescent the chance to experience giving and receiving support. It is probably also important that these interactions occur with adults and with peers.

Successful social support prevention and intervention programs have used a number of activities and techniques to achieve their goals. The majority of these programs rely on didactic group discussion, on cognitive and interpersonal problem-solving skill building, and on methods to impart their message and effect change (Barth & Schinke, 1984; Schinke, Barth, Gilchrist & Maxwell, 1986). Ward (1986), in describing his British social action intervention, and Gottlieb (1988) suggest that the use of role play, video work, and script writing are also helpful for allowing adolescents to express personal feelings and concerns and work somewhat better in achieving this than does direct personal discussion. In addition these interactions should provide an adolescent with opportunities to diagnose problems, to practice the thinking and language associated with problem solving and successful coping, to show affection, and to provide critical and caring feedback to others.

The Carnegie Council on Adolescent Development (Price, 1988) recently reviewed several promising social support intervention programs for adolescents and identified several common key features of these programs. They indicate that a program should: (1) allow participation that is nonstigmatized so that opportunities to advance and not existing deficits are emphasized; (2) initially provide comprehensive services and focus on basic life and survival needs, if necessary; (3) provide caring nonparental adults who provide mentoring functions and act as role models; (4) be community based and coordinated with other service systems for adolescents; and (5) be empowering by providing opportunities for both leadership and cultural expression. One program, offered by Felner and colleagues, focuses on removing barriers in school and classroom systems. It provided support to homeroom teachers and reorganizing the social matrix of students so that the expression of stable and consistent support in that setting is more likely to occur (Price, Cowen, Lorion & Ramos-McKay, 1988).

There is little evidence to suggest that a specific temporal ordering should be followed when implementing the network therapy strategies described briefly above. Responsible clinical practice would dictate that a service provider be sensitive to constructing a logical hierarchical plan for engaging an adolescent or group of adolescents in these activities. This plan would be based on a current and complete assessment of the situation in which the intervention or prevention effort is to occur.

Evaluating the efficacy of network intervention. Efforts to evaluate the efficacy of network intervention/prevention efforts should be fairly straightforward. Using specific observable behavioral outcomes one can examine the pre-intervention, immediate and post intervention frequency of desired behavior. Subjective determinations of how relationships function between adults and adolescents and between pairs or within groups of adolescents will also help to provide some formative evaluation data. It also may be useful to test the adolescent's knowledge regarding the critical functions of support. Gottlieb (1988) has suggested that evaluation research in this area needs to involve comparisons between different programmatic elements offered in a specific intervention or across interventions. These comparisons should focus on differences in attracting and sustaining participation of adolescents, in providing meaningful help to meet supportive needs, and in effecting desirable adjustment outcomes.

Social network assessment. The success of the proposed social network intervention will depend on the quality of assessments used with this population. Several types of assessments are needed to provide the information necessary to assist adolescents in managing stress and in achieving adult goals. At the onset of any intervention it is necessary to obtain a descriptive profile of the structural and supportive characteristics of the adolescent's social network. One method for obtaining these assessments is to use self-report measures that allow adolescents to describe members of the network and how they interact with them. Several examples of self-report measures have been used successfully with adolescents (Blyth et al., 1982; Blyth & Foster-Clark, 1987; Coates, 1985,

1987; Cauce et al., 1982, Rosen, 1982; Schinke, Barth, Gilchrist & Maxwell, 1986; Schinke, Schilling & Snow, 1987). The validity of adolescent self-report measures is an important issue and has been examined by Coates (1985) for social network reports and by Crockett, Schulenberg, and Petersen (1987) for height, weight, and school grade self-reports. Both report that comparisons of two kinds of data generally support the validity of adolescent self-reports. Coates (1985) found that day-to-day phone-recorded diary reports of social experience are fairly consistent with a self-report social network measure. The Crockett et al. (1987) validity data indicate that while some response error is present the majority of this error was random and did not vary as a function of grade or gender.

A significant psychometric problem that has not been addressed with adolescent populations concerns item scaling of social support item responses. The issue involves the underlying social support constructs and whether social competence outcomes can be expected to vary as a function of social support. Donald and Ware (1984) provide extensive data and methodology descriptions on the scaling of a measure of social support. This measure has been linked to estimates of well-being as an independent or outcome variable for adults. Their psychometric data provide some clarification of the issues involved in the development of a measure of social support using a questionnaire approach. However, it raises some questions about the assumed relationship between such measures of social support and well-being. The data of Donald and Ware (1984) underscore the importance of further investigating the psychometric properties of social network assessments that are conceptually linked to adolescent competence. In addition, we have little data available for adolescents that provide details on the stability of social network characteristics, the derivation of scale values for measures of social contact and resources that generalize across population subgroups, or the conceptually and empirically distinct aspects of social network characteristics. An additional validity issue involves determining the veridicality of social support. Antonucci and Israel (1986) have provided some data, from a study of adults over 70, on the relationship between responses about the network provided by a focus adult and those provided by members of this adult's network. Congruence in the perception of supportive functions between those with whom an adolescent interacts and the target adolescent is useful in planning a clinical intervention program. The psychometric properties of this congruence need to be explored further. This may greatly improve the quality of assessments available to those providing intervention or prevention services.

In assessing the descriptive characteristics of the network it is also important to gather information on the family environment. While numerous family environment characteristics are important to adolescent development, two seem significant for assessing the supportive potential of family members: (1) parenting style (Dornbusch, 1988; Marjoribanks, 1979), and (2) status of family dynamics as influenced by family structure, composition, and the interactional stage in the family life cycle (Preto & Travis, 1985). These assessments will help in planning how to involve the family or to augment critical family supports that may not be available. The assessment of several other adolescent characteristics are potentially useful in planning social network interventions or in evaluating the impact of these interventions. These characteristics are: self-esteem, self-concept, or self-efficacy (see recent review on clinical applications by Giblin, Poland & Ager, 1988); stress level; subjective responsiveness to stress and to offered social support (Gottlieb, 1988; Marziali & Pilkonis, 1986); family and personal background characteristics and social competence.

Directions for Future Research in Network Intervention

Network intervention is an emerging community mental health tool. Several unanswered questions can be identified that require further research in order to build an informed basis for clinical practice. There are several promising lines of inquiry that need exploration and only a few are mentioned here. Epidemiological studies, conducted in natural settings, are needed to identify specific component features of the adolescent social network. Once identified these factors can be examined to determine which are effective stress buffers for adolescents. These buffers can also be linked to specific stress reactions. Further study is also needed to examine how effective these network characteristics are as a function of cultural, ethnic, gender, and developmental variation. Based on this information randomized quasiexperimental trials should be conducted, where ethically possible, to determine whether these naturally occurring network buffers work to reduce stress and whether they are related to any of the generally accepted developmental tasks required to achieve adult status. It is also important to find out whether or not some of these naturally occurring buffers can be introduced to adolescents who do not use them. An additional question central to this line of inquiry involves testing the efficacy of the intervention for long-term and short-term outcomes.

The examination of individual differences in perceptions of support, reactions to stress, and susceptibility to efforts at intervention is also required as a basis for the design of sensitive implementation strategies. A concurrent line of inquiry is needed that will produce practical case studies utilizing small clinical trials. These studies would help to offer clarity regarding this source of variation by examining the resiliency and attachment patterns of very high-risk youngsters, early in life and during adolescence.

Longitudinal studies are also necessary in order to investigate the social support predictors of very high-risk behaviors. Block, Block, and Keyes (1988) have demonstrated that distinct social and personality antecedents of adolescent drug use can be identified. This suggests that it might be important to determine which characteristics of the social network are linked to drug use, delinquency, or other risk-taking behavior. These studies may help to understand when and how to intervene to prevent these negative outcomes. There is also a need to explore how children learn coping behaviors or how to use their networks to garnish support. As Compas (1987) suggests, it is not clear whether children learn their coping behavior through observations of parents or other significant figures. This learning process has received very limited empirical investigation. Likewise, as Gottlieb (1988) suggests, we need to examine whether one type of support is perceived as more helpful if offered by one network member rather than another. In this context Gottlieb (1988) also points out that it is important to pursue research that helps to shed light on how support is communicated to others and on what basis do networks need to be organized to facilitate the transfer of support from network members to the target adolescent. It is also important, as Gottlieb (1988) suggests, to identify the processes by which well-functioning adults maintain supportive relationships that come to their aid when necessary. Answers to these questions are critical to our understanding of how to intervene with vulnerable adolescents and with well functioning adolescents.

A network intervention model and a rationale for such a model has been presented. This model suggests that perceived and actual social interactions can be influenced to promote healthy adolescent adjustment. Some limited data on social networks among African-American adolescents is presented. These and other recent data support the assumption that well-adjusted and less stressed adolescents differ in support from those who have poor adjustment or more stress. The extensive literature on stress, adaptability, coping, and skill building was reviewed. A case was made for assuming that interventions can be effectively implemented to reduce support deficiencies resulting in improved social competency. The discussion presented presumes important intervention distinctions between social support, social network characteristics, and the social environment. Network intervention may be uniquely beneficial to African-American youth. This benefit may be because of the paradoxical social limitations and social advantages they face as a result of racism and extended kin/friend bonds necessary to cope with racism. While this conceptual model holds some promise a number of studies are necessary, as described, to build an appropriate practical and theoretical basis for this model.

ACKNOWLEDGMENTS

The author wishes to thank Peter Vietze and Brigit vanWidenfelt for helpful comments on earlier versions of this chapter.

REFERENCES

Allen, W. R. (1978a). The search for applicable theories of black family life. *Journal of Marriage and the Family, 47,* 117–128.
———. (1978b). Black family research in the United States: A review, assessment and extension. *Journal of Comparative Family Studies, 11,* 167–189.

Antonucci, T. C. & Israel, B. A. (1986). Veridicality of social support: A comparison of principal and network members responses. *Journal of Consulting and Clinical Psychology, 54*, 432–437.

Ball, R. E. (1983). Family and friends: A supportive network for low-income American black families. *Journal of Comparative Family Studies, 14*, 51–65.

Bandura, A. (1977). *Social learning theory.* Englewood Cliffs, NJ: Prentice-Hall.

Banks, W. C., McQuarter, G. V. & Hubbard, J. L. (1979). Toward a reconceptualization of the social-cognitive bases of achievement orientations in blacks. In A. W. Boykin, A. J. Franklin & M. F. Yates (Eds.), *Research directions of black psychologists* (pp. 294–311). New York: Russell Sage.

Baptiste, D. A. (1986). Counseling the pregnant adolescent within a family context: Therapeutic issues and strategies. *Family Therapy, 13*(2), 163–176.

Barth, R. (1983). Social support networks in services for adolescents. In J. K. Whittaker & J. Garbarino (Eds.), *Social support networks: Informal helping in the human services* (pp. 329–331). New York: Aldine Publishing Company.

Barth, R. P. & Schinke, S. P. (1984). Enhancing the social supports of teenage mothers. *Social Casework, 65*(9), 523–531.

Bedrosian, R. C. (1981). Ecological factors in cognitive therapy: The use of significant others. In G. Emery, S. D. Hollon & R. C. Bedrosian (Eds.), *New directions in cognitive therapy: A casebook* (pp. 239–254). New York: Guildford Press.

Block, J., Block, J. H. & Keyes, S. (1988). Longitudinally foretelling drug usage in adolescence: Early childhood personality and environmental precursors. *Child Development, 59*, 336–355.

Blyth, D. A. & Foster-Clark, F. S. (1987). Gender differences in perceived intimacy with different members of adolescents' social networks. *Sex Roles, 17*, 689–718.

Blyth, D. A., Hill, J. P. & Thiel, K. S. (1982). Early adolescents' significant others: Grade and gender differences in perceived relationships with familial and non-familial adults and young people. *Journal of Youth and Adolescence, 11*, 425–450.

Boissevain, J. (1974). *Friends of friends: Networks, manipulators and coalitions.* Oxford: Basil Blackwell & Mott.

Bott, E. (1955). Urban families: Conjugal roles and social networks. *Human Relations, 8*, 345–383.

Brown, D. R. & Gary, L. E. (1987). Stressful life events, social support networks, and the physical and mental health of urban black adults. *Journal of Human Stress, 13*,(4), 165–174.

Brownell, A. & Shumaker, S. A. (1984a). Social support: An introduction to a complex phenomenon. *Journal of Social Issues, 40*, 1–10.

———. (1984b). Where do we go from here: The policy implications of social support. *Journal of Social Issues, 40*, 111–122.

Cauce, A. M., Felner, R. D. & Primavera, J. (1982). Social support in high-risk adolescents: Structural components and adaptive impact. *American Journal of Community Psychology, 10*(4), 417–428.

Coates, D. L. (1981). *The Social Network Record.* Washington, DC: Catholic University, Center for the Study of Youth Development.

———. (1985). Relationships between self-concept measures and social network characteristics of black adolescents. *Journal of Early Adolescence, 5*, 319–338.

————. (1987). Gender differences in the structure and support characteristics of black adolescents' social networks. *Sex Roles, 17,* 667–687.

Cohen, F. & Lazarus, R. S. (1979). Coping with the stress of illness. In G. C. Stone, F. Cohen & N. Adler (Eds.), *Health Psychology.* San Francisco: Jossey-Bass.

Cohen, S. & Wills, T. A. (1985). Stress, social support and the buffering hypothesis. *Psychological Bulletin, 98,* 310–357.

Compas, B. E. (1987). Coping with stress during childhood and adolescence. *Psychological Bulletin, 101*(3), 393–403.

Compas, B. E., Slavin, L. A., Wagner, B. M. & Vannatta, K. (1986). Relationship of life events and social support with psychological dysfunction among adolescents. *Journal of Youth and Adolescence, 15*(3), 205–221.

Conger, J. J. (1978). *Adolescence and Youth,* New York: Harper and Row.

Cooper, C. R. (1987). Conceptualizing research on adolescent development in the family: Four root metaphors. *Journal of Adolescent Research 2,* 321–330.

Crockett, L. J., Schulenberg, J. E. & Petersen, A. (1987). Congruence between objective and self-report data in a sample of young adolescents. *Journal of Adolescent Research 2,* 383–392.

d'Abbs, P. (1982). *Social support networks: A critical review of models and findings.* Institute of Family Studies. Monograph No. 1. Melbourne: Institute of Family Studies.

Dean, A. & Ensel, W. M. (1983). The epidemiology of depression in young children: The centrality of social support. *Journal of Psychiatric Treatment and Evaluation, 5,* 195–207.

Donald, C. A. & Ware, J. E (1984). The measurement of social support. *Research in Community and Mental Health, 4,* 325–370.

Dornbusch, S. M., Ritter, P. L., Leiderman, H., Roberts, D. F., & Fraleigh, M. J. (1988). The relation of parenting style to adolescent school performance. *Child Development, 56,* 1244–1257.

Feiring, C. & Coates, D. L. (1987). Social networks and gender differences in the life-space of opportunity. *Sex Roles, 17,* 611–620.

Felner, R. D., Aber, M. S., Primavera, J. & Cauce, A. M. (1985). Adaptation and vulnerability in high-risk adolescents: An examination of environmental mediators. *American Journal of Community Psychology, 13*(4), 365–379.

Fischer, C. S., Jackson, R. M., Stueve, C. A., Gerson, K., Jones, L. M. & Baldassare, M. (1977). *Networks and places: Social relations in the urban setting.* New York: Free Press.

Gad, M. T. & Johnson, J. H. (1980). Correlates of adolescent life stress as related to race, SES, and levels of perceived social support. *Journal of Clinical Child Psychology, 9*(1), 13–16.

Garbarino, J. (1983). Social support networks: RX for the helping professional. In J. K. Whittaker & J. Garbarino (Eds.), *Social support networks: Informal helping in the human services* (pp. 3–28). New York: Aldine Publishing Company.

————. (1985). *Adolescent development: An ecological perspective.* Columbus, OH: Charles E. Merrill Publishing Company.

Gesten, E. L. & Jason, L. A. (1987). Social and community interventions. *Annual Review of Psychology, 38,* 427–461.

Giblin, P. T., Poland, M. L. & Ager, J. W. (1988). Clinical applications of self-esteem and locus of control to adolescent health. *Journal of Adolescent Health Care,* *9*(1), 1–14.

Gilchrist, L. D. & Schinke, S. P. (1983). Coping with contraception: Cognitive and behavioral methods with adolescents. *Cognitive Therapy and Research, 7,* 379–388.

Goldfried, M. R. (1979). Anxiety reduction through cognitive-behavioral intervention. In P. C. Kendall & S. D. Hollon (Eds.), *Cognitive-behavioral interventions: Theory, research and procedures* (pp. 117–152). New York: Academic Press.

Gottlieb, B. (1988). *Issues related to interventions based on social support networks.* Paper presented at the Carnegie Council on Adolescent Development Workshop on the Potential of Social Support Networks for Preventive Interventions during Adolescence, June 1988, Washington, DC.

Greenberger, E. & Sorensen, A. B. (1974). Toward a concept of psychosocial maturity. *Journal of Youth and Adolescence, 3,* 329–358.

Groves, G. (1982). Stress disorders. In S. M. Turner & R. T. Jones, *Behavior modification in black populations: Psychosocial issues and empirical findings* (pp. 279–300). New York: Plenum.

Hamberg, B. A. (1974). Early adolescence: A specific and stressful stage of the life cycle. In G. V. Coelho, D. A. Hamberg & J. E. Adams (Eds.), *Coping and adaptation.* New York: Basic Books.

Hamberg, D. A., Coelho, G. V. & Adams, J. E. (1974). Coping and adaptation: A synthesis of biological and social perspectives. In G. V. Coelho, D. A. Hamburg, & J. E. Adams (Eds.), *Coping and adaptation.* New York: Basic Books.

Hansell, S. (1985). Adolescent friendship networks and distress in school. *Social Forces, 63,* 698–715.

Harrison, A., Serafica, F. & McAdoo, H. (1984). Ethnic families of color. In R. Parke (Ed.), *Review of Child Development Research Vol. 7* (pp. 329–371). Chicago: University of Chicago Press.

Heller, K., Swindle, R. W. & Dusenbury, L. (1986). Component social support processes: Comments and integration. *Journal of Consulting and Clinical Psychology, 54,* 466–470.

Hirsch, B. J. & Rapkin, B. D. (1988). The transition to junior high school: A longitudinal study of self-esteem, psychological symptomatology, school life and social support. *Child Development, 56,* 1235–1243.

Hollon, S. D. & Kendall, P. C. (1979). Cognitive-behavioral interventions: Theory and procedure. In P. C. Kendall & S. D. Hollon (Eds.), *Cognitive-behavioral interventions: Theory, research and procedures* (pp. 445–454). New York: Academic Press.

Holmes, T. H. & Rahe, R. H. (1967). The Social Readjustment Rating Scale. *Journal of Psychosomatic Research, 11,* 213–218.

Kaplan, B. H., Cassel, J. C. & Gore, S. (1977). Social support and health. *Medical Care, 15,* Supplemental: 47–58.

Kelley, M. L. & Stokes, R. F. (1982). Contingency contracting with disadvantaged youth: Improving classroom performance. *Journal of Applied Behavioral Analysis, 15,* 447–454.

Kinney, B. A. (1988). *Individuation in late adolescent and young adult women as a function of psychosocial maturity and interpersonal competence.* Doctoral Dissertation, Catholic University of America, Washington, DC.

Problems & Perspectives

tworks for Preventive Interventions during Adolescence, June 1988, Washing-
, DC.

H., Cowen, E. L., Lorion, R. P. & Ramos-McKay, J. (Eds.) (1988). *Four-
n ounces of prevention: A casebook for practitioners.* Washington, DC:
nerican Psychological Association.

J. M. (1985). Friendship and its implications for mental health or social com-
tence. *Journal of Early Adolescence, 5,* 383–391.

. H. (1982). Childhood support networks: A study of pediatric and psychiatric
tpatients. *Clinical Proceedings CHNMC, 38,* 314–329.

R. (1979). *Networking families in crisis.* New York: Sciences Press.

. P. (1981). Cognitive therapy "in vivo." In G. Emery, S. D. Hollon &
. C. Bedrosian (Eds.), *New directions in cognitive therapy: A casebook* (pp.
71–287). New York: Guilford Press.

S. P., Barth, R. P., Gilchrist, L. D. & Maxwell, J. S. (1986). Adolescent
nothers, stress, and prevention. *Journal of Human Stress, 12,* 162–167.

, S. P., Barth, R. P., Gilchrist, L. D., Whittaker, J. K., Kirkham, M. A.,
Senechal, V. A., Snow, Wh. H. & Maxwell, J. S. (1986). Definitions and
methods for prevention research with youth and families. *Children and Youth
Services Review, 8*(3), 257–266.

, S. P., Schilling, R. F. and Snow, W. H. (1987). Stress management with
adolescents at the junior high transition: An Outcome evaluation of coping skills
intervention. *Journal of Human Stress, 13*(1), 16–22.

V. C. (1982). *Adolescent social development: Functional dynamic interaction.*
Lexington, MA: Lexington Books.

L. T. (1985). Afrikanity, cognition and extended self-identity. In M. B. Spencer, G. K. Brookins & W. R. Allen (Eds.), *Beginnings: The social and affective
development of black children* (pp. 173–183). Hillsdale, NJ: Lawrence Earlbaum
Associates Publishers.

ger, J. S. & Schoeneman, T. J. (1979). Symbolic interactionist view of self-
concept: Through the looking glass darkly. *Psychological Bulletin, 86,* 314–329.

nan, S., Seiffge-Krenge, I. & Sameat, N. (1987). Adolescent coping style as a
function of family climate. *Journal of Adolescent Research, 2,* 367–381.

aker, S. A. & Brownell, A. (1984). Introduction: Social support interventions.
Journal of Social Issues, 40, 1–4.

ions, R. G., Burgeson, R., Carlton-Ford, S. & Blyth, D. (1988). The impact of
cumulative change in early adolescence. *Child Development, 56,* 1220–1234.

ghter, D. T. & McWorter, G. A. (1985). Social origins and early features of the
scientific study of Black American families and children. In M. B. Spencer,
G. K. Brookins & W. R. Allen (Eds.), *Beginnings: The social and affective
development of black children* (pp. 5–18). Hillsdale, NJ: Lawrence Earlbaum
Associates Publishers.

k, J. L. & Speck, R. V. (1985). Social network intervention with adolescents. In
M. P. Mirkin & S. L. Koman (Eds.), *Handbook of adolescents and family therapy* (pp. 149–160). New York: Garner.

vack, G., Platt, J. J. & Shure, M. B. (1976). *The problem-solving approach to
adjustment.* San Francisco: Jossey-Bass.

vens, J. H. (1988). Social support, locus of control, and parenting in three low-

Laumann, E. O. (1973). *Bonds of pluralism*. New Y

Lazarus, R. S. & Folkman, S. (1984). *Stress, a*
Springer.

Lerner, J. V., Hertzog, C., Hooker, K. A., Hassil
longitudinal study of negative emotional states
hood through adolescence. *Child Development,*

Lin, L. (1985). Modelling the effects of social su
M. Ensel (Eds.), *Social support, life events a*
demic Press.

Lindblad-Goldberg, M. & Dukes, J. L. (1985). Socia
single-parent families: Normative and dysfuncti(
of Orthopsychiatry, 55, 42–58.

Little, V. L. & Kendall, P. C. (1979). Cognitive-beha
quents: Problem solving, role-taking and self-con
Hollon (Eds.), *Cognitive-behavioral interventions*
dures (pp. 81–115). New York: Academic Press.

Mahoney, M. J. & Arnkoff, D. B. (1978). Cognitive
S. L. Garfield & A. E. Bergin (Eds.), *The har*
behavior change. New York: John Wiley.

Marjoribanks, K. (1979). Family environments. In H. J.
environments and effects (pp. 15–37). Berkeley: M

Martin, E. P. & Martin, J. M. (1978). *The black extended*
of Chicago Press.

Marziali, E. A. & Pikonis, P. A. (1986). The measureme
stressful life events. *Journal of Human Stress, 12,* 5

McAdoo, H. (1981). *The supportive networks of single blac*
at the Sixth Conference on Empirical Research in E
University, Rochester, MI.

Mechanic, D. (1974). Social structure and personal adaptatio
Hamburg, & J. E. Adams (Eds.), *Coping and adap*
York: Basic Books.

Newton, C. R. & Barbaree, H. E. (1987). Cognitive changes
treatment: The use of a thought-sampling procedure. *C*
search, 11(6), 635–651.

Ogbu, J. U. (1985). A cultural ecology of competence amo
M. B. Spencer, G. K. Brookins & W. R. Allen (Eds.)
and affective development of black children (pp. 45–6
rence Earlbaum Associates Publishers.

Ollendick, T. H. & Cerny, J. A. (1981). Cognitive procedures
In T. H. Ollendick & J. A. Cerny (Eds.), *Clinical beha*
dren. New York: Plenum Press.

Peterson, G. (1987). Role transitions and role identities during ad
interactionist view. *Journal of Adolescent Research, 2,* 23

Preto, N. G. & Travis, N. (1985). The adolescent phase of the
M. P. Mirkin & S. L. Koman (Eds.), *Handbook of adoles*
apy. New York: Gardner Press.

Price, R. H. (1988). *Chairman's Overview*. Comments presented a
cil on Adolescent Development Workshop on the Potenti

Ne
to

Price, R.
te
A

Reisman
p

Rosen, R
o

Rueveni
Sacco, V
R
2

Schinke

Schinke

Schink

Seltzer

Semaj

Shrau

Shuln

Shun

Simn

Slau

Spe

Spi

Ste

income groups of mothers: Black teenagers, black adults and white adults. *Child Development, 59,* 635–642.

Thoits, P. A. (1986). Social support as coping assistance. *Journal of Consulting and Clinical Psychology, 54,* 416–423.

Tolor, A. & Fehon, D. (1987). Coping with stress. A study of male adolescents coping strategies related to adjustment. *Journal of Adolescent Research 2,* 33–42.

Tolsdorf, C. C. (1976). Social networks, support, and coping: An exploratory study. *Family Process, 15,* 407–417.

Turk, D. C. & Genest, M. (1979). Regulation of pain: The application of cognitive and behavioral techniques for prevention and remediation. In P. C. Kendall & S. D. Hollon (Eds.), *Cognitive-behavioral interventions: Theory, research and procedures* (pp. 287–318). New York: Academic Press.

Wahler, R. G. (1980). Parent insularity as a determinant of generalized success in family treatment. In S. Salzinger, J. Antrobus & J. Glick (Eds.), *The ecosystem of the "sick" child: Implications for classification and intervention for disturbed and mentally retarded children* (pp. 187–197). New York: Academic Press.

Wahler, R. G., Berland, R. M., Coe, T. D. & Leske, G. (1976). Social systems analysis: Implementing an alternative behavioral model. In A. Rogers-Warren & S. F. Warren (Eds.), *Ecological perspective in behavior analysis* (pp. 211–228). Baltimore: University Park Press.

Wahler, R. G., Leske, G. & Rogers, E. S. (1979). The insular family: A deviance support system for oppositional children. In L. A. Hamerlynck (Ed.), *Behavioral systems for the developmentally disabled: School and family environments.* New York: Bruner/Mazel.

Walker, L. S. & Greene, J. W. (1987). Negative life events, psychosocial resources, and psychophysiological symptoms in adolescents. *Journal of Clinical Child Psychology, 16*(1), 29–36.

Ward, D. (1986). Integrating formal and informal social care: Social action approach. Anglo/American Study Course: Integrating formal and informal care. The utilization of social support networks. *British Journal of Social Work, 16*(supplement), 149–165.

Wellman, B. (1979). The community question. *American Journal of Sociology, 84,* 1201–1231.

Windle, M. (1987). Stressful life events, general mental health and temperament among late adolescent females. *Journal of Adolescent Research 2,* 13–31.

Youniss, J. (1980). *Parents and peers in social development: A Sullivan-Piagetian perspective.* Chicago: University of Chicago Press.

2

Psychosocial Stress, Coping, and Development of Hispanic Immigrant Children

Luis M. Laosa

Loss, separation, and the requirement to adapt to new and changing life circumstances are interpersonal processes—often traumatic—to which all individuals and families are subjected at various points during their lifetimes. There are, however, other events of extraordinary intensity that involve personal uprooting, loss, and separation—circumstances that frequently induce family disruption and mental suffering and that cause markedly abrupt social and cultural discontinuities. These events place enormous demands on the individual for personal change and adaptation. One such event is immigration; and among those who feel the impact of this experience are Hispanic children who immigrate to the United States. These children and their families must adapt to a new and markedly different social, cultural, linguistic, and climatic environment. Although there is generally no agreed-upon definition of the term *stress* (see Garmezy & Rutter, 1983), almost everyone will agree that immigration is a potentially severe stressful process.

There has been a surge in Hispanic immigration in recent years, and the Hispanic population is expected to continue to grow at a much more rapid rate than perhaps any other segment of the population (Moore & Pachon, 1985;

Work on portions of this chapter was supported by a grant from the William T. Grant Foundation, which the author gratefully acknowledges.

U.S. Bureau of the Census, 1986, 1988). Demographic, social, political, and economic factors in Central and South America and in the Caribbean are such that, by all indications, these regions will continue to be a prime source of both documented and undocumented immigration. The United States will attract, in large numbers, families and individuals from the many Spanish-speaking nations that have population pressures and where the future appears troubled (Inter-American Dialogue, 1988; Morris, 1985).

Some children from Hispanic immigrant families adapt quite successfully to their new environment, and, in spite of unusually difficult circumstances, some even outperform the academic and social norms of U.S. natives. But many others fare less well; for example, many adapt poorly to their role as students in U.S. schools, thus further complicating their prospects and limiting their opportunities once they become adolescents and young adults. Indeed, the prevalence of educational and mental health problems among Hispanic children appears to rise as a function of length of stay in this country (Baral, 1979; Borjas & Tienda, 1985; Canino, Earley & Rogler, 1980; Fernandez & Nielsen, 1986; Valdez, 1986). Although there are some differences among the many U.S. Hispanic ethnic groups (for example, Mexican-Americans, mainland Puerto Ricans, Cuban-Americans, Dominican-Americans, and Salvadoran-Americans, to name a few) with regard to such sociodemographic variables as educational and occupational attainment, there is also considerable overlap, and the intragroup variation is generally greater than that among group averages (U.S. Bureau of the Census, 1988). Similarly, anecdotal evidence suggests a broad range of variation in the coping strategies, adjustment, development, and adaptation of Hispanic immigrant children. These children also vary widely in their apparent vulnerability to the events and processes associated with their immigration and settlement experiences. Briefly consider two Hispanic children, Andrés and Gualberto—keep in mind, however, that the contrast between them is but a mere hint at what is indeed a highly diverse population with a very broad and complex spectrum of particular circumstances.

Andrés

Andrés attends the sixth grade class of a U.S. public school. It is early spring, and the snow is beginning to melt. Andrés had never seen snow until two years ago, when he first arrived in this country with his family. The decision to emigrate took place in the aftermath of his uncle's death. His uncle had been a bystander discharging his daily duties as postman when he was caught in the crossfire between a band of urban guerrillas and government forces. Andrés's parents have not yet established close relationships here, but Andrés has already developed warm friendships with other children in the neighborhood.

Andrés spoke no English when the family first arrived in the United States, and his father spoke only a little learned from a Business English course. Nevertheless, Andrés is described today by his teachers as very attentive, industrious, and well behaved in class. They further describe him as highly motivated to master the English language, to learn the subject matter, to do the daily assignments, and to become familiar with "the way of doing things" here. He receives some help from Mrs. Vincent, an English-as-a-Second-Language (ESL) teacher. However, as a result of cutbacks in federal funding, the amount of time that Mrs. Vincent is able to devote to Andrés is very limited. She is the only ESL or bilingual-education teacher in the school district this year, and she must divide her time among four different school buildings.

At age twelve, Andrés is a confident, seemingly happy child, who performs well in his schoolwork.

Gualberto

Gualberto, too, is in a sixth grade class. His parents enrolled him last summer, shortly after their arrival in this country. Gualberto's father had decided to leave their closely-knit extended family and come to the United States because he was very dissatisfied with his career opportunities in his country and was frustrated about their insecure economic prospects.

Gualberto was an above-average student in his country. However, here he is having serious difficulties in school. He is frequently caught fighting with other students and is described by his teachers as uncooperative. Language is not much of a problem, because he had learned a fair amount of English from a tutor in his native community. Indeed, he and his sister already speak English with one another at home, thus frustrating their mother, who does not understand the new language.

Meanwhile, Gualberto's school problems are getting worse. At age eleven-and-a-half, he expresses considerable dislike for school, does poorly in his schoolwork, is frequently absent, and quarrels often with his classmates.

Why did these two Hispanic children with histories of loss, separation, and physical dislocation emerge at opposite ends of the academic and social adjustment spectrum by the sixth grade? Specifically, what factors allowed Andrés to excel against multiple odds? What variables explain why Gualberto has adapted so poorly to his role as student in the new environment? And more generally, what factors can prevent the downward trend experienced by, and often expected of (Orum, 1986), so many U.S. Hispanic children?

Prompted by these considerations, this chapter focuses on the general question: Which forms of experience associated with immigration and settlement are likely to influence the course of adaptation, adjustment, and development of Hispanic immigrant children? Several lines of research and theory on psychosocial stress, coping, and human development are reviewed, and their relevance to our understanding of the processes implied by this question are explored. Some answers are suggested, and clues identified, about protective and risk factors (Garmezy, 1985; Rutter, 1979) in the adaptation and development of these children and their families. In order to provide a vehicle for venturing into this broad and complex topic, an evolving conceptual framework is elaborated, and testable hypotheses are derived from it. The principal aims of the chapter are heuristic: (a) to add some measure of conceptual clarity to the topic, (b) to stimulate further research, and (c) to raise the consciousness level of applied professionals and policymakers. The topic reflects a fundamental element of this nation's character—the effective incorporation of new arrivals into the ongoing social order.

TOWARD PREVENTIVE APPROACHES

When applied to other problems, research approaches that seek to identify risk factors have yielded useful information by identifying variables linked to the probability of developmental problems. Such factors include, for example, intense stress in the caregiving environment resulting from parental mental illness, family discord, or economic deprivation (for recent reviews, see Farran & McKinney, 1986; Garmezy & Rutter, 1983; Honig, 1984). Although the tendency has been to focus on the "things that go wrong," the potential for prevention lies in increasing our knowledge and understanding of the reasons "why some children *are not* damaged" (Rutter, 1979, p. 49). For even under the most severely disruptive circumstances or handicaps, some children appear to develop stable, healthy, and productive personalities, thus displaying a marked degree of *resilience*—that is, the ability to recover from or adjust easily to misfortune or sustained life stress (Werner, 1984).

In their search for the factors that account for such resilience, some researchers are turning their attention to the coping patterns of children of divorced parents (e.g., Hetherington, Cox & Cox, 1978, 1982). Others have uncovered sources of strength and gentleness among children affected by contemporary wars (for reviews see Garmezy, 1983; Werner, 1984). And a few have studied the lives of (nonimmigrant) minority children who did exceptionally well in school in spite of chronic poverty and discrimination (e.g., Clark, 1983; Gándara, 1982; Shipman, Boroson, Bridgeman, Gant & Mikovsky, 1976).

Among children undergoing unusually severe or prolonged stressful events, there are some who have demonstrated unusual, exemplary performance. Something about their individual or family characteristics, or characteristics of people and situations outside the family, or some pattern or combination of these characteristics either compensated for, challenged, or protected them against the adverse effects of stressful life events. Their performance has inspired some writers to refer to them in such eloquent terms as stress-resistant (Garmezy & Tellegen, 1984), invulnerable (Anthony, 1974), and vulnerable but invincible (Werner & Smith, 1982).

The reasons for such heartening outcomes are not yet known. We have some clues and hypotheses, however, as we shall see.

A MULTIVARIATE MODEL

A recent review of family stress theory and data over the past three decades (McCubbin & Patterson, 1983) suggests that individual and family outcomes following the impact of stressors and crises are the byproduct of the interaction

Figure 2.1
Conceptual Framework of Influences on the Psychosocial and Educational
Adaptation, Development, and Adjustment of Immigrant Schoolchildren

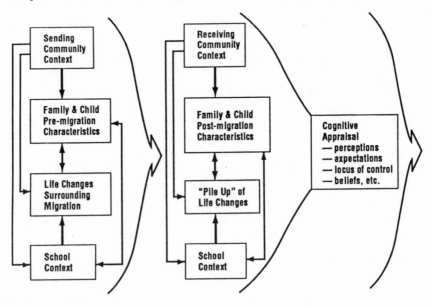

of multiple factors (see also Canino et al., 1980; Cervantes & Castro, 1985; Rogler, Gurak & Cooney, 1987). This conclusion implies that a promising research strategy for studying coping and adaptation among immigrant children is to employ a multivariate model where several domains of variables—identified not only from prior research studies but also from less systematic observations—are addressed simultaneously. In this way, the individual and collective contributions of these variables can be ascertained. The overarching research question then becomes: What kinds of circumstances or events, mediated by what perceptions thereof, interacting with what characteristics of the individual, the family, and the "sending" and "receiving" communities, shape the course of the Hispanic immigrant child's coping strategies, adaptation, adjustment, and development in the new society?

The conceptual model here proposed is depicted schematically in Figure 2.1. A central feature of this model is that it postulates the presence of moderator or mediating variables between the stresses of immigration and the child's adaptation, adjustment, and development over time. To illustrate, it is helpful to borrow Rahe's metaphor of optical lenses and filters (1974). Adapting the metaphor to the issue at hand, we can think of environmental events as light rays representing an individual's exposure to life changes. Some characteristics of the individual—such as the manner of perceiving (i.e., interpreting) certain life events—may act as light filters that alter the intensity of various life events.

Figure 2.1 (Continued)

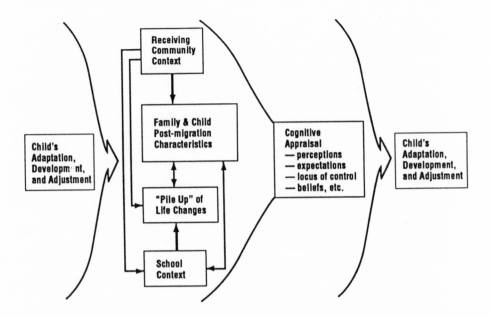

For example, a particular perception, expectation, or belief may intensify the impact of a life change, whereas a different perception or expectation may lessen it. The impact of some life-change events will be diffracted away by a subsequent experience or a contextual variable; others will pass through with little deflection. Along this pathway there are several chances for life changes to be handled in such a way that they never have a negative impact on the Hispanic immigrant child's psychosocial or educational development, or in a manner that they instead provide a stimulus for superior achievement. Another characteristic of the model proposed here is its emphasis on continuous change, development, and reciprocal influences as ongoing processes over time.

Let us now turn to some specific variables and hypotheses.

Characteristics of the Sending Community

We should expect to find considerable diversity in the characteristics of the Hispanic immigrants' communities of origin. For example, the sending communities[1] are likely to vary in population density, degree of urbanicity, intensity of political/military strife, type of economy and political system, and economic circumstances and prospects. These and other (objective and perceived) characteristics of the sending community are likely to be associated—directly or indirectly—with other factors in the model, including the choice of coping strategies and the course of adjustment and adaptation in the receiving community. The mechanisms accounting for this association are hypothesized to hinge on the contrasts between the receiving and sending communities. The discontinuity hypothesis (see, e.g., Laosa, 1977b, 1979, 1982) predicts that such contrasts will partly explain the course of adaptation. A similar prediction can be made from person-environment fit theory (see, e.g., French, Doehrman, Davis-Sacks & Vinokur, 1983). That is, the greater the articulated continuity between the sending and receiving community contexts or the fit between the characteristics of the person and those of the host environment, the more rapid and successful the adaptation and the healthier the adjustment.

We should also expect to find wide diversity in the circumstances surrounding immigration. In many instances, these circumstances will arise from characteristics of the sending and receiving communities. Consider that the causes of movements of human populations are quite diverse, including, for example, flows of skilled technicians and professionals in search of opportunities denied them in their homelands; displacements of manual labor moving permanently or temporarily to meet labor needs in the receiving economy; and refugee movements forced by political repression (Portes & Bach, 1985). Although typically such diversity is studied at the level of central tendencies between national-origin groups, significant individual differences, no doubt, occur within groups. It seems important to recognize explicitly the distinct character of each individual's or family's immigration and to assess the influence of its particular circumstances.

Family Premigration Life-Style and Background Characteristics

Social antecedents, that is, background characteristics referring to the "stock of human capital" that immigrants bring with them must be considered in evaluating or predicting how successfully they adjust. Among such characteristics are formal education level, specific marketable skills, occupational experience, English-language proficiency, age, and physical health. These, like other variables in the model, can have both direct and indirect effects. For example, formal schooling level is likely to be important not only in fulfilling requirements for occupational level entry—as Rogg and Cooney (1980) found was true of Cuban émigrés in West New York—but the more highly schooled immigrants may be more likely to adhere to such U.S. mainstream values as individualism and futurism, which in turn may influence their choice of coping strategies (see also Laosa, 1982).

The nature of the child-family relationships in the sending community, including those aspects related to the child's intellectual stimulation, are likely to be predictive not only of similar qualities of family life in the receiving community, but also predictive of the child's scholastic achievement (see, e.g., Henderson, 1981; Laosa & Sigel, 1982; Marjoribanks, 1979).

"Pile Up" of Stressors

A "piling up" of life changes during the period preceding, attending, and following immigration is also expected to account for variance in the child's adaptation and adjustment. Rutter (1979) has noted with insight that most research data are not analyzed in such a way as to reveal the cumulative and interactive effects of single stresses. The usual analytic approaches permit us to assess whether or not a particular stress has a statistical effect after taking into account its association with other forms of stress or disadvantage. Whereas the results of such analyses can reveal whether the stressor has an effect over and above that of other factors, they do not tell us whether or not the stressor has an effect when it occurs on its own. Using a different type of analysis, Rutter obtained interesting and surprising results, revealing that children with only one risk factor—that is, those with a single stressful event or situation— were no more likely to show psychiatric disorder than children with no risk factors at all. On the other hand, when two stressors occurred together, the risk increased fourfold, and with yet more concurrent stresses, the risk rose several times further. This finding led Rutter to the conclusion that "the stresses *potentiated* each other" so that the combination of stresses "provided very much more than a summation of the effects of separate stresses considered singly" (1979, pp. 52–53).

For an immigrant child, a piling up of stresses may well occur in connection with the events and experiences surrounding the immigration and settlement. On the basis of Rutter's finding, it is reasonable to hypothesize that such a pile up will have the effect of magnifying the stressful effects of immigration—all other things being equal—and thus, for example, increase the probability of physical illness or psychological problems during the settlement period.

Characteristics of the Receiving Community

Reception factors in the receiving community, such as relevant employment opportunities, the presence of a Hispanic enclave, the availability of community-based social supports, and community attitudes toward the newcomers must be considered among the variables that can influence the family's coping strategies and course of adaptation and development.

Social supports. A series of research reviews published in the mid-1970s (Caplan, 1974; Cassell, 1974; Cobb, 1976; Haggerty, Roghmann & Pless, 1975) sparked the interest in social supports. The evidence reviewed in these works suggested a causal link between social support and mental and physical health. Neighborhoods, family and kinship, and mutual self-help groups are among the major social support networks that have been studied (for reviews see House, Landis & Umberson, 1988; McCubbin, Joy, Cauble, Comeau, Patterson & Needle, 1980).

Poignant insights into some of the roles of social supports are provided by

Melville's anthropological study (1981) of Mexican women who had migrated to Houston, a major urban metropolis in the southwestern United States. The outstanding source of stress among these women was the loneliness caused by the separation from the extended family, from familiar and predictable neighbors, and from well-known, culturally meaningful surroundings; this separation from a customary social network and from frequent and numerous social contacts created a strain. It was not always possible to find housing near relatives or friends who had previously immigrated. Loneliness was compounded for those women who had to remain at home all day to care for the children. Their contacts were often limited to a neighbor or two, and for some, it was difficult to find these. As one of Melville's informants put it, "Here, people have air conditioning and leave their doors and windows closed" (1981). Social support factors that bear on the parents and influence their psychological well-being (e.g., depression) are likely to affect the quality of the parent-child relationship, and hence, indirectly influence the child's own adjustment, adaptation, and development in the new environment.

Studies pointing to the presence of familial ties as buffers against health breakdown suggest that a small, densely interconnected network of intimate ties is critical to individual well-being (Pilisuk & Parks, 1983). But such ties, however important, may be insufficient for certain types of psychosocial transition (Granovetter, 1973, 1983). For example, job loss is an event for which the dense, kinship-dominated network can typically provide consolation but not reassurance or assistance in finding new employment. Thus, for the immigrant parent to branch out into the new areas of commitment required by the receiving community, a larger network of weaker ties may also be critical to the family's successful adaptation.

Additional evidence of the importance of social supports and related situational and contextual factors comes from clinical studies of children who underwent displacement and evacuation during World War II and in more recent civil strife in the Middle East and Ireland (Garmezy, 1983). The evidence generally points to the quality of the relationship between the child and family members as a key variable distinguishing between children who were best able to sustain uprooting and those who had more difficulty. Another type of protective factor that can help contain the effects of stress resulting from uprooting is the model behavior presented by significant others in the child's life, including parents, guardians, teachers, counselors, and peers (Garmezy, 1983). The literature also makes reference to the role of communal ideology expressed by adults and to the efforts of significant adult figures to inculcate a sense of security in the children. Other evidence comes from studies of minority persons whose educational and occupational achievements have surpassed even the norm of those from more privileged backgrounds (e.g., Clark, 1983; Gándara, 1982; Shipman et al., 1976); these studies, too, point to the influence of the parent-child relationship or of some other aspect of the home environment.

In the framework proposed here, the concept of social support includes three major categories of support: (1) interpersonal transactions that provide emotional support and esteem, leading the individual to believe that he or she is cared for, loved, and esteemed and that he or she belongs to a network of communication involving mutual understanding (Cobb, 1976); (2) information disseminated with regard to problem solving and new social contacts for help (Granovetter, 1973, 1983); and (3) service agencies and other sources of material aid and tangible services such as child care, tutoring, language lessons, help with school homework, financial aid, and housing.

Both the availability and accessibility of social supports and their ability to provide support have been found to vary greatly (McCubbin et al., 1980), and such variability is likely to increase for Hispanic immigrant families. For example, the relationship between Hispanic immigrants and social supports can be affected by such variables as language proficiency and cultural beliefs and values.

Attitudes toward newcomers. Negative attitudes, stereotypes, and prejudices are sometimes associated with certain ethnic, racial, and language groups in the United States. By virtue of mere membership in such a group, the immigrant may be denied the same opportunities and experiences that normally are extended readily to, say, white, native English speakers. Being the subject of prejudice or discrimination, whether subtle or overt, can change and intensify the meaning and impact of normative societal stressors (McAdoo, 1983; Peters & Massey, 1983). The phenomenon may go beyond person-to-person interaction in the neighborhood, in the school, or on the work site. Indeed, negative images about particular groups may be part of the mainstream culture and hence difficult to escape, for they are projected continuously throughout the society— through TV, school textbooks, ethnic jokes, and personal experiences when different groups come in contact with one another (McAdoo, 1983). These concerns are important reasons for considering the role of community attitudes toward the immigrant group and, conversely, the manner in which the immigrant responds to and copes with prejudice and discrimination when they emerge. Stereotyped images may surface, for example, when teachers implicitly do not expect as much from the immigrant child and therefore are given less in return (Brophy & Good, 1974; Laosa, 1977a) or when employers do not consider members of certain groups capable of doing a job regardless of their individual ability or training. Moreover, the *duality* that immigrants may experience as they strive to obtain a balance between their educational or economic aspirations, often found only in the mainstream world, and their cultural and language roots may engender psychological conflict and thus further stress (Fordham, 1988; McAdoo, 1983).

The impact of stressors may depend in part on one's cognitive appraisal of the situation, as the following discussion suggests.

Cognitive Appraisal and Coping

It now appears that life events cannot be meaningfully studied without reference to how the individual perceives (construes) such events. Research suggests that one's cognitive appraisal of life events strongly influences how one responds to them (for reviews of research see Hamilton & Warburton, 1979). The same event may be perceived by different persons as irrelevant, benign, and positive, or threatening and harmful. Hinkle (1974) cites the example of the Hungarian refugees at the time of their flight during their revolt in the mid-1950s. Hinkle reports that for many of them, the physical dislocation and the many changes they experienced during the revolt and subsequent flight were accompanied by an element of pleasurable excitement and anticipation and by an improvement in their general health and well-being; for others, however, such life changes can be painful, with negative consequences. The general hypothesis here is that two individuals may differ widely in their perception (construal) of the same or a similar event, and that this difference is likely to result in divergent ways of coping and implications for adaptation.

Accordingly, we should expect to find wide variation among Hispanic immigrants' cognitive appraisals of the events surrounding their losses, dislocation, and life in the new environment. Where some of them will see opportunities and challenges to be mastered, others will see unwanted circumstances to be resisted or passively endured. The Hispanic immigrants' cognitive appraisals of the events and prospects surrounding their immigration and settlement are hypothesized to be important factors contributing to their choice of coping strategies and their adaptation to the new environment.

Primary and secondary appraisal. Lazarus (1984; Lazarus & Folkman, 1984) has identified two kinds of cognitive appraisal—primary and secondary.[2] The term *primary appraisal* is given to the process of evaluating the significance of an event for one's well-being. Primary appraisals of events can be one of three forms—irrelevant, benign-positive, or stressful. Three kinds of stressful appraisal are postulated: harm/loss, threat, or challenge. *Harm/loss* refers to injury or damage already done, as in the loss of a loved one or damage to physical function, social esteem, self-esteem, existential meaning, and so on. *Threat* can refer to the same kind of injuries, but the term signifies that they are anticipated but have not yet occurred. *Challenge* means an opportunity for growth, mastery, or gain. A hypothesis about the causal antecedents of threat and challenge is that the former is more likely when one assumes that the specific environment is hostile and dangerous and that one lacks the resources for mastering it. Challenge, on the other hand, arises when the environmental demands are seen as difficult but not impossible to manage, and that drawing upon skills that one has or can acquire offers a genuine prospect for mastery. In Lazarus's framework, the distinction between harm/loss, threat, and challenge may be very important not only in affecting the coping process itself and the effectiveness with which coping skills are used, but also in their divergent consequences for morale and somatic health.

Another form of appraisal also appears to be important. The term *secondary appraisal* refers to conceptualizing the implications of the event in terms of coping and resource options (Folkman, Schaefer & Lazarus, 1979). In secondary appraisal, the answer to the question, "What can I do about the trouble?" centers on evaluating the availability of suitable coping strategies—that is, on the goodness of fit among task demands, coping resources, and personal agendas. If coping is defined as "efforts, both action oriented and intrapsychic, to manage (i.e., master, tolerate, reduce, minimize) environmental and internal demands and conflicts among them, which tax or exceed a person's resources" (Folkman et al., 1979, pp. 282–283), then the range of coping processes that can be employed is broad. Such processes encompass at least four main categories—information search, direct action, inhibition of action, and intrapsychic modes. These coping processes can have at least two main functions—to alter the person-environment relationship (instrumental or problem-solving) or to regulate the stress and distress reaction (palliative).

Coping resources can be drawn from within the person or from the environment, and they include at least five categories—health/energy/morale, problem-solving skills, social networks, utilitarian resources (e.g., money, social agencies), and beliefs (Folkman et al., 1979). Thus, an important point is to distinguish between coping resources and the specific coping processes actually used in a given situation. The presence of coping resource does not mean that it inevitably will be used when required.

Self-efficacy and locus of control. Of the five categories of coping resources that Lazarus and associates (Folkman et al., 1979; Lazarus & Folkman, 1984) mention, one in particular, which they label *beliefs,* has psychocultural implications. In addition to perceptions and assumptions about specific events and environments (already discussed and labeled *primary appraisal*), people may have very general beliefs about themselves and the environment that will influence their appraisal of the specific events and environments (Lazarus, 1984). For example, Bandura (1977, 1982) and others have emphasized the belief in self-efficacy as a general, overarching resource that is hypothesized to be critical in coping. The self-efficacy construct seems conceptually related to the locus-of-control variable discussed by Rotter (1966) and Lefcourt (1976; see also Lefcourt 1981, 1983, 1984). Both refer to individual differences in adherence to the conviction that reinforcements are contingent on one's own behavior rather than being the result of luck, chance, or fate, which are unpredictable. A prediction from these theories is that to disbelieve in one's own efficacy should generate passivity and disengagement; at its extreme, such disbelief should be associated with a sense of helplessness and hopelessness, which can in turn be linked to depression (Folkman et al., 1979; Seligman, 1975). Experimental research suggests that it does not matter whether one actually has control; the important factor is thinking, or believing, one has control (Maier, 1984).

Locus of control was one of the variables that distinguished resilient from other high-risk children in the longitudinal study on the island of Kauai (Werner & Smith, 1982). Although it is always difficult to determine the directionality of correlations, a longitudinal design such as this one can provide a reasonable basis for causal interpretations. The resilient adolescents in this study, especially girls, seemed to have greater faith in their own control of the environment than did adolescents with serious coping problems. Achievement and psychological well-being appeared to be closely related to what the youngsters believed about their environment; that is, whether they believed, as the resilient ones appeared to do, that the environment would respond to reasonable efforts, or whether they believed, as those with serious problems appeared to do, that events were random and immovable.

Some beliefs may stem from historic-sociocultural premises. Attitudes, beliefs, and values shared within a culture provide a common basis for socialization of the child in that culture (see Sigel, 1985). Díaz-Guerrero (1975, 1982) has proposed that these implicit attitudes, beliefs, and values constitute historic-sociocultural premises that are fundamental determinants of shared personality characteristics within a given culture. These premises are deep-seated beliefs or assumptions about life transmitted from one generation to the next and are held by a majority belonging to the culture, subculture, or group. An example of an important dimension reflecting a historic-sociocultural premise is the variable labeled *affiliative obedience vs. active self-assertion*. Research by Díaz-Guerrero and his colleagues has revealed striking cross-national differences along this dimension. In a study of fourteen-year-old boys, for example, these researchers found that the majority in the United States subscribed to active self-assertion, whereas their Mexican counterparts preferred affiliative obedience. The most striking differences between cultures appeared for the low socioeconomic strata, suggesting that this segment of the population is the primary carrier of traditional sociocultural premises inherited from the past (Holtzman, Díaz-Guerrero, & Swartz, 1975).[3]

To the extent that historic-sociocultural premises may influence behavior, cultural groups can be expected to differ in their choice of coping strategies. An immigrant child may already possess a well-developed repertoire of coping strategies (or competencies), which are effective in and appropriate to the child's native cultural context. The same coping strategies and competencies may nevertheless differ in critical ways from those preferred by members of the host culture. They may even be ineffective, inappropriate, or offensive when applied within the context of the host culture, leading the members of that culture to view the immigrant child as incompetent, unmotivated, or perversely uncooperative (Laosa, 1979).

Rogler and Cooney (1984) examined certain historic-sociocultural premises among first- and second-generation Puerto Rican parents in the (mainland) United States, in particular a belief that events are more often contingent upon chance, luck, or fate than upon one's actions. The research results showed a stronger disagreement with this belief in the second than in the first generation, implying the effects of acculturation. The data also showed that, regardless of generation, those with more years of formal schooling appeared less strongly committed to sociocultural premises associated with traditional Puerto Rican culture than those with fewer years of education, suggesting, at least partly, the effects of schooling on traditional culture (cf. Laosa, 1982). Also, first-generation men who experienced upward mobility after leaving Puerto Rico and during their lives in the United States expressed significantly less adherence to these premises than those experiencing little or downward mobility. To the extent that beliefs may influence behavior, we should hypothesize that the historic-socio-cultural premises of an immigrant child's native culture will predispose that child to a particular pattern of coping, adaptation, and adjustment in the receiving society.

Expectancies and causal attributions. Explanations of behavior that include cognitive appraisal as a theoretical construct bear a conceptual resemblance to those that posit motivation as a variable. The early search for an understanding of the motivational/attitudinal determinants of achievement-related behavior was stimulated by the expectancy-value theory (Atkinson, 1958; for a review see Spence & Helmreich, 1983). This theory focuses on individual differences in the motive to achieve and on the effects of subjective expectancy on both this motive and the incentive value of success. Although some investigators, using new techniques to measure achievement motives, have continued to explore the implications of motivational mediators for achievement (see Spence & Helmreich, 1983), much of the work in the last decade has shifted attention away from motivational constructs to cognitive constructs, such as casual attributions, subjective expectancies, self-concepts of abilities, perceptions of task difficulty, and subjective task value (e.g., Eccles, 1983). Theoretical models that fit into this tradition, such as that of Eccles (1983), are built on the assumption that it is not reality itself that most determines one's expectancies, values, and behavior, but rather one's interpretation of that reality. The influence of reality on achievement outcomes and future goals is assumed to be mediated by causal-attribution patterns for success and failure, perceptions of one's own needs, values, and identity, as well as perceptions of characteristics of the task. Each of these factors, according to this view, plays a role in determining the expectancy and value associated with a particular task. Expectancy and value, in turn, are seen as influencing a whole range of achievement-related behaviors, for example, choice of the activity, intensity of the effort expanded, and actual performance.

Numerous studies have demonstrated the importance of expectancies for a variety of achievement behaviors, including academic performance, task persistence, and task choice (for reviews see Eccles, 1983; Spence & Helmreich, 1983). In her theoretical model, Eccles (1983) has proposed that students' expectancies are influenced most directly by their self-concept of ability and by their own estimate of task difficulty. Historical events, past experiences of success and failure, and cultural factors are hypothesized to be mediated through the individual's interpretations of these past events, perceptions of the expectancies of others, and identification with the goals and values of existing cultural role structures. Eccles's data on schoolchildren already provide some empirical evidence in support of her model. Although neither her theory nor her data focuses on immigrants' performance, the mentioned features of her model bear attractive promise for the testing of hypotheses regarding immigrant children's adaptation and academic development.

The School Context

Much has been written and debated about the effects of schools, and a spate of reports on the need to upgrade educational standards in U.S. schools has recently been issued by various national and regional commissions (e.g., Board of Inquiry, 1985; National Commission on Excellence in Education, 1983; Regional Policy Committee on Minorities in Higher Education, 1987; Youth and America's future, 1988). The public controversy over whether schools make a difference in reducing social inequalities has swung from the extreme pessimism of the late 1960s to the current optimistic view about the effects of schools on student progress. Among the issues that underlie the expressed concerns in today's view is the academic performance of ethnolinguistic minority students, who represent a growing proportion of the total school-age population.

Research studies and anecdotal observations by parents, educators, and students point to a variety of school contextual factors that are likely to affect the Hispanic immigrant child's coping and adaptation. These factors range from the nature of available services specifically geared to serve foreign, limited English-proficient, and cultural minority students, to school climate and organization variables that are likely to affect all students, to structural qualities such as the ethnolinguistic composition of the student body and teaching staff, and still other variables such as teacher expectancies, the frequency and nature of school-initiated and family-initiated parent–teacher contact, parental involvement in the child's formal education, and peer tutoring (for research reviews see Baker & de Kanter, 1983; Brophy & Good, 1986; Good, 1983; Good & Brophy, 1986; Gotts & Purnell, 1986; Haskins & Adams, 1983; Rutter, 1983a; Williams, Richmond & Mason, 1986; Willig, 1985). School contextual variables are hypothesized to contribute significantly to Hispanic immigrant children's adjustment and adaptation to their role as students.

Other Relevant Variables

Space considerations do not permit a discussion of all the variables or their many complex interrelationships that are directly relevant to the conceptual model proposed and schematized in brief outline in Figure 2.1. Only three more variables are discussed, therefore, before we turn to a consideration of developmental issues, which suffuse the entire model, pertaining as they do to virtually all the variables in it. These three final variables are among those reflecting individual characteristics of the child and the family.

Sex. A potentially important variable is sex. It appears that males are more vulnerable to physical stresses, and they seem in some respects to be also more susceptible to psychosocial traumata (LeCorgne & Laosa, 1976; Rutter, 1979; Werner & Smith, 1982), at least insofar as the effects are expressed at certain ages. Little is known about the reason for these apparent differences. The topic has recently attracted the attention of the Committee on Child Development Research and Public Policy of the National Academy of Sciences, and a committee project was organized to review the available evidence. The research evidence indicates that boys may respond more negatively than girls to some forms of psychosocial stress (Zaslow, 1987; Zaslow & Hayes, 1986). Practically nothing is known, however, about sex differences in vulnerability to immigration stresses among Hispanic schoolchildren.

Temperament. Temperament is another constitutional factor that has been implicated as relevant to the study of stress. It is perhaps a worthwhile variable to study in this regard, although the research evidence on the relationship between temperament and response to stress is limited (see Rutter, 1974, 1983b), and conceptual and methodological problems plague the field of temperament research (Hubert, Wachs, Peters-Martin & Gandour, 1982). A provocative discussion by Thomas, Chess, Sillen, and Mendez (1974) suggests the potential relevance of temperament to the adjustment of immigrant children. They reported a higher frequency of arrhythmic temperament (irregularity of biological functions) among their low-income New York Puerto Rican sample than in their non-Hispanic white middle-class (predominantly Jewish) sample. They attributed this group difference to more permissive socialization practices regarding the establishment of feeding and sleeping schedules among the former. That is, arrhythmicity as a temperamental characteristic during the preschool years was a major source of parental concern when it occurred in the middle-class non-Hispanic families, but not when it occurred in the low-income Puerto Rican sample. Later, however, when the children entered school and were expected to adhere to its system of inflexible schedules, arrhythmicity became a serious problem of adaptation in the Puerto Rican sample. Apparently, the early parental concern with arrhythmicity was translated into attempts by the non-Hispanic sample to control or modify such behavior when it occurred in their young children. It thus seems that there may exist cultural or socioeconomic group differences in parental reactions to emerging temperamental characteristics, differences that may have consequences for the children's later adaptation to extrafamilial environments such as the school. Although these particular findings on temperament are intriguing and intuitively appealing, they apparently have not been replicated.

Legal status. The final variable to be considered here that warrants examination because of its potential relevance to the psychosocial adaptation and adjustment of immigrant children is the status of their own or their family's presence in the country. *Undocumented aliens* is a term referring to persons illegally in the United States, namely, without residential, immigrant, or refugee status. An illegal alien is subject to deportation. Probably the largest group of undocumented aliens are among the Hispanics, particularly Mexican Americans. The aliens are often thought to consist mainly of single male migratory workers, but it appears that a large number are families with children; many have been here for a long time (Jenkins, 1983). Children in this status may have family-based emotional supports and economic support from working parents, but these families are likely to lack security, a sense of permanence, and social acceptance. They may feel threatened by the loss of health and education services because of their uncertain legal position.

There is some empirical support for the hypothesis that undocumented status adds significantly to the stressors generally experienced by immigrants in the United States. In a study of comparative stress among documented and undocumented Mexican families, Salcido (1979) found a high stress level for 52 percent of the undocumented families studied, but for only 20 percent of the documented families. The problems become more complex when some members of the family are documented and others not. An undocumented alien mother, for example, may have a child born in the United States in need of health services, but treatment for the citizen child could subject the mother to possible deportation (Jenkins, 1983). There have been recent changes in immigration policies. The effect of these policy changes on the well-being of immigrant children and families bears study.

Fundamental to the conceptual model proposed in this chapter is a developmental perspective on the individual, a view to which we now turn.

TOWARD A DEVELOPMENTAL APPROACH

Stressful experiences generally involve a *changing* relationship between person and environment, as the encounter unfolds (Lazarus & Folkman, 1984). The appraisal and coping processes and the emotional reactions to them, for example, may not remain the same over time because of changes in the situation or in the subjective evaluation of its significance or meaning. Social supports, too, change and develop as time elapses from the day of the immigrant's arrival and opportunities for contact with the new environment accrue. It is important, therefore, to consider coping, adaptation, and adjustment as processes that occur over time. In this way, one's data pertaining to the mediating or moderator variables in the conceptual model can reflect how such variables change the status and outcome of the stress process in the temporal flow of events (Lazarus & Folkman, 1984).

It is also important to consider the immigrant person as a developing organism. At the same time that the child is experiencing the events of immigration and settlement, he or she is also undergoing normative developmental changes along cognitive, personality, and physical dimensions. In this regard, it is helpful to view human development as a process and a product of the interaction and organization between the individual's characteristics (e.g., abilities, needs, behavioral style) and the environment (e.g., societal expectations, demands, opportunities) (Laosa, 1979).

Psychosocial theories (see Newman & Newman, 1984) emphasize the capacity of the person to contribute to his or her own development as a continuing process across the life span from infancy through later adulthood. Each phase in this development contains its own developmental tasks, namely, a set of skills and competencies that are acquired as the person gains increased mastery of the environment. Mastery of the tasks of later phases of development often depends on the acquisition of earlier ones. Language development, for example, is a primary task of toddlerhood, when many of the elements of language skill emerge. A *psychosocial crisis,* in Erikson's theory (1963), refers to one's psychological efforts to adjust to the demands of the social environment at each stage of development. The word crisis in this context refers to a normal set of stresses and strains rather than to an extraordinary set of punishing events. The society in which one lives makes certain psychic demands on the individual at each stage of development. These demands, which differ from stage to stage, are experienced as mild but persistent guidelines and expectations for behavior. This process produces a state of tension within the person that must be reduced in order for the person to proceed to the next stage. It is this tension that produces the psychosocial crisis. The crisis of a stage forces the individual to use developmental skills that have recently been mastered, and the resolutions of previous crises influences resolutions of current and future crises (Newman & Newman, 1984). Mastery of the appropriate skills and successful resolution of the normative crisis propels the person toward healthy development and adaptation.

The Eriksonian concept of psychosocial crisis is useful in considering the immigrant child's development. In contrast to the normative events in the life of a nonimmigrant child, the experiences of immigrant children are extraordinary. Indeed, settlement in a new and different cultural, social, and linguistic environment places *extraordinary* psychosocial demands on the individual. These demands can profoundly affect the course of the person's development. The outcomes can be positive or deleterious. The immigrant is bombarded by competing, and sometimes conflicting, normative demands between the culture of origin and the host society. How these extraordinary psychosocial crises are resolved will depend on how these diverse demands are negotiated by the individual.

Szapocznik and his colleagues (Szapocznik, Scopetta & King, 1978) observed certain of these extraordinary psychosocial crises among Cuban émigré families in the United States. In their research and clinical practice, these psychologists identified some apparent differences in value orientations between Cuban émigrés and mainstream U.S. Anglo Americans, pointing out their implications for successful psychosocial adaptation and mental health in the former. Their clinical experience suggested that behavioral disorders (such as drug abuse and antisocial behavior) in adolescent Cuban clients tended to be accompanied by the breakdown of the culturally sanctioned (Cuban) pattern of interpersonal relations within the family. This is a problem that was caused apparently by conflicts stemming from the youngsters' more rapid acculturation to the U.S. mainstream culture than their parents'. In order to treat these clients, Szapocznik and his associates developed a psychotherapeutic method designed to resolve these particular problems, as follows. First, the therapist attempts to restore the traditional Cuban relational pattern in the home. Once this relational pattern is thus restored and reaffirmed, the family is taught the skills necessary to negotiate the youngster's differentiation from the family. "It is within this culturally sanctioned framework," argue Szapocznik et al., "that the [developmental] process of individuation of the youngster must take place" (p. 117). The work of Szapocznik et al. is conceptually appealing because of the attempt it represents both (a) to embed individual and family development within a particular sociocultural context; and (b) to link, by this contextedness, a developmental process to adaptation and adjustment.

SUMMARY AND CONCLUSIONS

International migration and settlement are potentially stressful processes, frequently involving events of extraordinary intensity inducing loss, separation, mental suffering, and family disruption, and generally placing enormous demands on the individual for personal change and adaptation to a new and markedly different social, cultural, linguistic, and climatic environment. Among those affected by these experiences are children and families who come from Spanish-speaking countries to the United States. Hispanic immigration to the United States has increased significantly in recent years, and by all indications it will continue to surge. Although some children from immigrant Hispanic families adapt quite successfully in spite of often extraordinarily difficult circumstances, many others fare less well, as evidenced by the statistics on the academic underachievement and school dropout rate for this group.

This chapter was organized around the general question: Which forms of experience associated with immigration and settlement are likely to influence the adaptation and adjustment of Hispanic immigrant children? Several lines of research and theory on psychosocial stress, coping, and development were reviewed and examined for their relevance to our understanding of the processes involved in the adaptation and adjustment of immigrants to their new environment. Some answers were suggested and clues identified regarding both protective and risk factors in the psychosocial and educational adaptation and development of these children. In an attempt to give structure to this broad and complex topic, an evolving theoretical framework was elaborated, and testable hypotheses were derived from it. A central feature of the model is that it postulates the presence of two types of variable: (1) variables antedating immigration and (2) moderator or mediating variables between the stresses surrounding immigration and settlement, on the one hand, and on the other, the child's adaptation, development, and adjustment over time. Among the variables considered in the discussion are the characteristics of the community of origin, the characteristics and lifestyle of the child and family both before and after emigrating, the life changes surrounding immigration, the characteristics of the community where the family settles, the piling up of life changes, the school characteristics in both the community of origin and the receiving community, and the child's and family's cognitive appraisal of their situation. The present approach also emphasizes examining the psychosocial and environmental processes as they occur over time and the importance of considering the immigrant as a developing organism interacting reciprocally with the environment. In addition, this view brings forward the need to consider the particular point in the person's life cycle when the immigration takes place. Clearly, it would not be feasible for an investigator to include in a single empirical study all the variables discussed or implied in this chapter. The intention is, rather, to build our knowledge base systematically by accumulating answers to various pieces of the model across different studies—and thence to further articulate and adjust our conceptual understanding.

The study of immigrant adaptation embodies a myriad of issues and challenges. Necessarily, many variables and issues have been omitted from consideration here. Given the highly textured fabric of immigration and settlement experiences, we should expect to find a high degree of differentiation in the nature and range of these experiences and attendant stressors, coping patterns, and outcomes. Despite these complexities, the coping, adaptation, and development of immigrant children and families is an accessible and exciting area of study with implications for applied practice in mental health, education, and allied professions as well as for social planning and policy.

DIRECTIONS FOR FUTURE RESEARCH

Research on the factors influencing Hispanic immigrant children's adaptation, adjustment, and development is in its infancy. So much so, indeed, that it is difficult to identify priorities for future research; so many issues pertaining to the topic are in urgent need of inquiry. In this final section there is space to emphasize only a few general issues and concerns. Specific ideas for future studies have been brought forward—some explicitly, others implicitly—throughout the chapter.

High on the agenda for future research should be efforts to increase the methodological sophistication of psychological and educational research on immigration. Too often, research advances on important substantive issues are slowed or impeded by a lack of adequate or appropriate measurement instruments, a dearth of relevant psychometric research, and an absence of the demographic knowledge required to draw adequate samples. Equally prominent on the agenda should be endeavors toward further conceptual advances and theoretical developments. We also need to continue to look deeper through the surface manifestations of culture (Laosa, 1979, 1981, 1983, 1988, in press) and to dispel—theoretically and empirically—one-sided notions of the processes and outcomes of immigration and settlement.

Particularly welcome would be studies with implications for the *prevention* of psychosocial maladjustment and educational failure, problems that continue to face so many U.S. Hispanic children and youth (Laosa, 1985). Both risk and protective factors need consideration, emphasizing a search for those variables that mediate or moderate the impact of the stresses of immigration and settlement and that predict successful adjustment and optimal development. The focus should be not only on the negative experiences and pathological effects but also on the possibility that positive outcomes may result from negative changes if these are handled adaptively (Johnson, 1986). Perspectives are needed that will orient us to the potential for extraordinary positive growth that can be stimulated by the remarkable ranges of experience inherent in emigration and in entry to a new and vastly different cultural, social, and linguistic environment. Inquiry must also be aimed, however, at uncovering the psychological costs that immigrants can—unwittingly but insidiously—sometimes incur in their efforts to attain success as such attainment is defined by the host culture. Also needed are developmental approaches to the study of immigration, including perspectives that consider the life changes of immigration and settlement in view of their timing in relation to co-occurring developmental processes in the individual. Finally, resources must be funnelled into formulating and evaluating policies and services especially designed to increase the likelihood that all immigrant children will have the options and the opportunities to develop optimally and to cope adaptively and creatively with the cumulative psychosocial stresses of immigration and settlement. The ultimate aim is to enable, nay empower every immigrant child to realize his or her own full potential to contribute significantly to his or her adoptive country, this nation of immigrants.

NOTES

1. In sociology and demography the terms *sending* and *receiving communities* are used to refer, respectively, to the immigrant person's community of origin and the community where he or she settles upon arrival. These terms are not to be taken literally, for the literal sense may imply an inevitably passive role for the immigrant.

2. The labels *primary* and *secondary* do not indicate that one form of appraisal is more important or that it precedes the other in time (Lazarus & Folkman, 1984).

3. Intriguing but as yet unexplored parallels can be seen between Mexican psychiatrist Díaz-Guerrero's and Soviet psychologist L. S. Vygotsky's views (cf. Díaz-Guerrero, 1982, 1984; Luria, 1976; Scribner, 1985; Vygotsky, 1978; Wertsch, 1981, p. 27.).

REFERENCES

Anthony, E. J. (1974). The syndrome of the psychologically invulnerable child. In E. J. Anthony & C. Koupernik (Eds.), *The child in his family: Vol. 3. Children at psychiatric risk* (pp. 529–544). New York: Wiley.

Atkinson, J. W. (Ed.). (1958). *Motives in fantasy, action, and society*. Princeton, NJ: Van Nostrand.

Baker, K. A. & de Kanter, A. A. (1983). Federal policy and the effectiveness of bilingual education. In K. A. Baker & A. A. de Kanter (Eds.), *Bilingual education: A reappraisal of federal policy* (pp. 33–86). Lexington, MA: Lexington Books.

Bandura, A. (1977). Self-efficacy: Toward a unifying theory of behavioral change. *Psychological Review, 84,* 191–215.

———. (1982). Self-efficacy mechanism in human agency. *American Psychologist, 37,* 122–147.

Baral, D. P. (1979). Academic achievement of recent immigrants from Mexico. *Journal of the National Association for Bilingual Education, 3*(3), 1–13.

Board of Inquiry (1985). *Barriers to excellence: Our children at risk*. Boston: National Coalition of Advocates for Students.

Borjas, G. J. & Tienda, M. (Eds.). (1985). *Hispanics in the U.S. economy*. New York: Academic.

Brophy, J. E. & Good, T. L. (1974). *Teacher-student relationships: Causes and consequences*. New York: Holt, Rinehart and Winston.

———. (1986). Teacher behavior and student achievement. In M. C. Wittrock (Ed.), *Handbook of research on teaching* (pp. 328–375). New York: MacMillan.

Canino, I. A., Earley, B. F. & Rogler, L. H. (1980). *The Puerto Rican child in New York City: Stress and mental health*. New York: Hispanic Research Center, Fordham University.

Caplan, G. (1974). *Support systems and community mental health: Lectures on concept development*. New York: Behavioral Publications.

Cassell, J. (1974). Psychosocial processes and "stress": Theoretical formulation. *International Journal of Health Services, 4*(3), 471–482.

Cervantes, R. C. & Castro, F. G. (1985). Stress, coping, and Mexican American mental health: A systematic review. *Hispanic Journal of Behavioral Sciences, 7,* 1–73.

Clark, R. M. (1983). *Family life and school achievement: Why poor Black children succeed or fail*. Chicago: University of Chicago Press.

Cobb, S. (1976). Social support as a moderator of life stress. *Psychosomatic Medicine, 38,* 300–314.

Díaz-Guerrero, R. (1975). *Psychology of the Mexican: Culture and personality*. Austin: University of Texas Press.

———. (1982). The psychology of the historic-sociocultural premise. *Spanish-Language Psychology, 2, 2,* 383–410.

———. (1984). The psychological study of the Mexican. In J. L. Martinez, Jr. & R. H. Mendoza (Eds.), *Chicano psychology* (2nd ed., pp. 251–268). New York: Academic.

Eccles, J. (1983). Expectancies, values, and academic behaviors. In J. T. Spence (Ed.), *Achievement and achievement motives: Psychological and sociological approaches* (pp. 75–146). San Francisco: Freeman.

Erikson, E. H. (1963). *Childhood and society* (2nd ed.). New York: Norton.

Farran, D. C. & McKinney, J. D. (Eds.). (1986). *Risk in intellectual and psychosocial development*. New York: Academic.

Fernandez, R. M. & Nielsen, F. (1986). Bilingualism and Hispanic scholastic achievement: Some baseline results. *Social Science Research, 15,* 43–70.

Folkman, S., Schaefer, C., & Lazarus, R. S. (1979). Cognitive processes as mediators of stress and coping. In V. Hamilton & D. M. Warburton (Eds.), *Human stress and cognition: An information processing approach* (pp. 265–298). New York: Wiley.

Fordham, S. (1988). Racelessness as a factor in Black students' school success: Pragmatic strategy or pyrrhic victory? *Harvard Educational Review, 58,* 54–84.

French, J. R. P., Jr., Doehrman, S. R., Davis-Sacks, M. L. & Vinokur, A. (1983). *Career change in midlife: Stress, social support, and adjustment.* Ann Arbor: Institute for Social Research, University of Michigan.

Gándara, P. (1982). Passing through the eye of the needle: High-achieving Chicanas. *Hispanic Journal of Behavioral Sciences, 4,* 167–179.

Garmezy, N. (1983). Stressors of childhood. In N. Garmezy & M. Rutter (Eds.), *Stress, coping, and development in children* (pp. 43–84). New York: McGraw-Hill

———. (1985). Broadening research on developmental risk: Implications from studies of vulnerable and stress-resistant children. In W. K. Frankenburg, R. N. Emde & J. W. Sullivan (Eds.), *Early identification of children at risk: An international perspective* (pp. 45–58). New York: Plenum.

Garmezy, N. & Rutter, M. (Eds.). (1983). *Stress, coping, and development in children.* New York: McGraw-Hill.

Garmezy, N. & Tellegen, A. (1984). Studies of stress-resistant children: Methods, variables, and preliminary findings. In F. J. Morrison, C. Lord & D. P. Keating (Eds.), *Applied developmental psychology* (Vol. 1, pp. 231–287). New York: Academic.

Good, T. (1983). Research on classroom teaching. In L. S. Shulman & G. Sykes (Eds.), *Handbook of teaching and policy* (pp. 42–80). New York: Longman.

Good, T. L. & Brophy, J. E. (1986). School effects. In M. C. Wittrock (Ed.), *Handbook of research on teaching* (pp. 570–602). New York: Macmillan.

Gotts, E. E. & Purnell, R. F. (1986). Communication: Key to school-home relations. In R. J. Giffore & R. P. Boger (Eds.), *Child rearing in the home and school* (pp. 157–200). New York: Plenum.

Granovetter, M. (1973). The strength of weak ties. *American Journal of Sociology, 78,* 1360–1372.

———. (1983). The strength of weak ties: A network theory revisited. In R. Collins (Ed.), *Sociological theory* (pp. 201–233). San Francisco: Jossey-Bass.

Haggerty, R. J., Roghmann, K. J. & Pless, I. B. (1975). *Child health and the community.* New York: Wiley.

Hamilton, V. & Warburton, D. M. (Eds.). (1979). *Human stress and cognition: An information processing approach.* New York: Wiley.

Haskins, R. & Adams, D. (Eds.). (1983). *Parent education and public policy.* Norwood, NJ: Ablex.

Henderson, R. W. (1981). Home environment and intellectual performance. In R. W. Henderson (Ed.), *Parent-child interaction: Theory, research, and prospects* (pp. 3–32). New York: Academic.

Hetherington, E. M., Cox, M. & Cox, R. (1978). The aftermath of divorce. In J. H. Stevens, Jr. & M. M. Mathews (Eds.), *Mother/child father/child relationships* (pp. 149–176). Washington, DC: National Association for the Education of Young Children.

———. (1982). Effects of divorce on parents and children. In M. E. Lamb (Ed.),

Nontraditional families: Parenting and child development (pp. 233–288). Hillsdale, NJ: Erlbaum.

Hinkle, L. E., Jr., (1974). The effect of exposure to culture change, social change, and changes in interpersonal relationships on health. In B. S. Dohrenwend & B. P. Dohrenwend (Eds.), *Stressful life events: Their nature and effects* (pp. 9–44). New York: Wiley.

Holtzman, W. H., Díaz-Guerrero, R. & Swartz, J. D. (1975). *Personality development in two cultures: A cross-cultural longitudinal study of school children in Mexico and the United States.* Austin, TX: University of Texas Press.

Honig, A. S. (1984). Risk factors in infants and young children. *Young Children, 39*(4), 60–73.

House, J. S., Landis, K. R. & Umberson, D. (1988). Social relationships and health. *Science, 241,* 540–545.

Hubert, N. C., Wachs, T. D., Peters-Martin, P. & Gandour, M. J. (1982). The study of early temperament: Measurement and conceptual issues. *Child Development, 53,* 571–600. See errata in ibid., *54,* 251.

Inter-American Dialogue (1988). *The Americas in 1988: A time for choices.* Lanham, MD: University Press of America.

Jenkins, S. (1983). Children who are newcomers: Social service needs. In M. Frank (Ed.), *Newcomers to the United States: Children and families* (pp. 39–47). [*Journal of Children in Contemporary Society, 15*(3).] New York: Haworth.

Johnson, J. H. (1986). *Life events as stressors in childhood and adolescence.* Beverly Hills, CA: Sage.

Laosa, L. M. (1977a). Inequality in the classroom: Observational research on teacher-student interactions. *Aztlán—International Journal of Chicano Studies Research, 8,* 51–67.

———. (1977b). Socialization, education, and continuity: The importance of the sociocultural context. *Young Children, 32*(5), 21–27.

———. (1979). Social competence in childhood: Toward a developmental, socioculturally relativistic paradigm. In M. W. Kent & J. E. Rolf (Eds.), *Primary prevention of psychopathology: Vol. 3. Social competence in children* (pp. 253–279). Hanover, NH: University Press of New England.

———. (1981, October). *Statistical explorations of the structural organization of maternal teaching behaviors in Chicano and non-Hispanic White families.* Invited paper presented at the Conference on the Influences of Home Environments on School Achievement, Wisconsin Research and Development Center for Individualized Schooling, School of Education, University of Wisconsin, Madison.

———. (1982). School, occupation, culture, and family: The impact of parental schooling on the parent-child relationship. *Journal of Educational Psychology, 74,* 791–827.

———. (1983). Parent education, cultural pluralism, and public policy: The uncertain connection. In R. Haskins & D. Adams (Eds.), *Parent education and public policy* (p. 331–345). Norwood, NJ: Ablex.

———. (1984). Social policies toward children of diverse ethnic, racial, and language groups in the United States. In H. W. Stevenson & A. E. Siegel (Eds.), *Child development research and social policy* (Vol. 1, pp. 1–109). Chicago: University of Chicago Press.

———. (1985, July). *Ethnic, racial, and language group differences in the experiences of adolescents in the United States.* Invited paper presented at the Workshop on Adolescence and Adolescent Development, convened by the Committee on Child Development Research and Public Policy of the National Academy of Sciences, Woods Hole, MA.

————. (1988). *Population generalizability and ethical dilemmas in research, policy, and practice: Preliminary considerations* (Research Rep. No. RR-88-18). Princeton, NJ: Educational Testing Service.

————. (in press). Population generalizability, cultural sensitivity, and ethical dilemmas. In C. B. Fisher & W. W. Tryon (Eds.), *Ethics in applied developmental psychology.* Norwood, NJ: Ablex.

Laosa, L. M. & Sigel, I. E. (Eds.). (1982). *Families as learning environments for children.* New York: Plenum.

Lazarus, R. S. (1984). The stress and coping paradigm. In J. M. Joffe, G. W. Albee, & L. D. Kelly (Eds.), *Readings in primary prevention of psychopathology: Basic concepts* (pp. 131–156). Hanover, NH: University Press of New England.

Lazarus, R. S. & Folkman, S. (1984). *Stress, appraisal, and coping.* New York: Springer.

LeCorgne, L. L. & Laosa, L. M. (1976). Father absence in low-income Mexican-American families: Children's social adjustment and conceptual differentiation of sex role attributes. *Developmental Psychology, 12,* 470–471.

Lefcourt, H. M. (1976). *Locus of control: Current trends in theory and research.* Hillsdale, NJ: Erlbaum.

————. (Ed.). (1981). *Research with the locus of control construct: Vol. 1. Assessment methods.* New York: Academic.

————. (Ed.). (1983). *Research with the locus of control construct: Vol. 2. Developments and social problems.* New York: Academic.

————. (Ed.). (1984). *Research with the locus of control construct: Vol. 3. Extensions and limitations.* New York: Academic.

Luria, A. R. (1976). *Cognitive development: Its cultural and social foundations.* Cambridge, MA: Harvard University Press.

Maier, S. (1984). *Stress: Depression, disease and the immune system.* (Science and Public Policy Seminar, March 16, 1984; edited transcript.) Washington, DC: Federation of Behavioral, Psychological, and Cognitive Sciences.

Marjoribanks, K. (1979). *Families and their learning environments: An empirical analysis.* Boston: Routledge & Kegan Paul.

McAdoo, H. P. (1983). Societal stress: The Black family. In H. I. McCubbin & C. R. Figley (Eds.), *Stress and the family: Vol. 1. Coping with normative transitions* (pp. 178–187). New York: Brunner/Mazel.

McCubbin, H. I., Joy, C. B., Cauble, A. E., Comeau, J. K., Patterson, J. M., & Needle, R. H. (1980). Family stress and coping: A decade review. *Journal of Marriage and the Family, 42,* 855–871.

McCubbin, H. I. & Patterson, J. M. (1983). The family stress process; The double ABCX model of adjustment and adaptation. In H. I. McCubbin, M. B. Sussman & J. M. Patterson (Eds.), *Social stress and the family: Advances and developments in family stress theory and research* (pp. 7–37). [*Marriage and Family Review, 6*(1 & 2).] New York: Haworth.

Melville, M. B. (1981). Mexican women adapt to migration. In A. Ríos-Bustamante

(Ed.), *Mexican immigrant workers in the U.S* (pp. 119–124). Los Angeles, CA: Chicano Studies Research Center, University of California.

Moore, J. & Pachon, H. (1985). *Hispanics in the United States*. Englewood Cliffs, NJ: Prentice-Hall.

Morris, M. D. (1985). *Immigration: The beleaguered bureaucracy*. Washington, DC: Brookings Institution.

National Commission on Excellence in Education (1983). *A nation at risk: The imperative for educational reform*. Washington, DC: U.S. Government Printing Office.

Newman, B. M. & Newman, P. R. (1984). *Development through life: A psychosocial approach* (3rd ed.). Homewood, IL: Dorsey.

Orum, L. S. (1986). *The education of Hispanics: Status and implications*. Washington, DC: National Council of La Raza.

Peters, M. F. & Massey, G. (1983). Mundane extreme environmental stress in family stress theories: The case of Black families in White America. In H. I. McCubbin, M. B. Sussman & J. M. Patterson (Eds.), *Social stress and the family: Advances and developments in family stress theory and research* (pp. 193–218). *[Marriage and Family Review, 6*(1 & 2).] New York: Haworth.

Pilisuk, M. & Parks, S. H. (1983). Social support and family stress. In H. I. McCubbin, M. B. Sussman & J. M. Patterson (Eds.), *Social stress and the family: Advances and developments in family stress theory and research* (pp. 137–156). *[Marriage and Family Review, 6*(1 & 2).] New York: Haworth.

Portes, A. & Bach, R. L. (1985). *Latin journey: Cuban and Mexican immigrants in the United States*. Berkeley: University of California Press.

Rahe, R. H. (1974). The pathway between subjects' recent life changes and their near-future illness reports: Representative results and methodological issues. In B. S. Dohrenwend & B. P. Dohrenwend (Eds.), *Stressful life events: Their nature and effects* (pp. 73–86). New York: Wiley.

Regional Policy Committee on Minorities in Higher Education (1987). *From minority to majority: Education and the future of the Southwest*. Boulder, CO: Western Interstate Commission for Higher Education.

Rogg, E. M. & Cooney, R. S. (1980). *Adaptation and adjustment of Cubans: West New York, New Jersey*. New York: Hispanic Research Center, Fordham University.

Rogler, L. H. & Cooney, R. S. (1984). *Puerto Rican families in New York City: Intergenerational processes*. Maplewood, NJ: Waterfront.

Rogler, L. H., Gurak, D. T. & Cooney, R. S. (1987). The migration experience and mental health: Formulations relevant to Hispanics and other immigrants. In M. Gaviria & J. D. Arana (Eds.), *Health and behavior: Research agenda for Hispanics* (pp. 72–84). *[Simon Bolivar Research Monograph Series, 1.]* Chicago: Simon Bolivar Hispanic-American Psychiatric Research and Training Program, University of Illnois.

Rotter, J. B. (1966). Generalized expectancies for internal versus external control of reinforcement. *Psychological Monographs, 80*(Whole No. 609).

Rutter, M. (1974). Epidemiological strategies and psychiatric concepts in research on the vulnerable child. In E. J. Anthony & C. Koupernik (Eds.), *The child in his family: Vol. 3. Children at psychiatric risk* (pp. 167–179). New York: Wiley.

————. (1979). Protective factors in children's responses to stress and disadvantage. In M. W. Kent & J. E. Rolf (Eds.), *Primary prevention of psychopathology: Vol. 3. Social competence in children* (pp. 49–74). Hanover, NH: University Press of New England.

————. (1983a). School effects on pupil progress: Research findings and policy implications. *Child Development, 54,* 1–29.

————. (1983b). Stress, coping, and development: Some issues and some questions. In N. Garmezy & M. Rutter (Eds.), *Stress, coping, and development in children* (pp. 1–41). New York: McGraw-Hill.

Salcido, R. M. (1979). Undocumented aliens: A study of Mexican families. *Social Work, 24*(4), 306–311.

Scribner, S. (1985). Vygotsky's uses of history. In J. V. Wertsch (Ed.), *Culture, communication, and cognition: Vygotskian perspectives* (pp. 119–145). Cambridge: Cambridge University Press.

Seligman, M. E. P. (1975). *Helplessness: On depression, development, and death.* San Francisco: Freeman.

Shipman, V. C., Boroson, M., Bridgeman, B., Gant, J. & Mikovsky, M. (1976). *Disadvantaged children and their first school experiences. ETS-Head-Start Longitudinal Study: Notable early characteristics of high and low achieving Black low-SES children* (Project Rep. No. PR-76-21). Princeton, NJ: Educational Testing Service.

Sigel, I. E. (Ed.). (1985). *Parental belief systems: The psychological consequences for children.* Hillsdale, NJ: Erlbaum.

Spence, J. T. & Helmreich, R. L. (1983). Achievement-related motives and behaviors. In J. T. Spence (Ed.), *Achievement and achievement motives: Psychological and sociological approaches* (pp. 7–74). San Francisco, CA: Freeman.

Szapocznik, J., Scopetta, M. A. & King, O. E. (1978). Theory and practice in matching treatment to the special characteristics and problems of Cuban immigrants. *Journal of Community Psychology, 6,* 112–122.

Thomas, A., Chess, S., Sillen, J. & Mendez, O. (1974). Cross-cultural study of behavior in children with special vulnerabilities to stress. In D. F. Ricks, A. Thomas & M. Roff (Eds.), *Life history research in psychopathology* (Vol. 3, pp. 53–67). Minneapolis: University of Minnesota Press.

U.S. Bureau of the Census (1986). *Projections of the Hispanic population: 1983 to 2080* (Current Population Reports, Series P-25, No. 995). Washington, DC: U.S. Government Printing Office.

————. (1988). *The Hispanic population in the United States: March 1988 (advance report)* (Current Population Reports, Series P-20, No. 431). Washington, DC: U.S. Government Printing Office.

Valdez, R. B. (1986, February). *A framework for policy development for the Latino population.* Testimony prepared for the 2nd Annual California Hispanic Legislative Conference.

Vygotsky, L. S. (1978). *Mind in society: The development of higher psychological processes.* Cambridge, MA: Harvard University Press.

Werner, E. E. (1984). Resilient children. *Young Children, 40*(1), 68–72.

Werner, E. E. & Smith, R. S. (1982). *Vulnerable but invincible: A longitudinal study of resilient children and youth.* New York: McGraw-Hill.

Wertsch, J. V. (1981). The concept of activity in Soviet psychology: An introduction.

In J. V. Wertsch (Ed.), *The concept of activity in Soviet psychology* (pp. 3–36). Armonk, NY: Sharpe.

Williams, B. I., Richmond, P. A. & Mason, B. J. (Eds.). (1986). *Designs for compensatory education: Conference proceedings and papers*. Washington, DC: Research and Evaluation Associates.

Willig, A. C. (1985). A meta-analysis of selected studies on the effectiveness of bilingual education. *Review of Educational Research, 55,* 269–317.

Youth and America's Future: The William T. Grant Foundation Commission on Work, Family, and Citizenship (1988). *The forgotten half: Non-college youth in America. An interim report on the school-to-work transition*. Washington, DC: Author.

Zaslow, M. J. (1987). *Sex differences in children's response to parental divorce*. Paper commissioned by the Committee on Child Development Research and Public Policy of the National Academy of Sciences. Washington, DC: National Research Council.

Zaslow, M. J. & Hayes, C. D. (1986). Sex differences in children's response to psychosocial stress: Toward a cross-context analysis. In M. E. Lamb, A. L. Brown & B. Rogoff (Eds.), *Advances in developmental psychology* (Vol. 4, pp. 285–337). Hillsdale, NJ: Erlbaum.

3

Asian/Pacific-American Mental Health: Some Needed Research in Epidemiology and Service Utilization

Stephen S. Fugita

The specific aims of this chapter are (1) to critically review the available psychiatric epidemiology and mental health services utilization data on Asian/Pacific Americans and, based on this review, (2) to suggest directions for future research in these areas.

In order to provide a helpful context for discussing these mental health issues, some key demographic and historical characteristics of Asian/Pacific Americans will be presented. First, Asians currently make up some 1.7 percent of the total U.S. population. Significantly, from a political and service provision point of view, the group is rapidly increasing in size because of the 1965 Immigration Law and political instability in many of the countries of origin. The 1965 law, which took effect in 1968, emphasized family reunification and job skills and a larger quota for the Eastern hemisphere. In addition, in the aftermath of the Vietnam War, the number of refugees from Southeast Asia also soared. Barring any new restrictive immigration legislation, these trends are likely to continue (Gardner, Robey & Smith, 1985).

As Table 3.1 data shows, the three largest groups, each with over 20 percent of the total Asian/Pacific population are, in order, the Chinese, Filipino, and Japanese. Note that the size of the Japanese population increased only slightly from 1970 to 1980, while the Chinese and Filipino populations doubled and the number of Koreans increased some fivefold. Given the huge increases in

Table 3.1
Asian Population: 1980, 1970, and 1960

United States	Number			Percent		
	1980	1970	1960	1980	1970	1960
Total Asian Population	3,466,421	1,426,149	877,934	100.0	100.0	100.0
Chinese	812,178	431,583	237,292	23.4	30.3	20.0
Filipino	781,894	336,731	176,310	22.6	23.6	52.9
Japanese	716,331	588,324	464,332	20.07	41.3	...
Asian Indian	387,223	(NA)	(NA)	11.2	...	...
Korean [a]	357,393	69,510	(NA)	10.3	4.9	...
Vietnamese	245,025	(NA)	(NA)	7.1	...	...
Other Asians	166,377	(NA)	(NA)	4.8	...	...
Laotian	47,683	(NA)	(NA)	1.4	...	...
Thai	45,297	(NA)	(NA)	1.3	...	...
Cambodian (Kampuchea)	16,044	(NA)	(NA)	0.5	...	...
Pakistani	15,792	(NA)	(NA)	0.5	...	...
Indonesian	9,618	(NA)	(NA)	0.3	...	...
Hmong	5,204	(NA)	(NA)	0.2	...	...
All other	26,657	(NA)	(NA)	0.8	...	...

Sources: Bureau of the Census, U.S. Department of Commerce (1983). *1980 Census of Population.* Vol. 1, Characteristics of the Population, U.S. Summary, Chapter C, detailed Population Characteristics, Section A. Washington, DC: U.S. GPO; Bureau of the Census, U.S. Department of Commerce (1973). *1970 Census of Population.* Vol. 1, Characteristics of the Population, Part 1, U.S. Summary. Washington, DC: U.S. GPO; Bureau of the Census, U.S. Department of Commerce (1964). *1960 Census of the Population.* Vol. 1, Characteristics of Population, Part 1, U.S. Summary, Washington, DC: U.S. GPO.

[a]The 1970 data on the Korean population excluded the State of Alaska.

these three groups, it is not surprising that there are more foreign-born (58.6%) Asian/Pacific Americans than American born. Asian/Pacific Americans are the only major American minority in which this is the case. Further, more than 90 percent of the Chinese, Filipino, Korean, and Vietnamese over five years of age speak their native language at home (Bureau of the Census, 1983).

Second, the groups that fall under the Asian/Pacific-American rubric are very diverse. One estimate is that there are twenty-nine distinct cultural groups included in this category (Yoshioka, Tashima, Chew & Murase, 1981). Some, such as the Hmongs from Laos, come from a preliterate society, while others, such as the Japanese, come from very industrialized and technologically advanced ones. For instance, while the total U.S. percentage of high school graduates is 67 percent, 90 percent of Indonesians are graduates as compared with 22 percent of the Hmongs.

Third, generational differences further complicate the picture. For instance, among the Chinese, one may have to consider five generations, ranging from the highly acculturated descendants of those who came during the California gold rush to newly arrived immigrants. These variations not only pose very different communication problems, but markedly disparate mental health issues.

Fourth, although the per capita income for Asian/Pacific Americans overall is higher than for other minorities but somewhat lower than for whites, both native-born and immigrant Asian Americans are spread throughout the class structure. When we examine the percentage of individuals below the poverty level, the same general pattern of heterogeneity shows up. Further, note that Latin American, African, and Asian immigrants have substantially higher poverty rates than recent European immigrants. Among the Asian immigrants, the postfall of Saigon Vietnamese have had an extremely high level of poverty, some 41 percent in 1979. Clearly, these differences are critical in shaping the mental health needs and service utilization patterns of the various Asian groups.

Asian/Pacific Americans, like the Hispanics, are highly urbanized, over 90 percent living in metropolitan areas. Finally, except for Asian-Indians who are primarily found in the Northeast, Asian Americans are concentrated in the West. However, they are increasingly dispersing into other regions of the country.

PSYCHIATRIC EPIDEMIOLOGICAL DATA

Given the demographic and historical background information presented above, attention can now be focused on available psychiatric epidemiological data on Asian/Pacific Americans.

Treated Prevalence

There are no good probability sample data of true prevalence rates among Asian/Pacific Americans. Asians were not separately enumerated, as were Hispanics and blacks, in the landmark National Institute of Mental Health (NIMH) Epidemiologic Catchment Area (ECA) studies, the results of which have been recently published. Therefore, at this time, the best we can do is to piece together other types of information, however limited, to obtain a picture of the mental health of Asian Americans.

The 1980 Census provides estimates of the number of persons in various ethnic groups who were institutionalized in mental hospitals, thus we have some treated prevalence data. Asian/Pacific males have an age-adjusted commitment rate of .45/1000 compared to 1.20/1000 for white males. Asian females have a rate of .24/1000, white females .70/100. Black and Hispanic males have age-adjusted rates of 2.44/1000 and 1.00/1000, females 1.02/1000 and .49/1000 respectively. The rate for Native Americans males is 2.40/1000, females .63/1000.

Estimates of True Prevalence

It should be noted that institutionalization data provide a limited picture of true prevalence rates in the community because of the numerous selection factors that influence who seeks professional treatment in the United States. Three such factors that may be particularly important in the case of Asians are the potentially large number who return home to obtain more culturally syntonic treatment (Liu & Yu, 1985; Yeh, Chu, Klein, Alexander & Milton, 1979), ethnocentric therapists who make it more likely that minority clients will not return for treatment (Yamamoto, James, Bloombaum & Hattem, 1967), and the fact that Asians appear to keep mentally disordered family members in their homes unless they are acting out (Lin, Tardiff, Donetz & Goresky, 1978).

As previously noted, there has been no comprehensive epidemiologic survey of Asian/Pacific Americans. When researchers take on this challenge, they will face significant measurement problems. A major difficulty in determining true prevalence rates is the lack of standard case findings methods. The release in 1981 of the Diagnostic Interview schedule (DIS) that is keyed to Diagnostic Statistical Manual, Edition 3 (DSM 3) made available a major case-finding tool that is being used to assess mental disorders in large, community-based surveys, specifically the NIMH Epidemiological Catchment Area Studies. The DIS has been translated into a number of Asian languages and is or has been utilized in Taiwan, Mainland China, Hong Kong, Korea, and Manila (Liu & Yu, 1985). One measurement issue that further complicates matters is the finding that Asians respond differently to decontextualized instruments than Western subjects; that is, Asians have greater difficulty answering the abstract questions that are found on most standardardized questionnaires and interview schedules. They tend to focus more on the evaluative potential of their responses (Koh, Sakauye, Koh & Murata, 1983).

Finally, as Liu and Yu (1985; 1988) argue, the type of prevalence figures that would be most useful are those of total prevalence. So-called true prevalence rates miss those who have committed suicide or are committed to either mental or correctional institutions. Moreover, given that the Asian population currently consists of a large proportion of foreign born, there is the possibility that, because of selective migration factors, they are constitutionally different from nonimmigrant groups. Also, as previously mentioned, it appears that many of the impaired return to institutions in their home country, thus depressing prevalence rates found in community surveys.

Depression

Probably the best work on depression among Asian Americans is Kuo's recent study (1984) utilizing the NIMH Center for Epidemiology Studies scale for depression (CES-D). He used a telephone directory/organization list/snowball sampling procedure in Seattle to interview approximately equal numbers of Chinese, Filipinos, Japanese, and Koreans (n = 499). The mean CES-D score for Asian/Pacific Americans was 9.38. This is higher than the scores of white samples (Frerichs, Aneshenel & Clark, 1981; Radloff, 1977; Vernon & Roberts, 1982). However, this Asian-American score is lower than those for other minority groups reported by these investigators (11.71 to 9.49).

In Kuo's study, Koreans had the highest mean (14.37), then came Filipinos (9.72), Japanese (7.30), and Chinese (6.92). Even controlling for sex, marital status, age, and nativity, statistically significant differences between the groups remained. This study should be replicated using probability sampling procedures. Telephone directory samples are known to eliminate up to 40 percent of potential respondents in urban areas. Moreover, those who have unlisted telephone numbers are also those who have demographic characteristics that are likely to be positively correlated with mental disorders (Glasser & Metzger, 1975; Rich, 1977). To assure the generality of the findings, it should also be replicated in other parts of the country.

The Kuo study also illustrates other difficulties inherent in doing pioneering work on Asian/Pacific-American depression. It is very problematic interpreting the scores of culturally different groups on standardized instruments normed and validated on mainstream populations. A recent study by Crittendon, Fugita, Bae, Lamug, and Lin (submitted for publication) illustrates this point. These researchers administered the Zung Self-Report Depression Scale (SDS), a widely utilized twenty-item depressive symptom scale, to college students in three Asian countries (Korea, the Philippines, and Taiwan) and the United States. In the Philippines and Korea, some 56 percent and 71 percent had scores that indicated at least mild depression compared to 42 percent and 40 percent in the United States and Taiwan respectively. Is it likely that 71 percent of Korean college students are depressed? Certainly such a conclusion is premature without norms and validity data for this cultural group utilizing both clinical and community populations.

A conceptually interesting study of depression that illustrates some additional complexities of studying the issue cross-culturally was done by Tanaka-Matsumi and Marsella (1976). They compared the subjective meaning of depression across Japanese national, Japanese-American, and Caucasian-American college students. The Japanese and Caucasian Americans were asked to give their word associations to the word *depression* while the Japanese nationals were similarly asked to give associations to the Japanese equivalent word *yuutsu*. The results showed that the Japanese nationals gave associations that tended to be external, concrete referents (e.g., rain, dark, worries), while the Japanese and Caucasian Americans produced associations that referred to internal, negative mood states (e.g., sadness, lonely, down). Tanaka-Matsumi and Marsella attempted to explain their results by postulating that the Japanese perception of self includes the larger social context that surrounds the individual. This is in contrast to the independence-oriented concept of self of mainstream Americans. Although this study was carefully done and utilized an impressive number of subjects (454), there are two major ambiguities. First, all of the uncertainties associated with translation are present. Second, the cross-cultural meaningfulness of the word association procedure is not known.

Alcoholism

Kitano (1982), in his review of Asian-American drinking, concludes that Asians do not consume as much liquor as other Americans. Sue, Zane, and Ito (1979) point out that, if it is true that there is a lower rate of alcoholism among Asian Americans, this could be due to genetic differences in sensitivity to alcohol or to differences in culturally based attitudes toward its use. Evidence suggests that Asians metabolize alcohol quicker, hence, the flushing facial response (Inoue, Fukunaga, Kiriyama & Komura, 1984).

Sue et al. proposed a cultural explanation suggesting that Asian-American values limit alcohol consumption. This explanation would be supported if it were found that drinking habits differed according to degree of assimilation and stated values of one's parent and oneself. To test this, Chinese-American, Japanese-American, and Caucasian-American college students were surveyed. The Chinese-American and Japanese-American students reported less drinking than the Caucasians. Two of the three crude indices of assimilation were significantly related to amount of drinking. Asians who could speak their ethnic language drank less than those who could not. Also, the shorter time a generation had been in the United States, the less alcohol they consumed. Moreover, the Asian-Americans reported that they and their parents had more negative attitudes toward drinking than did the Caucasians.

The Sue et al. study has several limitations that should be noted. First, many of the students surveyed were under the legal drinking age. It is possible that Asian Americans were less willing to break the law. There is also the broader issue of the accuracy of self-report information on this topic. Studies that have correlated self-report measures with unobtrusive indices of alcohol consumption suggest that verbal reports significantly underestimate actual consumption (Rathje & Hughes, 1975). Perhaps Asian-Americans are less likely to admit their drinking.

Taylor (1988) has recently reported data collected among Chicago Korean males that indicates that they drink more heavily than whites. Ten percent reported drinking daily, almost half (48.6 percent) drank at least once a week, over a quarter (28.1 percent) drank at least once a month, and only 13 percent drank as rarely as once a year. The chronological order in which Korean men who drank developed drinking problems was very similar to that of American men with drinking problems. As in so many other areas, one needs to take into account the wide variation among Asian/Pacific-American groups in their drinking patterns and culturally based supports for and prohibition against alcohol consumption. With respect to treatment, even though there are clear indications of need in this area, at present, Asians do not seem responsive to what services are available (Kitano, 1980; Okano, 1977; Sekiguichi, 1975).

Suicide

Liu and Yu (1985) have produced the best current information about Asian/Pacific-American suicide. They have extracted data from death certificates submitted to the National Center for Health Statistics. Unfortunately, among Asians, only information about the Chinese, Japanese, and Filipino is currently available. The overall age adjusted suicide rates per 100,000 for these three groups and whites are 7.97, 7.84, 3.71, and 12.54 respectively. It should be noted that these figures exclude those who are neither permanent residents nor citizens of the United States. There are some cross-group reversals. For instance, a number of older Asian groups exceed the older white suicide rate.

Two older studies have looked at suicide and its concomitants among Asian Americans. Bourne (1973) examined suicide among Chinese Americans in San Francisco for a sixteen-year period (1952–1968). Their suicide rate (27.9/100,000) was significantly different from that of the San Francisco population as a whole but was almost three times higher than the national average (10/100,000). However, the number of Chinese suicides was decreasing while it was increasing for the city as a whole. Bourne reported that the peak suicide rate for these Chinese occurred from age 55 to 65 for both men and women. Almost four times as many men as women committed suicide, although this gap was narrowing. These men tended to be unmarried and either unemployed or retired. Over twice as many foreign born committed suicide as compared with American born.

King (1982) compared suicide rates for Chinese born in the United States, foreign-born U.S. Chinese, and Hong Kong/Singapore Chinese during 1959–1961. United States-born Chinese had rates similar to those of whites. Interestingly, the U.S.-foreign-born Chinese had a much higher suicide rate than did the Hong Kong/Singapore Chinese. Most of this effect was accounted for by the high rate of suicide among the foreign born over 55. King speculates that this is a result of the differences in status and respect accorded to older persons in the United States as compared to China.

THE UTILIZATION QUESTION

Utilization Rates

Probably the most frequently asked question in the Asian-American mental health literature addresses the frequency with which Asians utilize mental health facilities. The results of these studies are convincingly consistent. Asian Americans underutilize such services (Chen, 1976; Hatanaka, Watanabe & Ono, 1975; Kim, 1978; Kinzie & Tseng, 1978; Mochizuki, 1975; Shu, 1976; Sue & McKinney, 1975; True, 1975; Wong, 1977; Yamamoto, 1982). Unfortunately, it is less clear exactly why the utilization rates are low. However, in several instances where publicized, accessible, culturally appropriate services have been made available for the first time, rates of utilization have been shown to dramatically increase (Hatanaka, Watanabe & Ono, 1975; Sue & McKinney, 1975; Wong, 1977).

With regard to visits to nonfederally employed physicians with office practices, 3.1 percent of all visits in the United States were to psychiatrists. More white (3.2 percent) than blacks (1.7 percent) or Asian/Pacific Americans (.6 percent) visited such a psychiatrist in 1979. Moreover, when the data were broken down by the type of service provided not only by psychiatrists but by all physicians, psychotherapy, or psychotherapeutic listening was provided during 4.6 percent of the visits made by whites, 3.1 percent of the visits made by blacks, and 2.5 percent of those made by Asian/Pacific Americans (Yu & Cypress, 1982).

Explanations for the Low Utilization

Since much of the work in this area has had as its primary goal the documentation of underutilization, there has been much less empirically based analytic research of the specific processes involved. However, a number of possible explanations have been proffered to explain the underutilization phenomenon, most having some demonstrated validity. One set of factors has to do with the cultural differences in definitions of mental illness. Chen's work in Los Angeles's New Chinatown (1976) is one of the most extensive efforts on this topic. His interviews with 100 mostly recent immigrants in Chinatown showed that this group was able to identify several forms of mental illness. However, even after judging a person a paranoid schizophrenic, only about one-half of the respondents would recommend a community mental health or medical facility as the preferred method of treatment. Most often family and friends were considered the appropriate coping methods, particularly when the person was not acting out. Similar results have been reported by Lin, Tardiff, Donetz, and Goresky (1978).

Another factor that Chen found inhibited the use of the community Mental Health Research Center (CMHC) was the respondents' lack of knowledge about it (44 percent), even though it was located near the center of New Chinatown. Half saw transportation as a problem. The majority expected language (87 percent), money (78 percent), and losing face (76 percent) to also be problematic. Although Chen's study is one of the most informative with regard to the underutilization issue, its generalizability is limited to a Chinatown population.

Another reason for underutilization is the tendency to retain and manage all but those who are severely disruptive within the family setting. This has a consequence consistent with the findings from a number of studies. These indicate that, by the time the mental health treatment system does contact Asian clients, they are more disturbed than whites (Kinzie & Tseng, 1978; Lin, Tardiff, Donetz & Goresky, 1978). Even in a college population, Sue and Sue (1974) report that the Minnesota Multiphasic Personality Inventory (MMPI) scores of Asians who do go to a university psychiatric clinic indicate more severe problems than their white counterparts.

Asians have more collectivistic cultures (Haines, Rutherford & Thomas, 1981) and extended families (Cheung & Dobkin de Rios, 1982) than members of the core American culture. Certainly, consistent with conventional wisdom, in many instances the Asian/Pacific family serves as an important source of social support. However, there are some instances where it appears to be an impediment. We need to know when the family is a resource as opposed to a source of stress. As a case in point, Bourne (1975) argues that isolated Chinese college students experience a great deal of stress that is the result of academic achievement pressures being transmitted through the family. Lin, Inui, Kleinman, and Womack (1982) show that mentally ill Asians delay their contact with the formal mental health care system due, in part, to the persistent, heavy involvement of their families. They argue that in Asian cultures, the family, not the individual, is the basic unit of society. Thus, the mental illness of one individual is perceived to be a threat to the homeostasis of the entire family. All in all, it is as yet unclear under what specific circumstances Asian Americans' strong familism is therapeutic as opposed to counterproductive.

Chen (1976) found that the majority of his Chinatown respondents felt that mental illness is strongly related to environmental circumstances and were optimistic about the outcome of treatment. Contrary to what might be expected, this sample did not show support for either the family or traditional Chinese medicine as being effective resources in treating the mentally ill. Instead, attitudes were more favorable to Western medicine and psychotherapeutic approaches. Although over 90 percent would encourage a friend or relative to go to a mental health agency for treatment, only about 73 percent would consider going to one themselves. Further, 78 percent of the respondents thought that

Table 3.2
Ethnic Distribution of Psychiatrists in the United States, as of September 1, 1984, by APA Membership

	Total		Percent	
	N	Percent	APA Members	Non–APA Members
Total	41,460	100.0	72.4	27.6
White	35,140	84.7	73.5	26.5
Black	739	1.8	65.6	34.4
Native Americans	87	0.2	88.5	11.5
Mexicans	108	0.3	62.0	38.0
Puerto Ricans	176	0.4	56.0	44.0
Spanish	1,543	3.7	72.8	27.2
Asian-Indians	1,806	4.4	66.3	33.7
Filipinos	918	2.2	48.4	51.6
Chinese and Japanese	118	0.3	88.1	11.9

Source: W. T. Liu and E. S. H. Yu (1985). Ethnicity and mental health. In J. Moore and L. Maldonado (Eds.), *Urban ethnicity*. Beverly Hills: Sage.

most Chinese Americans would avoid going to a mental health service even when they were in need of such help.

Another probable factor in the underutilization of formal mental health services by Asian-Americans is a product of the lack of culturally syntonic providers. Recent figures from the American Psychiatric Association show that 8.6 percent (3,550) of their membership is Asian. However, of this number, 51 percent are Asian-Indians while 23 percent are either Chinese or Japanese (Liu & Yu, 1985). This represents a distribution problem as the Chinese and Japanese are two of the three largest Asian groups yet they make up less than one-quarter of the Asian psychiatrists. With regard to psychologists, the most recent American Psychological Association survey shows that in 1982, of those who provided only health services or health and educational services, only 1.0 percent were Asians.

Given that 59 percent of Asian/Pacific Americans are foreign born and the majority speak their native tongue at home, it is clear that language barriers are a major impediment to services for this group. Although definitive research has not been done, anecdotal evidence suggests that the use of interpreters produces substantial distortions in the psychotherapy process (Liu & Yu, 1985; Marcos, 1979; Sabin, 1975). An innovative procedure that shows promise of being able to help deal with situations where no bilingual/bicultural staff person is available has been developed by Yamamoto, Lam, Choi, Reece, Lo, Hahn & Fairbanks (1982). They have created Chinese, Japanese, and Korean audio-visual versions of the Psychiatric Status Schedule that can be used by personnel who cannot speak these languages. Thus, this procedure can skirt the severe problems associated with the use of translators. Moderate reliability was demonstrated between standard translated versions of the instrument and the audio-visual versions. More work is needed to produce material of this type so that at a minimum, Asians can be reliably diagnosed where no linguistically appropriate providers are available.

Another factor that needs to be taken into account are Asian/Pacific differences in presenting concerns. In a recent study by Tracey, Leong and Glidden (1986), they found that college Asian-American counseling center clients were much more likely to perceive themselves as having educational/vocational concerns, whereas white clients were more likely to report personal/emotional concerns. The authors' preferred explanation is that for Asian-American students, academic concerns have much greater role salience. They also note the possibility of greater sensitivity to the stigma attached to personal/emotional concerns among Asian Americans (Minatoya & Sedlacek, 1981). Since the data for this study were collected at the University of Hawaii where Asian Americans make up over 50 percent of the student body, caution needs to be exercised in generalizing the results to a mainland population.

Organization of Services

Sue (1977) and Uba (1982) have similarly raised the issue of what type of organizational structure, broadly conceived, is optimal for providing services to the Asian/Pacific-American community. Should we train everyone in mainstream agencies (probably minimally) to provide services to Asians, train specialists in a given agency, create separate parallel agencies, or facilitate the development of new forms of service delivery? Uba argues that effective integration of services for Asian Americans into mainstream facilities is highly unlikely due to the major revamping that would be required in the training of all mental health personnel. Another option would be to create parallel services that are physically separate and independent from existing facilities but are similar to them in structure and function. These would most likely be established in communities where there are large Asian-American populations. Since a specially selected staff would be used in these facilities, the problem of retraining would be minimized. Services would be specifically tailored to the ethnic community in which the facility resides (Sue, 1977). One potential problem in providing segregated services is the legal issue of preferential treatment.

Yet another possible approach to providing culturally sensitive mental health services to Asian/Pacific Americans is the utilization of nonparallel services. This would include new therapeutic forms, services, and/or agencies. Examples of this are unique community networks that are specifically formed to deal with mental health problems (Sue & Morishima, 1982). A wide variety of individuals (e.g., teachers, community leaders, folk healers) might work together to develop appropriate mental health programs. This approach increases the opportunity to utilize all available expertise, particularly existing community resources. It also, of course, raises issues about coordination and insuring the quality of services. At a minimum, careful study of the present interface between the sometimes relatively well developed (e.g., Japanese) and sometimes poorly developed (e.g., recent Southeast Asian refugees) systems of informal support resources among Asian/Pacific Americans and formal providers should be an excellent vehicle for understanding some of the processes involved in this type of alternative service delivery system.

Murase (1981) summarized an extensive study of 50 Asian/Pacific-American mental health agencies located in four western cities. These agencies provide mental health services which were specifically developed to respond to Asian/Pacific-American needs. The programs are located in Asian communities, have bilingual/bicultural staffing, and are governed by indigenous representatives. Murase concludes that to develop this type of community based service, it is necessary to: mobilize community support; influence the local political system; expect incremental growth; utilize existing resources; have a diversified funding base; and build coalitions for support.

With respect to thinking about what kinds of research should be encouraged in the area of utilization and organization of services, our approach would be to ask the question in a broad, integrated way. That is, now that it has been documented that Asian/Pacific Americans underutilize a particular type of public mental health service, that of Community Mental Health Centers, we believe attention ought to be focused on not only why they underutilize this particular type of facility, but if they are receiving equivalent help from other sources such as private practitioners and, among certain groups, indigenous healers. It certainly seems plausible that if general practitioners act as gatekeepers, there would be a tendency to refer clients to colleagues in private practice except in situations where the income of the client prohibits this. Given the diverse socioeconomic status found among this group, a substantial segment may seek out the best service for family members and therefore rely on the recommendations of trusted professionals and community leaders. In this way the potential stigma of being seen by others as having a "mental problem" and also using government facilities would be minimized.

Thus, it appears that not only are studies needed to examine clients' perceptions, social influence networks, and decision-making processes, but also those of professionals and community members relevant to dealing with mental health problems. In addition, as previously noted, we need to research both the structure of organizational and individual linkages between the ethnic community and formal providers. If the ethical problems can be surmounted, it may be helpful to conduct follow-back studies of how a client ended up in a particular facility or with a particular practitioner. These data would help place the planning of service provision on a firmer foundation.

CONCLUSIONS

The Asian/Pacific-American group is very heterogeneous, a fact that markedly increases the difficulty of documenting their mental health status and needs. At the current time, data from probability samples or true prevalence data are unavailable. In addition, significant cross-cultural measurement problems remain to be resolved.

Currently, Asian/Pacific Americans underutilize mainstream mental health facilities. The specific reasons for this are unclear. However, it appears that the low utilization rates can be substantially increased if a concerted effort is made to provide culturally appropriate services. One factor that no doubt contributes to this problem is the scarcity of culturally syntonic Asian/Pacific providers for most of the groups included in this diverse category.

DIRECTIONS FOR FUTURE RESEARCH

1. What may be the most fundamental and ultimately useful data are those that tell us, using a national probability sample, the prevalence and correlates of psychological disorders among Asian/Pacific Americans. However, given the diversity of the category and our current state of knowledge of some of the newer and smaller groups, such a study may, at the present time, be premature. Our recommendation would be to study the better-researched groups in an area or areas in which they are somewhat concentrated. At the same time, other parameter-establishing, foundation studies could be mounted on the newer groups so that similar, cost-effective studies on these rare populations can subsequently be done. In conjunction with this, standardized instruments that measure stress, disorder, and social support need to be validated for this population. These studies should be integrated for conceptual, methodological, and administrative continuity. This might be done by utilizing a multisite approach, with a single research center acting as a coordinating unit.

2. As the underutilization of mental health facilities has been well documented in the literature, we need to go further and link measures of specific needs to utilization (Casas, 1985; Lopez, 1981). Further, we should relate admission rates to termination patterns in treatment, as groups may not only have different dropout rates but different positive and negative outcome patterns (Sue, 1977; Goodman & Siegel, 1978).

3. Studies of Asian/Pacific-American kinship structure should be undertaken to better understand culture-specific influence processes and obligatory help relationships. In addition, other forms of community social support need to be understood. As these groups have formed many mutual aid societies, ways of interfacing formal support systems effectively with them need to be developed. The emerging general literature on linking informal and formal support systems (Froland, Pancoast, Chapman & Kimboko, 1981) should be useful here.

4. Most studies of Asian/Pacific-Americans have been done in areas of high ethnic concentration on the West Coast. As economic mobility and assimilation occur, it is likely that individuals will become isolated not only from kin, but from other quasikin community members. Some studies show that as Japanese and Japanese Americans become more culturally and structurally assimilated, they also become more prone to coronary heart disease. This effect holds after physiological and behavioral controls are introduced (Marmot & Syme, 1976; Marmot, Syme, Kagan, Kato, Cohen & Belsky, 1975; Winkelstein, Kagan, Kato & Sacks, 1975). Thus, it appears worthwhile to explore the mental health consequences of increasing ethnic isolation. Rabkin (1979) has shown that low ethnic concentration among blacks and Puerto Ricans in New York City is associated with increased mental health disorders.

5. Given the downward mobility experienced by so many recent immigrants and refugees in this group, particularly males, the familial and psychological consequences of this process need to be studied. Similarly, research is needed to suggest ways of dealing with the frequently disparate rates of acculturation among the various members of immigrant families. When this happens, it is likely that the family becomes less important and the ethnic community a more important influence on the more rapidly acculturating members of the family, most likely children. Thus, ethnic community leaders who can act as bridges to the wider society, both bringing resources into the ethnic community and making available opportunities in the larger society are crucial.

REFERENCES

Bourne, P. G. (1973). Suicide among the Chinese in San Francisco. *American Journal of Public Health, 63,* 744–750.

———. (1975). The Chinese—acculturation and mental illness. *Psychiatry, 38,* 269–277.

Bureau of the Census, U.S. Department of Commerce (1983). 1980 Census of Population. Vol. 1, Characteristics of the Population, United States Summary, Chapter C, Detailed Population Characteristics, Section A: Washington, DC: U.S. Government Printing Office.

Casas, J. M. (1985). A reflection on the status of racial/ethnic minority research. *The Counseling Psychologist, 13,* 581–598.

Chen, P. W. (1976). *Chinese-Americans view their mental health.* Unpublished doctoral dissertation, University of Southern California, Los Angeles.

Cheung, F. & Dobkin de Rios, M. (1982). Recent trends in the study of the mental health of Chinese immigrants to the United States. In C. B. Marrett & C. Leggon (Eds), *Research in race and ethnic relations* (Vol. 3). Greenwich, CT: JAI Press.

Crittendon, K. S., Fugita, S. S., Bae, H., Lamug, C. B. & Lin, C. (in press). A cross-cultural study of self-report depressive symptoms among college students. *Journal of Cross-Cultural Psychology*.

Frerichs, R. R., Aneshenel, C. S. & Clark, V. A. (1981). Prevalence of depression in Los Angeles County. *American Journal of Epidemiology, 1113*, 691–699.

Froland, C., Pancoast, D. L., Chapman, N. J. & Kimboko, P. J. (1981). *Helping networks and human services*. Beverly Hills: Sage.

Gardner, R. W., Robey, B. & Smith, P. C. (1985). Asian Americans: Growth, change, and diversity. *Population Bulletin, 40*, No. 4 (Population Reference Bureau, Inc.: Washington, DC).

Glasser, G. J. & Metzger, G. D. (1975). National estimates of nonlisted telephone households and their characteristics. *Journal of Marketing Research, 12*, 359–361.

Goodman, A. B. & Siegel, C. (1978). Differences in white-nonwhite community mental health center service utilization patterns. *Evaluation and Program Planning, 1*, 51–63.

Haines, D., Rutherford, D. & Thomas, P. (1981). Family and community among Vietnamese refugees. *International Migration Review, 15*, 310–319.

Hatanaka, K. H., Watanabe, B. Y. & Ono, S. (1975). The utilization of mental health services in the Los Angeles area. In W. H. Ishikawa & N. H. Archer (Eds.), *Service delivery in pan Asian communities*. San Diego: Pacific/Asian Coalition.

Inoue, K., Fukanaga, M., Kiriyama, M. & Komura, S. (1984). Accumulation of acetaldehyde in alcohol-sensitive Japanese: Relation to ethanol and acetaldehyde oxidizing capacity. *Alcoholism: Clinical and Experimental Research, 8*, 319–322.

Kim, B. L. C. (1978). *The Asian Americans: Changing patterns, changing needs*. Montclair, NJ: Association of Korean Christian Scholars.

King, H. (1982). Mortality among foreign- and native-born Chinese in the United States. In A. K. Murata & J. Farquhar (Eds.), *Issues in Pacific/Asian American health and mental health*. Chicago: Pacific/Asian American Mental Health Research Center.

Kinzie, J. D. & Tseng, W. S. (1978). Cultural aspects of psychiatric clinic utilization: A cross-cultural study on Hawaii. *International Journal of Social Psychiatry, 24*, 177–188.

Kitano, H. H. L. (1980). *Social service needs of Asian Americans in the West Los Angeles area*. Paper presented to the United Way of Los Angeles.

———. (1982). Alcohol drinking patterns: The Asian Americans. In *Special Population Issues* (Alcohol and Health Monograph Series, No. 4, pp. 411–430). Rockville, MD: U.S. Department of Health and Human Services, National Institute on Alcohol Abuse and Alcoholism.

Koh, S. D., Sakauye, K., Koh, T. & Murata, A. (1983). Reflections on the study of Asian American Elderly by Asian American researchers. *Pacific/Asian American Mental Health Research Center Research Review, 2*, 7–9.

Kuo, W. (1984). Prevalence of depression among Asian Americans. *Journal of Nervous and Mental Diseases, 172*, 449–457.

Lin, K-M., Inui, T. S., Kleinman, A. M., & Womack, W. M. (1982). Sociocultural determinants of the helpseeking behavior of patients with mental illness. *Journal of Nervous and Mental Disease, 170,* 78–84.

Lin, T., Tardiff, K., Donetz, G. & Goresky, W. (1978). Ethnicity and patterns of help seeking. *Culture, Medicine and Psychiatry, 2,* 3–13.

Liu, W. T. & Yu, E. S. H. (1985). Ethnicity and mental health. In J. Moore and L. Maldonado (Eds.), *Urban ethnicity.* Beverly Hills: Sage. 211–247.

———. (1988). Ethnicity and mental health: An overview. In W. T. Liu (Ed.), *The Pacific/Asian American Mental Health Research Center: A decade review of mental health research, training, and services* (pp. 3–18). Chicago: Pacific/Asian American Mental Health Research Center.

Lopez, S. (1981). Mexican-American usage of mental health facilities: Underutilization considered. In A. Baron Jr., (Ed.), *Explorations in Chicano psychology.* New York: Praeger.

Marcos, L. R. (1979). Effects of interpreters on the evaluation of psychopathology in non–English-speaking patients. *American Journal of Psychiatry, 136,* 171–174.

Marmot, M. G. & Syme, S. L. (1976). Acculturation and coronary heart disease in Japanese-Americans. *American Journal of Epidemiology, 104,* 225–247.

Marmot, M. G., Syme, S. L., Kagan, A., Kato, H., Cohen, J. E. & Belsky, J. (1975). Epidemiologic studies of coronary heart disease and stroke in Japanese men living in Japan, Hawaii, and California: Prevalence of coronary and hypertensive heart disease and associated risk factors. *American Journal of Epidemiology, 102,* 514–525.

Minatoya, L. Y. & Sedlacek, W. E. (1981). Another look at the melting pot: Perceptions of Asian-American undergraduates. *Journal of College Student Personnel, 22,* 328–336.

Mochizuki, M. (1975). Discharges and units of services by ethnic origin: Fiscal year 1973–1974. *Columns and Rows.* (County of Los Angeles, Department of Health Services, Mental Health Services), *3* (11).

Murase, K. (1981). *Issues and strategies in the delivery of mental health services to Asian/Pacific Americans.* Paper presented at A Symposium on Asian and Pacific Islander Mental Health Issues, sponsored by Asian Human Services, Denver.

Okano, Y. (1977). *Japanese Americans and mental health.* Los Angeles: Coalition for Mental Health.

Rabkin, J. G. (1979). Ethnic density and psychiatric hospitalization: Hazards of minority status. *American Journal of Psychiatry, 136,* 1562–1566.

Radloff, L. S. (1977). The CES-D Scale: A self-report depression scale for research in the general population. *Applied Psychological Measurement, 1,* 385–401.

Rathje, W. L. & Hughes, W. W. (1975). The garbage project as a nonreactive approach: Garbage in . . . garbage out? In H. W. Sinaiko & L. A. Broedling (Eds.), *Perspectives on attitude assessment: Surveys and their alternatives.* Washington: Smithsonian Institution.

Rich, C. L. (1977). Is random digit dialing really necessary? *Journal of Marketing Research, 14,* 300–305.

Sabin, J. E. (1975). Translating despair. *American Journal of Psychiatry, 132,* 197–199.

Sekiguichi, B. (1975). *A preliminary assessment of the mental health needs of the Jap-

anese American community in the City of Gardena. Unpublished MSW Thesis, University of California, Los Angeles.

Shu, R. L. H. (1976). *Utilization of mental health facilities: The case for Asian Americans in California.* Chicago: Asian American Mental Health Research Center.

Sue, S. (1977). Community mental health services to minority groups: Some optimism, some pessimism. *American Psychologist, 32,* 616–624.

Sue, S. & Morishima, J. K. (1982). *The mental health of Asian Americans.* San Francisco: Jossey-Bass.

Sue, S. & McKinney, H. (1975). Asian Americans in the community mental health care system. *American Journal of Orthopsychiatry, 45,* 111–118.

Sue, S. & Sue, D. W. (1974). MMPI comparisons between Asian-American and non-Asian students utilizing a student health psychiatric center. *Journal of Counseling Psychology, 21,* 423–429.

Sue, S., Zane, N. & Ito, J. (1979). Alcohol drinking patterns among Asian and Caucasian Americans. *Journal of Cross-Cultural Psychology, 10,* 41–56.

Tanaka-Matsumi, J. & Marsella, A. J. (1976). Cross-cultural variations in the phenomenological experience of depression: I. Word association studies. *Journal of Cross-Cultural Psychology, 7,* 379–396.

Taylor, J. (1988). Activities of the Scholar. In W. T. Liu (Ed.), *The Pacific/Asian American Mental Health Research Center: A decade review of mental health research, training, and services.* (133–143). Chicago: Pacific/Asian American Mental Health Research Center.

Tracey, T. J., Leong, F. T. L. & Glidden, C. (1986). Help seeking and problem perception among Asian Americans. *Journal of Counseling Psychology, 13,* 331–336.

True, R. H. (1975). Mental health services and a Chinese American community. In W. Ishikawa & N. Archer (Eds.), *Service delivery in Pan Asian communities.* San Diego: Pacific/Asian Coalition.

Uba, L. (1982). Meeting the mental health needs of Asian Americans: Mainstream or segregated services. *Professional Psychology, 13,* 215–221.

Vernon, S. W. & Roberts, E. (1982). Use of SADS-RDC in a triethnic community survey. *Archives of General Psychiatry, 39,* 47–52.

Winklestein, W. Jr., Kagan, A., Kato, H. & Sacks, S. T. (1975). Epidemiologic studies of coronary heart disease and stroke in Japanese men living in Japan, Hawaii, and California: Blood pressure distributions. *American Journal of Epidemiology, 102,* 502–513.

Wong, H. Z. (1977). Community mental services and manpower and training concerns of Asian Americans. Paper presented to the President's Commission on Mental Health, San Francisco, June 21.

Yamamoto, J. (1982). Mental health needs of Asian Americans and Pacific Islanders. In A. K. Murata & J. Farquhar (Eds.), *Issues in Pacific/Asian American health and mental health.* Chicago: Pacific/Asian American Mental Health Research Center.

Yamamoto, J., James, Q. C., Bloombaum, M. & Hattem, J. (1967). Racial factors in patient selection. *American Journal of Psychiatry, 124,* 630–636.

Yamamoto, J., Lam, J., Choi, W. I., Reese, S., Lo. S., Hahn, D. S. & Fairbanks, L. (1982). The psychiatric status schedule for Asian Americans. *American Journal of Psychiatry, 139,* 1181–1184.

Yeh, E.-K., Chu, H.-M., Klein, M. H., Alexander, A. A. & Milton, H. (1979). Psychiatric implications of cross-cultural education: Chinese students in the U.S.A. *Acta Psychological Taiwanica, 21,* 1–26.

Yoshioka, R. B., Tashima, N., Chew, M. & Murase, K. (1981). *Mental health services for Pacific/Asian Americans.* San Francisco: Pacific Asian Mental Health Research Project.

Yu, E. S. H. & Cypress, B. (1982). Visits to physicians by Asian/Pacific Americans. *Medical Care, 20,* 809–820.

Part II

Advances in Assessment

Introduction

Andrew I. Schwebel

For many students and practicing professionals, the term *assessment* brings to mind an image of a client, a psychometrician, a battery of standardized tests, and perhaps, a schedule containing a structured, diagnostic interview. Much like the picture many people have, the standard operating procedures in many educational settings and mental health centers typically involve the routine administration of certain measurement instruments. While this approach brings the advantage of efficiency, once assessment procedures are institutionalized and in place for a period of time, they often are taken as givens—and this can be a drawback. Specifically, if the standard assessment procedures do not take into account the cultural background of ethnic minorities, or if the instruments used were not designed to serve minority clients, they may not be effective in eliciting the information that assessment specialists need to fully understand and make the most appropriate recommendations for ethnic minority clients. The three chapters in Part II address this critical issue.

The issue of black students' pervasively poor performance on measures of quantitative reasoning is the subject of the first chapter, by Lloyd Bond. He begins with a review of studies that attempted to increase performance on measures of scholastic aptitude by providing specific instruction. Such studies, he notes, have paid insufficient attention to both the actual knowledge and skill requirements of the tests involved and to adequate diagnosis beforehand of the students to be coached. He then presents a summary of recent research in cognitive psychology directed toward understanding competence in mathematics using concepts from information-processing theory. Finally, he describes a research program that seeks to characterize the knowledge and skills that low-scoring students bring to the test situation, how that knowledge affects performance, and ways in which problem solving and quantitative reasoning may be facilitated through instruction.

Hispanic children's test performance is the focus of a chapter by Ernesto M. Bernal. Bernal examines the issue of validity and the interrelated question of test bias, with a view toward bringing new perspectives to bear on the old problems. He reviews the voluminous research literature in this field, with emphasis on its relevance to Hispanic children and youth. In addition, he identifies sources of mismeasurement in practical situations. Finally, he suggests better assessment procedures and directions for new departures from traditional psychometric research.

Rebecca del Carmen completes this section by first reviewing the research literature on Asian-American families, highlighting treatment-relevant issues that have been neglected in clinical studies. She then examines aspects of family systems theory and therapy relevant to the assessment of Asian-American families, including recent work on family life-cycle development. Finally, she proposes a familial and sociocultural context for assessment of Asian-Americans that is clearly linked to treatment.

Taken as a group, the chapters in this section suggest one and the same conclusion: Across a broad spectrum, many widely used assessment procedures fail to take into account the culture and unique life experiences of ethnic minority clients. This implies that assessment specialists should not interpret test results of minority clients in the same way as they would those of majority clients. Instead, they have to depend heavily on themselves and their understandings of ethnic minority individuals in developing their reports and in making recommendations.

On an optimistic note, Bernal, Bond, and del Carmen have taken important steps in the process of developing theory and practice in the area of ethnic minority mental health assessment. Further, they have suggested what should be the next steps in terms of needed research. The success of these contributors' work shows that, although the area is a broad one, the development of culturally sensitive assessment procedures is possible. However, much work lies ahead. A major commitment will be needed if we are to advance knowledge to the point where assessment procedures will provide maximum benefit to minority clients from every background and, therefore, to society as a whole.

4

Understanding the Black/White Student Gap on Measures of Quantitative Reasoning

Lloyd Bond

Of particular concern in this chapter is the pervasively poor performance of black students on measures of quantitative reasoning. Explanations involving cultural bias are reviewed and largely dismissed as inadequate. The chapter describes a program of research currently under way that explains such performance deficits from the perspective of modern information-processing theory. It is argued that a process-based conception of mathematical aptitude is possible and that such an approach implies the design of practical instructional treatments.

Few issues in education have received more public and media attention than the failure of our educational institutions to retain minority youth in school and to respond to their educational needs. The problem is both pervasive and acute. In some metropolitan areas, over 50 percent of minorities entering high school fail to graduate. To be sure, the causes for this are not entirely academic. Economic and social factors surely play a part. But academic factors can not and should not be minimized. Recent publications by the College Board reveal dramatically and in great detail what has been known only informally heretofore: Black students as a group score approximately 100 points (a standard deviation) below their white counterparts on both verbal and math sections of

The research reported here was supported by a grant from the College Board.

the Scholastic Aptitude Test. The reasons that have been advanced for these performance differences span the spectrum, from poor teaching to deficient home environments and, most controversially, to basic aptitude. The differences are reduced only modestly by the usual statistical adjustments, such as equating groups for comparable socioeconomic status.

Three considerations motivated this chapter. First, research on the effects of special preparation (coaching) on the performance of black students on such measures is meager and conflicting. Second, the nature of the educational deficiencies characteristic of many black students have never been systematically investigated, nor have these deficiencies been systematically related to the knowledge and skills required by the Scholastic Aptitude Test-Mathematics (SAT-M). Third, recent advances in cognitive psychology render possible a much more precise explication of the nature of expertise in problem solving, how competence and skill develop, and the conditions that foster their development.

First, I shall review attempts to increase performance on measures of scholastic aptitude by specific instruction. The next section summarizes recent research in cognitive psychology that attempts to understand competence in mathematics using concepts from information processing theory. The final section describes research that seeks to characterize the knowledge and skill that low-scoring students bring to the test situation, how that knowledge affects performance, and ways in which problem solving and quantitative reasoning can be facilitated through instruction.

THE EFFECTS OF SPECIAL PREPARATION

To what extent can the performance of students on standardized measures of quantitative reasoning be improved by instruction specifically designed to improve that performance? There is extensive and growing literature on this general topic (Bond, 1989). With respect to black students in particular, the few studies conducted so far (Roberts & Oppenheim, 1966; Messick, 1980; Johnson, Asbury, Wallace, Robinson & Vaughn, 1985) represent a mixed bag. Roberts and Oppenheim (1966) carried out their study on eighteen predominantly black, low-achieving secondary schools in rural and urban Tennessee. The Preliminary Scholastic Aptitude Test (PSAT) was employed as both the pre- and post-test. Students in eight of the eighteen schools received special instruction in mathematics, students in six schools received special instruction in verbal material and students in four schools received no special instruction. In addition to the latter "controls," students within the fourteen treatment schools were randomly assigned to coached and uncoached groups. The treatment consisted of fifteen one-half hour sessions over a four to six week period. A total of 188 students constituted the experimental group for math coaching and 122 students served as controls. Students coached in mathematics showed a .81 PSAT point increase over their noncoached counterparts. These modest increases correspond to eight points on the SAT-M scale and are slightly lower than the estimated coaching gains for nonminority students.

Messick (1980), in a reanalysis of data from the Federal Trade Commission study (1978) of commercial coaching schools, found that coaching gains made by black students were substantially and significantly higher than those for whites. The average coaching effect for white students (N = 132) was $-.25$ on the 600-point SAT scale, while that for the black students (N = 13) was 46.5. This difference is significant despite the small sample sizes. Messick also undertook a separate analysis of the scores of the eight identifiable black students in a study by Alderman and Powers (1979). He found only minor differences in differential effectiveness for black students over whites at the same schools.

Johnson et al. (1985) in a series of studies sponsored by the NAACP found similarly conflicting results. The studies (conducted in Atlanta, New York City, and San Francisco) represented an organized effort to raise the SAT scores of a group of volunteer disadvantaged black youth through two series of semi-weekly instructional sessions of two-and-a-half to three hours each, for six weeks, or a total of about thirty hours of instructional time. The twelve sessions were equally divided between math and verbal instruction. Instructional materials were developed by the National Association of Secondary School Principals to prepare students for nationally standardized college admission tests and included instruction and practice in vocabulary, verbal analogies, reading comprehension, and basic algebraic and geometric concepts. At all three sites, random assignment to experimental and control groups was attempted, but, because of administrative difficulties, was successful at the San Francisco site only. Math score increases at the sites ranged from a low of 13 points to a high of 57 points.

The major deficiencies of the above studies (and in fact of most research reports on coaching) are that (1) instructional content has not been presented in sufficient detail to allow one to relate aspects of the instruction to performance increases, and (2) insufficient attention has been paid to both the actual knowledge and skill requirements of the SAT-M and to adequate diagnosis beforehand of the students to be coached.

It has long been recognized that the actual knowledge of mathematical facts and relationships (the declarative knowledge base) necessary for superior performance on the SAT-M is quite modest. The sheer amount of knowledge required is rarely beyond that taught in a first-year high school algebra course and an introductory semester of geometry. Why then do so many minority students, many of whom have performed reasonably well in even advanced secondary courses such as trigonometry, find the SAT-M so difficult? Modern cognitive psychology, drawing principally upon concepts from information-processing theory, has made significant progress in providing answers to this question.

THE NATURE OF SKILLED PERFORMANCE

An information-processing approach to the study of both computational skill and conceptual understanding assumes that (1) information is processed through a series of "memories," each subject to different limitations and each capable of different kinds of storage and processing; (2) the capacity to respond automatically to certain components of complex tasks, such as number facts and simple algorithms, reduces the processing load of the human memory system and thus contributes to efficient functioning; (3) problem-solving ability is not a general skill that some persons possess and others do not, but rather depends upon a specific, prerequisite knowledge base; (4) problem solving in a given domain (e.g., mathematics or physics) depends crucially upon how relevant knowledge is organized in long-term memory; and (5) problem solving is either retarded or facilitated by how people represent a problem internally. These elements will be discussed in turn.

The Two Memory Systems

Information-processing approaches to human thinking and problem solving traditionally conceive of the human memory system as being composed of two distinct types of memories. Long-term memory includes our knowledge of the world around us, names of significant others in our life, our birth date—in fact, an almost infinite variety of bits of knowledge acquired over our lifetime. Short-term memory, by contrast, includes such things as telephone numbers held temporarily in memory while they are dialed and then quickly forgotten. Without continued rehearsal, information in short-term memory is not available for later use. For educated persons, their long-term memory for basic mathematics would include such things as the procedures for multiplication, division, addition and subtraction, place value, and the many other routine algorithms generally used in everyday life.

Automaticity

Automaticity in carrying out a procedure is indicated by the speed with which a response is evoked as well as the absence of conscious control over the processes involved. Of the various factors influencing expert performance, the literature is clearest on the origin and development of automaticity. It is purely and almost exclusively a function of practice. In addition to speed of response, another distinguishing feature of automated responses is that they can be carried out in parallel, as distinct from controlled responses that must be executed serially. As a similar case, the beginning piano player cannot carry on a conversation while reading even the simplest piece of music. Accomplished pianists, however, can do so while reading even complex pieces. The complex set of motor reactions to the printed music have become automated. Similarly, a driver experienced with standard transmissions can easily carry on conversations and perform other tasks requiring conscious attention while at the same time watch surrounding traffic, smoothly execute the complex set of coordinated movements required to operate the vehicle, and so on. It is in this sense that automated routines free up working memory during problem solving. To the extent that certain procedures can be executed automatically, without the need for direct attention, more space becomes available in working memory for processes that do require attention. On the SAT-M and other speeded measures of quantitative problem solving, automaticity of number facts and mathematical algorithms is essential for high-level performance.

The Prerequisite Knowledge Base

In fields as diverse as physics (Larkin, 1977), avionics (Gitomer, 1984), and baseball knowledge (Voss, Vesonder & Spilich, 1980), it has been repeatedly demonstrated that the development of problem-solving ability and conceptual understanding depends upon the acquisition of sufficient declarative knowledge in the domain in question, and the procedural skills to use that knowledge. Since the distinction between declarative knowledge and procedural knowledge plays a prominent role in the present research, it may be useful to discuss these important concepts a bit further.

Declarative knowledge is the factual knowledge about a concept, group of concepts, or an entire subject matter domain, as well as knowledge about objects and the perceptual features of things. Anecdotal and episodic memories about daily events, knowledge of names of everyday objects, knowledge of the Pythagorean theorem, or the number of degrees in a circle, are all instances of declarative knowledge. It is the *what* of long-term memory. By contrast, procedural knowledge is the knowledge of *how* to do something. Driving a car, setting up a series of equations to represent a word problem, manipulating and rehearsing information and routines in working memory, and internally monitoring the effectiveness with which these actions are implemented are all examples of procedural knowledge. Organizing and arranging geometry axioms and theorems to reach a proof is a good (and relevant) example of procedural knowledge.

As indicated earlier, problem solving is not a general, abstract ability that some persons possess and others do not. Rather, expertise in problem solving is predicated upon a richly elaborated, declarative knowledge base. Stored subject-matter knowledge and procedures are necessary but not sufficient, however, for skilled performance; the knowledge must also be organized in ways that facilitate access and use.

Knowledge Structure and Organization

In order to deal with the human capacity to solve problems, to understand, to generalize, and to invent, modern cognitive psychology has had to develop a richer, more elaborated conception of how people store and retrieve knowl-

Figure 4.1
Two Knowledge Structures for Division and Multiplication

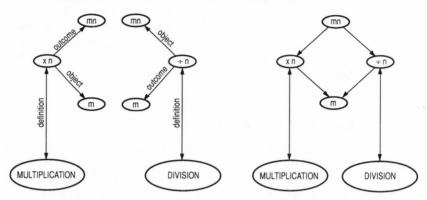

edge in memory. Clearly, if facts in memory are stored simply as an unordered list, retrieving relevant information from the list during problem solving would be both exhausting and inefficient. Available evidence suggests that for many subject matters, poor problem-solving performance is characterized by retrieval actions which closely approximate such a random search. By contrast, skill in problem solving has been shown to be facilitated by items in memory that are organized and related to each other in definable and therefore meaningful ways (Resnick & Ford, 1981; Glaser, 1981).

An example from Greeno (1978) and Resnick and Ford (1981) may help to illustrate this point for the domain of mathematics. It is possible to store information on the procedures for division and multiplication separately in memory, so that their inverse relationship goes unrecognized. Novice math students often do just this. With increasing sophistication and practice, the separate knowledge structures on the left in Figure 4.1 are replaced with the unified structure on the right.

According to the structure shown in Figure 4.1, multiplication is defined by the operation "times-n" (xn). The operation has an object, n, the entity upon which the operation is performed, as well as an outcome (mn), the result of performing the operation. Division is similarly represented. The unified structure on the right shows how knowledge might be organized for a person with an integrated structure for the two operations. Specifically, if a quantity (m) is multiplied by some number (n) and the outcome (mn) is divided by the same number (n) the original quantity is again obtained. Many persons apprehend this principle at some surface level. For example, if the original quantity involved is a one digit numeral, 8, then the action times 3 generates the product $8 \times 3 = 24$. The original quantity (8) will be reproduced if the action divided by 3 is performed on the product (24).

More elaborated knowledge structures that combine the four basic operations in the general domain of arithmetic (multiplication, division, addition, and subtraction) characterize persons with well-developed knowledge structures. Memory structures for the domain of algebra (Greeno, 1984), geometry (Greeno, 1984), physics (Larkin, 1977; Chi, Feltovich & Glaser, 1981) and electronics (Sussman, 1977) have also been investigated. The essential point to note is that elaborated knowledge structures, because they facilitate the recognition of the interrelationships among procedures and concepts, have the effect of directing, and hence constraining, memory search during problem solving.

Problem Representation

Intimately related to how knowledge is stored in memory is how specific problems to be solved are represented internally. As indicated earlier, stored subject-matter knowledge alone is not sufficient to solve problems. There must also be a mechanism to direct mental search through the network to retrieve information and a mechanism to generate and test relations among concepts and structures when the needed information is not stored in the form that is required.

The first step in any problem-solving situation is to build an internal representation of the problem, to recognize problem features and encode them in such a way that they are interpretable by the information-processing system. As is well known, constructing mathematical models of word problems is, for students who have mastered algebraic algorithms, the major intellectual hurdle in solving them.

For simple well-structured problems (e.g., solve for x in the equation $2x + 15 = 65$), the need to represent the problem internally is minimal. More complex, verbally presented problems, however, require the student to generate subgoals, to recognize constraints, and in general to plan. Initial problem representation is essential to this process.

RATIONALE AND DESIGN OF THE PRESENT STUDY

The study to be described was undertaken to investigate the usefulness of an information-processing approach in explaining the performance of minority students on the SAT-M and similar measures. In addition, the author wished to test the notion that poor performance in general (that is, for both black and white students) is primarily a function of a lack of procedural skills and not the absence of an adequate declarative knowledge base. This notion derives in part from the popular criticism that high school mathematics—as currently taught and learned—tends to emphasize the acquisition of the declarative knowledge necessary for problem solving, but that the next pedagogical step (systematic and sustained instruction in using that knowledge to solve problems) has either not been attempted or, if attempted, has been unsuccessful, thereby resulting in the virtual absence of procedural problem-solving skills.

Figure 4.2
A Retired SAT-Math Item Requiring Modest Declarative Knowledge, but
Extensive Procedural Knowledge

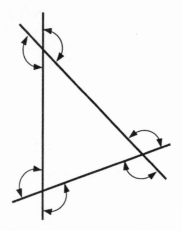

In the above figure, what is the sum of the indicated angles?

a) 360
b) 540
c) 720
d) 900
e) not enough information given to determine

Since the distinction between procedural and declarative knowledge is central
to the discussion that follows, an example using an item from a recently retired
form of the SAT-Math (see Figure 4.2) will help to illustrate these two concepts. If we exclude nonanalytic procedures (such as attempts to estimate the
requested sum by inspection), the student, in order to solve this problem, must
know the following facts (declarative knowledge) from introductory geometry:

F1. The number of degrees in a circle is 360.

F2. The interior angles of a triangle sum to 180°.

F3. When two straight lines intersect, the opposite angles are equal.

The vast majority of students who have recently completed geometry have this
knowledge. Yet, this problem is quite difficult for all SAT test takers (less than
25 percent get the item correct). It will be argued here that one of the principal
reasons for the inability to solve the problem, despite having the relevant

knowledge to do so, is that the students have not acquired the indicated "how" knowledge needed in this problem:

1. Around each vertex of the triangle, there are 360°, for a total of 1080°. F1
2. Subtract 180° from 1080°, courtesy of F2.
3. Subtract an additional 180°, courtesy of F3.

The purposeful organizing and arranging of integrated facts in memory toward the solution of a problem is the essence of procedural knowledge. The correct answer to this item is choice c.

Courses taken and grades received can be considered rough proxies of the knowledge a student has of high school mathematics. Using median splits, four patterns of combined course work/SAT performance are possible:[1]

1. below average course work/below average SAT;
2. below average course work/above average SAT;
3. above average course work/below average SAT;
4. above average course work/above average SAT.

Students with these performance patterns correspond in a general way to students with varying combinations of declarative and procedural knowledge. Students with performance pattern (1), for example, are likely to be both deficient in their knowledge of basic mathematical rules and procedures (declarative knowledge) as well as in their ability to formulate and execute efficient plans during problem solving (procedural knowledge). Students with performance pattern (3) are likely to have sufficient declarative knowledge but deficient procedural knowledge. This particular performance pattern, it turns out, is an extremely common one among all students but is more pronounced among black students and female students. The commonness of this pattern is one of the reasons for the belief that instruction in problem solving lags behind instruction in subject-matter knowledge.

Sample

The sample for the current study consisted of twenty-eight black high school students (seventeen girls and eleven boys) who volunteered to participate in the study. For comparative purposes, comparable data were also collected on six white students. All had taken a year of algebra (algebra 1) and a year of geometry. At the time of the study, all were taking algebra 2. Twenty students (fifteen black and five white) had obtained grades of B or better in both prior math courses. Of the remaining eight students, one had obtained Cs in both courses, and the remaining seven had received one B and one C. As indicated above, of particular interest were students who had performed well in math courses (B or better) but performed poorly on SAT-M (below 400). Only ten of the minority students, and two majority met these conditions exactly. However, if we defined low SAT to include scores below 450, then twenty-five of twenty-eight minority students satisfied the SAT criterion. Five of these students had at least one C in either algebra or geometry.

Method

Students participated individually in two separate laboratory sessions. In the first session, all subjects took a retired form of the SAT-M. They then took a twenty-five-item open-ended test of basic high school algebra and geometry. This test consisted entirely of straightforward factual items requiring no extensive quantitative reasoning or insight, as is typically found on the SAT-M. Rather, the brief test was administered as a check on the assumption that grades are a reasonable proxy for a working knowledge of high school mathematics. Typical algebra items required the student to simplify an algebraic expression or to solve for X in a linear equation. Typical geometry items required basic knowledge of the Pythagorean theorem, and the basic geometry of circles and triangles.

In the second session students were asked to solve 13 selected items from retired forms of the SAT. In this session subjects were requested to "think aloud" during problem solving and recorded verbal protocols were obtained. A protocol is a detailed description of the activities, ordered in time, that a subject engages in while performing a task. Verbal protocol analysis has been employed extensively and to great advantage in analyzing the knowledge and strategies individuals use in problem solving (Ericsson & Simon, 1980).

Results

Algebra and geometry pretest. The mean and standard deviation of scores on the twenty-five-item test of basic algebra and geometry was 14.2 and 3.1, respectively. This represents a mean performance of only 57 percent and is somewhat lower than expected. Grades, per se, are at best rough proxies for a working knowledge of high school mathematics. In the debriefing, several students said that they had simply forgotten many of the basic facts from geometry and some algebraic rules (e.g., the laws of exponents, the algebra of inequalities). Further questioning revealed that, with rare exception, the students did not practice or otherwise engage any of the skills learned in algebra 1 or geometry. Many claimed to be "rusty" in spite of the fact that they were currently enrolled in algebra 2. (It should be noted that the version of the SAT-M administered in this study actually provides the student on the first page of the test booklet with basic geometric formulas (area, circumference, and number of degrees in a circle; area and sum of the interior angles of a triangle; the Pythagorean theorem).

SAT-M. The mean and standard deviation of the sample of black students on the SAT-M were 419 and 78, respectively. (Corresponding figures for the small sample of white students was 452 and 91.) This figure compares with an average score of 384 for all black high school students who took the SAT in 1988. An average of 45 of the 60 items on the SAT-M were attempted by the students. Only three students had time to attempt every item.

Protocols. Space does not permit a complete description of all the protocols collected in this study. Table 4.1 summarizes the performance of black students on selected protocol items. The first figure in parenthesis to the right of each item is the percentage of the national sample who got the item correct. The second figure is the number (out of twenty-two) in the sample who correctly solved the problem. (The performance of the white comparative sample is discussed below.) It should be noted that by correct I mean that the experimenter did not intervene or query the student in ways that would aid the student in solving the problem. Many of the items were simply too difficult for the students. In fact, some were extremely difficult for all high school students.

Two protocols that are quite representative of the group will be discussed in some detail. The first one is from a student who obtained a B in algebra 1 and an A in geometry. His score on the SAT-M was 390. The problem he was attempting to solve is given below:

If X is an odd number what is the sum of the next two odd numbers greater than $3X + 1$?

(a) $6X + 8$

(b) $6X + 6$

(c) $6X + 5$

(d) $6X + 4$

(e) $6X + 3$

In the following transcription, S and E stand for the subject and the experimenter, respectively.

S: [Reads problem, rereads problem, long pause].

E: What are you thinking about?

S: Well, I'm trying to reason out this problem. Uh, ok I was . . . If X is an odd number, what is the sum of the next two odd numbers greater than 3X plus 1? So . . . I don't know, let's see [long pause] I need some help here.

E: Ok, hint: If X is an odd number, is 3X even or odd?

S: Odd.

E: OK. Is 3X plus 1 even or odd?

S: Even.

E: Now, does that help you?

Table 4.1
Sample Algebra and Basic Math Protocol Items

(1) The number 99,999,999 is NOT divisible by

    (a) 9   (b) 11   (c) 99   (d) 111   (e) 9,999

                                                   [.82, 21]

(3) Of the following numbers, which is the LEAST?

    (a) 0.102   (b) 0.11   (c) .1201   (d) 0.101   (e) 0.1001

                                                   [.65, 21]

(6) If x is an odd number, what is the sum of the next

    two odd numbers greater than $3x + 1$?

    (a) 6X+8   (b) 6X+6   (c) 6X+5   (d) 6X+4   (e) 6X+3

                                                   [.19, 2]

(7) In a race, if Bob's running speed was 4/5 Alice's, and

    Chris's speed was 3/4 Bob's, then Alice's speed was how

    many times the average (arithmetic mean) of the other

    two runners' speeds?

    (a) 3/4   (b) 7/10   (c) 40/31   (d) 10/7   (e) 5/3

                                                   [.10, 0]

(8) If 14 is 5 more than x and 12 is 3 less than y,

    then $x - y =$

    (a) 24   (b) 6   (c) 0   (d) –2   (e) –6

                                                   [.72, 14]

(9) If $3 = b^x$, then 3b must equal

    (a) b^{x+1} (b) b^{x+2} (c) b^{x+3} (d) b^{2x} (e) b^{3x}

                                                   [.19, 3]

(10) Jim is now twice as old as Polly. In 2 years Jim will

    be n years old. In terms of n, how old will be Polly

    be then?

    (a) n/2   (b) (n/2)+1   (c) (n/2)+2   (d) n+2   (e) 2n

                                                   [.13, 2]

Answers: (1) d;   (3) e;   (6) b;   (7) d;   (8) e;   (9) a;   (10) b

Note: Seven of thirteen retired SAT-M items used in the protocol study.

S: Yeah [long pause].

E: Repeat what you know.

S: Uh, let's see . . . uh, 3X is odd, 3X plus 1 is . . . even [long pause].

E: What is the next odd number greater than 3X plus 1?

S: Three? Put in three for X . . . and add it. So it would be ten?

E: Well, we've established that 3X plus 1 is even, right?

S: Yeah.

E: Now, what is the next odd number greater than that?

S: Five?

E: Well, X can be ANY odd number, 7 say. So if 3X plus 1 is even, what is the next odd number greater than 3X plus 1?

S: I don't know.

E: How about 3X plus 2?

S: [Pause] Oh, Oh. Aw, man [mutual laughter].

S: I was trying to figure out this 3X. . . . I see.

E: So what's the next odd number after 3x plus 2?

S: 3X plus 3.

E: The next ODD number.

S: Next ODD number? Oh, oh. You skip that number . . . 3X plus 4. So let's see [long pause].

E: Read the question.

S: [reads question] Oh, you add. Let's . . . It's b. It's 6X plus 6. Dag, man. *(Total time: 4 min, 46 sec).*

Three points are readily apparent from this protocol. The first is that, at the start, the student does not apprehend the very structure of the problem. This is so despite the fact that the generic character of the correct answer (that is, in the expression 6X + 6, X may be *any* odd number) can be deduced from the answer set. The second point to note is that the student could not generate, on his own, a goal structure for the problem. Yet, when prompted by the experimenter, the subject could provide the correct answers to all relevant subproblems. Finally, the student tended to represent the problem internally as a problem with a specific rather than a general solution. Hence, we see the student responds to the experimenter's query with a specific number (i.e., 10). He was apparently substituting the specific odd number 3 into the equation 3X + 1. (Even here the student misunderstood the question and simply gave the numeric answer after substituting 3 for X, rather than responding with 11, the correct specific answer to the question. This was obviously a simple misunderstanding that was corrected later.) The tendency of the student to respond to the queries with specific numeric answers rather than an algebraic expression in terms of X is typical. For example, eleven students gave specific, numeric answers to the query. In fact, four of the eleven students gave the same wrong answer (i.e., 10) to the query.

The above protocol is also typical in its overall structure. The students were generally unable to generate on their own the series of subgoals that lead to the correct answer, but experienced little difficulty in responding correctly to each question posed by the experimenter. This inability to generate an appropriate plan of action and system of subgoals, coupled with the ability to answer relevant questions posed externally tended to characterize the majority of protocols for these students.

Compare the above with the following protocol by one of only two students in the sample (one black, one white) who scored above 600. The protocol is that of a black female student (SAT-M = 610) who obtained As in both prior math courses:

S: [reads question, pause, rereads question] Let's see. If X is odd, then 3X must be odd. And plus 1 must be . . . even. Is that right? Yeah . . . So . . . what is the sum of the next two odd . . . so that's [pause] 3X plus 2 and . . . 3X plus . . . four. So . . . you add. It's b, it's 6X plus 6. *(Total time: 52 seconds).*

This protocol is virtually identical to that provided by the only other student to obtain above 600 on the SAT-M, and is also very similar to that of a colleague of the author who has a Ph.D. in mathematics and who served as the resident expert. Her protocols served as standards against which to evaluate others.

As a general rule, problems like those above (that is, problems that require the student to have in long-term memory a generic knowledge structure and a set of readily accessible routines that can be quickly searched during problem solving) presented extreme difficulties for the students. (It should be noted that such problems tend to be difficult for all students, regardless of race.) This point is illustrated clearly by the following problem:

At a certain college, X liters of milk are needed per month for each student. At this rate, Y liters of milk will supply Z students for how many months?

(a)   Y / XZ

(b)   Z / XY

(c)   XY / Z

(d)   YZ / X

(e)   XYZ

This problem is very difficult for all high school students. Less than 20 percent get the item correct. Of the total of twenty-eight students in the sample only three produced protocols of any length. The other twenty-five could not begin to attack the problem. The three protocols were similar in that each student attempted to solve the problem backwards by substituting in a specific example. One was successful on the first attempt. Because of minor errors, the other two were incorrect in their first answer.

Approximately halfway through the series of laboratory sessions, the experimenter presented subjects with the following problem after they had attempted the above problem:

At a certain college, five liters of milk are needed per month for each student. At this rate, 200 liters of milk will supply four students for how many months?

(a) 5

(b) 8

(c) 9

(d) 10

(e) 12

Note that this problem is a strict isomorph (Hayes and Simon, 1976) of the one that precedes it. The two differ only in their surface features. But the two are decidedly different in difficulty. Of the twelve students who were presented the latter problem after attempting to solve the former, ten solved the problem with little hesitation and virtually without mistakes. The following protocol (SAT-M $=$ 420) is representative:

S: [reads problem, laughs]. This is the same as the other one. [pause] But, let's see. Five liters for one student. So . . . 200, let's see. [pause] It would be twenty liters for four students. . . . So at a certain college five liters of milk are needed per month for each student. At this rate . . . you divide into 200. So it would be . . . uh, ten, d. *(Total time: 51 sec)*.

Seven of the twelve students were able to return to the generic item and solve it through substitution. It is important to stress here that the operations required in both problems are identical. As with all problem isomorphs, the deep structure of the two problems are one and the same.

A striking feature of many protocols was that most students had not automated many algorithms and routines from basic math and algebra. This fact was also evident from the basic math pretest, which contained numerous student errors in addition, multiplication, and division. Moreover, if simple linear equations involving one unknown (e.g., $5X - 8 = -4$) were encountered as a subgoal in the solution of a problem, these were rarely attempted mentally and generally consumed a significant portion of total solution time.

To what extent does the above description apply uniquely to black students attempting to solve quantitatively reasoning problems? Do majority and minority youngsters with similar grade/SAT performance patterns attack problems in the same way? That is, do they represent problems in similar ways, having similar misconceptions and making similar mistakes? The small sample of six white students was included in the study to obtain at least preliminary answers to this question.

It would appear that, at least on the basis of this small sample, the answer to the above question is yes. The protocols of the four white students who exhibited the high grades/low SAT pattern were virtually indistinguishable from those of black students with this pattern. Below is the protocol of a white female attempting to solve the first problem above. She obtained As in both algebra 1 and geometry and had an SAT-M of 440:

S: [reads problem, long pause] . . . uh . . . [long pause]. I'm not sure how to start getting into this one.

E: OK. What do you know first?

S: OK, uh, X is an odd number.

E: And what are they asking you?

S: What is the sum of the next two odd numbers greater than 3X plus 1 [long pause].

E: Is 3X even or odd?

S: Even.

E: What's the next odd number greater than 3X plus 1.

S: Eleven.

E: That's a specific one. What is the next. . . .

S: Oh, 3X plus . . . 2?

E: OK. Read the question.

S: [reads question] . . . So 3X plus 2 and . . . 3X plus . . . four?

E: OK. so. . . .

S: I would add those two . . . 6X plus 6. *(Total time: 2 min, 19 sec).*

While there are fewer errors and a bit less prompting, the similarity of this protocol to the first one above is readily apparent. In examining the transcriptions of black and white students with similar performance profiles, it was impossible to distinguish who was who. Inasmuch as these students were all from the same two algebra classes in the same school, this result may not be surprising. But it does suggest that, from an information-processing perspective, low-scoring white students and low-scoring black students tend to exhibit similar patterns of mistakes and have similar misconceptions about the structure of quantitative reasoning problems.

CONCLUSIONS

The present investigation was undertaken to shed some light on a persistent educational problem in American schools, the poor performance of black students on standardized measures of achievement, especially measures of quantitative reasoning. The paradigm guiding the research was specifically that of modern information processing. Although the investigation was preliminary, it nevertheless allows some tentative conclusions about the nature of mathematical knowledge that students who are doing well in school but perform poorly on measures of quantitative reasoning have, how that knowledge is organized and stored in memory, how it is accessed during problem solving, and how problems to be solved are represented internally.

First, it would appear that the presumption that grades in relevant math courses can be used as a proxy for the extent of one's declarative knowledge is only approximately correct. The students in this sample did not have many basic algebraic and geometric facts firmly in memory. Even so, the majority did have the relevant knowledge to solve the protocol problems.

The mathematical knowledge that these students have might best be described as inert, unintegrated knowledge. For example, they know that the interior angles of a triangle add up to 180°, and that an isosceles triangle has two angles that are equal. But if the third angle is given, they rarely combine the above two facts to determine the degree measure of the two equal angles. The two known facts about triangles tend to be isolated and unusable.

For the students in this sample, many arithmetic and algebraic routines were not yet automated. Numerous basic addition and multiplication errors were noted both in the pretest and in the protocols. The relevance of this to quantitative reasoning is that, for moderately speeded measures, much testing time, and in fact much of the student's working memory capacity, were consumed in solving routine subproblems. Students often lost track of the original problem and had to reread the problem often to retain the ultimate goal in working memory. The net effect is that the student would often solve the same subproblems two or three times during the course of the protocol.

Finally, unlike experts, the students in this sample rarely used external aids (e.g., geometric figures to represent the conditions of the problem) to facilitate and constrain memory search. Rather, if the problem was not immediately solvable, they tended to make a wild guess at the solution or to give up entirely.

It is noteworthy that, with very few exceptions, the students in this sample never practiced or honed math skills, other than when performing actual homework assignments. Moreover, they freely admitted to never attempting problems other than those assigned. Significantly, the two exceptions to the above were the two students who obtained scores above 600. Both of these students said during the debriefing that they often attempted to solve all of the problems in their texts. This difference in engaged time, cumulated over the years of formal schooling, may with further research prove to be a powerful explanatory variable.

FUTURE RESEARCH

This investigation was preliminary, but it demonstrates the utility of an information-processing approach to understanding the nature of the difficulties experienced by students attempting to solve quantitative reasoning problems. The study does not attempt explicitly to isolate the causes of the problems described here in terms of the subjects' instructional histories. Ethnographic studies both in the classroom and after school are needed to delineate such causes.

Experimental studies are now needed to further elaborate both the attributes of quantitative reasoning items that make them difficult as well as the instructional curricula that foster development of knowledge that is useful in problem solving. Attributes of items need to be systematically crossed with persons who have known knowledge structures. We must begin to link current thinking and research in cognitive psychology and instruction to a very serious practical problem. By subjecting the performance of students on quantitative reasoning tasks to a rigorous cognitive analysis, a process-based definition of mathematical aptitude is possible. Such a definition and description should facilitate the design of instructional treatments that effectively adapt individuals' characteristics to the specific demands of academic tasks.

NOTE

1. The categories "above" and "below" average course work and SAT scores are not intended to be tight dichotomies with well defined cut points. For purposes of exposition, the reader may consider (1) "below average course work" as being below a C in Algebra I and Geometry; and (2) "above average course work" as a B or better in these courses. With respect to the SAT, a median split would probably elucidate the pattern described in the text, although "below 400" and "above 500," would demonstrate the point made in the text even more clearly.

REFERENCES

Alderman, D. L. & Powers, D. E. (1979). The effects of special preparation on SAT-Verbal scores. *American Educational Research Journal, 17,* 239–251.

Bond, L. (1989). The effects of special preparation on measures of scholastic ability. In R. Linn (Ed.), *Educational Measurement* (3rd ed.). New York: Macmillan/American Council on Education. 429–446.

Chi, M. T. H., Feltovich, P. J. & Glaser, R. (1981). Categorization and representation of physics problems by experts and novices. *Cognitive Science, 5,* 121–151.

Ericsson, K. A. & Simon, H. A. (1980). Verbal reports as data. *Psychological Review, 87,* 215–251.

Federal Trade Commission. (1978). Staff memorandum of the Boston Regional Office of the FTC: *The effects of coaching on standardized admissions examinations.* Boston: Federal Trade Commission, Boston Regional Office.

Gitomer, D. (1984). *A cognitive analysis of a complex troubleshooting task.* Unpublished doctoral dissertation, University of Pittsburgh, PA.

Glaser, R. (1981). The future of testing: A research agenda for cognitive psychology and psychometrics. *American Psychologist, 36,* 923–936.

Greeno, J. G. (1978). Understanding and procedural knowledge in mathematics education. *Educational Psychologist, 12*(8), 262–283.

———. (1984). *Forms of understanding in mathematical problem-solving* (Report 1984/

26). Pittsburgh: University of Pittsburgh, Learning Research and Development Center.

Hayes, J. R. & Simon, H. A. (1976). Psychological differences among problem isomorphs. In N. Costellan, Jr., D. Pisoni & G. Potts (Eds.), *Cognitive Theory*. Hillsdale, NJ: Lawrence Erlbaum.

Johnson, S. T., Asbury, C. A., Wallace, M. B., Robinson, S. & Vaughn, J. (April 1985). *The effectiveness of a program to increase Scholastic Aptitude Test scores of black students in three cities*. Paper presented at the Annual Meeting of the National Council on Measurement in Education, Chicago.

Larkin, J. H. (1977). *Skilled problem-solving in physics: A hierarchical planning model*. Unpublished manuscript, University of California at Berkeley.

Messick, S. (1980). Effectiveness of coaching for the SAT: Review and analysis of research from the fifties to the FTC (ETS RR 80-8). Princeton, NJ: Educational Testing Service.

Resnick, L. B. & Ford, W. W. (1981). The psychology of mathematics for instruction. Hillsdale, NJ: Lawrence Erlbaum.

Roberts, S. O. & Oppenheim, D. B. (1966). The effect of special instruction upon test performance of high school students in Tennessee (ETS RR 66-36). Princeton, NJ: Educational Testing Service.

Sussman, G. J. (1977). Electrical design: A problem for artificial intelligence research. *Proceedings of the International Joint Conference on Artificial Intelligence*, 894–900.

Voss, J. F., Vesonder, G. T. & Spilich, G. J. (1980). Text generation and recall by high-knowledge individuals. *Journal of Verbal Learning and Verbal Behavior*, *19*, 651–667.

5

Increasing the Interpretative Validity and Diagnostic Utility of Hispanic Children's Scores on Tests of Achievement and Intelligence

Ernesto M. Bernal

Despite a plethora of research on the usefulness and validity of individually administered tests of achievement and intelligence, school psychologists and diagnosticians continue to ask, "How can I best interpret the scores of Hispanic children? Would individuals score higher on a test in Spanish? How far should I stick my neck out to make a 'clinical judgment'?"

For a great many psychologists and others who work in assessment or evaluation, the current literature on test bias has effectively closed the questions of test appropriateness and adaptation for ethnic minority students. For these professionals, tests of achievement (including minimal competency tests) and IQ tests should be administered in a standard fashion, except where required by law, for example, to satisfy the regulations under P.L. 94-142 for nondiscriminatory assessment. But even here, Maldonado-Colon (1984) and Garcia (1985) have indicated that the requirements to assess the child in his or her stronger or native language is routinely disregarded in some school systems.

Although various summaries of the literature on test bias already exist (e.g., Jensen, 1980; Reynolds & Brown, 1984), these have not provided a broad treatment of the direct, interpretative validity of test scores for nondominant ethnic groups. This is especially true regarding Hispanics, because most of the research has not accounted for certain psychometrically relevant characteristics of linguistic minority populations. This chapter will (1) examine the issues of validity and the interrelated question of bias with a view to bringing new perspectives to bear on the old problems; (2) identify sources of mismeasurement in practical situations; and (3) suggest better assessment practices and new departures for psychometric research.

CULTURAL LOADING, TEST BIAS, AND TEST FAIRNESS

Many authors have variously defined and used the terms *culture-free, culturally reduced,* and *culturally loaded* to classify tests. Their research indicates that although it is possible to frame culture-free tests—instruments that are not dependent upon knowledge commonly shared in a particular society—such instruments are useless as diagnostic indicators or predictors of cognitive performance (Anastasi, 1966), especially when these tests are nonverbal in nature (Rulon, 1966). Tests may, however, be roughly scaled along a continuum of culture-loading, from culturally loaded to culturally reduced (Jensen, 1980), depending upon how much culture-specific content they incorporate. The predictive validity of culturally loaded tests depends upon the extent to which the criterion is also culturally loaded (Green, 1975). For example, the vocabulary subtest of the Wechsler Intelligence Scale for Children-Revised (WISC-R) is at least moderately culturally loaded and has high predictive validity for achievement in English reading.

Clarizio (1979) differentiates between a test's cultural loading and a test's cultural bias, which he would determine by checking a test's internal characteristics and *predictive* validity (that is, the ability of the test to predict important outcomes, such as success in school). Green (1975) and Messick (1980) would also require the psychometrician to examine a test's content and construction validation as well to see if bias exists. Jensen (1980) distinguishes between test bias, which, like Clarizio's definition, is defined psychometrically, and test fairness, which has to do with the appropriateness of a test's use or application.

Mercer (1984) presents a model of nondiscriminatory assessment that integrates the notions of bias and fairness. She presents eight criteria to determine a test's potential for nondiscriminatory acculturation. Her criteria are stringent when taken in their totality, but fall within the spirit of the American Psychological Association's *Standards* (1985) for psychological tests. Furthermore, these criteria would seem to protect the legitimate societal interests of nondominant ethnic groups as a whole and of minority persons whose ''individual life trajectories'' (Mercer, 1984, p. 295) may be affected through the application of test results. Clearly, a variety of terms and concepts have been used to discuss the characteristics of tests and their use with various subpopulations of Americans.

TEST BIAS: THE TRADITIONAL VIEWPOINT

Historically the test bias issue was raised because of the clear abuses of "mental" tests with European populations immigrating to the United States early in this century (Kamin, 1974). Hispanic and Native American populations were also subjected early to such abuses (see Sanchez, 1934). These studies were often cited by racists of the day to prove the inferior genetic potential for intelligent behavior of Jewish, southern and eastern European, Asian, Native American, and Mexican groups. It was feared that their presence would diminish the "hybrid vigor" of the American "melting pot."

What alerts present day psychologists and humanitarians to the possibility of test bias, of course, are (1) the large differences in mean intelligence scores between whites and almost every other group; (2) the obvious lack of comparable English proficiency of some of the groups subjected to mental testing in that language; (3) the real political and economic consequences to individuals and to groups who have been stereotyped, stigmatized, and discriminated against as a result of testing; and (4) the nagging intuition among some that most standardized tests underestimate significantly the abilities and accomplishments of minority individuals more often than they underestimate these traits among whites.

Still a socially blind psychometric field defends itself against charges of bias, even when faced with group differences that are often so large and so statistically reliable that they stand out in the annals of behavioral science. Specifically, Cleary, Humphreys, Kendrick, and Wesman (1975), Jensen (1980), and others have demonstrated that the mere presence of group differences is not prima facie evidence of bias. Sattler and Gwynne (1982), for instance, found large average differences in errors made on the Bender Visual Motor Gestalt Test between blacks and whites, blacks and Hispanics, and some differences between Hispanics and whites at different ages, but they reported no bias.

A popular way to criticize tests is to find a number of items on a particular test that appear to be biased in one or more ways and to use these to condemn the test or, for that matter, all tests of the same genre. Again, some psychometricians point out that a test "may still turn out fair . . . so long as negative and positive biases for the different groups cancel each other out" (Bernal, 1983b, p. 4). Furthermore, it has been empirically demonstrated that armchair judgments about individual items, even when these are made by knowledgeable ethnic reviewers, are frequently in error (e.g., Miele, 1979; Sandoval & Millie, 1980).

Studies of Test Bias

Psychometricians have been investigating the issue of test bias for a long time (e.g., Anastasi, 1966; Cronbach, 1972). Cleary et al. (1975), in their *American Psychologist* position paper, probably sparked a rash of elaborations and modifications of commonly used techniques including those of McCornack (1983), a *t*-test of mean errors of estimation and an F-test of the mean squared errors, Scheuneman's chi-square (1979) based on the probability of a correct response across groups of similar ability levels, and Reynolds and Gutkin's application of the Potthoff procedure (1980), which provides a simultaneous test of slope and intercept values. Readers who wish to delve into the more technical and modern methods for detecting test bias are referred to Berk (1982), Fuchs (1985), Jensen (1980), Messick (1980), Reynolds and Brown (1984), Seong and Subkoviak (1987), Shepard, Camilli, and Williams (1985), and Wright (1986).

In general, the research literature suggests that commonly used tests are not biased against Hispanics. This has been found to be the case for the Illinois Test of Psycholinguistic Abilities (Perez, 1980), Raven Progressive Matrices (Carlson & Jensen, 1981; Corman & Budoff, 1974; Valencia, 1984), and the Kaufman Assessment Battery for Children or K-ABC (Reynolds, Willson, & Chatman, 1984; Valencia & Rankin, 1985). Even the Wechsler Intelligence Scale-Revised (WISC-R)—a test that has generated considerable legal and professional controversy due to its extensive use in diagnosis, educational placement, and research on group differences—has been acquitted of ethnic bias (Dean, 1977; Kaufman, 1979a, 1979b; Oakland & Feigenbaum, 1979; Reschly & Reschly, 1979; Reschly & Sabers, 1979; Ross-Reynolds & Reschly, 1983; Sandoval, 1979). Finally, Hennessy and Merrifield (1976) found that on a battery of ten ability and achievement group tests, nearly 3,000 black, Hispanic, Jewish, and Anglo high school seniors had similar structures of mental abilities, evidence for a lack of bias.

Although the literature supports the position of no bias in the principal tests used with Hispanic students, a few points are worth noting. First, there is a reluctance among most authors to say that a test is biased when their data yield mixed results; these authors are content when biases cancel each other out (see Cotter & Berk, 1981) or tend to reach one general conclusion about a test's bias according to the majority of the results of the analyses conducted, thereby assuming that all analyses of bias are of equal weight, importance, or applicability. Second, and more important, these studies seem either to restrict the Hispanic samples to more or less proficient speakers of English or fail to account for the language characteristics of their Hispanic subjects altogether. Important substudies of the validity of these measures for Hispanics who are limited English proficient (LEP) or, worse yet, non-English proficient (NEP) were not conducted. Perhaps these authors were ignorant about the Hispanic population's linguistic diversity, or felt that the tests are inappropriate for LEP/NEPS anyway (Kaufman, 1979a; Reynolds & Brown, 1984) and therefore, excluded them; assumed that anyone who can speak English can be tested in English (Cummins, 1982, 1984; Padilla, 1979); or believed that somehow the experimentally confounding effect of bilingualism was accounted for by the sophistication of their statistics (see Lawshe, 1969), as if analysis were a substitute for design. The summary point is inexorable: the generalization of these studies to all Hispanics is invalid.

THE NEED FOR A RECONCEPTUALIZATION OF BIAS

Reynolds (1982) categorized traditional definitions of test bias as follows: (1) inappropriate content, (2) inappropriate standardization samples, (3) examiner and language bias, (4) inequitable social consequences, (5) measurement of different constructs, and (6) differential predictive validity.

Related definitions that appear to come closer to the practical domain are the following: A test is biased when some characteristic of the test interacts with some characteristic of the test taker in such a way as to distort the meaning of the test score for some group of examinees (Shepard, 1980); and "Bias in testing occurs when a circumstance or condition—usually one which has no relevance to the intended purpose of the measurement—works systematically to distort the results enough to misrepresent the true condition of an individual or a definable group of individuals" (Bernal, 1983b, p. 4). While carefully pointing out that lower scores are not necessarily indicators of bias, Flaugher and Anderson admit that "Bias in measures can also stem from irrelevant difficulties" (1975, p. 44), which affect performance on individual items and thus, possibly impact upon total scores. They note that motivation, attitude, test anxiety, and the testing process or environment can also affect test performance and thus "lead to inaccurate inferences about the knowledge, skills, or other attributes of an individual or group" (Flaugher & Anderson, 1975, p. 43). Messick (1980) points out that tests that have not been validated constructually may not yield interpretable results when scores are low because the possibility that irrelevant factors have influenced low scoring individuals cannot be ruled out.

Traditional psychometricians (e.g., Hunter et al., 1984) would doubtlessly argue that if these statements were true, the "real" abilities or characteristics of the individuals or groups in question would show up in some other measurable way, such as in criterial performance. But they would miss the point that the criteria may be biased not only in ways that may easily be detected (see Schmitt & Lappin, 1980), but also in subtler ways that are difficult to detect because they may restrict the very expression of the competence or ability, except through narrowly defined, culturally bound practices (see Bernal, 1983b; Mercer, 1979). For instance, the use of highly atomized approaches to teach English reading to marginally English proficient Hispanic students, a practice that steals meaning from the reading experience of LEP students (Cummins, 1984; Kaminsky, 1976), inadvertently promotes their failure and ultimately relegates them to the slowest reading groups. Similarly, the popular use of basal readers with controlled vocabularies that consist mostly of monosyllabic words with Saxon roots might actually pose more difficulties for LEP Hispanic students than books with ostensibly harder polysyllabic words in English that have true French and Latin cognates and are therefore more similar to Spanish. (For related ideas see Au & Jordan, 1981; Thonis, 1970). Even the verbal part of the SAT shows differential item functioning among bilingual Hispanics, depending on whether items have true or false cognates (Schmitt, 1986).

Some testing situations, in short, cause the prophesy of the predictor to come true (see Brogden & Taylor, 1950; Green, 1975). And if such a test is used for selection or differential placement, as in admissions to college or graduate school, it will tend to preserve the extant system, since persons who might succeed, if the system were modified to accommodate other styles or modalities of expression, would be excluded or sent elsewhere (Cronbach, 1972; Messick, 1980). Bergan and Parra (1979) would study the relationship between IQ and academic learning under different instructional conditions, and Bernal (1983b) proposes that predictive validity studies should be long-term and comparative under a variety of educational settings, some of which would be culturally and linguistically appropriate for ethnic minority children.

Still some promising applications need to be considered. Gamache (1984) illustrated the use of factorial invariance as a criterion for cross-cultural construct validation and the determination of test bias. Valencia and Rankin (1985) investigated the possibility of content bias in English and Spanish versions of the McCarthy Scales of Children's Abilities with a carefully defined sample of dominant English-speaking and dominant Spanish-speaking Mexican-American preschool children from low socioeconomic status (SES) backgrounds. To analyze the results they used the item-group (partial) correlation method suggested by Lord and described in Angoff (1982). It involves calculating the correlation between the item and the group membership, with the contribution of the general ability true score partialed out. The item under investigation is not included in the true score. The test for bias is the significance of the item-partial correlation with subgroup membership controlling for total score, age, and sex. This method has the same result as matching on ability. It has the added advantages of controlling for regression toward the mean, reducing the number of subjects lost because of difficult matches, and partialing out sex and age differences at the same time that general ability is controlled (Valencia & Rankin, 1985, p. 199). Effect sizes were also calculated. Using these techniques, Valencia and Rankin determined that six of the McCarthy Scales' sixteen subtests were biased, two against English-dominant Chicano students and four against the Spanish-dominant.

The consequential outcomes of these subtler aspects of test bias are perhaps best observed in settings where diagnoses and placement decisions are made in large part on the basis of test scores, or when research psychologists impute group differences to genetically controlling factors. Mercer (1984) criticizes several psychologists for "treating [intelligence tests] scores as if they have genetic equivalents" (p. 312). After all, "the heritability index is but a hypothetical construct to which [psychologists], perhaps by default, assign that part of systematic variance which our research designs . . . and scientific imaginations cannot otherwise explain'' (Bernal, 1981, pp. 4–5).

Anastasi (1982) reminds us that (1) changes in environmental conditions can alter the heritability index, (2) a heritability index computed for one ethnic group is not applicable to evaluate mean differences in test scores between two groups, and (3) the heritability index does not include the degree of modifiability of any given trait. IQ, for example, ''is amenable to modification by environmental interventions'' (Anastasi, 1982, p. 351).

Then do the scores made by economically disadvantaged, linguistically distinct, nondominant ethnic children mean the same as similar scores derived from children belonging to the dominant ethnic group? Given the following: two ten-year-old children of the same gender, one an upper-middle-class white English monolingual from Midwest suburbia, the other a bilingual Chicano migrant farmworker from rural south Texas; both have the same Full Scale IQ, or FSIQ (105), the same Verbal IQ, or VIQ (90), and Performance IQ, or PIQ (124) on the WISC-R; who is the most educationally, socially, and economically advantaged? The white, of course. Who is most likely to complete a postsecondary training program in a community college? Again, the white. But who is smarter, who has the higher intellectual potential and the lesser chance of being learning disabled?

So, do these scores mean the same? This author does not think so. In the case of the Anglo and Chicano children above, could one intelligently compare their scores directly as if they were from the same ethnic or socioeconomic group? Could one reach certain clinical or diagnostic interpretations about their potential for intelligent behavior without taking their different backgrounds and experiences into account? These are basic issues in construct validity.

And so far as predictive validity is concerned, does knowledge about their IQs significantly alter the forecast that the advantaged white child will achieve greater ''success'' than the disadvantaged Chicano child, despite the greater likelihood that the Chicano has more of whatever it is that the IQ test is supposed to measure? What is more, if these two youngsters were part of a group being studied with classic regression techniques, the traditional psychometricians would probably conclude that a common regression line would underpredict the Anglo means, implying that somehow the test favored the Chicanos. Here is a hypothetical illustration of criterion bias in the raw, the very thing about which Mercer (1984) warns us to be vigilant.

SOURCES OF TEST BIAS

What are the sources of some of these biases? One source seems to be the failure of some test makers to remove items that show biases for any major group. Nungester (1977) reports that the removal of items with unacceptable discrimination or difficulty indices improved both the reliability and the validity of tests to a greater extent than the removal of items detected as biased by three other widely used psychometric methods.

CTB/McGraw-Hill (1977) used the inclusion of an extra choice in a multiple-choice format quite successfully in the item selection phase for the CTBS Forms S and T, eliminating the distractor that was least effective or the one whose deletion would affect the item's characteristics in a desired way. A related procedure was used by McArthur (1981) and McArthur and Hafner (1982), who examined the patterns of wrong answers made by separate groups of respondents, a technique that is reminiscent of Fruchter's factor analysis of right and wrong scores (1953). "Within the multiple choice format, differences between groups in the attractiveness of incorrect responses signal that the item's wrong choices may be differentially distracting" (McArthur, 1981, p. 11).

Working with bilingual adults (some English-dominant, the rest Spanish-dominant) in administrative secretarial training, Gonzalez-Tamayo (1984) administered the vocabulary subtest of the California Achievement Test and used it to predict a composite criterion on which there was no difference between the English-dominant and Spanish-dominant groups. The CAT had about equal rs for both groups but produced higher mean scores for the English-dominant group. He then debiased the vocabulary test by removing eight of the thirty items that did not have fairly exact equivalents in Spanish. Both groups scored similarly on the debiased CAT test. Furthermore, the shorter instrument proved to be a slightly more accurate predictor of the composite criterion for both groups of trainees.

Fuchs (1985) laments that most research on test bias tends to focus only on the test instrument and ignores the context in which assessment occurs. After conducting a meta-analysis of fourteen selected studies on the effects of examiner unfamiliarity, Fuchs found that the average, weighted, unbiased effect-size was only .05 (n.s.) for Caucasian examinees, whereas the effect of an unfamiliar examiner was .72 for black and Hispanic subjects. What this means is that, "given a normative test . . . with a population mean of 100 and a standard deviation of 15, the use of a familiar examiner would raise [an average-scoring] minority student's score from 100 to 111" (Fuchs, 1985, p. 11).

Bernal's experience in testing bilingual children and in evaluating compensatory educational programs suggests to him that bias may exist in the test as a whole. He offers the view that one way of evaluating a multiple-choice test's appropriateness is to compare the proportions of different ethnic groups who score at or below the expected chance-score (Bernal, 1983b).

For Hispanic groups, what might be some of the factors that bias a test as a whole? One is the cultural loading of the test content, a second is the language register (degree of formal English) used in the test (when that is not what the test is intended to measure), and a third has to do with adequacy of the directions (Cabello, 1981; CTB/McGraw-Hill, 1977). Test speededness (the extent to which speed is a factor in completing the test), a potential fourth factor, shows ambiguous results. (Compare Knapp, 1960, and Rincon, 1979). And

Burger (1969) suggests that the interrogative face-to-face situation—a fifth factor—is at least somewhat inappropriate to many Chicanos, whose behavior in these circumstances is erroneously interpreted to be shy.

The ethnicity of the examiner and the language of administration may also be important considerations. Anastasi and Cordova (1953), after giving English and Spanish versions of the Cattell Culture Free Intelligence Test in a counter-balanced design to Puerto Rican children, found an order effect by sex, but attributed the difference to levels of acculturation, where the more acculturated boys did better with the English-speaking examiner and the less acculturated girls scored higher when the examiner was Spanish speaking.

Garcia and Zimmerman (1972) tested bilingual Mexican-American children on a routine task and found that matching examiner and examinee by ethnicity improved performance. But Alley and Foster (1978) do not believe that such matching is enough to overcome the attitudinal references that may exist between the psychometrist and client. Nevertheless, some Hispanic children reliably get higher IQ scores when examiners encourage them to actively participate, to verbalize, and to persevere (Thomas, Hertzig, Dryman & Fernandez, 1971).

When the purpose of the test is to assess learning ability, language factors should not be permitted to interfere with tested performance (Olmedo, 1981). Alderman (1982) finds that English proficiency is indeed critical in predicting test performance itself: SAT scores were best predicted for certain bilinguals by performance on a Spanish-language college aptitude test when English proficiency was treated as a moderator variable. Figueroa (ca. 1981) could predictively rank Hispanic students' test scores on the basis of the System of Multicultural Pluralistic Assessment (SOMPA) Sociocultural Scales' determination of language dominance.

Language thus seems to act as a moderator variable, especially where questions of proficiency in English or in both languages are concerned. Certain bilinguals—those who demonstrate high levels of proficiency in both languages, whose bilingualism is additive (Cummins, 1979)—seem to cross a threshold and enjoy certain cognitive advantages over monolinguals (Cummins, 1984), while other bilinguals suffer the negative cognitive effects of semilingualism in both languages. Accurate estimations of proficiency in both languages would seem to be crucial covariables in any study of a test's predictive validity with bilingual Hispanic subjects.

Training in test-taking skills has shown mixed results. Jensen (1980) summarized the literature and concluded that minority scores improved with training but did not come to equal those of whites. Powers (1982) conducted training sessions in test-taking skills with black, Hispanic, Native American, and Anglo students in grades three, five, and seven. He found that (1) test-taking skills before training were the same for all groups once reading ability and SES were controlled; (2) gains in these skills were comparable for all ethnic groups; (3) this training did not affect reading comprehension scores; and (4) training in test-taking skills was more closely related to gains in these skills than to gains in achievement scores. Oakland (1972), working with a small group of disadvantaged preschoolers, demonstrated that experimental gains on training in test-taking skills can be matched by young children's normal development over a few months' time.

Ortar (1960), however, coached disadvantaged Israeli children on a nonverbal intelligence test and increased the correlation of these scores with school marks and with the VIQ of the WISC. Later, Ginther (1978) demonstrated that pretraining on test-taking strategies improved both the reliability and the predictive validity of the Arithmetic Reasoning Test for seventh-grade Chicano students but not for non-Chicanos. Similarly, Maspons and Llabre (1983), working with over 500 Hispanic college students, who were divided randomly into test-taking skills training and control groups, found that a slightly lower internal consistency on the computation test of the College Guidance and Placement Program was obtained by those in the experimental groups, but that predictive validity of their results was significantly increased. Blakely (1983) found that there is a significant difference in the amount of time required for limited English proficient (LEP) students to acquire the requisite test-taking skills, that the brief demonstrations during group achievement testing are insufficient for LEP students to perform their best; hence, these skills need to be taught ahead of time.

Carlson (1983) and Carlson and Wiedl (1980) administered the Coloured Progressive Matrices (CPM) and some Piagetian measures to 434 Anglo, black, and Hispanic second- and fourth-graders under six different conditions: (1) standard, (2) verbalization during and after solution, (3) verbalization after solution, (4) simple feedback from the examiner, (5) elaborated feedback/explanation by the examiner, and (6) verbalization during and after solution followed by elaborated feedback. Anglo-black differences in subjects' initial responses on Piagetian tasks were most pronounced under condition 1, zero under condition 6 (although it is not clear if this was due to possible ceiling effects, which occur when many individuals get virtually every item correct); all groups improved under condition 6, and condition 2 seemed effective only for the fourth-graders. For the CPM, the verbalization conditions all produced higher results than did the standard or feedback conditions (simple or elaborated); condition 2 produced superior results for all three ethnic groups, followed by condition 3; however, Anglo-black and Anglo-Hispanic differences in favor of Anglos continued to be evident on the CPM. Regrettably, neither SES nor the language proficiency of the Hispanic subgroups were controlled or studied.

Related to the effect of test-taking skills is the possibility that a significant proportion of minority examinees may respond to the testing environment poorly (Flaugher, 1970) or process the test questions differently. The data of Haggard (1954) suggest that "deprived" children really did not know how to take IQ tests. Before he trained them (and subsequently raised their scores), Haggard noted that many children simply hurried through the test as if to get it over with and thereby remove themselves from an unpleasant situation. (See also Zigler & Butterfield, 1968). Haggard's work illustrates that, contrary to Jensen's presumption (1980, 1984) about adequately developed test-taking skills among minorities, experience with tests may merely serve to reinforce minority students' bad test-taking habits. Gitmez (1972), for example, demonstrated how different sets of directions on multiple-choice tests can alter the performance levels of children whose experience with tests has been restricted. He rejects "the commonly held belief that, for all practical purposes, instructions to Ss provide an adequate control of motivational and mental sets. The ability of an individual to solve problems is not free from . . . situational demands, nor from his perception of the costs and rewards of his action" (Gitmez, 1972, p. 159).

Pascual-Leone and Smith (1969) demonstrated the importance of experimental repertoire control through pretraining in order to reduce the effects of experiential and stylistic differences on Piagetian tasks, a view also reflected in the work of Van de Flier (1972), who would reduce culture-specific skill differences in order to tap true abilities. Zimmerman and Rosenthal (1972), for example, showed that both Anglo and Chicano children showed improvement in concept-attainment tasks under conditions of modeling and repetition of test directions. Cole and Bruner (1971) note that cultural deprivation arises when persons must perform in a manner that is not consistent with their backgrounds, a situation that turns differences into deficits.

Ulibarri (1982) takes the matter even further. He believes that a "culture-loaded" item is one that calls for information-processing strategies on the part of minority test takers that are different from the ones employed by majority subjects. In this fashion Ulibarri seems to complement the work of McArthur and Hafner (1982), who view test bias as "a systematic but unanticipated pattern of responses to a multiple-choice test found for an entire group of test-takers" (p. 7). Such pattern-differences, they maintain, raise the possibility that different groups use different strategies to arrive at their answers. Ulibarri trained a mixed group of children to select and use appropriate strategies for solving certain types of problems, specifically those items with p-values that were lower for minorities, and succeeded in raising minorities' overall scores significantly. McArthur (1981) and McArthur and Hafner (1982) also identified difficult items and taught fifth-grade Asian and Hispanic students the intellectual skills necessary to select the correct responses to the Reading Comprehension subtest of the California Test of Basic Skills (CTBS). Estes (1974) suggested that such differences in cognitive processing, if they exist, need to be studied from the perspective of learning theory, so that the sources of poor performances may be isolated.

Further evidence of processing differences involving language has surfaced, indicating that language plays a significant role even on tests that ostensibly rely very little on English. Llabre and Cuevas (1983) gave the Comprehensive

Tests of Basic Skills to bilingual Hispanics in grades four and five who were taught predominantly in English and whose reading comprehension in English and Spanish had been previously assessed and found to be at least minimally functional. They found an interaction between the Reading Comprehension subtest of the CTBS and the Concepts and Applications subscales (when Concepts exceeded Applications), which they interpreted as indicating that the difference between concepts and applications scores decreased as levels of English reading comprehension increased (Llabre & Cuevas, 1983). Taylor and Partenio (1984) tested almost 650 black, Hispanic, and white children, ages five to eleven, with the Bender-Gestalt and either the Wechsler Preschool and Primary Scale of Intelligence (WPPSI) or the WISC-R. While they neither measured nor controlled for Hispanics' language proficiency, they reported that Performance IQ was significantly related to Bender-Gestalt test performance of the black and white subjects, whereas Verbal IQ was significant for only the Hispanic group (Taylor & Partenio, 1984), indicating the greater verbal loading of the Bender for the Hispanic children. In a related study of children aged six to eleven, Taylor, Zigler, and Partenio (1984) found that the Hispanic group had a significantly greater Verbal versus Performance (V-P) IQ discrepancy on the WISC-R than did either the black or white groups. The authors caution that the use of V-P discrepancies in the special education classification of Hispanic students is clearly inappropriate (Taylor et al. 1984), although common and documented experience indicates that such misuse occurs frequently.

The question of whether to test the child in English or in Spanish, with bilingual examiners or with interpreters, was partly resolved by Swanson and DeBlassie (1979), who compared three conditions of test administration by testing ninety second-grade, Spanish-dominant bilingual children. They found that for the Verbal section of the WISC, a standardized English administration yielded higher scores than an interpreted administration, which in turn yielded a higher mean than a Spanish administration. In the Performance subtests, however, the use of Spanish yielded the highest scores in Picture Arrangement, Block Design, and Object Assembly. They concluded that, "In general, administration of the Verbal phase of the WISC in English and the Performance phase in Spanish appears to be most efficacious in terms of eliciting optimum performance of Mexican-American children" (Swanson & DeBlassie, 1979, p. 235). This finding may seem counter intuitive, but it underscores the claims of Figueroa (1981) about the power of the language of the test and demonstrates, dramatically in my opinion, that translations of verbal tests are not as good as original instruments that truly reflect both the language and the cultural repertoire of the ethnic-minority bilingual child (see Hardy, Glad, Bernal, and Cordova, 1978). Chavez (1982) also found lower scores on unofficially translated versions of the Peabody Picture Vocabulary Test (A&B); a trial-by-language interaction, furthermore, suggests that "responding to an English version of the test first may decrease performance on the Spanish version" (Chavez, 1982, p. 1337).

Finally, there are affective or personality factors that influence minority children's test performance. Hill and Eaton (1977) note that in general highly anxious children score poorly on cognitive and ability tests because of motivational difficulties, not because of learning deficiencies. Children who were highly anxious about being tested performed well on math problems when the threat of failure was removed, when they were allowed to pace themselves without time pressure, and when they did not perceive the testing condition as highly evaluative. Attributions of success and failure also play a role in motivation to perform well on maximal performance tests, but anxiety is believed to play the most influential role in affecting test-related outcomes (Fyans, Wise, Magee & Siebermann, 1980). For minority children, furthermore, high test anxiety or self-deprecating attributions may actually increase with age, again contrary to the assertions of Jensen (1980).

Willig, Harnisch, Hill, and Maehr (1983) studied almost 400 black, Anglo, and Hispanic students in grades four to eight. For Hispanic children, "high test anxiety scores are associated with low defensiveness scores, low math scores, the tendency to attribute failure to lack of ability (the most debilitating failure attribution) and to task difficulty, with a greater incidence of family mobility . . . and with being female" (Willig et al., 1983, pp. 392–393). The least acculturated Hispanics tend to attribute failure to luck, not to lack of effort, but do tend to attribute success to effort. Both Hispanic and black children who seem to be most at risk are the ones in the process of acculturating. "It is the moderately acculturated group that stands out in terms of debilitating attributions, higher defensiveness, and anxiety scores" (Willig et al., 1983, p. 400).

Bernal (1984a) built upon some of the foregoing studies to examine test bias from a more holistic perspective. The subjects (N = 192) were eighth-grade Anglos, blacks, Chicanos monolingual in English, and bilingual Chicanos, all matched on gender and SES (3 classes). They were randomly divided into two groups. The control group took a shortened version of the multiple choice Letter Sets Test (LST) and the completion Number Series Test (NST), two measures of higher order cognitive processing, in standard fashion. The experimental group was given a brief practice session with the items taken from the longer LST and NST tests, then took the shortened versions. During these practice sessions, examiners were matched both ethnically and linguistically with small groups of examinees. Efforts were made to establish rapport. The examinees practiced with time limits, received feedback regarding the accuracy of their choices. Also, the students with the correct solutions were asked to articulate and explain their answers to their peers, and additional explanations were provided as necessary. Under the control/standard condition, Anglos consistently outperformed the minority groups on both measures, and a definite SES effect was present. Under the experimental condition Anglo performance on both tests was essentially unchanged. However, the minorities' scores increased so dramatically that ethnic differences were no longer detectable, an unusual if not unique finding in the literature (see also Miller and Swanson, 1960).

Bernal (1984a) suggested that some differences in mean ethnic test scores are artifacts of the tests themselves and that the standard testing ambience itself could be biased. Jensen (1984) trenchantly criticized this conclusion because the ethnic-by-treatment interactions on NST and LST were not significant. Bernal (1984c) reanalyzed the data, making an exact test of the interaction, and concluded that the results were ambiguous, since the interaction term for the Number Series Test was significant, but the result for the Letter Sets Test was not. Bernal, however, pointed out that if Jensen and other hereditarians had more data like his to review, they could not support the principal thrust of their work, the genetic interpretation of ethnic differences in intelligence. Clearly some circumstances can substantially and differentially increase the test performance of minority students.

Perhaps the most creative, recent experimental investigation into the nature of traditional psychometric definitions of bias was conducted by Harrington (1984). Harrington borrowed an animal research model from the biomedical field. He selected a genetically homogeneous group of rats, used different maze configurations as test items, and established a separate maze-running set of trials as the criterion measure to examine the inherent validity of the tests he would construct. Essentially, Harrington randomly assigned the rats to six groups, noted their performance on the different maze items, then varied the proportional representation of each group for the various item analyses he would use to select the final set of items. He devised six tests using this procedure. His results indicate (1) "a significant positive association between the test performance of a group and representation in the population used for item analysis and the ensuing item selection" (p. 124); and (2) "increasing predictive validity with increasing minority group representation" (p. 125). Thus, two different forms of minority test bias occur as psychometric artifacts from the use of standard psychometric procedures (Harrington, 1984, pp. 126–127).

Since an independent measure of maze running had already been established, it was possible to compare item correlations, not only with total scores on the test but also to the criterion measure. The results indicated that some groups were clearly discriminated against. More specifically, "a minority effect was found that depresses both test scores and test validity in a way that cannot be corrected simply by using different norms" (Harrington, 1984, p. 129). If, furthermore, the predictor and the criterion are both subject to similarly biased selection (and one cannot help but draw the parallel to school or college), then "bias in both . . . will result in common intercepts and common slopes" (p. 133), a typical finding in the literature that reports no bias.

Harrington, then, may have demonstrated the oft-suspected circularity of item-total procedures which relate performance on an item to performance on the total test in a way that calls into question their general use with heterogeneous groups, as well as with less represented subgroups of an ostensibly homogenous sample of a population. Jensen (1980) himself suggests that "comparable item selection procedures [be] performed separately within each subgroup" of approximately equal size "or at least large enough to permit comparable statistical inferences regarding the psychometric properties of the test" (p. 373) as a whole. But McArthur and Hafner (1982) are quick to point out that no test on the market has been constructed in this fashion.

Harrington's work was quickly put to an empirical test with human subjects. Using the standardization sample of the Kaufman Assessment Battery for Children (K-ABC), Hickman and Reynolds (1986–1987) did an elaborate simulation and constructed separate tests for black and white subjects along the same lines as the K-ABC subtests, using similar selection criteria for the items which constituted these two tests, believing that by using "the most extreme of nonproportionate sampling methods [exclusion of the other group], the probability of locating the Harrington Effect should be at its maximum" (Hickman & Reynolds, 1986–1987, p. 420).

It is unfortunate that these authors chose this particular tack, because Harrington's work can in no way be taken to imply that he advocates different tests for different ethnic groups. Quite to the contrary, his work is predicated upon the interacting presence of several groups in the item-tryout sample. So instead of asking if the different tests for blacks and whites represent significantly different collections of items, Hickman and Reynolds should have constructed a "new" K-ABC, using equal representation of ethnic groups and asking to what extent does this test differ from the extant K-ABC, which was developed using only proportional representation. As it was, the separate tests they devised had some 80 to 90 percent overlap and the authors concluded that this is evidence of no bias in proportional sampling, when what should have been done is a test of significance in proportions of items selected to see if the ten to twenty percent discrepancies were enough to be different.

Ethnic mean differences were reduced in the Hickman and Reynolds study for all subparts of the test except the Simultaneous Processing (SP) scales, where whites scored higher than blacks on both the white SP scale and the black SP scale (a similar finding to that of Green, 1972). Predictive validities for the two tests were calculated against the K-ABC's achievement test, and the Potthoff analysis indicated no differences in regression slopes but differences in intercepts, the classic condition that leads Hickman and Reynolds to conclude that a common regression line would overpredict the achievement scores of blacks and underpredict the achievement of Anglos—again.

And so tests produce biased scores, often supported by biased criteria, and continue to be used more or less appropriately with minority ethnic groups. An Hispanic school psychologist put it well:

What can I do with an IQ of 70 obtained by a twelve-year-old boy without any formal education, who recently immigrated directly to Chicago from a ranch in Mexico, where he was employed as a cowboy, working alongside his father? His teachers say he's a slow learner, reticent, and maladjusted. The other members of the staffing team think he should be placed in special ed., where he can get some individualized help (Personal Communication, F. Palomo, April 1, 1986).

Reynolds (1982) notes that practicing clinicians tend to overestimate the IQs of blacks; furthermore, when IQ and achievement are held constant, black children are currently less likely to be recommended for placement in special education than white children. He believes that this reflects psychologists' reluctance to place blacks in undesirable settings, but an alternative interpretation of this practice is that psychologists sense that black students' scores on these tests of maximal performance do not match other manifestations of their adaptive and intelligent behaviors. For example, Hardy, Welcher, Mellits, and Kagan (1976) administered the WISC under standard and informal (testing-of-limits) conditions and noted how many times inner-city children seemed to know the answers to items they had previously gotten wrong. While such informal assessments turn the standardized IQ test into a sort of criterion-referenced test with relatively unspecified conditions of administration (Kaufman, 1979a), thereby vitiating any possible comparisons under controlled conditions, the assumption here is that this technique, which is ordinarily reserved for difficult-to-test whites and other individuals, yields unexpectedly higher raw scores for disadvantaged children, thereby further documenting the inappropriateness of the test for many of them.

Bernal (1986) illustrates this inappropriateness in an evaluation report on a special program for potentially gifted elementary- and high-school migrant students (Hispanic, Hmong, and Laotian) who speak a minority language. In a central California school district, the Otis Lennon School Ability Test (OLSAT) was used to screen students for the gifted program. Nominated students had to score at least one standard deviation above the mean (SAI = 116) on the OLSAT to be administered a Wechsler test, the results of which would figure prominently in the selection decision. Qualifying students would ordinarily have to have a FSIQ of at least 130. Only one of thirty-four bilingual, Hispanic, migrant children nominated for this special program scored 116 or higher on the OLSAT, but since the services of a school psychologist were available to the project, all thirty-four children were also tested with the WISC-R, and twelve were deemed qualified for admission to gifted classes. Using the Wechsler score as the preferred criterion to define this population, the OLSAT screening criterion identified only 8.3 percent of the eligible Hispanic children.

So in cooperation with the school district's gifted program a study of the OLSAT's screening effectiveness was undertaken: thirty non-Hispanic, nonmigrant students who were also recently nominated for the gifted program were tested with both the OLSAT and the WISC-R. The results indicated that the OLSAT correctly screened in (true positives) thirteen of the twenty-two children who qualified for placement, or 59.1 percent. A test of the OLSAT's positive diagnostic screening accuracy for the two groups (N = 64) yields a significant result: a test for nonindependent proportions yields a z of 3.62, $p <$ .0005. Reducing the cutoff score to SAI > 107 (or +.5 z) would improve the proportion of correctly screened individuals to .86 for non-Hispanic, nonmigrants and to .54 for the language-minority migrants by reducing the number of false negatives. But even under these simulated, relaxed standards the difference in the proportions of correctly screened children may still be said to discriminate against the language minority, Hispanic migrant population, since the difference in the proportions of correctly screened students is still significant: $z = 3.104$, $p <$ .003. Furthermore, the overall screening efficiency of the OLSAT would be reduced because the number of false positives for the entire group (N = 64) increases from 5 percent to 17 percent. The OLSAT may thus be considered a biased test for screening migrant, language-minority, Hispanic children for programs for the gifted.

And so another definition of test bias emerges in the realm of applied measurement: A test is biased if the diagnostic use of the same cut score with two or more groups results in statistically significant proportional differences in the screening accuracy of true positives and false negatives (pq). Such analyses can be made whenever one has access to an independently validated criterion score or diagnostic category at the time of the assessment, or when follow-up data reveal the true conditions of these individuals.

Gordon (1977), Marion and Bernal (1985), and others have documented the adding-points phenomenon that some psychologists use to try to compensate the low IQ scores earned by certain minority individuals. Such procedures suffer from their lack of objectivity and do not correct the basic problem of content bias or alter the predictive validity of these tests. The System of Multicultural Pluralistic Assessment (SOMPA), designed to correct obtained scores for bias and improve the diagnostic utility of the standard IQ test (see Mercer, 1979), has failed to satisfy traditional criteria of predictive validity against achievement measures (see, for example, Oakland 1980). But as Figueroa (ca. 1981), Harrington (1984), Marion and Bernal (1985), and Mercer (1984) indicate, studies such as Oakland's will probably not support the adaptation of traditionally derived scores when it is likely that similar sources of bias simultaneously infect IQ scores, achievement scores, and grade point averages.

Clearly the diagnostic utility of many tests is suspect, since scores, whatever their short-term predictive validity, cannot be interpreted directly to form a nomological net of evidence to support a diagnostic conclusion (Mercer, 1984) when scores are low and the individual client is atypical.

McNemar (1942) revealed that for the 1937 revision of the Stanford-Binet, items were selected to balance for interactions of sex with item difficulty to ensure that the scale would not show mean group differences based on gender. Donlon, Hicks, and Wallmark (1980) were able to determine that the content of Graduate Record Examination items, rather than the type of item, was an important determinant of systematic differences between males and females, and that it is possible to influence the magnitude of these differences by controlling the selection of item material.

Why, then, do we not undertake studies that could help identify the key factors in mean score differences by ethnicity on tests of maximal performance? The Mantel-Haenszel procedure and the standardized difference technique employed by Educational Testing Service (ETS) are closely related statistics (Wright, 1986) that rely on matching two groups on some objective criterion such as total score on the test in question, dividing the groups of examinees into score intervals, calculating and comparing the probability of each group's getting an item correct at each interval, and then summing across intervals to determine if an overall differential item functioning (dif) exists (Dorans, 1986). Once items that exhibit dif have been identified, they may be examined to try to determine why these positive or negative difs exist, as exemplified by the studies of Bleistein and Wright (1986) on Asian-American examinees and Schmitt (1986) on Hispanic examinees who took the Scholastic Aptitude Test. A technical shortcoming of these techniques is their need for large samples (to accommodate many score intervals for a finer grained analysis). Their advantages lie in the fact that they in effect partial out ability differences in groups to see if the other grouping factor (e.g., ethnicity or gender) is biasing the results (Holland & Thayer, 1986). The biggest problem with these procedures may be in how they are applied. Their complete focus on individual items may make investigators lose sight of the fact that an imbalance of positive and negative dif items has real consequences for a student's total scores. Of the studies cited above on Hispanic and Asian examinees, not one psychometrician ever reached the conclusion that these SAT forms were inappropriate for any language minority group, possibly because they did not study the effects of the biased items on the mean scores of the majority and minority groups.

Scheuneman's recent work (1987) also represents an effort to identify the key factors in differential performance by ethnic group. She examined numerous hypotheses about sources of bias through the Graduate Record Exam (GRE) and thus transcended the limitations of examining individual items post-hoc. Sets of pairs of parallel items, one of which embodied a potentially biasing factor and one that did not, were administered in different forms of the GRE to different combinations of black and white examinees to study the effects of these factors on the two groups. One hypothesis, for example, tested the notion that the placement of the strongest distractor before the key or correct choice, rather than after it, would have a different impact. Another hypothesis checked the effects of using diagrams to supplement verbal descriptions of quantitative items. Numerous interactions were found between ethnic group, item version, and even particular items, which tended to make the results ambiguous though the general notion that test items can be deliberately altered to affect average minority-majority differences in performance was supported.

While the validity of debiased tests was not investigated by Scheuneman, this study illustrates the feasibility of debiasing tests by altering the specifications for content, format, and operations. Scheuneman's research, despite its limitations, is an imaginative attempt to break the stalemate in the study of test bias by focusing not merely "on the peculiarities of the items identified" but also "on the communalities that may exist among them" (p. 98). She argues that "the causes of bias that are likely to be important . . . are those that lie in characteristics common to several items in a test" (Scheuneman, 1987, p. 99).

IMPLICATIONS FOR PRACTICE

At present, what can we do to improve the use of tests of maximal performance with Hispanic children? The study of the OLSAT and the WISC-R described previously (Bernal, 1986) and a base of shared experiences over the years lead to my first recommendation for test use with Hispanic students: do not employ less reliable (presumably less valid) instruments to screen out Hispanic children from taking a more reliable (presumably more valid) diagnostic procedure. If cost is a problem, work to improve the quality of the referral process prior to psychological testing, but always use the best instruments available and the most thorough assessment procedures which are appropriate for the diagnosis of the suspected condition.

Second, obtain oral language-proficiency estimates in both first (L-1) and second (L-2) languages for LEP/NEP and bilingual children early in the assessment process in order to anticipate the need for further bilingual assessment, establish rapport and familiarity, ensure that the essential test-taking skills or repertoire are established, and help interpret the scores on tests of maximal performance. Having parents or teachers complete a language background questionnaire is a good first step (Payan, 1984), and may identify native English speakers—monolinguals—from Hispanic backgrounds. For all others, bilingual proficiency testing is necessary.

Commercially available tests of language proficiency are relatively unreliable, usually measure only surface aspects of language (Bernal, 1980, 1983a, 1984b; Cummins, 1984; Marion & Bernal, 1985; Politzer, Shohamy & Mc-Groarty, 1983), and do not have adequate concurrent validity (Dieterich, Freeman & Crandall, 1979; Ulibarri, Spencer & Rivas, 1981). Furthermore, many of these instruments fail to measure some children's communicative competence by arbitrarily discounting valid, sensible answers expressed in a mixture of L-1 and L-2 (Bernal, 1983a). As Hayes (1982) has noted, no two language-proficiency tests give the same information about a child, and low L-1, low L-2 scores may be artifacts of the tests themselves. Hence, informal assessments may have to supplement or supplant the use of formal measures. The interview is one technique that has been carefully researched and may be used to advantage (see Clark, 1978; Mendoza, 1983). In any case, the language-proficiency assessment should emphasize communicative competence on familiar topics such as school activities (Politzer et al., 1983) and employ such techniques as role playing and story telling (Hayes, 1982)—procedures that on the one hand allow the students considerable initiative and imagination to show us what they know, and on the other hand also tap or demonstrate cognitively demanding content (Cummins, 1982). Older children may also be given filling in blanks in sentences tests, or oral dictation tests, or may be asked to write a composition (Mendoza, 1983).

Third, promote the acquisition of test-taking skills by clients prior to formal assessment, and ensure they understand both the procedural vocabulary of the tests and what is implicitly expected of them.

Fourth, use experienced bilingual examiners to identify items and even sections of tests that are possibly biased or that at least need to be interpreted with considerable caution. In testing, as in any other profession, experience counts. The techniques used by test developers to identify potentially biased items by "expert" judges should be used with experienced psychometrists to see if their opinions converge on certain items, item-types, or sections of a test.

Fifth, do not interpret the IQ and achievement test scores of LEP/NEP children as if they were obtained by fluent speakers of English, whether they were tested in English or in their native language, unless the test was specifically designed for these students initially, or has demonstrated its validity and appropriateness for these groups. Cummins (1982, 1984) cites numerous examples of psychological reports where psychologists all but ignore the language and residence backgrounds of bilingual children, assume that casual, interpersonal fluency in English is sufficient for IQ assessment through that language, and interpret scores and make placement recommendations as if children's low VIQs implied low abilities instead of low verbal development in English. Many practitioners, unfortunately, simply do not appreciate the confounding effects that a child's language and culture may have on tested performance, especially when contextually reduced, verbally loaded items are presented. The psychological research of Willig et al. (1983) and of linguists such as Cummins (1979, 1982, 1986) are important breakthroughs in this regard. The focus of clinical/diagnostic assessment should be on why the child scored as she or he did, not on how well he or she did (Kaufman, 1979b).

Still, a few tests have been demonstrated to be effective with Hispanic children. The K-ABC for English-proficient children has already been discussed. For young Spanish-speaking children the CIRCO battery (Hardy et al., 1978) also has promise. This series of eleven tests includes some instruments that were translated from the English CIRCUS to Spanish, others which were adapted from English to Spanish, and a few which were designed especially for this population, including two tests in English. It also includes a language check to ensure that the child knows sufficient Spanish to be tested with this battery. Some 15,000 Mexican-American, Puerto Rican, and Cuban American children were involved in test development and norming, and the results helped to dispel the myth that a common test for the various ethnic and regional dialects of

Spanish could not be designed. More tests like these, with academically relevant content, need to be developed.

Sixth, supplement all formal assessments with informally gathered diagnostic information. Guerin and Maier (1983) have provided a useful compendium of such informal procedures, including diagnostic teaching. But care needs to be taken that techniques such as task analysis do not reduce the task to meaningless units of activity, since this seems to negatively affect LEP children's motivation and understanding (see Cummins, 1984). Similarly, testing-of-limits may be employed with individually administered IQ and achievement tests after formal assessment has taken place, and other diagnostic teaching measures such as test-teach-retest (Feuerstein, Miller & Jensen, 1980) may also be used to great advantage by a diagnostician (Marion & Bernal, 1985). Bernal and Tucker (1981) point out that with LEP/NEP students one must look for contraindications of exceptionality as well, especially in the cognitive and language domains.

Seventh, use English and Spanish judiciously in individualized testing to enhance the understanding and performance of the bilingual client. Some psychometricians argue that any departure from the prescribed English administration and scoring criteria makes the test uninterpretable in a standard way, but my experience with CIRCO and other individualized testing suggests that this is not always so. Performance scales generally can be administered in translated form, I believe, without compromising their basic validity, although the translated directions may be expected to be approximately 15 percent longer in Spanish than in English (Cortada de Kohan, 1972). Verbal scales, on the other hand, should be administered first in English if the client shows basic English proficiency, then perhaps readministered informally in Spanish with the assistance of an interpreter or with the aid of a script prepared by a master translator, checked by a bilingual-biliterate psychometrist, and administered by a bilingual-biliterate examiner. Correct answers in English, Spanish, or a blend of both, furthermore, should be accepted. Since the order of administration that seems to produce the higher scores is Spanish-English, administer the performance subtests first.

Eighth, try to anticipate and control the affective factors that impact test performance: (1) choose fluent and literate bilingual examiners, (2) preferably of Hispanic origin, who (3) take a personal interest in the client, (4) establish rapport easily with Hispanics of widely differing social circumstances, (5) can get the children to articulate their thoughts in L-1 or L-2, and (6) encourage them to keep trying. These factors are especially important for socially mobile clients, who may exhibit greater anxiety and defensiveness.

IMPLICATIONS FOR FUTURE RESEARCH

There are many research issues in the assessment of Hispanic children that psychometricians need to address. The principal issues found in the literature have been discussed in this chapter. In my opinion there is one central problem that will require a particularly creative solution involving both research and development: how to simultaneously produce unbiased, diagnostically/nomologically valid tests for the majority and the most numerous ethnic minority groups. Various techniques to achieve this goal have been enumerated in this chapter.

Certainly debiasing tests for several groups simultaneously without first doing some targeted research to guide our efforts would be costly. But an intelligent plan, based on a program of cross-cultural research (see Eckensberger, 1972), could be put together. Techniques such as latent-trait models, the study of patterns of wrong answers on multiple-choice tests, the control of language proficiency in language-minority samples, analyzing equal numbers or large samples with proportional weighing from all major ethnic groups in test development and norming, and validity studies of deliberately debiased tests could be employed. The resultant tests should not be culture-free, but should aim to eliminate irrelevant sources of difficulty in content and administration. Finally tests which tap other, related abilities should be tried out simultaneously to see if culturally different examinees can bring their unique strengths to bear on meaningful and fair criterial performance.

CONCLUSION

Since so many psychometricians have chosen to devote considerable energies to the defense of intelligence and achievement tests against charges of bias, instead of to the deliberate improvement of these instruments, one cannot help but suspect that the characterization by Mercer (1979) of psychometricians as power elites within American society is essentially correct. Techniques exist that have the potential to produce tests of maximal performance that are both equitable and valid, but Garcia (1981) believes that test developers are waiting to see how American society feels about psychometric equality before they finally design tests of intelligence and aptitude that yield parity with validity for different ethnic groups.

The need to devise valid alternative tests and practices for LEP/NEP children is urgent. And if it can be done ethically, psychometricians need to subject standardized (English) tests that have been administered to LEP/NEP children to critical analyses of their diagnostic utility. If such studies are not within ethical limits because of the possible consequences to LEP/NEP subjects, or if it is determined that the effort would be futile because of the restricted range of test scores, or if for any other reason such studies cannot or should not be conducted, then it should be incumbent on all professional organizations of psychologists and measurement specialists to say so and to demand that test publishers explicitly prohibit the use of their instruments for the formal assessment of LEP/NEP children. The alternative is to wait for aggrieved parties to file suits, to allow court cases and compromised consent agreements to settle the disputes legally, whether or not they provide the best psychometric solutions (see Green, 1975; Kaufman, 1979a).

But a general synthesis and a practical demonstration need to be realized if psychometrics is to move soon from defending its tests against charges of bias to designing broadly valid and easily interpretable tests that lend themselves more to the treatment of human affliction, the recognition and promotion of human talent, and the study of the human condition than to the questionable enterprise of making Americans comfortable with their ethnic prejudices.

REFERENCES

Alderman, D. (1982). Language proficiency as a moderator variable in testing academic aptitude. *Journal of Educational Psychology, 74,* 580–587.

Alley, G. & Foster, C. (1978). Nondiscriminatory testing of minority and exceptional children. *Focus on Exceptional Children, 9,* pp. 1–16.

American Psychological Association (1985). *Standards for educational and psychological testing.* Washington, DC: Author.

Anastasi, A. (1966). Some implications of cultural factors for test construction. In A. Anastasi (Ed.), *Testing problems in perspective.* Washington, DC: American Council on Education.

———. Anastasi, A. (1982). *Psychological testing* (5th ed.). New York: Macmillan.

Anastasi, A. & Cordova, F. A. (1953). Some effects of bilingualism upon the intelligence test performance of Puerto Rican children in New York City. *Journal of Educational Psychology, 44,* 1–19.

Angoff, W. H. (1982). Use of item difficulty and discrimination indices for detecting item bias. In R. A. Berk (Ed.), *Handbook of methods for detecting test bias* (pp. 96–116). Baltimore, MD: Johns Hopkins University Press.

Au, K. H. & Jordan, C. (1981). Teaching reading to Hawaiian children: Finding a culturally appropriate solution. In H. Trueba, G. P. Guthrie, & K. H. Au (Eds.), *Culture and the bilingual classroom: Studies in classroom ethnography.* Rowley, MA: Newbury House.

Bergan, J. R., & Parra, E. B. (1979). Variations in IQ testing and instruction and the letter learning and achievement of Anglo and bilingual Mexican-American children. *Journal of Educational Psychology, 76,* 819–826.

Berk, R. A. (Ed.). (1982). *Handbook of methods for detecting test bias.* Baltimore, MD: Johns Hopkins University Press.

Bernal, E. M. (1980, May–June). *Testing Spanish native language skills in bilingual education.* Paper presented at the Summer Symposium on Bilingual Multicultural Education Research, Buffalo, NY.

———. (1981, August). Discussion: Intelligence tests on trial. In J. Sattler (Chair), *Intelligence tests on trial: Larry P. and PASE.* Symposium presented at the meeting of the American Psychological Association, Los Angeles. (ERIC Document Reproduction Service No. ED 249 295)

———. (1983a, March). *Tests of language dominance and proficiency: A sampler and a critique.* Austin: The University of Texas at Austin, Bilingual Special Education Training Consortium.

———. (1983b, September). *Problems with traditional measures of cognitive abilities, achievement, adaptive behavior, and language proficiency* (training module). Austin: University of Texas at Austin, Bilingual Special Education Project.

———. (1984a). Bias in mental testing: Evidence for an alternative to the heredity-environment controversy. In C. R. Reynolds & R. T. Brown (Eds.), *Perspectives on bias in mental testing* (pp. 171–187). New York: Plenum.

———. (1984b). Gifted migrant students: An empirical system for their identification and selection. In A. Valencia (Ed.), *Viable strategies for advancing the education of gifted/talented migrants* (pp. 9–31). Fresno: California State University, Fresno.

———. (1984c). Postscript: Bernal replies. In C. R. Reynolds & R. T. Brown (Eds.), *Perspectives on bias in mental testing* (pp. 587–593). New York: Plenum.

———. (1986, February). *Evaluation report: Migrant and Gifted Impact Center (MAGIC)*. Fresno: California State University, Fresno.

Bernal, E. M. & Tucker, J. A. (1981, February). *A manual for screening and assessing students of limited English proficiency*. Paper presented at the Council for Exceptional Children's Conference on the Exceptional Bilingual Child, New Orleans. (ERIC Document Reproduction Service No. ED 249 295).

Blakely, M. M. (1983, October). *Teaching test-taking skills to elementary ESL students*. Paper presented at the ORTESOL Conference, Portland.

Bleistein, C. A. & Wright, D. (1986, April). *Assessment of unexpected differential item difficulty for Asian-American examinees on the Scholastic Aptitude Test*. Paper presented at the meeting of the National Council on Measurement in Education, San Francisco.

Brogden, H. E. & Taylor, E. K. (1950). A theory and classification of criterion bias. *Education and Psychological Measurement, 10,* 159–186.

Burger, H. G. (1969, April). *"Ethno-lematics": Evoking "shy" Spanish-American pupils by cross-cultural mediation*. Paper presented at the meeting of the Society for Applied Anthropology, Mexico City.

Cabello, B. (1981). *Potential sources of bias in dual language achievement tests*. Los Angeles: University of California, Center for the Study of Evaluation.

Carlson, J. S. (1983, January). *Application of dynamic assessment to cognitive and perceptual functioning of three ethnic groups*. (Final report: NIE-G-81-0081.) (ERIC Document Reproduction Service No. ED 233 040).

Carlson, J. S. & Jensen, C. M. (1981). Reliability of the Raven Colored Progressive Matrices Test: Age and ethnic group comparisons. *Journal of Consulting and Clinical Psychology, 49,* 320–322.

Carlson, J. S. & Wiedl, K. H. (1980, May). *Dynamic assessment: An approach toward reducing test bias*. Paper presented at the meeting of the Western Psychological Association, Honolulu. (ERIC Document Reproduction Service No. ED 191 884).

Chavez, E. L. (1982). Analysis of a Spanish translation of the Peabody Picture Vocabulary Test. *Perceptual and Motor Skills, 54,* 1335–1338.

Clarizio, H. F. (1979). In defense of the IQ test. *School Psychology Digest, 8,* 47–62.

Clark, J. L. D. (Ed.) (1978). *Direct testing of speaking proficiency: Theory and application*. Princeton, NJ: Educational Testing Service.

Cleary, T. A., Humphreys, L. G., Kendrick, S. A. & Wesman, A. (1975). Educational uses of tests with disadvantaged students. *American Psychologist, 30,* 15–41.

Cole, M. (1975). Culture, cognition, and IQ testing. *National Elementary Principal, 54,* 49–52.

Cole, M. & Bruner, J. (1971). Cultural differences and inferences about psychological processes. *American Psychologist, 26,* 867–876.

Corman, L. & Budoff, M. (1974). Factor structures of Spanish-speaking and non-Spanish-speaking children on Raven's Progressive Matrices. *Educational and Psychological Measurement, 34,* 977–981.

Cortada de Kohan, N. (1972). Test construction and standardization in different cultural settings. In L. J. Cronbach & P. J. D. Drenth (Eds.), *Mental tests and cultural adaptation.* The Hague: Mouton.

Cotter, D. E. & Berk, R. A. (1981, April). *Item bias in the WISC-R using Black, White, and Hispanic learning disabled children.* Paper presented at the meeting of the American Educational Research Association, Los Angeles. (ERIC Document Reproduction Service No. ED 206 631).

Cronbach, L. J. (1972). Judging how well a test measures: New concepts, new analysis. In L. J. Cronbach & P. J. D. Drenth (Eds.), *Mental tests and cultural adaptation.* The Hague: Mouton.

CTB/McGraw-Hill. (1977). *CTBS technical bulletin no. 2.* Monterey, CA: CTB/McGraw-Hill.

Cummins, J. (1979). Linguistic independence and educational development of bilingual children. *Review of Educational Research, 49,* 222–251.

———. (1982, February). Tests, achievement, and bilingual students [special issue]. *Focus* (9).

———. (1984). *Bilingual and special education: Issues in assessment and pedagogy.* San Diego, CA: College Hill.

———. (1986). Empowering minority students: A framework for intervention. *Harvard Educational Review, 56,* 18–36.

Dean, R. S. (1977). Reliability of the WISC-R with Mexican-American children. *Journal of School Psychology, 15,* 267–268.

Dieterich, T. G., Freeman, C. & Crandall, J. A. (1979, May). *A linguistic analysis of some English proficiency tests.* Paper presented at the meeting of the National Association for Bilingual Education, Seattle.

Donlon, T., Hicks, M. & Wallmark, M. (1980). Sex differences in item responses on the Graduate Record Examination. *Applied Psychological Measurement, 4,* 9–20.

Dorans, N. J. (1986, April). *Two approaches to assessing unexpected differential item performance: Standardization and the Mantel-Haenszel method.* Paper presented at the meeting of the National Council on Measurement in Education, San Francisco.

Eckensberger, L. H. (1972). The necessity of a theory for applied crosscultural research. In L. J. Cronbach & P. J. D. Drenth (Eds.), *Mental tests and cultural adaptation* (pp. 99–106). The Hague: Mouton.

Estes, W. K. (1974). Learning theory and intelligence. *American Psychologist, 29,* 740–749.

Feuerstein, R., Miller, R. & Jensen, M. R. (1980). *Can evolving techniques better measure cognitive change?* (Research Report). Israel: Hadassah-WIZO Canada Research Institute.

Figueroa, R. A. (1981). *Test bias and Hispanic children* (Validation of the SOMPA project). Unpublished manuscript, University of California at Davis.

Flaugher, R. L. (1970). *Testing practices, minority groups, and higher education: A review and discussion of the research.* (Research Bulletin 70-41). Princeton, NJ: Educational Testing Service.

Flaugher, R. L. & Anderson, S. B. Bias in testing (1975). In S. B. Anderson, S. Ball, & R. T. Murphy (Eds.), *Encyclopedia of educational evaluation.* San Francisco: Jossey-Bass.

Fruchter, B. (1953). Differences in factor content of rights and wrongs scores. *Psychometrika, 18,* 257–265.

Fuchs, D. (1985, June). *You can take a test out of the situation, but you can't always take the situation out of the test: Bias in minority assessment.* Based on a paper presented at the Biennial Conference on Minority Assessment, Tucson, AZ, November, 1985. (ERIC Document Reproduction Service No. ED 274 707).

Fyans, L. J., Jr., Wise, C. J., Magee, V. L. & Siebermann, F. J., III. (1980, April). *Achievement related motives of educationally disadvantaged students.* Paper presented at the meeting of the American Educational Research Association, Boston. (ERIC Document Reproduction Source No. ED 191 866).

Gamache, L. M. (1984, April). *The examination of factorial invariance in the construct validation of a reading achievement test.* Paper presented at the meeting of the National Council on Measurement in Education, New Orleans, LA. (ERIC Document Reproduction Service No. ED 261 062).

Garcia, A. B. & Zimmerman, B. J. (1972). The effect of examiner ethnicity and language on the performance of bilingual Mexican American first graders. *Journal of School Psychology, 87,* 3–11.

Garcia, J. (1981). The logic and limits of mental aptitude testing. *American Psychologist, 36,* 1172–1180.

Garcia, S. B. (1985, Fall). Characteristics of limited English proficient Hispanic students served in programs for the learning disabled: Implications for policy, practice and research (Part 1). *Bilingual Special Education Newsletter,* pp. 1, 3–6.

Ginther, J. R. (1978). Pretraining Chicano students before administration of a mathematics predictor test. *Journal of Research in Mathematics Education, 9,* 118–125.

Gitmez, A. S. (1972). Instructions as determinants of performance: The effect of information about the task. In L. J. Cronbach & P. J. D. Drenth (Eds.), *Mental tests and cultural adaptation.* The Hague: Mouton.

Gonzalez-Tamayo, E. (1984). *An item content criterion of debiasing a test.* (ERIC Document Reproduction Service No. ED 247 240).

Gordon, E. W. (1977, Winter). Human diversity, program evaluation and pupil assessment. *IRCD Bulletin,* pp. 1–7.

Green, D. R. (1972). *Racial and ethnic bias in test construction.* Monterey, CA:: CTB/ McGraw-Hill.

————. (1975, March). *What does it mean to say a test is biased?* Paper presented at the meeting of the American Educational Research Association, Washington, DC.

Guerin, G. R. & Maier, A. S. (1983). *Informal assessment in education.* Palo Alto, CA: Mayfield.

Haggard, E. A. (1954). Social status and intelligence. *Genetic Psychology Monographs, 49,* 141–186.

Hardy, J. B., Welcher, D. W., Mellits, E. D. & Kagan, J. (1976). Pitfalls in the measurement of intelligence: Are standard intelligence tests valid instruments for measuring the intellectual potential of urban children? *Journal of Psychology,* *94,* 43–51.

Hardy, R., Glad, D., Bernal, E. M & Cordova, F. (1978). *CIRCO technical report and manual.* Princeton, NJ: Educational Testing Service.

Harrington, G. M. (1984). An experimental model of bias in mental testing. In C. R. Reynolds & R. T. Brown (Eds.), *Perspectives on bias in mental testing* (pp. 101–138). New York: Plenum.

Hayes, Z. A. (1982, January). *Limited language proficiency: A problem in the definition and measurement of bilingualism.* Rosslyn, VA: InterAmerica Research Associates. (ERIC Document Reproduction Service No. ED 228 859).

Hennessy, J. J. & Merrifield, P. R. (1976). A comparison of the factor structures of the mental abilities in four ethnic groups. *Journal of Educational Psychology,* *68,* 754–759.

Hickman, J. A. & Reynolds, C. R. (1986–1987). Are rare differences in mental test scores an artifact of psychometric methods? A test of Harrington's experimental model. *Journal of Special Education, 20,* 409–430.

Hill, K. T. & Eaton, W. O. (1977). The interaction of test anxiety and success-failure experiences in determining children's arithmetic performance. *Developmental Psychology, 13,* 205–211.

Holland, P. W. & Thayer, D. T. (1986, April). *Differential item performance and the Mantel-Haenszel procedure.* Paper presented at the meeting of the American Educational Research Association, San Francisco.

Hunter, J. E., Schmidt, F. L. & Rauschenberger, J. (1984). Methodological, statistical, and ethical issues in the study of bias in psychological tests. In C. R. Reynolds & R. T. Brown (Eds.), *Perspectives on bias in mental testing* (pp. 41–99). New York: Plenum.

Jensen, A. R. (1980). *Bias in mental testing.* New York: Free Press.

———. (1984). Test bias: Concepts and criticisms. In C. R. Reynolds & R. T. Brown (Eds.), *Perspectives on bias in mental testing* (pp. 507–586). New York: Plenum.

Kamin, L. J. (1974). *The science and politics of IQ.* Potomac, MD: Lawrence Erlbaum.

Kaminsky, S. (1976). Bilingualism and learning to read. In A. Simoes, Jr. (Ed.), *The bilingual child* (pp. 155–171). New York: Academic Press.

Kaufman, A. S. (1979a). *Intelligent testing with the WISC-R.* New York: John Wiley & Sons.

———. (1979b). WISC-R research: Implications for interpretation. *School Psychology Digest, 8,* 5–27.

Knapp, R. R. (1960). The effects of time limits on the intelligence test performance of Mexican and American subjects. *Journal of Educational Psychology, 51,* 14–20.

Lawshe, C. H. (1969). Statistical theory and practice in applied psychology. *Journal of Personnel Psychology, 22,* 117–124.

Llabre, M. M. & Cuevas, G. (1983). The effects of test language and mathematical skills assessed on the scores of bilingual Hispanic students. *Journal for Research in Mathematics Education, 14,* 318–324.

Maldonado-Colon, E. (1984, August). *The role of language assessment data in diagnosis and intervention for linguistically/culturally different students.* Paper presented at the meeting of the American Psychological Association, Toronto. (ERIC Document Reproduction Service No. ED 254 987)

Marion, R. & Bernal, E. M. (1985). Working with culturally diverse children and families. In S. I. Pfeiffer (Ed.), *Clinical child psychology: An introduction to theory, research, and practice* (pp. 399–443). New York: Grune & Stratton.

Maspons, M. M. & Llabre, M. M. (1983, April). *Effect of pretraining Hispanic students on test-taking strategies on the reliability and predictive validity of a mathematics predictor test.* Paper presented at the meeting of the American Educational Research Association, Montreal. (ERIC Document Reproduction Service No. ED 229 431).

McArthur, D. (1981, November). *Test Design Project: Studies in test bias.* Los Angeles: University of California, Los Angeles, Center for the Study of Evaluation. (ERIC Document Reproduction Service No. ED 211 592).

McArthur, D. L. & Hafner, A. L. (1982, November). *Modifying test bias through targeted instruction.* Los Angeles: University of California, Center for the Study of Evaluation. (ERIC Document Reproduction Service No. ED 224 841).

McCornack, R. L. (1983). Bias in the validity of predicted college grades in four ethnic minority groups. *Educational and Psychological Measurement, 43,* 517–522.

McNemar, Q. (1942). *The revision of the Stanford-Binet scale: An analysis of the standardization data.* Boston: Houghton-Mifflin.

Mendoza, P. (1983, Summer). The role of language in psychological assessments of students. *Bilingual Special Education News,* pp. 1, 4–5.

Mercer, J. R. (1979). In defense of racially and culturally nondiscriminatory assessment. *School Psychology Digest,* 89–115.

———. (1984). What is a racially and culturally nondiscriminatory test? In C. R. Reynolds & R. T. Brown (Eds.), *Perspectives on bias in mental testing* (pp. 293–356). New York: Plenum.

Messick, S. (1980). Test validity and the ethics of assessment. *American Psychologist, 35,* 1012–1027.

Miele, F. (1979). Cultural bias in the WISC. *Intelligence, 3,* 149–164.

Miller, D. R. & Swanson, G. E. (1960). *Inner conflict and defense.* New York: Henry Holt.

Nungester, R. J. (1977). *An empirical examination of three models of item bias.* Unpublished doctoral dissertation, Florida State University.

Oakland, T. (1972). The effects of test-wiseness materials on standardized test performance of preschool disadvantaged children. *Journal of Psychology, 10,* 355–360.

———. (1980). An evaluation of the ABIC, pluralistic norms, and estimated learning potential. *Journal of School Psychology, 18,* 3–11.

Oakland, T. & Feigenbaum, D. (1979). Multiple sources of test bias on the WISC-R and Bender-Gestalt Test. *Journal of Consulting and Clinical Psychology, 47,* 968–974.

Olmedo, E. L. (1981). Testing linguistic minorities. *American Psychologist, 36,* 1078–1085.

Ortar, G. R. (1960). Improving test validity by coaching. *Educational Research, 2,* 137–142.

Padilla, A. M. (1979). Critical factors in the testing of Hispanic Americans: A review and some suggestions for the future. In R. W. Tyler & S. H. White (Eds.), *Testing, teaching, and learning: Report of a conference on testing.* Washington, DC: National Institute of Education.

Pascual-Leone, J. & Smith, J. (1969). The encoding and decoding of symbols of children: A new experimental paradigm and a neo-Piagetian model. *Journal of Experimental Child Psychology, 8,* 328–355.

Payan, R. (1984). Development of the bilingual special education interface. In L. M. Baca & H. T. Cervantes (Eds.), *The bilingual special education interface.* St. Louis, MO: Times Mirror/Mosby.

Perez, F. M. (1980). Performance of bilingual children on the Spanish version of the ITPA. *Exceptional Children, 46,* 536–541.

Politzer, R. L., Shohamy, E. & McGroarty, M. (1983). Validation of linguistic and communicative oral language tests for Spanish-English bilingual programs. *Bilingual Review, 10*(1), 3–20.

Powers, S. (1982, March). *The effect of testwiseness on the reading achievement scores of minority populations.* Tucson, AZ: Tucson Unified School District, Dept. of Legal and Research Services. (ERIC Document Reproduction Service No. ED 222 549).

Reschly, D. & Reschly, J. (1979). Validity of the WISC-R factor scores in predicting achievement and attention for four sociocultural groups. *Journal of School Psychology, 17,* 355–359.

Reschly, D. J. & Sabers, D. (1979). Analysis of test bias in four groups with the regression definition. *Journal of Educational Measurement, 16,* 1–9.

Reynolds, C. R. (1982). The problem of bias in psychological assessment. In C. Reynolds & T. Gutkin (Eds.), *The handbook of school psychology.* New York: John Wiley and Sons.

Reynolds, C. R. & Brown, R. T. (1984). Bias in mental testing: An introduction to the issues. In C. R. Reynolds & R. T. Brown (Eds.), *Perspectives on bias in mental testing* (pp. 1–39). New York: Plenum.

Reynolds, C. R. & Gutkin, T. B. (1980). A regression analysis of test bias on the WISC-R for Anglos and Chicanos referred for psychological services. *Journal of Abnormal Child Psychology, 8,* 237–243.

Reynolds, C. R., Willson, V. L. & Chatman, S. (1984). Relationships between age and raw score increases on the Kaufman-Assessment Battery for Children. *Psychology in the Schools, 21,* 19–24.

Rincon, E. T. (1979). *Test speededness, test anxiety, and test performance: A comparison of Mexican American and Anglo American high school juniors.* Unpublished doctoral dissertation, the University of Texas at Austin.

Ross-Reynolds, J. & Reschly, D. J. (1983). An investigation of item bias on the WISC-R with four sociocultural groups. *Journal of Consulting and Clinical Psychology, 51,* 144–146.

Rulon, P. J. (1966). A semantic test of intelligence. In A. Anastasi (Ed.), *Testing problems in perspective.* Washington, DC: American Council on Education.

Sanchez, G. I. (1934). Bilingualism and mental measures: A word of caution. *Journal of Applied Psychology, 18,* 765–772.

Sandoval, J. (1979). The WISC-R and internal evidence of test bias with minority groups. *Journal of Consulting and Clinical Psychology, 7,* 919–927.

Sandoval, J. & Millie, M. P. W. (1980). Accuracy of judgments of WISC-R item difficulty for minority groups. *Journal of Consulting and Clinical Psychology, 48,* 249–253.

Sattler, J. M. & Gwynne, J. (1982). Ethnicity and Bender Visual Motor Gestalt Test performance. *Journal of School Psychology, 20,* 69–71.

Scheuneman, J. D. (1979). A method of assessing bias in test items. *Journal of Educational Measurement, 16,* 143–152.

————. (1987). An experimental, exploratory study of causes of bias in test items. *Journal of Educational Measurement, 24,* 97–118.

Schmitt, A. P. (1986, June). *Unexpected differential item performance of Hispanic examinees on the SAT-Verbal, Forms 3FSA08 and 3GSA08* (Report No. SR-86-90). Princeton, NJ: Educational Testing Service.

Schmitt, N. & Lappin, M. (1980). Race and sex as determinants of the mean and variance of performance ratings. *Journal of Applied Psychology, 65,* 428–435.

Seong, T. & Subkoviak, M. J. (1987, April). *A comparative study of recently proposed item bias detection methods.* Paper presented at the meeting of the National Council on Measurement in Education, Washington, DC. (ERIC Document Reproduction Service No. ED 281 883).

Shepard, L. A. (1980, November). *Definitions of bias.* Paper presented at the Johns Hopkins University National Symposium on Educational Research, Washington, DC.

Shepard, L. A., Camilli, G. & Williams, D. M. (1985). Validity of approximation techniques for detecting item bias. *Journal of Educational Measurement, 22,* 77–105.

Swanson, E. & DeBlassie, R. (1979). Interpreter and Spanish administration effects on the WISC performance of Mexican-American children. *Journal of School Psychology, 17,* 231–236.

Taylor, R. L. & Partenio, I. (1984). Ethnic differences on the Bender-Gestalt: Relative effects of measured intelligence. *Journal of Consulting and Clinical Psychology, 52,* 784–788.

Taylor, R. L., Zigler, E. W., & Partenio, I. (1984). An investigation of WISC-R verbal performance differences as a function of ethnic status. *Psychology in Schools, 21,* 437–441.

Thomas, A. Hertzig, M. E., Dryman, I. & Fernandez, P. (1971). Examiner effect in IQ testing of Puerto Rican working-class children. *American Journal of Orthopsychiatry, 41,* 809–821.

Thonis, E. W. (1970). *Teaching reading to non-English speakers.* New York: Macmillan.

Ulibarri, D. (1982). Cognitive processing theory and culture-loading: A neo-Piagetian approach to test bias. Unpublished doctoral dissertation, University of California, Berkeley.

Ulibarri, D. M., Spencer, M. L. & Rivas, G. A. (1981, Spring). Language proficiency and academic achievement: Relationship to school ratings as predictors of academic achievement. *NABE Journal, 5*(3), pp. 47–80.

Valencia, R. R. (1984). Reliability of the Raven Coloured Progressive Matrices for Anglo and for Mexican-American children. *Psychology in the Schools, 21,* 49–52.

Valencia, R. R. & Rankin, R. J. (1985). Evidence of content bias on the McCarthy Scales with Mexican American children: Implications for test translation and nonbiased assessment. *Journal of Education Measurement, 77,* 197–207.

Van der Flier, H. (1972). Evaluating environmental influences on test scores. In L. J. Cronbach & P. J. D. Drenth (Eds.), *Mental tests and cultural adaptation.* The Hague: Mouton.

Willig, A. C., Harnisch, D. L., Hill, K. T. & Maehr, M. L. (1983). Sociocultural and educational correlates of success-failure attributions and evaluation anxiety in the school setting for Black, Hispanic, and Anglo children. *American Educational Research Journal, 20,* 385–410.

Wright, D. J. (1986, June). *An empirical comparison of the Mantel-Haenszel and standardization methods of detecting differential item performance* (Unpublished Report No. SR-86-99). Princeton, NJ: Educational Testing Service.

Zigler, E. & Butterfield, E. C. (1968). Motivational aspects of changes in IQ test performance of culturally deprived nursery school children. *Child Development, 39,* 1–15.

Zimmerman, B. J. & Rosenthal, T. L. (1972). Observation, repetition, and ethnic background in concept attainment and generalization. *Child Development, 43,* 605–613.

6

Assessment of Asian-Americans for Family Therapy

Rebecca del Carmen

Asian-Americans face many of the same stressors that any ethnic group confronts, including the multigenerational effects of migration and acculturation (Shon and Ja, 1982); cultural conflict, and related problems of identity (Sue, 1980); and discrimination (Toupin, 1980). Yet there is a striking pattern of underutilization of mental health services among members of this ethnic group (see Fugita, this volume). Studies indicate, however, an increase in the use of mental health service among Asian-Americans when culturally relevant programs are provided (Parron, 1982; Sue & McKinney, 1975; True, 1975). Different ethnic and cultural groups require different approaches or orientations in therapy (Dahlquist & Fay, 1984; Brown, 1979; Herrera & Sanchez, 1980).

In order to identify culturally relevant mental health programs for Asian-Americans, researchers have examined a broad range of issues, including problem perception (Tracey, Leong & Glidden, 1986; Lum, 1982; White, 1982); stereotypes (McGoldrick & Rohrbaugh, 1987); clinical assessment of symptoms (Marsella, 1980; Tseng & McDermott, 1981; Chin, 1983); facilitating therapy (Toupin, 1980; Root, 1985); and social support (Liu, 1986). Broadly speaking, a unifying theme emerging from this body of literature is that culturally relevant programs are those that recognize and utilize the important role of the family among Asian-Americans. However, recent attempts at assessment and treatment of Asian-Americans in the context of the family (Lee, 1982;

Kim, 1985; Ko, 1986) have not been linked to the available empirical literature concerning family structure, role expectations in the marriage and the family, and communication patterns. Furthermore, the relationship between assessment and treatment has not been defined clearly (H. Wong, 1986).

The aims of this chapter are: (1) to review the literature on Asian-American families highlighting treatment-relevant issues that have been neglected in clinical studies, including family structure, marital and parental role expectations, and family communication patterns; (2) to review aspects of family systems theory and therapy relevant to the assessment and treatment of Asian-American families, including work on family life-cycle development and ethnicity; and (3) to propose a familial and sociocultural context for assessment of Asian-Americans that is clearly linked to treatment approaches.

ASIAN-AMERICAN FAMILIES

Family Structure

Composition. In the past, the traditional Asian family has been characterized by a large and extended family structure, which included many siblings and their spouses who lived with their parents and other family members of two or three generations (B. Wong, 1985; Shon & Ja, 1982). However, surveys conducted in contemporary China and Japan indicate that this type of traditional, extended family is now quite rare in Asia where there has been a gradual shift toward the nuclear family in recent decades (Tseng, Kuotai, Hsu, Jinghua, Lian & Kameoka, 1988; Japanese Statistical Yearbook, 1984). These surveys indicate that approximately 60–75 percent of families in China and Japan are nuclear in structure. Shinohara (1981) used the phrase "nuclearization era" to describe contemporary Japan with respect to family structure.

In contrast, contemporary American society has witnessed major demographic changes influencing a shift away from the nuclear family structure toward alternative arrangements (e.g., more households headed by women) (Bureau of the Census, 1983). These changes include a dramatic rise in the proportion of births to unmarried women and the well-documented rise in divorce rate (Bureau of the Census, 1983; Momeni, 1984). Although these patterns are representative of the general American population, they do not represent trends in Asian-American families.

Several characteristics have been observed that appear unique to the Asian-American family. In comparison to other ethnic groups in the United States, Asian-Americans have the lowest proportion of households headed by a woman, the lowest rate of divorce, and the lowest rate of fertility (Momeni, 1984). The proportion of Asian families of divorced or widowed parents in the United States (5.7 percent) is lower than that of whites (9.3 percent), blacks (16.3 percent), Native Americans (13.0 percent), and Hispanics (9.1 percent) but still higher than Asians living in Asia (for example, 1.9 percent of Japanese families) (Momeni, 1984).

Although the vast majority of families living in Asia are nuclear, recent surveys have suggested that 27 percent of Japanese and 40 percent of Chinese families have retained some aspect of the traditional, extended family structure in the form of a "stem-family" with at least one grandparent living in the same home (Tseng et al., 1988; Sorifu, 1985). In contrast, it is estimated that only 3 percent of all American families include a grandparent in the same home (Schwalb, Imaizumi & Nakazawa, 1987). For the Asian-American family, Liu and Fernandez (1987) report that the proportion of households including at least one relative was 4.8 percent of Japanese, 10.0 percent of Chinese, 15.1 percent of Filipinos, and 7.6 percent of Koreans. For Japanese, the proportion increased to 7.2 percent for native-born families. For Chinese, Filipinos, and Koreans, proportions including relatives in the household remained the same or decreased slightly in native-born families, but proportions were no less than 6.7 percent. Thus, the first- and second-generation Asian-American family is less likely than the Asian family but more likely than the non–Asian-American family to include a grandparent or relative living at home.

Two additional family patterns have been observed among Asian-Americans. Researchers have described the "incomplete family" in which family members are temporarily separated over a number of months or years in the process of migration from Asia to the United States (B. Wong, 1985; Liu & Fernandez, 1987). Although the statistical proportions or psychological implications of such an arrangement have not been estimated, the fact that the majority of Asian-Americans are first generation or are foreign-born (Liu & Fernandez, 1987) suggests that many Asian-American families may have struggled with this arrangement in the immigration process. Another prevalent family pattern described by researchers is the nonresidential or "modified-extended" family in which the residential pattern is nuclear in its structure, but extended family ties are maintained with grandparents and other relatives living in close proximity (B. Wong, 1985).

In all the various arrangements observed, the structure and composition of Asian-American families continues to reflect the importance of strong family ties. Although the residential extended pattern is rare, the Asian-American family appears to have a nuclear family structure that retains some aspects of the extended family pattern. A large proportion of these families are first-generation Asian-Americans and at certain periods in the family cycle, family members may be separated from one another in the process of migration to the United States. Of importance to the clinician and researcher interested in the psychological well-being and family functioning of Asian-Americans are roles and expectations within the family.

Marital roles. Traditional Asian marital roles evolved out of Confucian role definitions that were hierarchical and patriarchal. Marriage did not symbolize the creation of a new family but rather a continuation of the male family line

(Shon & Ja, 1982). Women were expected to show unquestioned obedience toward their husbands. There is increasing evidence, however, that expectations regarding this traditional, patriarchal pattern are shifting toward more egalitarian views, especially among contemporary Asian and Asian-American women. Early findings suggested that contemporary Asian and Asian-American women readily adopted egalitarian perspectives toward husband-wife relations; however, their male counterparts persisted in more traditional and patriarchal orientations. Arkoff, Meredith, and Dong (1963) found that Japanese-American males held the most male-dominant, patriarchal attitudes regarding marital roles. Significant differences were not found in marital attitudes between the Japanese-American females and Caucasian-American females nor between the Caucasian-American males and females.

More recently, Chia, Chong, and Cheng (1986) reported that Chinese women living in Taiwan held more modern orientations and were more egalitarian with respect to marriage roles than their male counterparts. Although a similar finding was reported for Caucasians, the sex difference was not nearly as discrepant as it was for Asians. When marital attitudes of Chinese and American men and women in 1984 were compared to those in 1962, women in both cultures and at both time periods held more egalitarian orientations than their male counterparts (Chia, Chong, Cheng, Castellow, Moore, & Hayes, 1985). Chinese women in 1984 held attitudes regarding husband-wife relations more similar to the American men and women in the 1980s, unlike their male counterparts who held attitudes more similar to those of the American men and women in the 1960s. Chia et al. (1985) concluded that in contrast to stereotypes involving obedience, passivity, and submissiveness, Asian and Asian-American women are very progressive in their views regarding husband and wife relations, particularly in comparison to Asian men. Consistent with this view is research indicating that Asian-American women acculturate much faster into American society than Asian-American men (Arkoff, Meredith & Dong, 1963).

Arkoff et al. (1963) suggested that these discrepancies between men and women regarding marital roles may be a source of conflict in Asian and Asian-American marital functioning. In an early study by Jacobson (1952), Caucasian divorced couples were more discrepant in their marriage role attitudes than married couples. However, there is no evidence to support this claim within Asian or Asian-American marriages. When Tseng et al. (1988) assessed how Chinese view their marital relations in 697 families, nearly 70 percent described the relationship as very good, 28 percent as fair, 2 percent as poor; only 4 percent were divorced. In addition, as mentioned, Asian-Americans have relatively low divorce rates (Momeni, 1984).

How these attitudinal discrepancies regarding marital roles in Asian-American men and women actually translate into behavior and influence marital and family functioning remains unexplored in the literature, despite important clinical implications. Recently, Chow (1987) suggested that "cross-pressures" between ethnicity and gender have inhibited Asian-American women from expressing progressive or egalitarian views within American society. She noted that Asian-American women may perceive open expression of such attitudes as threatening to Asian-American solidarity, which might lead to "setbacks for the Asian American cause, cooptation into the larger society, and eventual loss of ethnic identity for Asian-Americans as a whole" (p. 288).

Only a few studies focus on the behavioral patterns in contemporary Asian-American marriages. Hsu, Tseng, Ashton, McDermott, and Char (1985) have observed decision-making patterns in Japanese-American and Caucasian couples. They found significant differences in decision-making style, with the Caucasian couples utilizing mutual consent and the Japanese-American couples making more unilateral decisions. The Caucasian couples also were more satisfied with their decision-making patterns than the Japanese-American couples.

Harrison, Serafica, and McAdoo (1984) indicated that the traditional pattern of relating is somewhat modified in second- and third-generation Japanese-American families. More acculturated husband-wife relationships tend to be complementary (Fujitomi & Wong, 1973), with the more educated and Americanized women enjoying a higher status within the family. Similarly, Yu and Kim (1983) have observed subtle changes in the marital roles of Korean Americans. The Korean-American husbands they interviewed were beginning to perform household tasks within the home and relate to their wives in untraditional ways, although it was difficult to ascertain whether these changes were the result of changing beliefs or of practical circumstances that necessitate change (e.g., maternal employment). The authors concluded that changing sex roles in husband-wife relationships among Asian-Americans will be an important area for future research. Gender-based roles and expectations within the marriage system may influence not only the marital relationship but also parental roles and expectations.

Parental roles. Traditionally, parental roles among Asians have been clearly defined (Shon & Ja, 1982). Like marital roles, they are derived largely from Confucian definitions of sex roles. In China, Ho (1987) indicated that these roles have been characterized by the popular saying, "Strict father, kind mother" (p. 230). In addition to being a provider, the Asian father also was expected to be responsible for educating and disciplining his children; the mother was the protective, nurturant figure in the family. In most traditional Asian cultures, sons have been more highly valued than daughters, and it was the father's duty to educate his eldest son in moral, occupational, and financial matters (Schwalb, Imaizumi & Nakawawa, 1987). The eldest son was expected to be a role model for his younger siblings and, eventually, take over the family leadership (Shon & Ja, 1982). In contrast, the daughter was socialized to be caretaker of the home and to later marry and be absorbed into her husband's family. Thus, socializing the eldest son was an important task of parents and, in particular, the father-son relationship took on added significance within the family.

Although there is evidence that some aspects of these traditional role definitions have been retained, many expectations appear to be changing among contemporary Asian and Asian-American parents. Currently, the relevant research literature on Asian parental roles and behaviors includes reports on children's perceptions of their parents' roles (Matsumoto & Smith, 1961; Benkart & Benkart, 1985), surveys of parental attitudes or values (Del Carmen & Serafica, 1985; O'Reilly, Tokuno & Ebata, 1986; Yu, 1984; B. Wong, 1985; McDermott, Char, Robillard, Hsu, Tseng & Ashton, 1983; Tseng et al. 1988), and a limited number of observational studies on family and parent-child interactions (Hsu et al., 1985; Caudill & Frost, 1974).

An early study on perceptions of parental roles among Japanese and American children suggested that the Japanese father was more often perceived as an intellectual authority and disciplinarian than the American father; the mother's role was similar in both cultural groups and involved activities such as child care and housework (Matsumoto & Smith, 1961). However, more recent surveys have indicated that Asian mothers also are involved in disciplining their children. One survey found that Japanese and Americans perceived both parents as sharing equally in disciplinary responsibilities (Sorifu, 1982). Similarly, Benkart and Benkart (1985) reported that Japanese mothers were perceived by children as more salient figures and closer in the day to day lives of the children than Japanese fathers. Such findings have led researchers to suggest that in contrast to popular views, the paternal role in contemporary Japan is not dominant at home and that Japanese fathers are not necessarily the primary disciplinarians (Schwalb, Imaizumi & Nakazawa, 1987).

Gender differences in the way children view their parents also have been reported. Matsumoto and Smith (1961) found that Japanese girls saw their mothers as more restrictive whereas Japanese boys viewed their fathers in that role. Fukaya and Fukaya (1975) reported that Japanese boys' ratings of their parents become less positive with age although salience for the paternal role increased with age. For girls, fathers' ratings were constant across the different school age groups but always were lower (less salient and positive) than ratings of their mothers. Furthermore, McDermott et al. (1983) reported that girls (13–20 years of age) across ethnic groups (Japanese-American and Caucasian-American) value family affiliation and closeness whereas boys seek independence and self-differentiation from parents and others.

Shon and Ja (1982) noted the importance in considering such factors as generation and social class in understanding Asian-American parental values. In a study of parental roles among old immigrant (arriving before 1965), new immigrant, and second-generation Chinese families living in New York, Wong (1985) found that as families adapt to the United States there is a general tendency to emphasize the husband-wife relationship over the traditional father-son dyad.

Similarly, when social class is considered, some ethnic differences in parental values and childrearing style diminish. For example, Yao (1985) reported few significant differences between Asian-American (Chinese, Korean, Filipino, Vietnamese, and East Indian) and Caucasian-American parents of high-

achieving children in middle and upper-middle class families. In both Asian-
and Caucasian-Americans, middle-class parents of high achievers possessed high
expectations of their children, stable family environments, and close-knit family relations. However, weekends were more structured and task-oriented for
the Asian-American family than for the Caucasian family. Asians pursued activities involving cognitive learning (e.g., language classes) whereas Caucasians engaged in activities involving affective and psychomotor development
(e.g., sports). Also, although both groups of parents were well-informed and
knowledgeable about their children's school activities, Asian parents were more
involved in their children's homework and school projects whereas Caucasian
parents made more school visits.

Other researchers have noted ethnic variations in parental values and beliefs
among Asian-American and Caucasian parents. O'Reilly et al. (1986) assessed
differences in values among Japanese-American and Caucasian parents. Japanese-Americans valued "behaving well" more than the Caucasian parents who
placed more value on openness to experience, self-direction, tolerance, and
sensitivity to feelings. Similarly, McDermott et al. (1983) found that Caucasian
parents were more likely to believe family members should share feelings. In
contrast, Japanese-American parents valued sharing deep thoughts rather than
feelings. The authors suggested that in a clinical setting, cognitive, task-oriented approaches may be more appropriate than those emphasizing the expression of affect.

Another major cultural value emphasized in the Asian parenting literature
(see Serafica, this volume) is that of filial piety, defined as loyalty, respect,
and devotion of children to their parents (Sih, 1961). Children are expected to
respect and obey their parents in a deferential manner (Kikumura & Kitano,
1980) as well as respect and care for family elders as they age (Huang, 1981).
Yu (1984) assessed how this value may be influenced by the acculturation process. She found that older Chinese immigrants in the United States (as opposed
to recent immigrants or native-born Asian-Americans) felt obligated to care for
their aging parents but did not expect their children to care for them as they
age.

Despite evidence for changing roles and family patterns among Asian-American parents in the direction of greater similarity to Caucasian-American values,
there also is some indication that ethnic values continue to play a significant
role in family life for many generations (McGoldrick, 1982). Further, one can
not always assume a loss of traditional values with increasing resident years in
the United States, across all areas of family functioning. Arkoff, Meredith, and
Iwahara (1964) found that Japanese-American men residing in the United States
held more traditional values regarding sex-roles in comparison to Japanese or
American men, although the difference was not quite statistically significant.
Similarly, Kitano (1961, 1964) reported that when comparing older and younger
Japanese mothers living in both Japan and the United States in childrearing
attitudes, the older group of Japanese-American mothers held more restrictive

attitudes toward childrearing than the older and younger mothers living in Japan. They were, however, more restrictive than the younger generation of Japanese mothers living in the United States, suggesting some loss of traditional values.

These findings suggest that Asian-American parents residing for many years in the United States may be more traditional in some areas of family functioning when compared to their counterparts living in Asia. One clinical implication is that there may be varying conscious or unconscious motivations among Asian-Americans regarding the need to reassert more traditional values, which warrant respect by the clinician. Perhaps as one's sense of identity is challenged by living in the United States for many years, one coping strategy may be to reassert certain traditional Asian values. More recent immigrants, however, may be less concerned about a loss of Asian identity and more involved with assimilating to American society. Alternatively, Asian-Americans may adhere to traditional roles still believing them to be the cultural standards because they are unaware that such standards have changed in their respective countries of origin.

Communication Patterns

Patterns of communication are critical in defining relationships and establishing roles within the family system (Nichols & Everett, 1986). In fact, many therapists believe that changing communication patterns is the single most important goal of family intervention (Group for the Advancement of Psychiatry, 1970). Although striking differences between Asian and American family communication patterns have been noted (Shon & Ja, 1982), few empirical studies have been conducted in this area. Personality studies indicate that Asian-Americans tend to exhibit lower levels of verbal and emotional expressiveness than Caucasian-Americans (Leong, 1986; Ayube, 1971; Fukuyama & Greenfield, 1983; D. Sue & Kirk, 1973). Such communication differences may be misunderstood by the clinician. For example, although silence and the avoidance of eye contact may be signs of respect from an Asian perspective, these characteristics may be signs of dysfunctional communication from an American perspective (Goldenberg & Goldenberg, 1985).

The determinants of communication patterns also may be different for Asians than for Americans. Characteristics of individuals such as age, sex, occupation, and marital status determine who initiates conversation, speaks more softly or loudly, or avoids eye contact. Shon and Ja (1982) have suggested that there is a greater reliance on these interpersonal cues in social interactions among Asian-Americans when compared to Caucasian-Americans. Ayube (1971) drew similar conclusions after assessing speaking behavior of Japanese-American and Caucasian-American female college students.

Nakanishi (1986) and Hsu et al. (1985) report more restraint when communicating with others among Asians. Nakanishi found that a high level of self-disclosure is viewed as less socially appropriate and is associated with less competence among Japanese. Similarly, after observing patterns of family interaction among Caucasian- and Japanese-Americans, Hsu et al. (1985) reported that not only were Japanese-American family members more cautious and indirect in communicating with one another, but also they showed more restraint and less warmth or affection. Although raters (who were both Asian-American and Caucasian) viewed these Asian family patterns as less healthy, the authors highlighted cultural differences in communication noting that the Japanese value "implicit, nonverbal, intuitive communication over explicit, verbal, and rational exchange of information" (p. 579). The authors also emphasized the Japanese distinction between a public self *(omote)* and a private self *(ura)*. They noted that a "lack of expression or affection in public should not be equated with a lack of affection in actuality" (p. 580). A challenging problem for the clinician and the researcher is ascertaining whether their observations (e.g., high levels of affective restraint) are a function of cultural differences in social desirability relating to the clinical and experimental situation or differences that represent truly distinct patterns of interaction found outside of the clinical or research setting.

The empirical literature on Asian and Asian-American roles, expectations, and communication patterns has largely been neglected by researchers in both family development and clinical assessment, although it has implications for understanding individual and family functioning among Asian-Americans and for meeting their mental health needs. A later section of the chapter examines how the research findings discussed above can be integrated into the assessment and treatment of Asian-Americans. First, however, the family systems approach and its relevance to the treatment of Asian-American mental health problems will be examined.

THE FAMILY SYSTEMS APPROACH

Traditional Approaches

The family systems approach is characterized by the identification of the family system as a whole, rather than the individual, as the target of assessment and intervention (Johnson, Rasbury & Siegel, 1986). Its origins can be traced to the early 1950s when researchers, exploring new ways to think about psychopathology, started investigating the relationship between factors in family functioning and schizophrenia. For example, the work of Bateson et al. on double bind interactions (1956), the conceptions of Lidz et al. of marital schism and marital skew (1957), Bowen's study of symbiotic mother-child relationships (1960), and the idea of Wynne et al. (1958) of pseudomutuality all contributed to understanding the role of family dynamics in the etiology of schizophrenia. As investigators began expanding their work to other problems (for example, delinquency), it became evident that similar family dynamics could be observed to some degree in all families (Johnson et al., 1986).

Varied approaches to family assessment and intervention have evolved that view the family as the major context for understanding problems and difficulties of individuals (Johnson et al. 1986). In the last two decades, this view has broadened in ways that have increasing relevance for understanding and treating the Asian-American family. Researchers have expanded the contextual variables to include family life cycle (Duvall, 1971; Haley, 1971; Glick & Kessler, 1980) and ethnicity (McGoldrick, Pearce & Giordano, 1982).

Evolving Approaches

Family life-cycle development. The family developmental approach is similar to the individual life span perspective in its focus on stages of development over time (Hill, 1970; Duvall, 1971; Barnhill & Longo, 1980; and Solomon, 1973). The approach was first introduced by sociologists (Duvall, 1971; Hill, 1970) and, in part, derived from an application of Erikson's model of psychosocial development to the family (1963). Researchers have conceptualized various "tasks" associated with different phases of family development, but most emphasize transitions that occur as families move through stages of formation (mate selection and marriage), parenting and expansion (pregnancy, childbearing, and childrearing), contraction (individuation and separation from children), and the postparental stages including retirement and old age (Nichols & Everett, 1982; Hetherington & Martin, 1986). "Normal" crises in family development are usually identified as those that occur around the addition or loss of a family member through birth, death, or symbolically, by change in activity or residence.

Some researchers have found this model useful in its orientation toward prevention, rather than pathology, by identifying predictable crisis points or in evaluating vulnerabilities in the family system that contribute to individual psychopathology (e.g., Hetherington & Martin, 1986). Others, however, have criticized the approach for its restrictiveness in terms of criteria used to define the different stages and in its linear assumptions (Steinglass, 1987; Nichols & Everett, 1986). Nichols and Everett (1986) proposed that there may be additional transitions involving marital dissolution, single-parent living, and step-family living. They emphasized concomitant systemic reorganization that occurs with the evolution of nontraditional family units.

Steinglass (1987) noted that a major limitation in applying Erikson's theory to family development is the theory's assumption of linearly arranged stages. He stated that families are complex, multigenerational systems with continuity ensured by the fact that individuals are simultaneously children in their families of origin and "founders" of their own families of procreation. Similarly, Nichols and Everett (1986) argued that issues relating to family development emerge and operate long after one has physically "left home" and that they continue to have an impact over several generations. This multigenerational view of family development is consistent with the conception of the family in Asian culture that emphasizes continuity of the family line through marriage. Examples of this changed emphasis are offered by Wynne (1984) and Steinglass (1987).

Ethnicity and family therapy. Despite variations in family values and lifestyles as a function of ethnicity, many family therapists have avoided issues of culture in their conceptual work on assessment and intervention. Goldenberg and Goldenberg (1985) suggested that avoidance of cultural issues may have been a reflection of attempts to minimize stereotyping and discrimination. They stated, "Perhaps they [practitioners] lean over backwards not to show prejudice or discriminate in the clinical setting, but the overall effect is to ignore a potentially rich source of data regarding individual and family functioning" (p. 313).

In the family therapy literature, two major works dealing with the complexities of ethnicity in a family therapy context are by Papajohn and Spiegel (1975) and McGoldrick, Pearce, and Giordano (1982). The former deals primarily with value conflicts within Puerto Rican-, Greek-, and Italian-American families, while the latter is an edited volume addressing working with families of nineteen different ethnic backgrounds, including Asian-American ones. These books have demonstrated the usefulness of incorporating the role of ethnicity in understanding family functioning. In particular, McGoldrick (1982) provided a useful framework for understanding the way ethnic patterns manifest themselves within the family life cycle. For example, migration may be disruptive to a particular stage in the family life cycle (e.g., coping with adolescence) by interfering with processes involving adjustment (e.g., establishing appropriate limits). Furthermore, a life-cycle transition or situational crisis can elicit ethnic identity conflicts since it puts family members into contact with the roots of their family traditions and challenges who they are. More research is needed to illustrate the ways family life cycle and ethnicity interact to influence family functioning and to explore how these variables can be assessed most usefully to match family problems with appropriate clinical approaches, particularly among Asian-Americans.

ASSESSMENT FOR FAMILY THERAPY

Traditional Approaches

Variables. Family therapists have struggled with defining the most appropriate variables to include in a thorough family assessment and relating these variables to treatment. As early family theorists shifted away from individual and medical-model conceptualizations of problems, there were reactions against formal diagnostic procedures (Goldenberg & Goldenberg, 1985), leading to a greater focus on clinical technique and intervention rather than assessment (Liddle, 1983). Currently, there is no single, systematic approach to family assessment (Johnson et al., 1986).

Fisher (1977) reviewed the literature from 1957–1977 on the assessment and classification of families and noted two emerging viewpoints. According to the first perspective, conflicts occur in families as a result of "life stage events plus external circumstances" (Haley, 1971, p. 426). The focus of the assessment is on evaluating stressors in the environment and the family's adjustment to these stressful circumstances.

The second view is derived from more clinically oriented work suggesting that assessment should focus on underlying pathology that emerges not solely in reaction to stress but as a function of the construction of the family itself, and that the developmental stage of the family may simply color its expression or define the nature of the symptoms.

Fisher (1977) specified that these two views have distinct implications for clinical intervention. The first would lead to environmental manipulation, education, prevention, or supportive services; the second suggests therapeutic approaches designed to change pathological family structure or patterns of interaction.

From the literature on ethnic minorities, Korchin (1980) also struggles with the issue of context in evaluating the significance of pathology. In his paper entitled "Clinical Psychology and Minorities," Korchin (1980) presented a "cross-cultural approach" that views behavior in terms of its meaning within particular subcultures and yet attempts to avoid the extremes of cultural relativism (e.g., Benedict, 1934; Scheff, 1966). Korchin noted that although cultural relativism in its full extension "cautions against" ethnocentric assumptions, it denies the possibility of defining a "panhuman criteria" of psychopathology. Korchin (1980) suggested that assessment should acknowledge the meaning of the behavior within a particular context or subculture and yet be ready to propose change in terms of more universal standards.

Both Fisher (1977) and Korchin (1980) have suggested the importance in delineating the relevant context of pathology in proposing change and directing the focus of intervention. For a culturally sensitive assessment, there is a need not only to identify the specific contextual variables but also to derive these variables from the empirical literature.

Measures. A variety of standardized measures for use in family assessment have been developed. For example, Moos (1974) developed the Family Environment Scale while Skinner et al. (1983) devised the Family Assessment Measure to evaluate strengths and weaknesses of various areas in family functioning. Finally, a broad range of family "classification" dimensions have been identified, including styles of adaptation, developmental family stage, initial problem identified, family theme, and type of marital relationship (Fisher, 1977).

Relating Assessment to Treatment

In reviewing the vast array of approaches toward assessment taken by family therapists, it is easy to lose sight of the purpose and function of assessment. Clinical assessment is a process for gaining understanding to make informed decisions (Korchin, 1976). These decisions relate to questions regarding whether or not therapy is needed, what kind of intervention, and with whom (Nichols and Everett, 1986). Liddle (1983) argues for model-specific assessment procedures from which to move into the corresponding treatment techniques. However, in this approach one runs the risk of trying to fit a given family problem into a specific theoretical framework. Research suggests that particular therapeutic approaches are more effective for certain problems than for others (Garfield, 1983; Kazdin, 1988). Moreover, most theories were derived from work on nonethnic samples and it has been only recently that the various theoretical assumptions in family therapy have been tested on Asian-Americans (e.g., Kim, 1985; Ko, 1986). Therefore, a culturally sensitive approach to family evaluation is one that involves maintaining a flexible, responsive orientation toward assessment (rather than a fixed, model-specific one), selecting assessment variables derived from the empirical literature on Asian-American families, and structuring the therapeutic approach and treatment goals around the specific problems observed.

The literature on relevant contextual variables including family structure, marital and parental role expectations, and communication patterns among Asian-Americans was discussed in the previous section. What follows is an attempt to clarify how assessment of these variables and related pathological features of the individual, family, and community subsystems among Asian-Americans can direct treatment goals.

A CONCEPTUAL FRAMEWORK FOR ASSESSMENT OF ASIAN-AMERICAN FAMILIES

Existing Formulations

Much of the work on assessment and treatment of Asian-Americans has focused on individual approaches (Chin, 1983; Sue & Sue, 1987; Leong, 1986), but there have been a few recent attempts to advance a family systems approach (Lee, 1982; Kim, 1985; Ko, 1986).

Lee (1982) presented a comprehensive framework for assessing and treating Chinese-American families. She identified three subsystems that define the "client system" (person, family, and community) and three interacting domains (physical, psychological, and sociocultural). Critical assessment information then emerge from these interacting variables. For example, in the "person system" Lee suggested that it is important to inquire about the physical (constitutional or somatic organization), the psychological (ego functioning and self-concept), and sociocultural (responses to rules and expectations of the society) factors. Similarly, for the family system, it is necessary to assess the same dimensions: physical (family composition, kinship network), psychological or structural (coping styles of family members, marital relations), and sociocultural aspects (intergenerational differences, migration history, extent of support system) aspects. Lee's framework is helpful in suggesting important variables for assessment. However, it is not based on empirical data.

Kim (1985) applies both a strategic (Haley, 1963) and a structural (Minuchin, 1974) framework to the assessment and treatment of Asian-American families. She suggests obtaining "baseline data" about the family and its members (e.g., place of origin, family structure, role expectations, communication patterns, stability prior to immigration) as well as "postimmigrational variables" if appropriate to assess any discrepancies between pre- and postimmigrational functioning.

A final contribution to Asian-American family therapy is presented by Ko (1986). She provided a case illustration of a Vietnamese refugee family, utilizing Minuchin's structural techniques for treatment (1974a). The case involved conflict between a married couple and the paternal in-laws. A major task in Minuchin's system is to develop clear boundaries between subsystems (e.g., between the married couple and the in-laws), by encouraging the married couple to separate and "unbalance" the structure of the family. Ko (1986) noted that this technique may not always be appropriate in Asian families given the strong values of filial piety and obedience. Therefore, Ko (1986) utilized Minuchin's "joining and accommodation" strategies by passing messages through the authority figures to separate and initiate change. She concluded by emphasizing the importance in working with the extended family and utilizing strengths found in the family in order to bring about change when working with traditional Chinese families.

There have been only a few attempts to apply a family systems perspective to Asian-American families, despite its potential as a culturally appropriate assessment and treatment approach. Lee's work (1982) is clear and comprehensive regarding assessment. Kim (1985) and Ko (1986) provide useful suggestions for conducting family therapy. However, these three works represent only a beginning attempt to understand and treat Asian-American families from a family systems approach, and they do not fully utilize empirical data on Asian-Americans in their conceptualizations of assessment and treatment. This is especially true with respect to relevant literature on family structure, marital and parental role expectations, and communication patterns. The available data could provide a sound rationale for selecting particular assessment variables and evaluating the risk for particular problems.

A related concern is that the current conceptualizations do not specify how assessment information can be utilized in treatment (H. Wong, 1986). How can the information obtained in a family assessment fit in to a treatment framework? Why is it being collected? These questions are important in any family assessment. For Asian-Americans, the added issues of "saving face" and ambivalence toward self-disclosure (Nakanishi, 1986) may require longer periods of time to develop an alliance and collect the assessment information. Given a general tension between the therapist's need to obtain information in order to be helpful and the client's need to be helped without undue delay (Nichols & Everett, 1986), specifying the link between assessment and treatment is critical.

As noted, Lee (1982) identified three aspects of the client system to be assessed from a social systems approach including the person, the family, and the community. H. Wong (1986) suggested linking this assessment information to treatment goals. From the empirical literature discussed in the previous section, critical variables emerge that can provide the basis for a culturally sensitive assessment of Asian-American families.

An Alternative Empirically Based Framework

A conceptual framework relating specific assessment variables to treatment approaches for Asian-American families is depicted in Table 6.1. This model for family assessment is based on several assumptions: (1) The empirical literature on Asian-American families can guide selection of culturally relevant assessment variables; (2) these variables can alert the clinician to particular problem areas and vulnerabilities; (3) the emergent problems or their precursors can then direct appropriate intervention. Information can be obtained to assess and intervene at the individual, family, and community subsystem levels.

The individual level. The literature suggests that a variety of individual characteristics determine the relationship and communication patterns among family members and that these may be different for Asians than for Americans. Among Asian-Americans, the critical assessment variables that emerge at the individual level include age, gender, education and occupation, ethnicity, level of acculturation (e.g., first generation, second generation), and gender-role orientation. Potential problems that may arise in relation to these variables include identity conflicts, low self-esteem, cultural conflicts, and cross-pressures between ethnicity and gender. For example, an Asian immigrant may be experiencing conflict relating to acceptance into American society whereas his more acculturated counterpart may be concerned about cultural or identity conflicts. In the former case, treatment may involve supportive counseling, educational resources, or changes in the environment to ease immigration transitions and make appropriate sociocultural adjustment. In contrast, the latter situation might involve psychotherapy, cognitive behavioral approaches, or group therapy to increase self-esteem and facilitate bicultural adaptation.

The literature suggests gender and generational differences need to be considered in assessing values and that social class or educational background may minimize cultural differences in some areas of life (e.g., valuing achievement, stability of family life). There appear to be wide variations in the need to

Table 6.1
Relating Assessment Information to Treatment Approaches

Subsystem Level	Critical Assessment Variable	Potential Problem	Treatment Approach
Individual	Age, gender, education/ occupation, ethnicity	Identity conflicts low self-esteem	Psychotherapy, Cognitive behavioral approaches, group therapy to improve self-esteem and identity
	level of acculturation	cultural conflicts, transition difficulties	Supportive counseling, support groups, education to facilitate bicultural awareness and ease transition
	gender-role orientation	cross pressures between ethnicity and gender	Counseling or group therapy to provide support, improve coping or (depending upon level of distress) to increase insight into conflicts
Family	family composition (e.g., nuclear, stem-family, incomplete, modified extended)	loss of family support: emotional / loss of family support: material	Family therapy (e.g., Bowenian, Existential), Network therapy, education regarding alternative support systems
	family structure, hierarchy, organization and leadership, (e.g., father-son or husband-	shifting family structure, ambiguous hierarchical organization, stressful family life cycle	Family therapy to define or improve organization and structure (Structural or Strategic), or improve

Table 6.1 (Continued)

Subsystem Level	Critical Assessment Variable	Potential Problem	Treatment Approach
Family	wife dyad emphasized).	transitions, varying levels of acculturation among family members	interfamilial relations (Bowenian)
	marital roles (egalitarian) marital relations	marital distress due to immigration or acculturation stress	Marital counseling sensitive to acculturation pressures
	parental roles, child-rearing attitudes	cultural conflicts regarding parenting, approaches discordant with larger society and not conducive to adaptation	Parent counseling sensitive to acculturation pressure, education regarding bicultural parenting, family therapy (Bowenian, Existential) behavioral parent training
	communication patterns, self-disclosure, language proficiency, direct expression of thoughts and feelings	communication problems within the family due to varying levels of language proficiency, acculturation-related differences in values regarding self-disclosure and communication	Interventions to improve skills in communication and interpersonal assertiveness and to increase opportunities for communication
Community	degree of social support, community involvement	isolation alienation	Education regarding community resources; involvement in community networks
	level of acceptance/ discrimination, degree of discordance of values with the wider community	perceived powerlessness	advocacy groups

155

maintain or reject more traditional Asian values that could be explored by the clinician.

Conflict may arise between one's gender-role orientation and ethnicity. For example, an Asian-American woman, like her American counterpart, may believe in highly egalitarian sex roles (Arkoff et al, 1964; Chia et al., 1985) but feel ambivalence and conflict about expressing such attitudes due to cultural values inhibiting such expression. In addition, she may believe ethnic issues take precedence over gender-role issues in coping with discrimination (Chow, 1987). Distress may arise as a result of major discrepancies between one's own values and societal expectations or stereotypes with respect to sex roles (Chia et al., 1985). For example, Chia et al. (1985) noted the striking contrast between the progressive views of Asian and Asian-American women and prevalent stereotypes involving passivity and submissiveness.

If conflict between ethnic or societal values and gender-role orientation emerges, treatment may include counseling or group therapy to provide support, increase insight into the conflict, and improve strategies to cope with external stressors such as discrimination. While some forms of group therapy may be helpful to share feelings and attitudes, data on patterns of communication (e.g., Nakanishi, 1986; Hsu et al., 1985) suggest that Asian-Americans may be more restrained and less comfortable than non–Asian-Americans in revealing their conflicts and concerns with much depth in groups. Those who feel restrained but still desire participation in group therapy could use the context of the group and assistance of the clinician to learn and practice assertiveness skills.

The family level. Many aspects of family functioning directly or indirectly reflect the family's values and norms derived from the culture or subculture to which the family belongs (Boszormenyi-Nagy & Ulrich, 1981). Immigration and acculturation may strain a family, particularly if there is major dissonance between the family (or subculture) and the broader host culture. At the family level, the literature suggests that critical assessment variables for Asian-Americans include family composition, family structure and hierarchy, marital role expectations, parental roles, and communication patterns. It is particularly important to determine the impact of cultural transition in these areas, since studies suggest variations based on ethnicity and level of acculturation. Although varied patterns of family composition have been observed among Asian-Americans (e.g., nuclear, stem (including at least one grandparent in the home), incomplete, and modified-extended), these patterns continue to reflect the importance of strong family ties. Immigration or acculturation may leave an Asian-American family with a loss of family support (e.g., no grandparent in the home, an incomplete family) (Liu & Fernandez, 1987; Wong, 1985). This loss may be perceived in terms of a decrease in emotional support or material support (child care, income). Thus, current family composition should be assessed along with preimmigration family composition. Who is living in the home? Is the family complete, extended, or nuclear? Were there major shifts in family composition that resulted from immigration or acculturation? What were the roles and responsibilities of absent family members? What are the perceptions of any shifts that occurred?

If necessary, treatment for problems that result in a perceived loss of family support might include supportive counseling or psychotherapy, family therapy, multiple family therapy, network therapy, or education regarding alternative resources (e.g., child care). Bowen's family therapy (1976) that emphasizes both emotional processes in family relationships and the family's response to stress may be useful in addressing problems in this area. Alternatively, the experiential approach to family therapy by Whitaker (1977) may help family members focus on the here and now in order to overcome obstacles and increase growth.

Other problems may result from varying levels of acculturation among family members, shifts in family structure or lines of authority, ambiguous hierarchical organization due to cultural conflict or changing family structure, and stressful family life cycle transition points. For example, studies suggest that Asian-American women acculturate much faster into American society than Asian-American men (Arkoff et al., 1963), and this gender difference may impact upon marital and family functioning. Many family therapeutic approaches have been developed to ease difficult transitions (e.g., Haley, 1971), improve family organization and structure, (e.g., Minuchin & Fishman, 1981), or improve interfamilial relations (e.g., Bowen, 1976). In particular, Haley's strategic approach (1971) highlighting family life-cycle transitions and Minuchin's strategic approach (1974a) emphasizing family structure and hierarchy both have been successfully applied to Asian-American families experiencing distress (Kim, 1985; Ko, 1986).

Also of importance in assessing the family are marital and parental roles, expectations, and relations. Regarding marital roles, research suggests that Asian-American men and women possess discrepant marital role attitudes (Arkoff et al., 1963; Chia et al., 1986), which may or may not be a source of conflict or tension in a marriage (Jacobson, 1952). These attitudes may have a subtle impact on marital and family functioning that could be explored by the clinician and contribute to the clinician's task of facilitating Asian-American marital and family functioning. For example, the clinician might alleviate tension within a marriage or facilitate insight in a couple by conveying that certain egalitarian attitudes are increasingly found among contemporary Asian and Asian-American women or that conflicts between ethnicity and gender have been reported by Asian-Americans.

With respect to parental values, studies show that both mothers and fathers are active disciplinarians and that the husband-wife relationship, rather than the traditional father-son dyad, is increasingly emphasized by Asian-American families. Gender influences family values with girls valuing family affiliation and closeness and boys seeking independence and self-differentiation from parents and others. Although there is evidence that certain family patterns have changed in the direction of greater similarity to American values, studies also suggest that there may be a reassertion of traditional values in some areas of family functioning (e.g., Kitano, 1964). Aspects of family life and parental functioning that are most or least resistant to change could be identified and explored by the clinician to reveal family members' particular needs and motivations.

Immigration and acculturation clearly may strain marital and family functioning, particularly if the couple or the parents have values and beliefs that are discordant with the larger societal values. Marital and parental counseling that is sensitive to acculturation pressure would be appropriate. Both Whitaker (1977) and Bowen (1976) have emphasized intergenerational themes while Haley (1971) and Minuchin (1974b) discuss extrafamilial pressures. Also, in view of cultural differences in childrearing values, behavioral parent training might be utilized with fewer cultural biases. For example, child management skills could be taught as the parent selects which behaviors are adaptive or maladaptive from an Asian or an Asian-American perspective (see Serafica, this volume).

Family communication patterns also are shaped by values derived from the family's cultural background. For Asian-Americans, critical variables include self-disclosure, language proficiency, and direct or indirect expression of thoughts and feelings. Studies show that Asian and Asian-Americans may rely more heavily upon interpersonal and social cues in social interaction (Ayube, 1971), view self-disclosure more negatively (Nakanishi, 1986), and show more restraint and caution in communicating with family members (Hsu et al., 1985) than non–Asian-Americans. These differences create special complexities for the clinician in evaluating and treating the Asian-American family. In a clinical setting, they may be misunderstood (e.g., viewing restraint or a lack of self-disclosure as resistance or defensiveness) if not considered from an Asian or Asian-American perspective. Also, Asian-American families may value sharing deep thoughts rather than feelings (McDermott et al., 1983) suggesting task-oriented, cognitive approaches may be more effective.

Community level. At the community level, relevant variables to assess are the degree of social support and community involvement, the degree of dissonance in terms of values and life-styles, and the level of acceptance or discrimination. Steinhauer (1987) emphasized the importance of the family "bonding" to the larger community. If such bonding does not occur, he suggests problems may arise such as isolation, alienation, and a loss of "existential significance" (p. 102). Thus, the therapist should assess how isolated, deviant, or alienated the family appears in relation to the subculture and the broader community. If indicated, treatment might involve providing useful information and education regarding community resources, encouraging involvement in community networks, or becoming involved in advocacy groups. Family therapy may also be useful for addressing problems of the family in relation to wider social systems (Minuchin & Fishman, 1981) or decreasing alienation (Whitaker, 1977). Involvement in community networks, religious affiliations, and extended family systems all have the potential to facilitate improved interrelationships that bind the family to the community and allow healthy functioning.

CONCLUSIONS

A review of the current literature on Asian-American families suggests that certain patterns of family composition, marital roles and expectations, child-rearing, and communication are unique to Asian-Americans. Not only do many of these findings contradict popular conceptions of Asian marital and family life, but also they have important implications for meeting the mental health needs of Asian-Americans. More specifically, the following empirical findings have clinical relevance:

1. The characterization of a large and extended Asian family is not an accurate description of contemporary Asians and Asian-Americans. However, the Asian-American family structure is more likely than that of the non–Asian-American family to be nuclear, stem, incomplete due to the immigration process, or modified (nonresidential) extended.

2. In contrast to stereotypes of Asian and Asian-American women involving submissiveness and passivity, there are data suggesting that Asian women are very progressive and egalitarian in their marital role expectations and that they acculturate more quickly into American society than their male counterparts.

3. The parenting literature suggests both mothers and fathers are active disciplinarians and that gender, social class, and level of acculturation may influence parental values and beliefs among Asian-Americans. While increasing resident years in the United States leads to a decrease in many traditional views with respect to parenting (e.g., restrictiveness), other Asian values and expectations are maintained (e.g., kinship and familial contact).

4. Differences in communication patterns between Asians and non-Asians exist, and these differences have important clinical implications. These include less self-disclosure, more restraint, and a greater reliance on interpersonal cues in social interactions among Asians than non-Asians. Also, expressing thoughts is more acceptable than expressing feelings.

It has been suggested that this neglected body of empirical work on Asian-American families as well as the theoretical work in family therapy can provide the conceptual basis for a culturally meaningful approach to the assessment and treatment of Asian-Americans. Although there have been a few attempts to apply a social systems approach to treating Asian-American families, the relationship between assessment and treatment has not been clearly specified. By examining empirically based assessment variables that have been highlighted in this chapter, the clinician can remain sensitive to cultural differences as well as related problems that may direct treatment at the individual, family, or community level among Asian-Americans.

DIRECTIONS FOR FUTURE RESEARCH

In reviewing the literature on Asian-American families with a view toward assessment and treatment from a family systems perspective, several neglected areas become apparent.

Marital and parental roles as well as expectations vary as a function of cultural background, gender, family life-cycle phase, and generation. Clearly, more studies are needed to elucidate aspects of Asian-American family life and parental functioning that are modified or retained in the process of acculturation, and the role of social class in what gets modified or retained. Further, there is a need for studies that will explore how observed cultural differences in family structure, marital and parental roles and expectations, and communication patterns affect mental health and family functioning.

The findings of research on Asian-American families have implications for conceptualizing a culturally sensitive assessment and intervention approach, but the data remain underutilized by clinicians and clinical researchers. Future research needs to integrate empirically derived knowledge about Asian-Americans with clinical work. Designing assessment measures and intervention methods more closely tied to empirically derived data on normality and pathology among Asian-Americans can provide a clinical approach that is both scientifically valid and less culturally biased. In this way we can advance toward more meaningful clinical theory, research, and practice that respects the cultural integrity of Asian-American families.

REFERENCES

Arkoff, H., Meredith, G. & Dong, J. (1963). Attitudes of Japanese American and Caucasian Americans and Caucasian-American students toward marriage roles. *Journal of Social Psychology, 59*, 11–15.

Arkoff, A., Meredith, G. & Iwahara, S. (1964). Male-dominant and equivalent attitudes in Japanese, Japanese-American students. *Journal of Social Psychology, 64*, 225–229.

Ayube, H. I. (1971). Deference and ethnic differences in voice levels. *Journal of Social Psychology, 85*, 181–185.

Barnhill, L. R. & Longo, D. (1980). Fixation and regression in the family life cycle. In J. G. Howells (Ed.), *Advances in family psychiatry* (Vol 11, pp. 51–64). New York: International Universities Press.

Bateson, G., Jackson, D. D., Haley, J. & Weakland, J. (1956). Towards a theory of schizophrenia. *Behavioral Science, 1*, 251–264.

Benedict, R. (1934). *Patterns of culture*. Boston: Houghton Mifflin.

Benkart, C. P. & Benkart, B. M. (1985). Japanese children's perceptions of their parents. *Sex Roles, 13*, 11–12, 679–690.

Boszormenyi-Nagy, I. & Ulrich, D. N. (1981). Contextual family therapy. In A. S. Gurman and D. P. Kniskern (Eds.). *Handbook of family therapy*. New York: Brunner/Mazel.

Bowen, M. (1960). The family concept of schizophrenia. In D. D. Jackson (Ed.), *The etiology of schizophrenia*. New York: Basic Books.

————. (1976). The use of family theory in clinical practice. *Comprehensive Psychiatry, 7*, 345–364.

Brown, J. (1979). Clinical social work with Chicanos: Some unwarranted assumptions. *Clinical Social Work Journal, 7*, 256–266.

Bureau of the Census, U.S. Department of Commerce (1983). 1980 Census of the Population, Vol. 1, Section A: United States. Washington, DC: U.S. Government Printing Office.

Caudill, W. & Frost, L. A. (1974). A comparison of maternal care and infant behavior in Japanese-American, American, and Japanese families. In W. P. Lebra (Ed.), *Youth, socialization, and mental health* (Vol. 3). Honolulu, Hawaii: University of Hawaii Press.

Chia, R. C., Chong, C. J. & Cheng, B. S. (1986). Relationship of modernization and marriage role attitude among Chinese college students. *The Journal of Psychology, 120*(6), 599–605.

Chia, R. C., Chong, C. J., Cheng, B. S., Castellow, W., Moore, W. & Hayes, M. (1985). Attitude toward marriage roles among Chinese and American college students. *The Journal of Social Psychology, 126*(1), 31–35.

Chin, J. L. (1983). Diagnostic considerations in working with Asian Americans. *American Journal of Orthopsychiatry*, Jan, *53*,(1), 100–109.

Chow, E. N. (1987). The development of feminist consciousness among Asian American women. *Gender and Society, 1*(3), 284–299.

Cohen, R. E. (1974). Borderline conditions: A transcultural perspective. *Psychiatric Annals, 4*, 7–20.

Connor, J. W. (1974). Acculturation and family continuities in three generations of Japanese Americans. *Journal of Marriage and the Family, 36*, 159–166.

Dahlquist, L. M. & Fay, A. S. (1984). Cultural issues in psychotherapy. In C. E. Walker (Ed.), *The handbook of clinical psychology: Theory, research and practice*. Homewood, IL: Dow Jones-Irwin.

Del Carmen, R. & Serafica, F. C. (1985). Locus of control and childrearing in Chinese- and Filipino-Americans. Paper presented at the Bienniel Meeting of the Society for Research in Child Development, Toronto, Canada.

Duvall, E. M. (1971). *Family development* (4th ed.). Philadelphia: J. B. Lippincott.

Erikson, E. H. (1963). *Childhood and society* (2nd ed.). New York: Norton.

Fisher, L. (1977). On the classification of families. *Archives of General Psychiatry, 34*, 424–433.

Fujitomi, I. & Wong, D. (1973). The new Asian-American woman. In S. Sue & N. H. Wagner (Eds.), *Asian Americans: Psychological perspectives* (Vol. 1). Palo Alto, CA: Science and Behavior Books.

Fukaya, M. & Fukaya, K. (1975). *Theory of modern childhood*. Tokyo: Yunikaku.

Fukuyama, M. A. & Greenfield, T. K. (1983). Dimensions of assertiveness in an Asian-American student population. *Journal of Counseling Psychology, 30*, 429–432.

Garfield, S. L. (1983). Effectiveness of psychotherapy: the perennial controversy. *Professional Psychologist: Research and Practice, 14*, 35–43.

Glick, I. D. and Kessler, D. R. (1980). *Marital and family therapy* (2nd ed.). New York: Grune and Stratton.

Goldenberg, I. & Goldenberg, H. (1985). *Family therapy: An overview.* (2nd ed.). Monterey, CA: Brooks/Cole Publishing Company.

Group for the Advancement of Psychiatry (1970). Washington, DC: GAP.

Haley, J. (1963). *Strategies of psychotherapy.* New York: Grune and Stratton.

————. (1971). Family therapy. *International Journal of Psychiatry, 9,* 233–242.

Harrison, A., Serafica, F. & McAdoo, H. (1984). Ethnic families of color. In R. D. Parke (Ed.), *Review of child development research,* Vol. 7, 329–371. Chicago, IL: The University of Chicago Press.

Herrera, A. & Sanchez, B. (1980). Prescriptive group psychotherapy: a successful application in the treatment of low-income Spanish-speaking clients. *Psychotherapy: Theory, Research, and Practice, 17,* 169–174.

Hetherington, E. M. & Martin, B. (1986). Family factors and psychopathology in children. In H. C. Quay and J. S. Werry (Eds.), *Psychopathological disorders of childhood* (3rd ed.) (pp. 332–390). New York: John Wiley and Sons.

Hill, R. (1970). *Family developments in three generations.* Cambridge. MA: Schenkman.

Hill, R. & Hansen, D. A. (1960). The identification of conceptual frameworks utilized in family study. *Marriage and Family Living, 22,* 299–311.

Ho, D. Y. F. (1987). Fatherhood in Chinese culture. In M. E. Lamb (Ed.), *The father's role: Cross-cultural perspectives* (pp. 227–246). Hillsdale, NJ: Lawrence Erlbaum Associates.

Hsu, J., Tseng, W., Ashton, G., McDermott, J. F. & Char, W. (1985). Family interaction patterns among Japanese-American and Caucasian families in Hawaii. *American Journal of Psychiatry, 142,* 5, 577–581.

Huang, L. J. (1981). The Chinese American family. In C. H. Mindel and R. W. Habenstein (Eds.), *Ethnic families in America.* New York: Elsevier.

Jacobson, A. H. (1952). Conflict of attitudes toward the roles of the husband and the wife in marriage. *American Sociological Review, 17,* 146–150.

Japanese Statistical Yearbook (1984). Tokyo: Statistics Bureau, Management and Coordination Agency.

Johnson, C. L. (1977). Indebtedness: An analysis of Japanese American kinship relations. *Journal of Marriage and the Family, 39,* 351–363.

Johnson, J. H., Rasbury, W. C. & Siegel, L. J. (1986). *Approaches to child treatment.* New York: Pergamon Press, 270–305.

Kazdin, A. E. (1988). *Child psychotherapy: Developing and identifying effective treatments.* New York: Pergamon.

Kikumura, A. & Kitano, H. H. L. (1980). The Japanese American family. In R. Endo, S. Sue, & N. Wagner (Eds.), *Asian-Americans: social and psychological perspectives* (Vol. 2). Palo Alto, CA: Science and Behavior Books.

Kim, S. C. (1985). Family therapy for Asian Americans: A strategic-structural framework. *Psychotherapy, 22,*(2), 342–348.

Kitano, H. H. L. (1961). Differential childrearing attitudes between first and second generation Japanese in the United States. *Journal of Social Psychology, 53,* 13–19.

————. (1964). Inter- and intra-generational differences in maternal attitudes toward childrearing. *Journal of Social Psychology, 63,* 215–220.

Ko, H. Y. (1986). Minuchin's structural therapy for Vietnamese Chinese families. *Contemporary Family Therapy, 8*(1), Spring, 20–32.

Korchin, S. (1976). *Modern clinical psychology*. New York: Basic Books.

———. (1980). Clinical psychology and minority problems. *American Psychologist, 35*, 262–269.

Landau, J. (1982). Therapy with families in cultural transition In M. McGoldrick, J. K. Pearce, and J. Giordano (Eds.), *Ethnicity and family therapy*. New York: The Guilford Press.

Lee, E. (1982). A social systems approach to assessment and treatment for Chinese American families. In M. McGoldrick, J. K. Pearce, and J. Giordano (Eds.), *Ethnicity and family therapy*. New York: The Guilford Press.

Leong, F. T. (1986). Counselling and psychotherapy with Asian-Americans: Review of the literature. *Journal of Counselling Psychology, 33*,(20), 196–206.

Liddle, H. A. (1983). Diagnosis and assessment in family therapy: A comparative analysis of six schools of thought. In J. C. Hansen (Ed.), *Diagnosis and assessment in family therapy* (pp. 1–33) Rockville, Maryland: Aspen Corporation.

Lidz, T., Cornelison, A., Fleck, S. & Terry, D. (1957). The intrafamilial environment of schizophrenic patients. II. Marital schism and marital skew. *American Journal of Psychiatry, 114*, 241–248.

Liu, W. T. (1986). Culture and social support. *Research on Aging, 8*(1), 57–83.

Liu, W. T. & Fernandez, M. (1987). Family reunification. In Liu, W. T. (Ed.), *The Pacific/Asian American Mental Health Research Center*. Chicago: University of Illinois at Chicago.

Lum, R. G. (1982). Mental health attitudes and opinions of Chinese. In E. E. Jones and S. J. Korchin (Eds.), *Minority mental health*. New York: Praeger Press.

Marsella, H. A. (1980). Depressive experience and disorder across cultures. In H. C. Triandis & J. G. Draguns (Eds.), *Psychopathology: Handbook of cross-cultural psychology* (pp. 237–289). Newton, MA: Allyn and Bacon.

Matsumoto, M. & Smith, H. (1961). Japanese and American children's perception of parents. *The Journal of Genetic Psychology, 98*, 83–88.

McDermott, J. F., Char, W. F., Robillard, A. B., Hsu, J., Tseng, W. & Ashton, G. (1983). Cultural variations and family attitudes and their implications for therapy. *Journal of the American Academy of Child Psychiatry, 22*, 5, 454–458.

McDermott, J. F., Robillard, A. B., Char, W. F., Hsu, J., Tseng, W. & Ashton, G. (1983). Reexamining the concept of adolescence: differences between adolescent boys and girls in the context of their families. *American Journal of Psychiatry, 140*, 1318–1322.

McGoldrick, M. (1982). Ethnicity and family therapy: An overview. In M. McGoldrick, J. K. Pearce, and J. Giordano (Eds.), *Ethnicity and family therapy*. New York: Guilford Press.

McGoldrick, M., Pearce, J. K. & Giordano, J. (Eds.) (1982). *Ethnicity and family therapy*. New York: Guilford Press.

McGoldrick, M. & Rohrbaugh, M. (1987). Researching ethnic family stereotypes. *Family Process, 26*(1), 89–99.

Minuchin, S. (1974a). *Families and Family Therapy*. Cambridge, MA: Harvard University Press.

———. (1974b). Structural family therapy. In S. Arieti and G. Caplan (Eds)., *American handbook of psychiatry: Child and adolescent psychiatry*. New York: Basic Books.

Minuchin, S., Montalvo, B. Guerney, B., Rosman, B. & Schumer, F. (1967). *Families of the slums*. New York: Basic Books.

Minuchin, S. & Fishman, H. C. (1981). *Family therapy techniques*. Cambridge, MA: Harvard University Press.

Momeni, J. A. (1984). Demography of racial and ethnic minorities in the United States: a political and sociodemographic review. In J. A. Momeni (Ed.), *Demography of racial and ethnic minorities in the United States*. Westport, CT: Greenwood Press.

Moos, R. H. (1974). *Combined preliminary manual: Family, work and group environment scales*. Palo Alto, CA: Consulting Psychologists Press.

Nakanishi, M. (1986). Perception of self-disclosure in initial interaction. *Human Communication Research, 13*, 2, 167–190.

Nichols, W. C. & Everett, C. A. (1986). *Systemic family therapy: An integrative approach*. New York: Guilford Press.

O'Reilly, J. P., Tokuno, K. A. & Ebata, A. T. (1986). Cultural differences between Americans of Japanese and European ancestry in parental valuing of social competence. *Journal of Comparative Family Studies, 17*, 1, 87–97.

Papajohn, J. & Spiegel, J. P. (1975). *Transactions in families: A modern approach for resolving cultural and generational conflict*. San Francisco: Jossey-Bass.

Parron, D. L. (1982) An overview of minority group mental health needs and issues as presented to the President's Commission on Mental Health. In Munoz, F. U. & Endo, R. (Eds.), *Perspectives on minority group mental health* (pp. 3–20). Washington, DC: University Press of America, 3–20.

Root, M. P. P. (1985). Guidelines for facilitating therapy with Asian American clients. *Psychotherapy, 22*, 349–356.

Satir, V. (1967). *Conjoint family therapy*. Palo Alto, CA: Science and Behavior Books.
———. (1972). *Peoplemaking*. Palo Alto, CA: Science and Behavior Books.

Scheff, T. J. (1966). *Being mentally ill*. Chicago: Aldine.

Schwalb, D. W., Imaizumi, N. & Nakazawa, J. (1987). The modern Japanese father: roles and problems in a changing society. In M. E. Lamb (Ed.), *The father's role: cross-cultural perspectives*. Hillsdale, NJ: Lawrence Erlbaum Associates.

Shinohara, T. (1981). The role of the father in the era of the nuclear family. In H. Katsura (Ed.), *The paternal role*. Volume 5, Tokyo: Kaneko Shobo.

Shon, S. P. & Ja, D. Y. (1982). Asian families. In M. McGoldrick, J. K. Pearce, and J. Giordano (Eds.), *Ethnicity and family therapy*. New York: Guilford Press.

Sih, P. K. T. (1961). *The Hsaio Ching*. New York: St. John's University Press.

Skinner, H. A., Steinhauer, P. D. & Santa-Barbara, J. (1983). The family assessment measure. *Canadian Journal of Community Mental Health, 2*, 91–105.

Solomon, M. A. (1973). A developmental, conceptual premise for family therapy. *Family Process, 12*, 179–188.

Sorifu (1985). *White paper on youth*. Tokyo: Prime Minister's Office.

Steinglass, P. (1987). A systems view of family interaction and psychopathology. In T. Jacob (Ed.), *Family interaction and psychopathology: Theories, methods, and findings*. New York: Plenum Press.

Steinglass, P., Bennett, L. A., Wolin, S. J. & Reiss, D. (1987). *The alcoholic family*. New York: Basic Books.

Steinhauer, P. D. (1987). The family as a small group: The process model of family functioning. In T. Jacob (Ed.), *Family interaction and psychopathology: Theories, methods, and findings*. New York: Plenum Press.

Sue, D. & Sue, S. (1987). Cultural factors in the clinical assessment of Asian-Americans. *Journal of Consulting and Clinical Psychology, 55*,(4), 479–87.

Sue, D., Sue, D. W. & Sue, D. M. (1975). Asian Americans as a minority group. *American Psychologist, 30,* 906–910.

————. (1983). Psychological development of Chinese-American children. In G. J. Powell, J. Yamamoto, A. Romero, & A Morales (Eds.), *The psychosocial development of minority group children.* New York: Brunner/Mazel.

Sue, S. (1980). Psychology theory and implications for Asian Americans. In R. Endo, S. Sue and N. N. Wagner (Eds.), *Asian-Americans: Social and psychological perspectives* (Vol. 1). Palo Alto, CA: Science and Behavior Books.

Sue, D. W. & Kirk, B. A. (1973). Differential characteristics of Japanese-American college students. *Journal of Counseling Psychology, 20,* 142–148.

Sue, S. & Kitano, H. (1973). Stereotypes as a measure of success. *Journal of Social Issues, 29,* 83–98.

Sue, S. & McKinney, H. (1975). Asian Americans in the community mental health care system. In Endo, R., Sue, S. & Wagner, N. (Eds.), *Asian-Americans: Social and psychological perspectives.* Palo Alto, CA: Science and Behavior Books, Inc.

Toupin, E. S. W. (1980). Counseling Asians: Psychotherapy in the context of racism and Asian-American history. *American Journal of Orthopsychiatry, 50*(10), January, 76–86.

Tracey, T. J., Leong, F. T. L. & Glidden, D. (1986). Help seeking and problem perception among Asian Americans. *Journal of Counseling Psychology, 33*(3), 331–336.

True, R. (1975). Mental health services in a Chinese American community. In W. Ishikawa and N. Archer (Eds.), *Service delivery in Pan Asian communities.* San Diego: Pacific Asian Coalition.

Tseng, W. S., Kuotai, J. H., Hsu, J., Jinghua, C., Lian, Y. & Kameoka, V. (1988). Family planning and child mental health in China: the Nanjing survey. *American Journal of Psychiatry, 145, 11,* 1396–1403.

Tseng, W. S. & McDermott, J. F. (1981). *Culture, mind and therapy: An introduction to cultural psychiatry.* New York: Brunner/Mazel.

Whitaker, C. A. (1977). Process techniques of family therapy. *Interaction, 1,* 4–10.

White, G. M. (1982). The role of cultural explanations in "somatization" and "psychologization." *Social Science and Medicine, 16,* 1519–1530.

Wong, B. (1985). Family, kinship, and ethnic identity of the Chinese in New York City, with comparative remarks on the Chinese in Lima, Peru and Manila, Philippines. *Journal of Comparative Family Studies, 16*,(2), 231–252.

Wong, H. Z. (1986). Clinical assessment of Asian Americans for family therapy. Presentation at the conference on Minority Mental Health, Ohio State University, Columbus, OH.

Wynne, L. C. (1984). The epigenesis of relational systems: A model for undertaking family development. *Family Process, 23,* 297–318.

Wynne, L. C., Ryckoff, I. M., Day, J. & Hirsch, S. I. (1958). Pseudomutuality in the family relationships of schizophrenics. *Psychiatry, 21,* 205–220.

Yao, E. L. (1985). A comparison of family characteristics of Asian-American and Anglo-American high achievers. *International Journal of Comparative Sociology, 3–4,* 198–208.

Yu, K. H. & Kim, L. I. C. (1983). The growth and development of Korean-American children. In G. J. Powell (Ed.). *The psychosocial development of minority group children.* New York: Brunner/Mazel.

Yu, L. C. (1984). Acculturation and stress within Chinese American families. *Journal of Comparative Family Studies, 15,*1, 77–94.

Part III

Advances in Treatment

Introduction

Richard K. Russell

This section presents three chapters examining important advances in the delivery of treatment services to ethnic minority clients. In the first chapter Janet E. Helms identifies three theoretical perspectives that have influenced the treatment literature on ethnic minorities. These perspectives include the client-as-problem, the therapist-as-problem, and racial/ethnic identity models. For each framework, Helms provides a review of the historical background and significance of the perspective, a critical analysis of the relevant literature, and conclusions and recommendations for additional treatment and research. In her review Helms emphasizes that any analysis of the therapeutic process in cross-cultural counseling must consider the interaction between the racial identity attitudes of both the therapist and the client.

The second chapter in this section is by Guillermo A. Argueta-Bernal. This chapter begins with a discussion of some of the unique stressors affecting the Hispanic population, and includes consideration of demographic factors, life events, and adjustment to migration. Argueta-Bernal next examines strategies for the assessment of stress and coping responses in Hispanics, noting that behaviorally oriented assessment techniques seem particularly reliable and valid in evaluating mental status in Hispanics. Finally, Argueta-Bernal presents findings from two treatment studies illustrating the application of behavioral medicine approaches to stress-related disorders with Hispanics. Both studies demonstrate the utility of biofeedback-assisted relaxation training strategies with Hispanics. This chapter concludes with a summary of some of the significant conceptual and methodological issues investigators must be aware of in studying stress-related disorders in the Hispanic population.

The final chapter in this section is by Felicisima C. Serafica. The chapter is divided into three main topics, beginning with an examination of the need for mental health services targeted toward Asian-American parents, especially immigrant parents. Next Serafica selectively reviews the Asian-American socialization research, examining the implications of these findings for parents struggling to raise children in multicultural society. In the third section Serafica presents a cultural-developmental approach to counseling designed to enhance Asian-American parenting. This approach stresses the importance of providing emotional support and education in working with parents and requires that the counselor be sensitive to the cultural experiences and pressures facing Asian-American parents. The chapter concludes with a summary of the key issues and a discussion of directions for future research.

The three chapters in this section serve to highlight the importance of specialized training experiences for persons providing treatment services to ethnic minority clients. This training should include the development of a theoretical knowledge of the cultural and societal influences affecting minority clients, as well as supervised training in service delivery. Clearly, it is imperative that graduate programs adapt to the need for these training experiences if we are to begin to be responsive to the mental health needs of ethnic minorities in the years ahead.

7

Three Perspectives on Counseling and Psychotherapy with Visible Racial/Ethnic Group Clients

Janet E. Helms

Three theoretical perspectives have characterized the literature on counseling and psychotherapy as it involves visible racial/ethnic groups (VREG).[1] These perspectives will be called the (1) client-as-problem (CAP), (2) therapist-as-problem (TAP), and (3) racial/ethnic identity (REI) strategies and/or models. Implicit in each of the three perspectives is a different philosophy concerning the operation of cultural factors in therapist-client interactions. Consequently, each of these three perspectives has had different implications for therapy service delivery which includes therapist-client relationship characteristics, client diagnosis, and therapy process and outcome considered more generally.

The purpose of this review is to examine these perspectives for what they can reveal about how best to treat VREG clients. In so doing, the focus of this chapter will be upon therapy dyads involving a VREG client and a single therapist of whatever race/ethnicity. However, the issues raised could, of course, be addressed with respect to other types of counseling and psychotherapy interventions and/or combinations of client and therapist race/ethnicities.

In this chapter, the expression "visible racial/ethnic group" (VREG) is used when referring to Asians, Blacks, Hispanics, and Native Americans collectively. As Cook and Helms (1988) have pointed out, alternative terminology is needed to replace "minorities", which implies an ethnocentric racial comparison in which Whites are the majority.

The chapter essentially consists of three major sections, one covering each of the perspectives. All three sections contain a general overview of the particular perspective including its assumptions regarding therapist and client cultural characteristics and their influence on the quality of the therapy relationship. Each section also includes an overview of the relevant research as well as a brief critique that attempts to tie together the theoretical and empirical themes inherent in each perspective. The chapter closes with general conclusions and recommendations for practice and research.

CLIENT-AS-PROBLEM (CAP) PERSPECTIVE

The CAP perspective is basically an approach that anticipates problems in the helping process involving VREGs but locates the source of the problems in the personality characteristics of the VREG client and/or the racial/ethnic group from which he or she is perceived to descend. For the most part, because it was stimulated by the social unrest of the Civil Rights era of the mid-1960s and early 1970s, the focus of this approach has been on describing how VREG clients might be expected to express their experiences of racial oppression and discrimination in the therapy process.

Two general modes of expression have been described in the literature. These might be called the "cultural scar hypothesis" and the "acting out client phenomenon." Each has contributed to different views of the therapy process; each has contributed to different empirical traditions.

Cultural Scar-Hypothesis

The cultural-scar hypothesis proposes that personality deficits caused by racial/ethnic discrimination, differential cultural socialization experiences, and perhaps genetic characteristics make VREG clients inappropriate candidates for traditional therapy at least in their natural state. At its worst, the cultural-scar hypothesis was deficit modeling run amok as it promoted negative stereotypes about VREG clients that resulted in therapists' viewing them as inferior beings with many liabilities and few, if any, cultural strengths. Furthermore, the idea of a group personality, that is, the notion that all members of a particular racial/ethnic group could be described by a modal set of personality characteristics, seems to have been nourished by this version of the CAP perspective.

By way of illustration, in describing the portrayal of Black clients in mental health literature, De La Cancela (1985), Gardner (1971), and Smith (1975) have called attention to the overwhelming negativity inherent in the descriptions of Black clients. Interestingly, though somewhat more recently, characterizations of Hispanics and Native Americans have followed similar directions. Thus, VREG clients, regardless of race/ethnicity, are frequently portrayed in the mental health literature as mistrustful, nondisclosive, poor, passive or apathetic, lacking in self-esteem, inarticulate, resentful, antisocial, and crippled by hypothetical cultural characteristics such as "cool" or "machismo," to mention only a few of the common descriptors one encounters in the relevant literature (Acosta, Yamamoto & Evans, 1982; Casas, Wampold & Atkinson, 1981; Kardiner & Ovesey, 1951; Rivera & Cespedes, 1983; Sue & Kitano, 1973).

Although use of group stereotypes and/or other similar cultural constructs promotes the viewpoint that therapists are attending to cultural issues in the therapy process, in fact, such constructs contribute to simplistic treatment strategies and over-reliance on therapeutic approaches for which there is no empirical support (see also Sue, 1988, and Sue & Zane, 1987). For instance, Valdes (1983), in writing about Hispanic clients, asserted that, "it has been *proven* [italics mine] that nondirective techniques are completely inappropriate for Hispanics in general" (p. 60). Similar conclusions have been offered for treating Asian, Black, and Native Americans as well (e.g., Acosta et al., 1982; Dinges, Trimble, Manson & Pasquale, 1981; Levine & Padilla, 1980; Tounsel & Jones, 1980; Trimble, 1981). Contradictory observations also have been offered (Bransford, 1982; E. Jones, 1978). Additionally, some empirical evidence, albeit limited, suggests that these absolutists' treatment prescriptions are not necessary for VREG clients (Acosta, 1979; E. Jones, 1978; Lerner, 1972; Parker & McDavis, 1983).

The premise underlying the cultural-scar hypothesis generally has concerned the VREG client's "problematic" cultural adaptations and the source of the "problem" has been viewed as the client's membership in a disfavored racial/ethnic group or category per se. Nevertheless, it is possible to argue that VREG clients develop particular attitudes, beliefs, coping strategies, or other psychological characteristics that may be correlated with racial/ethnic group membership, but are not necessarily caused by it. Reluctance to trust therapists of another race might be an example of a psychological characteristic that may be correlated with racial/ethnic group membership (Terrell & Terrell, 1984). Two models based on psychological characteristics rather than racial group membership have appeared in the cultural-scar literature. D. W. Sue (1978) proposed a diagnostic model in which the constructs of locus of control and responsibility are used to speculate about client characteristics. D. W. Sue and D. Sue (1977) attempted to use differences in VREG clients' cultural values and behavior patterns relative to those of White middle-class therapists (and clients) to describe sources of potential conflicts in the therapy relationship. With two exceptions (Cook, 1983; Giorgis & Helms, 1980), neither of these models has been examined in the empirical mental health literature. However, each potentially has some implications for how one treats VREG clients. For instance, D. W. Sue and D. Sue used their relationship model to note the absence of therapy technique matched to VREG client characteristics and recommended that "the counselor must be more action oriented in (a) initiating counseling, (b) structuring the interview, [and] (c) helping clients cope with pressing social problems of immediate concern to them" (p. 427).

Acting-Out Client Phenomenon

The central premise of the acting-out client phenomenon is that VREG clients can be expected to act out or demonstrate their rage and/or "cultural paranoia" in ways unfamiliar to traditional therapists (Adams, 1950; Kardiner & Ovesey, 1951; Ridley, 1984; Vontress, 1969). Grier and Cobbs (1968), who best exemplify this orientation, asserted that Black clients would feel too angry with Whites in general to focus on much other than rage in the presence of White therapists. Various authors (e.g., Ridley, 1984; Vontress, 1971) have developed models to explain the different styles VREG clients can be expected to demonstrate in cross-racial interactions.

In general, advocates of the acting-out client phenomenon contend that the VREG client's manner of coping with the therapy relationship is merely a continuation of her/his manner of coping with a lifetime of discrimination. In therapy situations, the therapist is hypothesized to symbolize the larger society in some manner (A. Jones & Seagull, 1977; Ridley, 1984) and clients are described as directing a variety of negative emotions including rage, hostility, anger, suspicion, fear, or frustration toward the therapist (Pinderhughes, 1973; Vontress, 1969, 1971). The writings by Pinderhughes and Vontress suggested that passivity and nonparticipation in the therapy, silence, challenging, and nonpayment of the therapist may be symbolic expressions of unexpressed feelings evoked by therapist or societal racism.

Recommended strategies for professionals who find themselves providing services to acting-out clients typically have centered around changing the VREG client's symbolic expression of feelings (e.g., increasing talkativeness) rather than on changing the underlying causes of the expressions (e.g., reactions to racism or racism itself). However, Boykins (1959) insists that to counsel Black (and presumably other VREG) clients effectively, the therapist must explore with each client the consequences of being a member of a VREG (a characteristic that she points out is not equivalent to lower socioeconomic status) in a society that devalues VREG's race/ethnicity. Several authors (Brown, 1951; Harper, 1973; Jackson, 1972) have recommended that racial/ethnic issues be addressed explicitly with special attention to the client's racial/ethnic identity and the social and political implications of living in a larger White society.

Client-as-Problem Research

Perhaps the largest set of studies that can be categorized as representing the CAP perspective are those that have attempted to determine how VREG clients' pretherapy expectations can be manipulated so as to make the clients more suitable for traditional therapy. The bulk of these studies have examined the effectiveness of manipulating pretherapy expectations as a means of preventing clients' premature termination from therapy; a smaller set have measured expectations and preferences as a means of determining how VREG clients differ from their Anglo counterparts.

Pretherapy expectations. Interestingly, in those studies that have attempted to manipulate pretherapy expectations, although samples have often consisted of a mixture of racial/ethnic groups, analyses based on this variable usually have not been reported. In examining "classic" studies in this area, one finds that 14 percent of Sloane, Cristol, Pepernick, and Staples' sample (1970) was Black; 12.5 percent of Hoehn-Saric, Frank, Imber, Nash, Stone, and Battle's sample (1964) was Black; a "similar percentage" of Strupp and Bloxom's sample of 122 (1973) was Black. In each of these studies, the remaining clients were white presumably. More recently, authors' samples (e.g., Zwick & Attkinson, 1985; Lambert & Lambert, 1984) have included a greater variety of VREG groups, but the race/ethnicity variable has been ignored in these studies as well. Consequently, the most that can be said at this time, based on currently available data, is that it is inappropriate to assume that the results of studies of prestructuring of therapy expectations necessarily pertain to any of the VREG-client groups.

Measured expectations. In those studies designed to determine whether these groups do, in fact, hold expectations for therapists or the therapy process that are incompatible with successful therapy, investigators have begun to compare the pretherapy expectations of specific racial/ethnic groups and occasionally to link these expectations with therapy outcome. When social class is controlled, results of these studies seem to indicate that VREG clients' therapy expectations may not differ very much from those of their Anglo counterparts.

For instance, Acosta (1979) found that lower socioeconomic Mexican-American and Anglo psychiatric outpatients were about equally likely to expect therapists mainly to ask them a lot of questions (49 percent vs 48 percent, respectively). Evans, Acosta, Yamamoto, and Hurwicz (1986) found that the expectations of Black, Hispanic, and White clients (of varied social class) were related to premature termination. Whereas the largest percentage of all three groups (Blacks = 55 percent; Hispanics = 43 percent; Anglos = 73 percent) sought therapy as a means of gaining insight and clarification, 26 percent of Hispanics and 15 percent of Blacks as compared to 9 percent of Whites sought the therapist's intervention in their social environment in some manner. This expectation for environmental intervention (81 percent of those with such expectations) was most strongly linked to the clients' terminating therapy without consulting their therapists.

Critique

Although it underlies the majority of the mental health literature on VREG populations, the CAP perspective has generated more theory and speculation than it has research. This speculative literature (and subsequent criticisms of it) frequently confounds general personality processes (e.g., development of self-concept), race/ethnicity, and economic factors (e.g., social class). Thus, one cannot tell whether recommendations and conclusions are intended to pertain only to members of particular racial/ethnic groups or people of particular social classes or people regardless of any of these cultural considerations.

Nevertheless, in spite of the relative lack of empirical information concerning the usefulness of the CAP perspective, this approach has raised investigators' awareness of intra- and cross-group racial/ethnic differences as possible sources of conflict in the counseling and psychotherapy process. It was in response to a perceived minimization of such intra-group differences and the overgeneralization of White cultural experiences to VREGs that researchers (e.g., Jackson & Kirschner, 1973; Gordon & Grantham, 1979) began to search for psychological variables (e.g., expectations, preferences) that could be used to operationalize client problems due to race/ethnicity more completely and diversely than was the case when the client's racial or ethnic group membership was blamed for all problems in the therapy and diagnostic processes. Moreover, acknowledgment of the possibility of VREG client diversity led to expanded consideration of therapist diversity as a potential source of whatever racial/ethnic barriers might occur in the therapy process.

THERAPIST-AS-PROBLEM (TAP) PERSPECTIVE

The basic premise of the TAP perspective is that if there are impediments to client progress or impasses in the therapy process, then these are largely due either to the (usually White) therapist's cultural insensitivity or his or her racial prejudice. The primary difference between insensitivity and prejudice seems to be that the former is a therapeutic error of omission (i.e., the therapist is unable to deliver adequate services because of her or his cultural naivete or ignorance) whereas the latter is an error of commission (i.e., the therapist is unable to deliver unbiased services because her or his own racial socialization experiences have contributed to automatic negative images of and perhaps behavior toward VREG clients). Obviously, these two categories of errors are not mutually exclusive, but are separated here for ease of discussion.

Therapist Insensitivity

In arguing their case for therapist insensitivity as the cause of friction in the helping process, various authors have asserted that White therapists as well as VREG therapists, trained in White institutions, lack awareness and understanding of and the competence to handle therapy situations resulting from the unique cultural experiences of VREG clients. Complaints have been lodged against mental health professional training programs for their lack of cultural content in curricula (Bernal, 1980; Bernal & Padilla, 1982; Boxley & Wagner, 1971; Wyatt & Parham, 1985); small numbers of VREG students and faculty (e.g.,

Atkinson, 1983a; W. Parham & Moreland, 1981); and lack of culture specific practica experiences (Guiterrez, 1982; Cook & Helms, 1988; Mitchell, 1970).

In a similar manner, professional mental health workers and organizations have been chided for their failure to attend to cultural factors in service delivery (Jackson, 1977; Wrenn, 1962; Wrenn, 1985). Thus a variety of writings suggest that it is hardly likely, for the most part, that therapists can competently offer culturally sensitive therapy unless they have acquired such competencies through self-education or osmosis of some sort.

As Hale (1977) points out, a prevailing norm in Anglo society is the "melting pot" philosophy, that is, the belief that immigrants and American VREGs should adapt the beliefs, customs, and behavioral patterns of Anglo society whether they want to or not. However, many VREG people value their racial/ ethnic distinctiveness and expect others to do so as well. Consequently, a problem can occur in therapy if the therapist, due to internalization of the melting pot norm, and/or lack of exposure to the life circumstances of VREGs, overlooks or minimizes the importance of race or culture to the client. Treatment barriers thought to evolve from insensitivity are (a) misunderstanding due to denial of the importance of racial/ethnic issues to the client; and (b) failure to understand the client's communications (Adebimpe, 1981; Block, 1981; Marcos & Alpert, 1976).

Treatment recommendations evolving from criticisms of therapist cultural insensitivity have been fairly consistent as to content and can be characterized as a series of vague generalities which have been summarized by E. Jones (1985) as follows: (1) "Develop a knowledge of the culture along with gaining experience in working with ethnic-minority clients. (2) Be prepared to adapt your techniques, especially the level of activity. (3) Communicate acceptance and respect for the client in terms that are intelligible and meaningful in his or her cultural frame of reference. (4) Be open to the possibility of more direct intervention in the life of the client than the traditional ethos of the psychological therapies might suggest" (p. 174).

Though one may criticize treatment generalities of the sort summarized by Jones on a number of grounds, two of the most serious are that there is currently no empirical evidence in support of these recommendations and there are no theoretical explanations for why the proposed treatment recommendations are more relevant to clients from VREGs than they are to Whites.

Therapist Prejudice

As a result of socialization in a discriminatory society, some authors contend that it is impossible for therapists to be entirely free of prejudice (A. Jones & Seagull, 1977; Rosen & Frank, 1972). Therefore, advocates of this position contend that therapists express their prejudice either overtly or covertly to clients in ways which do not differ markedly from the larger society and such expressions result in poor service delivery to VREG clients.

Specific treatment issues subsumed under this approach concern the extent to which therapists experience some form of "countertransference" that inhibits their ability to express accurate empathy when faced with a VREG client. A. Jones and Seagull (1977) summarized the ways in which countertransference might appear in the therapy relationship involving Black clients and White therapists. These include: (1) projecting unacceptable drives and impulses onto Blacks (e.g., they are over-sexed); (2) using a particular Black client to symbolize all Blacks; (3) seeking Black clients to allay guilt about one's own racism; (4) behaving in a paternalistic or authoritarian fashion; (5) discouraging the expression of anger; and (6) overzealousness in "helping" Blacks.

Additional authors have speculated about the probable impact of the therapist's countertransference on the therapy process. Possible communication barriers resulting therefrom have been hypothesized to include: (1) restricted diagnoses, for example, assuming that VREG clients necessarily have crippled personalities; (2) inflexible therapy process, for example, attribution of pathology to clients who express racial concerns; and (3) stereotypic therapist roles, for example, the "great White father syndrome" or belief that one must take care of VREG clients (Block, 1981; Smith, 1975; Vontress, 1971). Some immediate potential consequences to the client as a result of therapist countertransference include: (1) differential diagnoses in which Black and Native Americans receive more severe diagnoses than Whites (Abramowitz & Murray, 1983; Block, 1981; Hall & Maloney, 1983; Kleiner, Tuckman & Lovell, 1959), and (2) assignment to treatments requiring less therapist time and involvement such as crisis intervention and inpatient services rather than long-term outpatient psychotherapy (Mayo, 1974; Sue, McKinney, Allen & Hall, 1974).

Recommendations for what therapists should do if they are prejudiced seem to depend on how prejudiced they are. For instance, A. Jones and Seagull (1977), Kincaid (1969), and Barnes (1972) recommended that therapists with blatant racist attitudes should not counsel VREG clients, should leave VREG communities, and/or should be in therapy themselves. However, if it is true that some racism is inevitable, then questions arise as to how the therapist who is not a blatant racist should proceed. A. Jones and Seagull (1977) recommend the acquisition of self-knowledge through consultation with multiracial colleagues, participation in case conferences and discussion groups, and exposure to invited speakers with expertise in racial/ethnic psychology.

Therapist-as-Problem Research

The few studies with obvious implications for practice that have originated from the TAP perspective have occurred in response to the notion that insensitivity is the bugaboo in the therapy process. The empirical literature addressing insensitivity generally has examined the effects on VREG clients' perceptions of therapist credibility when the therapist's cultural awareness is increased.

In examining the consequences of teaching relevant cultural information to therapists, Evans, Acosta, Yamamoto, and Skilbeck (1984) exposed psychiatric residents and clinical psychology interns to a ten-and-one-half hour seminar series oriented toward the needs, cultural background, and expectations of working-class patients (mostly Black and Hispanic). Using the therapists as their own controls, Yamamoto, Acosta, Evans, and Skilbeck (1984) and Evans et al. found that therapists increased their factual knowledge of cultural issues and that clients, regardless of ethnicity, were more satisfied with the therapists after the therapists had received the culture-specific training. However, Christensen (1984), who exposed master's level counseling trainees to a training program, which sounds similar to those of Evans et al. and Yamamoto et al., found no differences between the trained group and a control group on judges' ratings of empathy and attending behavior. However, she did not obtain client evaluations of the counselor's performance. Perhaps cultural effects are most clearly demonstrable in those studies which use the reactions of participants (i.e., client or therapist) to evaluate effectiveness.

The role of therapist prejudice in the therapy process has been all but ignored in the empirical literature. In most therapy research since the mid-1960s, the responsibility for counselor prejudice has been shifted to the VREG client. Thus, rather than asking how therapists' prejudicial attitudes influence the therapy process (an omission noted by Sattler, 1977), researchers have tended to ask whether clients' preferences regarding race of therapist influence the therapy process. Most such investigations have been surveys or analogue studies in which VREG subjects react, usually by means of some sort of self-descriptive questionnaire (e.g., willingness to self-disclose to the therapist), to tapes, scripts, or descriptions of therapists alleged to be either White or from a VREG.

Several reviews of the counselor preference literature currently exist (e.g., Abramowitz & Murray, 1983; Atkinson, 1983b, 1985, 1986; Bryson & Bardo, 1973; Hall & Maloney, 1983; Harrison, 1975; Pine, 1972). Regardless of the race/ethnicity of the VREG samples being investigated, the results of this body of preference studies can generally be summarized as follows: Sometimes VREG clients prefer therapists of their own race/ethnicity and sometimes they do not. In passing, it should be noted that the preference literature actually reveals nothing about racial/ethnic prejudice—neither the therapist's nor the client's. It is at least possible that clients may prefer therapists of their own race/ethnicity without necessarily being prejudiced against therapists from other racial/ethnic groups.

Critique

Perhaps the primary contribution of the TAP perspective has been that the therapist is no longer considered to be omnipotent. Instead, it has become possible to recognize the therapist as a person who can be shaped by the same social influences that shape VREG clients. Thus, therapists can be seen as biased and insensitive almost to the same extent that clients can be perceived as resistant and hostile.

Yet missing from the TAP perspective, as it was from the CAP perspective, has been acknowledgment of the possible significance to the therapy process of the therapist's own cultural characteristics. Rather, therapists have continued to be viewed as merely reacting to VREG clients vis à vis clients' cultural or racial/ethnic issues. Thus, in a peculiar sort of way, cultural influences have continued to be considered as unidirectional—from VREG client to therapist. Nevertheless, in its advocacy of therapist insensitivity and racial/ethnic prejudice as contributors to therapy interactions, the TAP perspective has moved the field half a step closer to broadening the definition of race/ethnicity to include more than just the client's racial/ethnic category membership.

RACIAL/ETHNIC IDENTITY (REI) MODELS

The racial/ethnic identity models have evolved in response to the recognition that sociocultural and historical factors can contribute to diverse personality characteristics in therapists as well as clients. The racial/ethnic identity models represent the first systematic attempt to comprehend the diagnosis and treatment of VREG clients using culture-specific personality theory based primarily on psychological determinants (i.e., subjective and objective behavior) rather than racial/ethnic category.

In general, the REI models proposed that in the process of integrating the racial/ethnic aspect of themselves into their overall identity or self-concept, VREG members experience a variety of predictable life transitions and/or cultural adaptations. Some of these transitions or adaptations are viewed as being healthier and/or less psychologically damaging than others; each may have implications for the counselor's and client's behaviors during the psychotherapy process.

In the personality and psychotherapy theoretical literature, there exists at least one REI model for each of the major VREGs including Asian (Sue & Sue, 1971), Black (Cross, 1971), Hispanic (Szapocznik, Scopetta, Kurtines & Aranalde, 1978), and Native Americans (Runion & Gregory, 1984). Though the topic is beyond the scope of the present chapter, models for whites (Helms, in press) also have been proposed. Most of the VREG models are based on the underlying premise that the pressure to assimilate or acculturate into Anglo culture and/or the societal devaluation of VREG cultures is so great that sooner or later the VREG person must decide how he or she will cope with being a member of a disfavored group.

Generally, REI models can be classified as either typologies or stage models. Typologies postulate the existence of various psychological categories or modal personality styles of VREG people. Each category is generally assumed to represent an adaptation to some aspect of racial oppression. Different emotions or attitudes or values or behaviors are assumed to distinguish members of a particular category from those of other categories. Thus, to understand and/or predict a person's behavior, one must figure out which psychological category he or she belongs to. Presumably, belonging to a particular category constitutes a quite stable element of the person's identity.

Stage models postulate a (usually) linear process of racial/ethnic identity development that consists of specific identifiable stages. Predictable types of racial attitudes, emotions, values, and behaviors are assumed to vary with the person's stage of development. Therefore, to understand and/or predict a person's behavior, one must identify the person's stage of development. Later stages of development are assumed to be healthier and more enduring than earlier stages.

Since each of the models for the various VREGs appears to have been developed independently of the others, they probably all reflect attempts to operationalize a process common to the life-experiences of those VREGs who are subjected to racial/cultural discrimination. Elsewhere Helms (1990) has summarized several models for Blacks (and Whites). Table 7.1 summarizes the available models for the other major VREGs.

Diagnostic Use of the REI Models

The REI models have been used most often to diagnose or speculate about the characteristics of clients who display one form of identity development rather than another. For instance, if one were considering using a typology for diagnosing Native American clients, Table 7.1 shows that one could potentially choose from among four (i.e., Carroll, 1978; Chance, 1965; Lowrey, 1983; Spindler & Spindler, 1957). Notice that though the labels for the types differ, all agree that one type of person identifies with Native American culture exclusively (e.g., "Traditional People", "Native Type") and most agree that another type identifies with Anglo culture almost exclusively (e.g., "Non-Traditional," "Acculturated Types"). These are themes that are present in virtually all of the REI models regardless of whether they are typologies or stage models.

Although Lee (1988) has begun to investigate a stage model for Chinese and Korean Americans, for the most part, empirical study of stage models has been limited to Blacks. Of the various models for Blacks that have been proposed, (cf., Helms, 1990), Cross's Negro-to-Black conversion model (1971) has been used most frequently as the basis for defining the personality characteristics of Blacks as well as for speculating about the therapy process (cf., Cross, Parham & Helms, in press). Therefore, it might be useful to briefly summarize his model as modified by Helms (e.g., Helms, 1990, 1989, 1986, 1985, 1984). Cross (1971, 1978) proposed that en route to incorporating a positive Black identity, Black Americans in the United States go through a four- or five-stage racial identity developmental process. The process is more generally called "Nigrescence," meaning "to become Black," and has been evident in the culture-specific literature at least since the 1800s (cf. Cross et al, in press).

Nevertheless, as Cross et al. point out, the postulation of stage models initially occurred between 1968 and 1976, presumably in response to the Civil Rights activities of that era.

Cross's model (1971) proposes the following stages: (1) Preencounter, which is characterized by the denial of one's Blackness (that is, the person lacks a Black identity), devaluing of other Blacks and Black culture, and an idealization of Whites and White culture (i.e., internalization of a Euro-American identity); (2) Encounter, which is marked by a conscious decision to develop a Black identity and abandon one's White identity; (3) Immersion/Emersion, a stage in which the person "tries on" a new (often stereotypic) Black identity while denigrating Whites and White culture; and (4) Internalization, which is characterized by the development and internalizing of a positive personalized Black identity, a realistic valuing of Black culture as well as an acceptance of what is positive about White culture and a rejection of what is not; and (5) Internalization/Commitment, a stage in which the person engages in political and social activism aimed at eliminating cultural oppression of victims regardless of their race or ethnicity.

Each of the racial identity stages is assumed to have different attitudinal, behavioral, and affective consequences. For instance, the affect associated with the stages might include anxiety for Preencounter, euphoria for Encounter, anger for Immersion/Emersion, and none in particular for Internalization and Internalization/Commitment. Respective stage-related behaviors might include exclusive socializing with Whites, searching for Black associates, exclusive socializing with Blacks, or friendship selections not necessarily based on race.

Helms (1986) has recommended that the stages be considered to be world views, that is, nonconscious templates for organizing information about one's world. She further suggests that the stages are hypothetical personality constructs and are not directly assessable, just as other cognitive processes (e.g., intelligence) must be inferred from behaviors since they cannot be measured directly. Where racial/ethnic identity is concerned, Helms suggests that racial identity attitudes, feelings, behavioral styles, and other cognitions may be used to make inferences about the person's stage of identity. In operationalizing the Cross model, racial identity attitudes have been used most often to represent the stages, though they are not stages themselves, but merely one proposed correlate of them. The diagnostic implication of this interpretation is that rather than attempting to locate a person in a single stage on the basis of one type of attitude, it might be more useful to determine which types of attitudes are present in the person's personality configuration, since each type potentially influences the person's characteristics to some extent.

REI Models in the Therapy Process

Where the therapy process is concerned, the original attempts to use racial identity constructs to anticipate the psychotherapy process (e.g., Butler, 1975;

Table 7.1

Summary of Models of Racial/Ethnic Identity for Asians, Hispanics, and Native Americans

Author	Kind	Types/Stages		Personality Characteristics	
		Asian Americans			
Kitano (1982)	Typology	1.	negative Japanese-negative White	1.	identifies with neither White nor Japanese-American culture
		2.	positive White-negative Japanese	2.	identifies with White culture rejects Japanese-American culture
		3.	negative White-positive Japanese	3.	rejects White culture identifies Japanese-American culture
		4.	positive Japanese-positive White	4.	identifies with Japanese and White-American culture
Sue & Sue (1971)	Typology	1.	Asian-American	1.	idealizes Chinese American culture denigrates White culture
		2.	Traditional Chinese	2.	identifies with traditional Chinese culture
		3.	Marginal	3.	identifies with neither culture
		Hispanics			
Ruiz & Padilla (1977)	Typology	1.	Type A		committed to Hispanic and Anglo culture
		2.	Type B		strong commitment to Hispanic culture, weak commitment to Anglo culture
		3.	Type C		weak commitment to both cultures
		4.	Type D		strong commitment to Anglo culture, weak commitment to Hispanic culture
Szapocznik et al.	Typology	1.	Type 1	1.	identifies primarily with Anglo culture
		2.	Type 2	2.	identifies primarily with Cuban Culture
		3.	Type 3	3.	identifies with Cuban and Anglo culture
		4.	Type 4	4.	marginal person, identifies with neither culture

Table 7.1 (Continued)

Author	Kind	Types/Stages	Personality Characteristics
		Native Americans	
Carroll (1978)	Typology	1. Traditional Indian	1. rejects middle-class White values, favors present time orientation, harmony with nature, non-competitiveness and conformity
		2. Nontraditional	2. Wishes to be assimilated into White society and accepts White values such as future orientation, time consciousness, competitiveness, and nonconformity
Chance (1965)	Typology	1. Low, medium, high Western identification combined with low, medium, high intercultural contact	1. Nine types vary in the extent to which they prefer White cultural customs and have access to White community. Greater emotional disturbance is thought to be associated with low contact and high identification
Lowrey (1983)	Typology	1. Traditional People	1. takes pride in Indian culture, language, customs, beliefs; daily activities remain same as ancestors
		2. Acculturated People	2. straddles two cultures, pushes for change and White customs
		3. Autonomous People	3. bicultural, chooses positive values and beliefs from both Native and Anglo-American culture
Spindler Spindler (1957)	Typology	1. Native Type	1. immersed in Native American culture limited contact with White culture
		2. Reaffirmative Type	2. identifies with Native American culture as compensation for rebuffs by White culture
		3. Transitional Type	3. does not identify with Native American or White culture, shifts cultural loyalties unpredictably

Table 7.1 (Continued)

Author	Kind	Types/Stages		Personality Characteristics
		4.	Special Deviant Type	4. self-involved, uses religious ritual to resolve personal and cultural conflict
		5.	Acculturated Type	5. identifies with predominant local White group and uses achievement of success to submerge feelings and avoid aggressiveness

Parham & Helms, 1981) focused on client perceptions or preferences. That is, they attempted to determine whether diversity in the racial identity development of Black clients would differentially influence their view of cross-racial versus homoracial therapists.

Recently, Helms (1984) has begun to expand the REI theoretical orientation to explain situations more analogous to the psychotherapy process. Assumptions of her model are that (1) within racial/ethnic groups, the client's and therapist's racial group categories determine which REI model or models are applicable to each; (2) certain behaviors, attitudes, and emotions are differentially associated with the various stages of racial/ethnic identity; (3) one's manner of interacting with the client or therapist communicates information about one's level of racial identity development; and (4) the recipient (e.g., therapist or client) of such communications reacts in a manner congruent with her or his own level of racial identity development. Thus, in her Black/White interaction model, she proposes that therapists' and clients' respective stages of racial/ethnic identity development interact to determine the quality of the therapy interaction and its subsequent outcome for both participants.

Helms (1984) proposed four pure types of interactions or therapy relationships which she called "crossed," "parallel," "regressive," and "progressive." In crossed relationships, therapists and clients have opposite or contradictory racial identity world views; in parallel relationships, therapists and clients share similar racial identity world views; in regressive relationships, the client's cultural world view is more developmentally advanced than the therapist's world view; in progressive relationships, the therapist's racial identity world view is more developmentally advanced than the client's world view. Each type of dyad is hypothesized to result in predictable therapist-client relationship issues, therapist-client social influence strategies, and therapist-client outcome.

The proposed types of therapy relationships are hypothesized to occur within and across racial groups. So, for instance, if the client is Black and therapist is White, then parallel relationships are those in which they share analogous racial identity attitudes (e.g., Preencounter, Contact, etc.). It should be noted that Helms (1984) proposes different therapy dynamics, too numerous to repeat here, depending upon the particular combinations of attitudes expressed by therapist

Table 7.2

Examples of Therapy Relationship Types Involving Black Counselors and Clients

Preencounter-identifies with Whites rather than Blacks; has little or no regard for Blacks.	Preencounter-identifies with Whites rather than Blacks feels uncomfortable in relationships with Blacks.	Parallel-each reinforces the other's anti-Black/pro-White perspective.	Both counselor and client are afraid to be open because they fear one or the other will reveal stereotypic "Black" characteristics that are embarrassing to Blacks (e.g., weakness, hypersexuality). Both collude to avoid self-exposure.
Immersion/Emersion-rejects all that is not Black and to redefine relationships to fit a Black perspective.	Preencounter-rejects all that is not White and seeks to assimilate to White culture.	Crossed (Progressive)-Each struggles to hold onto an opposing world view.	Counselor attempts to raise client's racial consciousness often through haranguing; moralizing and lecturing client; is frightened by the message that he/she is defective in some mysterious way and reacts by withdrawing into his/her Euro-American identity and rejecting the "Black" counselor.
Encounter-wants to be Black; seeks role models to define a Black identity.	Immersion/Emersion-rejects all that is not Black; feels threatened by those who do not satisfy her/his conditions for Blackness.	Regressive-each wants to use the other to move forward in the identity process.	Counselor regards client as "noble savage" because of client's ability to identify with Black culture and express anger and rage. Counselor uses client as role model. Client regards counselor as naive and "too White" and defends self by becoming stereotypically Black
Internalization-does not have to prove self-worth through the client; encourages others to share their views of life.	Preencounter-is accustomed to rejecting Blacks and Blackness by stereotyping.	Progressive-each expects the therapist to to encourage change.	Counselor gently confronts blatant avoidance of emotional issues and structures the therapy experience for the client. Client admires competence, cannot neatly stereotype the counselor and gradually begins to examine racial identity issues.

and client. Accordingly, a parallel therapy dyad in which both participants share Preencounter attitudes should differ qualitatively from a parallel dyad in which they share Internalization attitudes. Presumably, the latter would be more therapeutic since participants could focus on the client's therapy issues rather than the therapist's and/or client's unresolved racial issues per se. Table 7.2 summarizes some outstanding characteristics of the four types of relationships when the therapists and clients are Black. The examples are elaborations of Hunt's descriptions (1987) of Black counselor–Black client supervision issues, though she did not actually use REI theory in her presentation.

Research Using the REI Models

Although theoretical formulations of the REI models preceded empirical investigations by many years, one can find the sprigs of two branches of research. The first concerns the extent to which racial identity can be used to describe the personality characteristics of VREG people, usually Blacks. The second concerns the manner in which racial identity influences various aspects of the therapy process. In both kinds of studies, racial identity attitudes have been used virtually exclusively to operationalize racial identity.

Personality characteristics. In the personality studies conducted by Helms and her colleagues, respondents use various personality measures to self-describe intrapsychic characteristics such as anxiety, self-esteem, and so on (cf., Helms, 1984). These measures are then correlated with responses to some version of the Racial Identity Attitude Scale (Helms & Parham, in press), a measure of four types of racial identity attitudes derived from Cross's model (1971). Support for Nigrescence theory would be differential correlations between the general personality characteristics and each of the types of attitudes.

In fact, some evidence does exist to suggest that the racial identity attitudes may be differentially related to intrapsychic characteristics. Parham and Helms (1985a, 1985b) found that Preencounter and Immersion/Emersion attitudes tended to be related to similar personality characteristics in similar directions. For instance, both tended to be associated with high anxiety and low self-esteem. However, Immersion/Emersion attitudes seemed to be uniquely related to anger. Thus, it is possibly the case that Preencounter attitudes are equivalent to an accommodationist reaction to racism whereas Immersion/Emersion attitudes may be equivalent to a militant reaction.

Carter and Helms (1987a) found that Black racial identity attitudes were predictive of Afrocentric cultural values (that is, having their roots in classic African culture), but not Eurocentric values (that is, having their roots in classic European culture). In particular, they found that Internalization attitudes were predictive of collateral social relationships, harmony with nature, and a "doing" activity orientation. Immersion/Emersion attitudes were also related to a belief in collateral or group-level social relationships. Based on Afrocentric theory (cf., Nobles, 1980), one would expect more "crystallized" or self-actualized Black identities to be related to Afrocentric values, a group rather than individual orientation in this case, and the results of Carter and Helms appear to have confirmed this expectation. Also, the active orientation associated with Internalization attitudes may be supportive of Cross's hypothesis (1971) that social activism is indicative of this stage of development of racial identity.

Furthermore, Carter and Helms (1987b) demonstrated that attitudes toward racial identity were not predicted by social class defined according to traditional (e.g., parents' education) and self-report measures. They interpret their results as evidence that social class and development of racial identity are not synonymous.

Thus, limited in quantity though it is, the existing empirical literature on the personality correlates of racial identity appears to indicate that the respective attitudes do tend to be related to different characteristics. Moreover, the relationships do seem to be consistent with current Nigrescence theory. Of course, more research is needed. In particular, the determination of the degree the REI models may be generalized requires some studies of other VREGs using relevant REI models.

Counseling process research. Researchers are gradually beginning to assess the applicability of racial identity theory to situations analogous to some aspect of the counseling process. The majority of these studies have used questionnaires (e.g., Parham & Helms, 1981; Morten & Atkinson, 1983) or vicarious participation analogues (e.g., Pomales, Claiborn & LaFromboise, 1986; Richardson, 1987). One study (Bradby & Helms, 1986) has examined therapy relationships.

The questionnaire studies have generally concerned Black respondents' preferences for counselors of the same race. In the first study that fits this genre, Parham and Helms (1981) administered a racial identity attitude inventory and a counselor preference measure to Black respondents. They found that Encounter and Immersion/Emersion attitudes tended to be predictive of preferences for Black counselors whereas Internalization attitudes did not; they also found that Preencounter attitudes tended to be related to preferences for White counselors. In a later study, using a Black racial identity model similar to the Cross (1971) models, Morten and Atkinson (1983) found support for a pro-Black/anti-White stage being associated with preference for Black counselors whereas their transcendent stage was not associated with preferences for counselors of a particular race. Ponterotto, Anderson, and Grieger (1986) found a tendency for Black men, but not women, to prefer a counselor of the same ethnicity if they were in the Encounter stage. Thus, taken together, the racial preference studies appear to support the usefulness of racial identity constructs in examining intragroup counselor preference and, if these findings generalize to actual counseling situations, may suggest that mental health settings might do well to consider such variables in matching Black clients and counselors.

Pomales, Claiborn, and LaFromboise (1986) published the first counseling analogue study in which the interaction of racial identity attitudes and content of the counseling session was examined. They used a videotaped analogue in which a White female counselor either did or did not discuss racial issues with a Black male client. Observers, who were classified as being either in the Encounter or Internalization stage of identity, evaluated the counselor in one of the sessions. Pomales et al. found that subjects with high Encounter attitudes preferred the counselor more when she discussed racial issues, whereas her discussion of racial issues made no significant difference for subjects whose Internalization attitudes were high. Their results may indicate that Encounter attitudes are the crucial factor in determining whether or not specific consideration of racial issues must occur in order for the Black client to be committed to the process. However, because subjects with Preencounter and Immersion/ Emersion attitudes were not included in their study and the observers were not actual clients, this conclusion remains speculative.

In apparently the only existing study of the relationship of clients' racial identity attitudes to their reactions to actual therapy interactions, Bradby and Helms (in press) measured twenty Black clients' racial identity attitudes prior to their first therapy session with White therapists. They also obtained client satisfaction ratings after a total of four or five sessions and counted the number of sessions clients actually attended. Bradby and Helms found that the various racial identity attitudes were related to different aspects of the therapy process: (1) Preencounter (denigrating Black/idealizing White) attitudes tended to be positively related to how many sessions clients attended therapy, such that the higher their Preencounter attitudes, the more sessions they attended; (b) Encounter (euphoric Black/confused White) and Internalization (transcendent) attitudes were significantly positively related to how satisfied clients were after five sessions. In other words, the higher their Preencounter attitudes, the more sessions with White therapists Black clients attended and the higher their Encounter and Internalization attitudes, the more satisfied the clients were with the early phase of therapy.

Bradby and Helms (in press) also measured therapist sensitivity to Black culture via Williams's Black Intelligence Test for Cultural Homogeneity (BITCH) (1972). An interesting incidental finding in their study was that to the extent that clients' Preencounter attitudes were high, their therapists' cultural sensitivity tended to be low. This might suggest that Black clients, who themselves lacked sensitivity to Black culture, were likely to be assigned, following the intake process, to a therapist whose Black cultural sensitivity also was low. Be that as it may, Bradby and Helms's findings appear to support somewhat Helms's argument (1984) that, in using racial/ethnic identity attitudes to analyze the counseling and psychotherapy process, one must take into account the interaction between the therapist's and the client's racial identity attitudes.

Critique

Taken together, the counselor preference, analogue, and therapy studies from the REI perspective suggest that racial identity attitudes may be useful constructs not only for promoting better therapist/client relationships (as the CAP and TAP perspectives intended), but also for deciding how the client should be treated and especially what the therapist should do once the client enters therapy. Nevertheless, more studies from this perspective using racial/ethnic groups other than or in addition to Blacks are needed so as to ascertain the applicability of REI constructs to a variety of VREG populations.

Some recommendations that can be derived from the REI perspective include the following: (1) the therapist should assess the client's racial identity either formally or informally to determine the extent to which the client's presenting problems may be aggravated by a lack of healthy racial/ethnic identity development. Cross et al., (in press) and Helms (1989) discuss some techniques in addition to attitudinal inventories that have been used for assessment purposes on an experimental basis; (2) the therapist should be familiar enough with the cultural variations and nuances of the VREG he or she is treating, as well as the societal stereotypes regarding the specific group, so that the therapist can avoid colluding with the client in maintaining a less than healthy identity. In this regard, most of the REI models advise that exclusive or primary identification with Anglo society should not be considered to be evidence of adequate psychological development for a VREG person; (3) the therapist, regardless of her or his race/ethnicity, should evaluate his or her own racial/ethnic identity development. Fortunately, workshops are becoming available by which such self evaluation can occur (cf., Carter, 1987; Helms, 1990; Katz & Ivey, 1977); (4) practitioners and researchers should begin to listen for and communicate to their colleagues the various ways that issues of racial identity development appear in the counseling and psychotherapy process so that such information can become a useful part of the lore of the mental health professions.

Admittedly these recommendations, as were those derived from the CAP and TAP perspectives, are based on a rather shaky empirical foundation. Yet it seems quite unlikely that effective psychotherapy approaches for VREG clients will become available until and unless therapists and researchers begin to use some systematic theoretical frameworks which encompass psychological variables to guide their interventions. The REI models seem to be excellent candidates for a theoretical perspective in which the particular life circumstances of the VREG client (and her or his therapist) can be incorporated into the counseling and psychotherapy process at multiple levels.

GENERAL CONCLUSIONS AND RECOMMENDATIONS

Though it has been expedient to consider the three major theoretical perspectives (CAP, TAP, REI) as though they are mutually exclusive, a more accurate portrayal is that they all overlap to some extent. At least in theory, each focuses in some way on psychological characteristics of the client and the counselor and the nature of the interaction between participants. They differ primarily in the amount of emphasis given to each of these aspects of the counseling process.

CAP Perspective

The CAP perspective that began as an attempt to ascertain how VREGs differed from Whites with respect to the counseling process is now being reformulated in ways that permit a broader definition of "the problem." Impasses in the process are not always considered to be attributable solely to the client's race/ethnicity per se. Instead, researchers and theorists are beginning to consider the role of cultural and sociopolitical factors in shaping the psychological characteristics with which VREGs enter the counseling process. They are also giving greater emphasis to the impact of the therapist and the broader society on the client's reactions and the subsequent therapy process.

Counseling process models that exhibit an expanded definition of the VREG clients' cultural adaptations are Sue and Sue's communication barriers model, (1977), Vontress's analysis (1971) of Black client/White therapist interactions, and Ridley's descriptions (1984) of various styles of Black client self-disclosure. None of these models has yet resulted in the use of theory-directed interventions where VREGs are concerned, but each offers a framework by which such interventions could be designed.

TAP Perspective

The TAP perspective originally evolved as an attempt to discover what was "wrong" with the therapist in terms of how he or she managed cultural issues in the therapy process. However, the source of potential difficulties was assumed to be the clients' and only occasionally the therapists' dysfunctional personality development. More recently, theorists and researchers (e.g., Evans et al., 1984; Arredondo-Dowd & Gonsalves, 1980; Johnson, 1987; Sue, Bernier, Durran, Feinberg, Pedersen, Smith & Vasquez-Nuttell, 1982) have begun to entertain the possibility that therapists' mismanagement of VREG clients' counseling issues may be due to deficits in skills rather than or in addition to deficits in personality development.

Greater attention to skill development does seem to have resulted in training models devoted to helping therapists become more comfortable in using their existing skills with VREG clients (Evans et al., 1984; Pedersen, 1977). Virtually missing from the mental health literature, however, is evidence that what the therapist does, that is, his or her skill usage, has any effect on the therapy process as it involves VREG clients. More descriptions of what therapists do (as opposed to how they feel) to help VREG clients is needed in the psychotherapy literature.

REI Perspective

The REI perspective seems to have the most potential for merging the various perspectives. It gives comparable attention to the characteristics of the client, the therapist, and their interaction. More importantly, it offers explanations for why people develop as they do that are equally applicable to clients and therapists from the same racial/ethnic groups. Consequently, whatever information one obtains about how clients function due to their racial/ethnic identity development ought also to be applicable to therapists of the same race/

ethnicity in some manner. Thus, a VREG client at a stage or level of racial/ethnic identity characterized by discomfort with therapists of their own racial/ethnic group might withdraw from the process by not showing up for subsequent appointments; therapists at the same stage might withdraw by referring the client or otherwise pushing him or her out of the process.

Although the REI models are gaining increasing popularity as frameworks for analyzing or diagnosing VREG clients' personality development (cf., Cross, Parham & Helms, in press; Lee, 1988), only one model (Helms, 1984) exists for anticipating how identity issues might influence the therapy process. Helms (1984) showed that her model can be used to analyze case studies retroactively, and Carter (1987) demonstrated that racial identity attitudes were differentially related to counselors' intentions and clients' reactions to therapists in counseling simulations; still there is currently no evidence that using REI models to conceptualize the therapy process from the beginning would make the process more responsive to the needs of VREG clients and/or their therapists. The hope is that practitioners will begin to use and write about their experiences in using such models to manage the therapy process.

GENERAL RESEARCH RECOMMENDATIONS

Where research and empirical investigations of racial/ethnic influences on the therapy process have been examined, with the exception of those operating from the REI perspective, counseling and psychotherapy researchers have tended to emphasize descriptive studies in which racial/ethnic group membership is used as the independent variable. In such studies, usually one VREG is compared to Whites on some single dependent variable considered to be crucial to the efficient functioning of the process (e.g., self-disclosure, talkativeness). To the extent that investigators obtain intergroup differences, they conclude that they have discovered something about the differential psychological characteristics of the groups being studied. However, in psychology, the term *psychological* is typically used to refer to overt and/or covert behavior; but knowledge of a person's racial group membership or classification actually reveals nothing about the person's behavior, particularly given that racial classifications are generally externally imposed in most existing research. That is, the researcher decides what racial/ethnic categories are germane and which physical characteristics mean that a person belongs to one group rather than another. Consequently, studies in which race/ethnicity has been used as an independent variable have generally contributed very little to our understanding of why VREG clients and their counselors behave as they do.

A psychological study of the effects of race/ethnicity on the therapy process minimally should involve three components: (1) racial classifications in which guidelines for determining how the researcher decided that the person belonged to one group rather than another are clearly specified; (2) at least one well defined psychological variable (e.g., behavior, attitude, personality characteristics) along with a theoretical explanation of why this variable is assumed to be differentially correlated with racial/ethnic group membership; and (3) a clearly described dependent variable whose contribution to the success of the counseling process is also outlined. In such a study, the second component would serve as the independent or predictor variable. In most research to date, this middle component has been missing. Nevertheless, investigators within each of the three perspectives recently have begun to remedy this omission by examining the relationships of hypothesized psychological correlates of race/ethnicity to particular aspects of the counseling and psychotherapy process.

CAP Perspective

Terrell and Terrell's study (1984) of the effect of Black clients' level of mistrust of Whites on their premature termination rates is a good exemplar of a psychological study from a CAP perspective for many reasons. In addition to incorporating a predictor variable for which they laid some theoretical foundation, they also conducted their study in an actual clinical setting. Studies of psychological predictor and criterion variables involving VREG clients in real-life settings are extremely rare. Moreover, Terrell and Terrell's findings suggest that if Black clients' level of mistrust of Whites could be used to match them with counselors according to race, then premature termination rates might be reduced. In addition, a more recent analogue study by Watkins and Terrell (1988) provides some information about the kinds of expectations Black clients might hold about White therapists when their levels of White mistrust are high. This kind of information could be useful in designing and testing interventions to improve rapport among Black clients and White counselors when race is an issue for the client.

More generally, expanding the numbers and quality of studies using psychological variables from the CAP perspective requires operationalizing and/or quantifying many of the personality variables that typically have been assumed to characterize VREG clients. By comparing clients whose levels of these kinds of variables differ, it should be possible to move beyond supposition about which client characteristics are impediments in the process.

TAP Perspective

An example of race-related psychological research from a TAP perspective is Berg and Wright-Buckley's study (1988) of the differential effects of racial similarity and interviewer disclosure on Black and White interviewees' self-disclosure. By manipulating the interviewers' behavior in their counseling analogue study (i.e., assuming that what the interviewer does may influence the process), they were able to show that Black interviewees were only nondisclosive when their White interviewers were also nondisclosive. Thus, for the researcher (or practitioner) interested in improving the quality of therapy relationships involving White therapists and Black clients, Berg and Wright-Buckley's findings suggest that the therapist's behavior might be one place to start.

Many studies of the therapists' contribution to the therapy process need to be conducted. Berg and Wright-Buckley (1988) provided one strategy that could be used to conduct such studies. By operationalizing other psychological variables in a similar manner one could probably obtain a clearer picture of what sorts of therapist-initiated interventions might improve the process.

Nevertheless, it should be noted that according to the TAP perspective, the therapists' feelings, behavior, and so on are alleged to influence their *own* reactions to the process. Berg and Wright-Buckley's study (1988) does not address therapist reactions. Few TAP studies do. Therefore, in the future, more studies are needed in which the therapists' reactions to racial/ethnic issues are the focus of inquiry.

REI Perspective

The REI perspective relies, of course, on psychological variables (e.g., attitudes, behaviors, etc.) to define the counseling diagnosis and therapy processes. What is needed from this perspective is more studies focusing on the behavioral implications of differential racial/ethnic identity development. That is, more knowledge is needed about whether or not knowledge of a person's level of racial identity attitudes (for instance) allows one to make meaningful predictions about any other aspect of the person's behavior.

Carter's studies (in press, 1987) of racial identity attitudes in counseling simulations provide several examples of how behavioral correlates of racial identity attitudes might be examined. In his studies he examined therapists' and clients' intentions and reactions, respectively, during participation in a counseling simulation concerning racial issues. In one set of studies, he correlated racial identity attitudes with counselors' and clients' self-reported levels of various intentions and reactions. His findings indicated that racial identity attitudes were differentially related to the kinds of intentions and reactions participants reported experiencing. Whereas most studies from the REI perspective have focused on diagnostic uses, that is, determining which client personality characteristics are related to which racial identity attitudes, Carter's studies suggest that it is possible to use the perspective to examine interactional or behavioral variables involving counselors and clients.

Although the quantity of research based on the three perspectives is quite limited, the emergence of attempts to redefine race/ethnicity in ways that have psychological meaningfulness does suggest that it ought to be possible to do so. Nevertheless, creating a larger data base from which to make inferences about how racial/cultural variables influence the therapy process will require greater methodological diversity than has been exhibited in the past. Yet if the mental health professions are to move out of the armchairs of futile speculation and into the arena of actually helping VREG clients, then it is necessary that researchers and practitioners dedicate themselves to creating and implementing more diverse ways of asking whether and how race and ethnicity matter in the counseling and psychotherapy process.

NOTE

The author wishes to thank Gordon Rice for his assistance in preparing this manuscript.

REFERENCES

Abramowitz, S. I. & Murray, J. (1983). Race effects in psychotherapy. In J. Murray and P. Abramowitz (Eds.), *Bias in Psychotherapy* (pp. 215–255). New York: Praeger.

Acosta, F. X. (1979). Pretherapy expectations and definitions of mental illness among minorities and low-income patients. *Hispanic Journal of Behavioral Sciences, 1,*(4), pp. 403–410.

Acosta, F. X., Yamamoto, J. & Evans, L. A. (1982). *Effective Psychotherapy for Low-Income and Minority Patients.* New York: Plenum Press.

Adams, W. A. (1950). The Negro patient in psychiatric treatment. *American Journal of Orthopsychiatry, 20,* 305–310.

Adebimpe, V. R. (1981). Overview: White norms and psychiatric diagnosis of Black patients. *American Journal of Psychiatry, 138*(3), 279–285.

Arredondo-Dowd, P. & Gonsalves, J. (1980). Preparing culturally effective counselors. *The Personnel and Guidance Journal, 59,* 376–378.

Atkinson, D. R. (1986). Similarity in counseling. *The Counseling Psychologist, 14,* 319–354.

———. (1985). Research on cross-cultural counseling and psychotherapy: A review and update of reviews. In P. Pedersen (Ed.), *Handbook of Counseling and Therapy* (pp. 191–197). Westport, CT: Greenwood Press.

———. (1983a). Ethnic minority representation in counselor education. *Counselor Education and Supervision, September,* 5–17.

———. (1983b). Ethnic similarity in counseling psychology: A review of research. *Counseling Psychologist, 11*(3), 79–92.

Barnes, E. J. (1972). The Black community as the source of positive self-concept for Black children: A theoretical perspective. In R. L. Jones (Ed.), *Black Psychology* (pp. 106–130). New York: Harper & Row.

Berg, J. H. & Wright-Buckley, C. Effects of racial similarity and interviewer intimacy in a peer counseling analogue. *Journal of Counseling Psychology,* 1988, *35,* 377–384.

Bernal, M. E. (1980). Hispanic issues in psychology: Curricula and training. *Hispanic Journal of Behavioral Sciences, 2*(2), 129–146.

Bernal, M. E. & Padilla, A. M. (1982). Status of minority curricula and training in clinical psychology. *American Psychologist, 37,* 783–787.

Block, L. B. (1981). Black Americans and the cross-cultural counseling and psychotherapy experience. In A. J. Marsella & P. B. Pedersen (Eds.), *Cross-Cultural Counseling and Psychotherapy* (pp. 177–194). New York: Pergamon Press.

Boykins, L. (1959). Personality aspects of counseling the Negro college student. *Quarterly Review of Higher Education among Negroes, 27,* 64–73.

Boxley, R. & Wagner, N. N. (1971). Clinical psychology training programs and minority groups: A survey. *Professional Psychology, 2,* 75–81.

Bradby, D. & Helms, J. E. (in press). Black racial identity attitudes and White therapist cultural sensitivity in cross-racial therapy dyads: An exploratory study. Paper submitted for publication.

Bransford, J. (1982). To be or not to be: Counseling with American Indian clients. *Journal of American Indian Education, 21,*(3), 18–21.

Brown, L. (1951). Psychoanalysis vs. the Negro people. *Masses and Mainstream, 4,* 16–24.

Bryson, S. & Bardo, H. (1973). Race and the counseling process: An overview. *Journal of Non-White Concerns in Personnel and Guidance, 4,* 5–15.

Butler, R. D. (1975). Psychotherapy: Implications of a Black-consciousness process model. *Psychotherapy: Theory, Research and Practice, 12,* 407–411.

Carroll, R. E. (1978). Academic performance and cultural marginality. *Journal of American Indian Education, October,* 11–16.

Carter, R. T. (in press). Does race or racial identity attitudes influence the counseling process? In J. E. Helms (Ed.), *Black and White Racial Identity:* Theory, Research, and Practice. Westport, CT: Greenwood Press.

———. (1987). *An empirical test of a theory on the influence of racial identity attitudes on the counseling process within a workshop setting.* Unpublished Doctoral Dissertation. University of Maryland, College Park, MD.

Carter, R. T. & Helms, J. E. (1987a). The relationship between racial identity attitudes and socioeconomic status. *Journal of Negro Education.* (Also ERIC, March 6, Microfilm No. ED 250 423).

———. (1987b). The relationship of Black value-orientations to racial identity attitudes. *Measurement and Evaluation in Counseling and Development, 19,* 185–195.

Casas, J. M., Wampold, B. E. & Atkinson, D. R. (1981). The categorization of ethnic stereotypes by university counselors. *Hispanic Journal of Behavioral Sciences, 3,* 75–82.

Chance, N. (1965). Acculturation, self-identification, and adjustment. *American Anthropologist, 67,* 372–393.

Christensen, C. P. (1984). Effects of cross-cultural training on helper response. *Counselor Education and Supervision, 23*(4), 311–320.

Cook, D. A. (1983). *A survey of ethnic minority clinical and counseling of graduate students' perceptions of their cross-cultural supervision experiences.* Unpublished doctoral dissertation, Southern Illinois University.

Cook, D. A. & Helms, J. E. (1988). Relationship dimensions as predictors of visible racial/ethnic group students' perceptions of cross-racial supervision. *Journal of Counseling Psychology, 35,* 268–274.

Cross, W. E., Jr. (1978). Models of psychological Nigrescence: A literature review. *Journal of Black Psychology, 5,* 13–31.

———. (1971). The Negro-to-Black conversion experience. *Black World, 20,* 13–27.

Cross, W. E., Jr., Parham, T. A. & Helms, J. E. (in press). Nigrescence revisited: theory and research. In R. L. Jones (Ed.), *Advances in Black Psychology* (Volume 1). Berkeley, CA: Cobb & Henry.

De La Cancela, V. (1985). Toward a sociocultural psychotherapy for low-income ethnic minorities. *Sociocultural Psychotherapy, 427–435.*

Dinges, N. G., Trimble, J. E., Mason, S. M. & Pasquale, F. L. (1981). Counseling and psychotherapy with American Indians and Alaskan Natives. In A. J. Marsella & P. B. Pedersen (Eds.), *Cross-Cultural Counseling and Psychotherapy* (pp. 243–276). New York: Pergamon Press.

Evans, L. A., Acosta, F. X., Yamamoto, J. & Hurwicz, M. (1986). Patient requests: Correlates and therapeutic implications for Hispanic, Black, and Caucasian patients. *Journal of Clinical Psychology, 42*(1), 213–221.

Evans, L. A., Acosta, F. X., Yamamoto, J. & Skilbeck, W. M. (1984). Orienting psychotherapists to better serve low income and minority patients. *Journal of Clinical Psychology, 40,*(1), 90–96.

Gardner, R. (1971). Therapeutic relationship under varying conditions of race. *Psychotherapy: Theory, Research, and Practice, 8,* 78–86.

Giorgis, T. W. & Helms, J. E. (1980). A comparison of the locus of control and anxiety level of African, Black American, and White American College Students. *Journal of College Student Personnel, November,* 503–509.

Gordon, M. & Grantham, R. J. (1979). Helper preference in disadvantaged students. *Journal of Counseling Psychology, 28,* 87–89.

Grier, W. & Cobbs, P. (1968). *Black Rage.* New York: Basic Books.

Guiterrez, F. (1982). Working with minority counselor education students. *Counselor Education and Supervision, 21,* 218–226.

Hale, J. E. (1977). De-mythicizing the education of Black children. In R. L. Jones (Ed.), *Black Psychology* (pp. 221–230). New York: Harper & Row.

Hall, G. C. N. & Maloney, N. H. (1983). Cultural control in psychotherapy with minority clients. *Psychotherapy: Theory, Research, and Practice, 20,* 131–142.

Harper, F. D. (1973). What counselors must know about the social sciences of Black Americans. *Journal of Negro Education, 42,* 109–116.

Harrison, D. K. (1975). Race as a counselor-client variable in counseling and psychotherapy: A review of the research. *Counseling Psychologist, 5,* 124–133.

Helms, J. E. (Ed.). (1990). *Black and White racial identity; Theory, research and practice.* Westport, CT: Greenwood Press.

———. (1989). Considering some methodological issues in racial identity research in counseling psychology. *The Counseling Psychologist, 17,* 227–252.

———. (1986). Expanding racial identity theory to cover the counseling process. *Journal of Counseling Psychology, 33,* 62–64.

———. (1985). Cultural identity in the treatment process. In P. Pedersen (Eds.), *Handbook of Cross-Cultural Counseling and Therapy* (pp. 239–245). Westport, CT: Greenwood Press.

———. (1984). Toward a theoretical model for assessing the effects of race on counseling: A Black-White interaction model. *The Counseling Psychologist, 12*(4), 153–165.

Helms, J. E. & Parham, T. A. (in press). The development of the Racial Identity Attitude Scale. In R. Jones (Ed.), *Handbook of Black Personality Measures.*

Hoehn-Saric, R., Frank, J. D., Imber, S. D., Nash, E. H., Stone, A. R. & Battle, C. C. (1964). Systematic preparation of patients for psychotherapy: I. Effects on therapy behavior and outcome. *Journal of Psychiatric Research, 2,* 267–281.

Hunt, P. (1987). Black clients' implications for supervision of trainees. *Psychotherapy, 21,* 114–119.

Jackson, G. G. (1977). The emergence of a Black perspective in counseling. *Journal of Negro Education, Summer,* 230–253.

———. (1972). Black youth as peer counselors. *Personnel and Guidance Journal, 51,* 280–285.

Jackson, G. G. & Kirschner, S. A. (1973). Racial self-designation and preference for a counselor. *Journal of Counseling Psychology, 20,* 560–564.

Johnson, S. D. (1987). "Knowing that" vs. "knowing how": toward achieving expertise in multicultural training for counseling. *The Counseling Psychologist, 15*(2), 320–331.

Jones, A. & Seagull, A. A. (1977). Dimensions of the relationship between the Black client and the White therapist: A theoretical overview. *American Psychologist, 32*(10), 850–855.

Jones, E. E. (1985). Psychotherapy and counseling with Black clients. In P. Pedersen (Ed.), *Handbook of Cross-Cultural Counseling and Therapy* (pp. 173–179). Westport, CT: Greenwood Press.

———. (1978). Effects of race on psychotherapy process and outcome: An exploratory investigation. *Psychotherapy: Theory, Research, and Practice, 15*(3), 226–236.

Kardiner, A. & Ovesey, L. (1951). *The mark of oppression: Exploration in the personality of the American Negro.* New York: Norton.

Katz, J. H. & Ivey, A. (1977). White awareness: The frontier of racism awareness training. *Personnel and Guidance Journal, 55,* 485–487.

Kincaid, M. (1969). Identity and therapy in the black community. *Personnel and Guidance Journal, 47,* 884–890.

Kitano, H. H. (1982). Mental Health in the Japanese American Community. In E. E. Jones & S. J. Korchin (Eds.) (1982), *Minority Mental Health,* New York: Praeger Publishers.

Kleiner, R. J., Tuckman, J. & Lovell, M. (1959). Mental disorder and status based on religious affiliation. *Human Relations, 12,* 273–276.

Lambert, R. G. & Lambert, M. J. (1984). The effects of role preparation for psychotherapy on immigrant clients seeking mental health services in Hawaii. *Journal of Community Psychology, 12,* 263–275.

Lee, S. R. (1988). *Self-concept correlates of Asian American cultural identity attitudes.* Unpublished doctoral dissertation, University of Maryland, College Park, MD.

Lerner, B. (1972). *Therapy in the ghetto: Political importance and personal disintegration.* Baltimore: Johns Hopkins University Press.

Levine, E. S. & Padilla, A. M. (1980). *Crossing cultures in therapy: Pluralistic counseling for Hispanics.* California: Brooks/Cole.

Lowrey, L. (1983). Bridging a culture in counseling. *Journal of Applied Rehabilitation Counseling, 14,* 69–73.

Marcos, L. R. & Alpert, M. (1976). Strategies and risks in psychology with bilingual patients: The phenomena of language independence. *American Journal of Psychiatry, 133,* 1275–1278.

Mayo, J. A. (1974). The significance of sociocultural variables in the psychiatric treatment of outpatients. *Comprehensive Psychiatry, 15*(6), 471–482.

Mitchell, H. (1970). The Black experience in higher education. *Counseling Psychologist, 2,* 30–36.

Morten, G. H. & Atkinson, D. R. (1983). Minority identity development and preference for counselor race. *Journal of Negro Education, 52*(2), 156–161.

Nobles, W. W. (1980). African philosophy: Foundations for Black psychology. In R. L. Jones (Ed.), *Black Psychology* (23–36). New York: Harper & Row.

Parham, T. A. & Helms, J. E. (1985a). Relation of racial identity attitudes to self-actualization and affective states of Black students. *Journal of Counseling Psychology, 32*, 431–440.

———. (1985b). Attitudes or racial identity and self-esteem of Black students: An exploratory investigation. *Journal of College Student Personnel, 26*, 143–147.

———. (1981). The influence of Black students' racial identity attitudes on preference for counselor's race. *Journal of Counseling Psychology, 28*, 250–257.

Parham, W. D. & Moreland, J. R. (1981). Nonwhite students in counseling psychology: A closer look. *Professional Psychology, 12*, 499–507.

Parker, W. M. & McDavis, R. J. (1983). Attitudes of Blacks toward mental health agencies and counselors. *Journal of Non-White Concerns in Personnel and Guidance, 56*, 94–100.

Pedersen, P. B. (1977). The triad model of cross-cultural counselor training. *Personal and Guidance Journal, 56*, 94–100.

Pinderhughes, C. A. (1973). Racism and psychotherapy. In C. U. Willie, B. M. Kramer & B. S. Brown (Eds.), *Racism and mental health* (pp. 61–121). Pittsburgh: University of Pennsylvania Press.

Pine, G. J. (1972). Counseling minority groups: A review of the literature. *Counseling and Values, 17*(1), 35–44.

Pomales, J., Claiborn, C. D. & LaFromboise, T. D. (1986). Effects of Black students' racial identity on perceptions of White counselors varying in cultural sensitivity. *Journal of Counseling Psychology, 33*, 58–62.

Ponterotto, J. G., Anderson, W. H. & Grieger, I. Z. (1986). Black students attitude toward counseling as a function of racial identity. *Journal of Multicultural Counseling and Development, 14*(2), 50–59.

Richardson, T. (1987). *The relationship of Black males' racial identity attitudes to perceptions of parallel counseling dyads.* Unpublished masters thesis, University of Maryland, College Park, MD.

Ridley, C. R. (1984). Clinical treatment of the nondisclosing Black client: A therapeutic paradox. *American Psychologist, 39*, 1234–1244.

Rivera, O. & Cespedes, R. (1983). Rehabilitation counseling with disabled Hispanics. *Journal of Applied Rehabilitation Counseling, 20*, 65–71.

Rosen, H. & Frank, J. D. (1972). Negroes in psychotherapy. *American Journal of Psychiatry, 119*, 456–460.

Ruiz, R. H. & Padilla, A. M. (1977). Counseling Latinos. *Personnel and Guidance Journal, 55*, 401–408.

Runion, K. & Gregory, H., Jr. (1984). Training Native Americans to deliver mental health services to their own people. *Counselor Education and Supervision, 23*(3), 225–233.

Sattler, J. M. (1977). The effects of therapist-client racial similarity. In A. S. Gurman and A. M. Razdin (Eds.), *Effective Psychotherapy: A Handbook of Research* (pp. 252–290). New York: Pergamon Press.

Sloane, R. B., Cristol, A. H., Pepernick, M. C. & Staples, F. R. (1970). Role preparation and expectation of improvement in psychotherapy. *Journal of Nervous and Mental Disease, 150,* 18–26.

Smith, E. J. (1975). Profile of the black individual in vocational literature. *Journal of Vocational Behavior, 6,* 41–59.

Spindler, G. D. & Spindler, L. S. (1957). American Indian personality types and their sociocultural roots. *Annals of the American Academy of Political and Social Science, 311,* 147–157.

Strupp, H. H. & Bloxom, A. (1973). Preparing lower-class patients for group psychotherapy: Development and evaluation of a role-induction film. *Journal of Consulting and Clinical Psychology, 41,* 373–384.

Sue, D. W. (1978). Eliminating cultural oppression in counseling: Toward a general theory. *Journal of Counseling Psychology, 25,* 419–428.

Sue, D. W., Bernier, J. E., Durran, A., Feinberg, L., Pedersen, P., Smith, E. J. & Vasquez-Nuttall, E. (1982). Position paper: Cross-cultural counseling competencies. *The Counseling Psychologist, 10*(2), 45–52.

Sue, D. W. & Sue, D. (1977). Barriers to effective cross-cultural counseling. *Journal of Counseling Psychology, 24,* 420–429.

Sue, S. (1988). Psychotherapeutic services for ethnic minorities: Two decades of research findings. *American Psychologist, 43,* 301–308.

Sue, S. & Kitano, H. H. L. (1973). Stereotypes as a measure of success. *Journal of Social Issues, 29*(2), 83–98.

Sue, S., McKinney, H., Allen, D. & Hall, H. (1974). Delivery of community mental health services to black and white clients. *Journal of Consulting and Clinical Psychology, 42*(6), 794–801.

Sue, S. & Sue, D. W. (1971). Chinese-American personality and mental health. *Amerasia Journal, 1,* 36–49.

Sue, S. & Zane, N. (1987). The role of culture and cultural techniques in psychotherapy: A critique and reformulation. *American Psychologist, 42,* 37–45.

Szapocznik, J., Scopetta, M. A., Kurtines, W. & Aranalde, M. D. (1978). Theory and measurement of acculturation. *Inter-American Journal of Psychology, 12,* 113–130.

Terrell, F. & Terrell, S. (1984). Race of counselor, client, sex, cultural mistrust level, and premature termination from counseling among Black clients. *Journal of Counseling Psychology, 31,* 371–375.

Tounsel, P. L. & Jones, A. C. (1980). Theoretical considerations for psychotherapy with Black clients. In R. L. Jones (ed.), *Black Psychology* (pp. 429–438). New York: Harper & Row.

Trimble, J. E. (1981). Value differentials and their importance in counseling American Indians. In P. Pederson, J. Draguns, W. Lonner, & J. Trimble (Eds.), *Counseling across cultures* (pp. 203–226). Honolulu: University of Hawaii Press.

Valdes, M. R. (1983). Psychotherapy with Hispanics. *Psychotherapy in Private Practice, 1*(1), 55–62.

Vontress, C. E. (1971). Racial differences: impediments to rapport. *Journal of Counseling Psychology, 18,* 7–13.

———. (1969). Cultural barriers in the counseling relationship. *Personnel and Guidance Journal, 48,* 11–17.

Watkins, C. E. & Terrell, F. (1988). Mistrust level and its effect on counseling expectations in Black client-White counselor relationships: An analogue study. *Journal of Counseling Psychology, 35,* 194–197.

Williams, R. L. (1972). The BITCH Test (Black Intelligence Test of Cultural Homogeneity). Black Studies Program, Washington University, St. Louis, MO 63130.

Wrenn, C. G. (1985). Afterword: The culturally encapsulated counselor revisited. In P. Pederson (Ed.), *Handbook of Cross-Cultural Counseling and Therapy* (pp. 323–329). Westport, CT: Greenwood Press.

———. (1962). The culturally encapsulated counselor. *Harvard Educational Review, 32,* 444–449.

Wyatt, G. C. & Parham, W. D. (1985). The inclusion of culturally sensitive course materials in graduate school and training programs. *Psychotherapy, 22,* 461–468.

Yamamoto, J., Acosta, F. X., Evans, L. A. & Skilbeck, W. M. (1984). Orienting therapists about patients' needs to increase patient satisfaction. *American Journal of Psychiatry, 141*(2), 274–276.

Zwick, R. & Attkisson, C. C. (1985). Effectiveness of a client pretherapy orientation videotape. *Journal of Counseling Psychology, 32,* 514–524.

8

Stress and Stress-Related Disorders in Hispanics: Biobehavioral Approaches to Treatment

Guillermo A. Argueta-Bernal

Stress is a term that in recent years has been studied extensively and has been seen as playing an integral role in the onset of many disorders. Included among these disorders are headaches, cardiovascular problems, gastrointestinal problems, borderline hypertension, and many other psychological and psychophysiological conditions (Cohen, Williamson, Monguillat, Hutchinson, Gottlieb & Waters, 1983; James, Hartnett & Kalsbeck, 1983; Whitehead & Basmajian, 1982).

There are three basic conceptual models that have been used to study stress: (1) stress as a dependent variable, (2) stress as an independent variable, and (3) stress as a lack of fit between the individual and the environment. The work of Selye (1956) characterizes the research on stress as a dependent variable. In this model the individual's response to a noxious environment is viewed as stress. This approach has influenced numerous researchers, including Holmes and Rahe (1967) and Holmes and Masuda (1974). The second conceptual model describes stress in terms of the stimulus characteristics of noxious environments. Weitz (1970) reviewed and classified different factors that have been viewed as stressful, including heat, cold, noise, and other environmental stimuli. The third model characterizes stress as the reflection of a lack of fit between the individual and the environment (Cox, 1979). In this schema, both the antecedents and the effects of stress are studied. The lack of fit is seen as occurring between the perceived and actual demand on the individual, and the perceived and actual capability of the individual. This lack of fit produces the experience of stress, and has various psychological, physiological, and behavioral consequences.

There is some evidence of high levels of stress among Hispanics (Vega, Warheit & Palacio, 1985). For example, Mexican-American males tend to have more alcohol-related arrests (Caetano, 1984), and to use the hospital emergency rooms more frequently than Anglos (Cornelius, Chavez & Jones, 1984). Considering that many sociological and psychiatric studies (Fabrega, 1969; Brody, 1970; Favazza, 1980) have linked such factors as poverty, ethnicity, and rapid social or cultural change to personal pathology, the Hispanic immigrant is clearly at high risk for general psychopathology (Cohen, 1979; Vega, Warheit, Buhl-Auth & Meinhardt, 1984) and its behavioral concomitants (Shannon & Shannon, 1973; Szapocznik, Scopetta, & King, 1978).

This chapter will selectively review the literature on stress and stress-related disorders in Hispanics, discuss conceptual and methodological issues relevant to this literature, and outline a conceptual model for the assessment and treatment of stress in the Hispanic population.

STRESSORS IN THE HISPANIC POPULATION

Many factors have been considered relevant to a conceptualization of stress in the Hispanic population. None of these factors by themselves can account for the psychological problems observed among Hispanics, but they can be conceptualized as marker variables (Price, 1981). These marker variables, in turn, can help researchers outline relevant problems and develop better research strategies and methods of clinical intervention. The most salient factors include demographic factors, life events, and the effects of migration.

Demographic Factors

Among the demographic factors associated with stress are socioeconomic status, education, occupation, and ethnicity. While few studies have investigated these demographic components with Hispanics, the work done with Anglo populations may, to a certain extent, be extrapolated to Hispanic populations. For example, the findings of Pearlin (1975) regarding depression among men and women may well apply to Hispanics. Specifically, low socioeconomic status Hispanics typically have large families and young children, both of which have been associated in Anglos with a high incidence of depression among women. Among men, depression has been linked to job dissatisfaction. In a similar context, the research of Dohrenwend and Dohrenwend (1969) has shown an inverse linear relationship between education and symptoms of psychological distress in Anglos. It is likely that this same relationship exists among Hispanic populations.

For many low-income Hispanics, another source of stress is the type of jobs they have. Usually these jobs are exhausting, physically dangerous, and often demeaning. The type and pace of work that Hispanics encounter from farm labor to sweat shops tends to reinforce marginal adjustment and a sense of powerlessness. In addition, inadequate income may lead to poor living and health conditions, as well as to life-styles that may produce destructive interpersonal relations.

Life Events

In the early work of Rahe and Arthur (1978), the role of life events was recognized as being influential in the development of stress disorders. Most of the research in the last twenty years has been based on variations of the model proposed by Holmes and Rahe (1967) and expanded by Rahe and Arthur (1978). These authors suggest that stress is caused by life changes that disrupt well-developed behavioral patterns. When faced with these disruptions, individuals seek to mobilize physiological, behavioral, and psychological efforts to cope with these changes. When the frequency or intensity of change exceeds the individual's ability to cope, illness follows.

The research in the area of life events and stress has been rather simplistic. In general, this research has treated life events as an undifferentiated and uni-dimensional construct, ignoring all the possible mediating variables that might affect the relationship between life events and stress-related disorders. More recently, the literature has begun to examine the relationship between specific types of life events and specific types of disorders. There appears to be, for example, a relationship between anxiety, depression, and negative events beyond the control of the individual (Sarason, Johnson & Siegel, 1978; Roth & Hough, 1979; Warheit, 1979).

Among the life events that may affect the Hispanics' mental health are sudden, unanticipated changes in personal circumstances such as accidents, death of close family members, severe illness, and unemployment. While few studies have examined the frequency and impact of these events among Hispanics, it may be hypothesized that this group is more likely to experience these changes since Hispanics are low in socioeconomic status, are transient, and are employed in unskilled jobs.

Vega, Hough, and Romero (1983) have documented the frequency with which stress due to life events occurs in immigrant Hispanics. Vega, Warheit, and Palacio (1985) surveyed the Mexican-American population and found that they tend to report higher numbers of stressful events. Furthermore, those experiencing the most stress also report more psychiatric symptoms. The strains and events of life are closely related (Pearlin & Schooler, 1978). Among Hispanics, stressors such as inability to speak English can precipitate events (e.g., loss of a job, trouble with the law), which in turn can result in stress. The six potential areas of strain identified by Pearlin (1983) may have applicability to minority groups. These include: (1) the problems an individual may have in carrying out the task to be performed; (2) interpersonal problems with role sets; (3) interpersonal problems as the result of having multiple role sets; (4) undesirable roles; (5) gain or loss of roles; and (6) restructuring and changing of role within role sets.

Few studies have addressed the issue of the relative importance of changes due to life events among Hispanics. Fairbank and Hough (1981) concluded in their review that ethnic minority individuals in the United States and in third world countries tended to rate life events having to do with economic and basic bodily needs as more stressful than those having to do with personal or interpersonal issues. An earlier study by Komaroff, Masuda, and Holmes (1968) found that blacks, Mexican-Americans, and Asians rated events quite differently from the Anglos studied by Holmes and Rahe (1967). The items on which there were significant differences in rating dealt with labor, income, and living conditions, all of which were seen by the ethnic minority groups as requiring some change and adaptation.

In another early study, Janney, Masuda, and Holmes (1977) compared the impact of a natural catastrophe, an earthquake, on the lives of individuals. Ratings of residents in two Peruvian cities were compared with those from individuals residing in El Salvador and Spain. Their findings also showed that minority individuals tended to rank events having to do with bodily needs higher than those having to do with personal or interpersonal relationships. Rosenberg and Dohrenwend (1975) found also that in New York, Puerto Ricans tended to rate four events having to do with bodily needs higher than Anglos did.

Migration

In examining the effects of immigration on Mexican-Americans, Fabrega (1969) has identified several sources of stress, including point of origin, migratory passage, and immigrant adjustment. At the point of origin, the stress factors may include motivation for leaving the country (voluntary or involuntary emigration), whether the family agrees to move or not, and whether or not the support network of the individual is disrupted. In migratory passage, the critical variable is the legality of the migration. The crossing of the border for undocumented Hispanics can be especially harrowing. Recently, the media have highlighted the increased incidence of violence and crime in border towns. Frequently, undocumented aliens are robbed, raped, and killed by individuals who are supposedly helping them cross the border. It is likely that the levels of psychological distress are extremely high among undocumented aliens, whether they successfully cross the border or are apprehended.

The personal adjustment of immigrants can be affected by several factors (Vega et al., 1984). One major stressor is the necessity of obtaining a job as soon as possible in order to survive. Because they lack entry-level skills and formal education, many immigrants encounter serious difficulties when they have to adapt to industrialization and urbanization. When this occurs, individuals are forced to change their earlier economic activities and relocate. As noted earlier, job dissatisfaction has been linked to depression among men. Thus, Hispanic men are likely to experience chronic stress and depression as a result of low levels of education and the inability to speak English, which leads to poor jobs. Another stressor is that undocumented immigrants are vulnerable to exploitation and abuse. Immigrants may also experience blatant discriminatory practices for the first time, which may intensify feelings of disappointment and disenchantment with their new home. The problems just described also can result from migratory patterns within the United States as, for example, among migratory workers.

The literature on stress has shown that when rapid social change occurs, as it does in migration, high levels of stress may be produced. For instance, when social institutions and the norms and belief systems that support them go through rapid alterations, it is likely that individuals' prior socialization will not be appropriate to the current environment. This is basically what Hispanic immigrants encounter. When the Hispanic individual is uprooted, he or she is likely to experience a weakening or destruction of social ties, and to have an alien culture imposed on or incorporated into his or her own. Moreover, serious disruption of marital and sex role patterns occur when Hispanic women go to work. Ybarra (1982) found that males experienced feelings of loss of control, while females experienced conflicts about their maternal roles. In addition, many fathers are forced to be absent from their families when they can find work only at distant locations. This situation often results in disrupted marriages and female-headed households.

Acculturation and different patterns of socialization between generations also may result in conflict between parents and children. Usually parents retain the cultural styles and beliefs of their original home, while children tend to become more acculturated and adherent to Anglo norms. As a result, parents may experience a loss of control over their children, which may manifest itself through a variety of psychological or somatic symptoms. To date, however, there are no firm data on the impact of acculturation as a stressor in Hispanic family relationships. An important variable related to the conflicts between parent and offspring is the age of the child. Adolescence, for example, may be a period when parent-child conflicts are particularly intense. Adolescent girls in Anglo families are allowed much more freedom than in Hispanic families. Acculturation of Hispanic adolescent girls may lead to defiance of parental controls, school truancy, and sexual experimentation. In an attempt to retain parental control, parents become overly concerned about their daughters' dress, makeup, and dating patterns (Szapocznik, Ladner & Scopeta, 1979). Finally, the research of Szapocznik et al. (1979) and Ramirez and Arce (1981) indicates that a significant variable affecting the potential abuse of drugs among Hispanic male adolescents is the degree of the acculturation gap between the parents and their adolescent offspring.

Before ending this section on the effects of immigration, it should be noted that how well the individual adapts to the immigration process and the new country is influenced by such factors as the integration between minority and host cultures, presence or absence of solutions to problems between cultures, and the rigidity of each cultural system (Fabrega, 1969). Furthermore, according to Myers, Lindenthal, and Pepper (1974), changes such as the ones cited above may leave people with a sense of loss of control over their lives, reducing their ability to predict their future. In addition, changes can impair their ability to interpret and derive meaning from experience and can serve to produce a deep sense of loss of the past. Although the work of Myers et al. was done with Anglo populations, the findings seem applicable to the experience of Hispanics. The important point is that the adverse effects of change do not stem from an inherent tendency among Hispanics to have problems but rather, problems themselves frequently are caused or exacerbated by the numerous losses produced by change.

PERCEIVING AND COPING WITH STRESS

Stress is a perceptual process that involves a dynamic interaction of components. There are various internal and external factors that determine whether a particular situation or condition will be perceived by the individual as stressful. Some of the internal factors affecting these perceptions are genetic predispositions, learning experiences, belief systems, and life-style. The external factors that may influence the perception of stress include noxious environments, and geographic and sociocultural conditions.

An individual's ability to cope with stress also depends on internal as well as external factors. Internal factors include genetic traits or predispositions and psychophysiological responsivity. Other internal factors include belief systems and learned cognitive patterns.

Belief systems can provide a way of explaining an ethnic group's thoughts and behaviors. For example, the notion of supernatural intervention is found among most Hispanic groups. Specifically, Mexican-Americans may seek the help of a *yerbero,* a Cuban may seek help from *santeros,* and Puerto Ricans, from *espiritistas.* The reliance and belief on prayer and the invocation of saints or spirits among Hispanics produces a sense of security and well being. It seems that these belief systems and practices constitute a means of reducing stress and tension among Hispanics (Garrison, 1975; Vega, 1980; Trotter & Chavira, 1982).

Learned cognitive patterns such as locus of control (Rotter, 1966) and self-efficacy (Bandura, 1982), vary across cultures. Among Hispanics it is common to externalize locus of control, as exemplified by the reliance on faith and prayer as a means of resolving problems. It is likely that this may affect Hispanics' sense of self-efficacy. Lefcourt (1976) has shown that individuals with an external locus of control may have less of an ability to decrease the impact of stress. In addition, learned helplessness and passive acceptance of victimization may be cognitive learned patterns frequently found among Hispanics. There are, however, no studies that clearly indicate the relationship between locus of control, self-efficacy, and cultural and socioeconomic variables among the various Hispanic ethnic groups.

External factors that influence the ability to cope with stress are socioeconomic factors, the presence or absence of support systems, and cultural norms. Regarding socioeconomic factors, it is well known that Hispanics may be poorer and less educated and, therefore, exposed to more environmental stressors. Lack of education, poor jobs, transient employment, and employment where labor laws are not enforced further influence the ability of individuals to cope with stress.

Support systems also have been seen as external factors mitigating the impact of stress (Cobb, 1976). Hispanics are perceived as having very large and supportive networks and therefore benefiting from the ''stress buffering'' aspects of social support. In addition to the stress buffering hypothesis, there is also a direct effect hypothesis about social support systems. The direct effect hypothesis suggests that social support contributes to the satisfaction of many personal needs for affiliation, belonging, respect, social recognition, affection, and nurturance (Aneshensel & Stone, 1982). The cultural characteristics of social support systems have been extensively reviewed (Valle, 1980; Ramirez & Castaneda, 1974). Hispanic support systems seem to have some general characteristics. Valle (1980) describes three types of natural support systems among Mexican-Americans: (1) aggregate, formalized mutual aid groups or organizations; (2) linkpersons or support systems based on friendship or coparenthood; and (3) kinship or support systems based on nuclear and extended family.

Magnusson and Statten (1978) clearly show the effects of cultural norms in a cross-cultural study of reactions to three different anxiety-provoking situations in Japanese, Hungarian, and Swedish children. The children rated their own reactions to the following situations: being in the woods at night, alone at home, and alone in the woods. The results indicated that all three groups of children differed not only on their mean level of anxiety across situations, but also on their characteristic profiles of reactions across situations.

Most cross-cultural research has been done without reference to specific situations, despite the fact that it is becoming increasingly clear that what is stressful depends upon the physical, social, and cultural environment in which individuals are reared and live. The literature indicates that certain culture-based factors may affect the psychobiological aspects of personality. Among these are diet, exercise, and health care habits. According to reports Mexican-Americans tend to be overweight (Schreiber & Homiak, 1981), their diets are high in saturated fats and sodium (Day, Lentner & Jaquez, 1978), and they are not likely to exercise (Roberts & Lee, 1980). These factors may affect health and body image and consequently may interfere with coping mechanisms.

Psychological coping mechanisms also are influenced by cultural values. For example, it is common among Hispanics to use *controlarse,* or control of oneself, to deal with unpleasant feelings, thoughts, and moods. This control of one's feelings may lead to resigning to one's fate, not thinking about a problem *(no pensar)* or attempting to overcome reactions to situations conducive to stress *(sobreponerse)* (Cohen, 1979).

A CONCEPTUAL MODEL OF STRESS

Any review of the literature on stress and the mental and physical health of Hispanics reveals a rather disorganized state of current information. This disorganization is, in part, due to lack of a unifying conceptual framework. In this section information will be presented on the Miranda and Castro model (1985), which is based on the life-stress illness paradigm (Andrews, Tennant, Hewson & Vaillant, 1978; Dohrenwend, 1975; Lazarus, 1968) as mediated by coping responses, individual resources, and social support systems.

Most models of stress have attempted to depict the relationship between life-stress and illness as flowing only in one direction, while the model devised by Miranda and Castro (1985) emphasizes a dynamic system with ongoing feedback loops between its different components (see Figure 8.1).

This model emphasizes the relationship between the level of perceived stress and mental health status as moderated by coping responses, personal resources, and social support. The model separates coping responses and personal resources from social support, even though all three affect the individual's mental health status. In this framework, the coping responses are affected by the individual's personal resources such as levels of self-esteem, self-concept, and sense of mastery. Social support is conceptualized as serving a buffer role because it may reduce the individual's sense of threat in relation to life-event changes. The effect of life-event changes also are mediated by factors such as socioeconomic status, level of acculturation, sex, and age of the individual experiencing the stressor. These factors must be taken into account if one is to understand the relationship between life events change and mental health status as it is affected by cultural and social factors.

Miranda and Castro (1985) detail several of the areas that need to be researched within their proposed model. According to the authors, the model seeks to identify life-events stressors and to determine how social support networks, coping responses, and personal resources mediate these stressors in the development of symptoms.

Although there is an extensive literature linking stressful life events to related symptoms and illness, little work, if any, has been done with Mexican-Americans and Hispanics. The types of stressors affecting Mexican-Americans and Hispanics appear to be different from those that have been studied in the majority of the population.

Figure 8.1
A Conceptual Model for Clinical Research on Stress and Mental Status

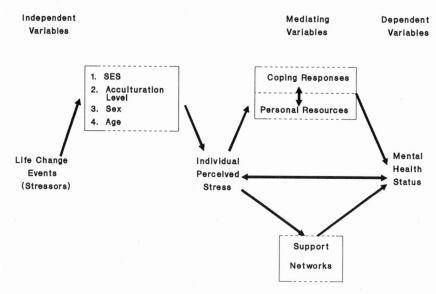

Source: "A conceptual model for clinical research on stress and mental status: From theory to assessment" by M. R. Miranda and F. Castro, 1985. In W. A. Vega and M. R. Miranda (Eds.), *Stress and Hispanic mental health research relating to service delivery,* p. 176. Copyright by U.S. Department of Health & Human Services, National Institute of Mental Health.

ASSESSMENT OF STRESS AND COPING IN HISPANICS

Functional Analysis of Behavior

Behavioral strategies such as the functional analysis of behavior may represent one of the most reliable and valid methods to assess mental status in Hispanics. The functional analysis of behavior seeks to discover the relationships between the maladaptive behavior shown by the patient and events occurring in the environment that may be controlling and maintaining that behavior. This type of behavioral assessment defines the behavioral excesses and/or deficits, as well as the resources available to the patient. The treatment program following this approach is problem-oriented, and follows a specific outline in determining both what behaviors will be changed and when treatment is completed. The goal of behavioral assessment is to determine which environmental events have a functional or controlling relationship to the maladaptive behavior. The assumption behind any behavioral assessment and treatment is that behavior, whether adaptive or maladaptive, is learned and maintained by events in the environment. To discover what events are maintaining a maladaptive behavior, the therapist must determine when and where the behavior occurs and what consequences follow the appearance of that behavior. In addition, cognitive behavioral approaches recognize the importance not only of observable behaviors, but also the role played by thoughts and beliefs in the development of psychological problems.

Although behavioral approaches represent an established perspective within clinical psychology, few if any studies have been done to utilize or modify this approach to achieve a culturally appropriate assessment method for Hispanics. The advantage of the behavioral perspective for researchers, of course, is that it focuses on maladaptive behaviors rather than on presumed underlying psychopathology in Hispanics. It also looks at environmental stimuli such as family and community that can affect an individual's behavior. An effective behavioral assessment is designed to lead to a specific treatment approach. For Hispanics, the behavioral terms and procedures may have to be translated into Spanish in such a way that they will be understood by individuals with different levels of education and acculturation. This may not be as great an obstacle as it may seem. In the section on treatment, two studies are cited where attempts have been made at developing simple instructions, drawings, and analogies to explain basic behavioral terms.

The types of stressors affecting Mexican-Americans are different from those that have been studied in the majority of the population. The stressors presented in most life-events checklists may not be relevant or the type confronting many Mexican-Americans (e.g., immigration, undocumentation, lack of language skills). A more appropriate scale needs to be developed along the lines of the Hassles and Uplifts Scales (Kanner, Coyne, Schaefer & Lazarus, 1981). This measure looks at the daily small but constant irritants and pleasant events that, when taken as a whole, may be a better predictor of ongoing and future stress symptoms than major life events.

Assessment of Coping Responses

Coping responses represent ways of thinking or behaving that a person can use to deal with stressful events or situations. These behavioral and cognitive patterns are used by the individual to attempt to modify a situation, to control the meaning of a stressful event, or to control the stress experience itself.

Among the personal coping resources of individuals that researchers have identified are self-esteem, self-denigration, and mastery (Pearlin & Schooler, 1978). When individuals are threatened or confronted by events or objects in their environment, they tend to rely on these resources. Self-esteem can be seen as the individual's positive attitude toward self, while self-denigration is the negative attitude toward self. Mastery can be defined as the degree to which an individual believes he or she can exercise control over events in the environment. There is a need to construct assessment instruments that would tap patterns of self-esteem and self-denigration among Mexican-Americans, perhaps drawing upon those already available for other groups.

Information about support systems seems especially important because it could serve to mobilize family support systems. In addition, the social support system beyond the family is another area that needs to be systematically examined. Assessment and intervention in these areas may reduce the number of treatment sessions required, as well as increase treatment effects by facilitating generalization to the home environment.

When developing a scale to assess social supports among Mexican-Americans, it is important to assess both the size of the network as well as the quality. These assessments would serve to measure both the emotional and informational structure of social support (Schaefer, Coyne & Lazarus, 1981). These aspects should be measured according to the type of help needed in situations that are culturally relevant to Mexican-Americans, and in situations that may differ in their degree of stress potential.

The assessment of coping responses is an important area since the behaviors and thought patterns that an individual relies upon can modify the situation, control the meaning of the stressful experience, or control the experience of stress itself. A scale that would measure coping responses would need to consider: (1) the situational context, (2) the coping response itself, (3) the negative or positive consequences, and (4) the personal demographics of the individual. It also would be important to measure how often and how successful these coping responses would be in dealing with stressful situations.

TREATMENT OF STRESS-RELATED DISORDERS IN HISPANICS

In this section, two pilot studies will be presented that illustrate the application of behavioral medicine approaches to stress-related disorders with Hispanics. Given that Hispanics are one of the largest-growing minority groups in the United States, and that they are likely to be exposed to multiple stressors, the need for cost-effective, short-term treatment protocols is important. It is well known that Hispanics are more likely to present physicians with somatic complaints rather than emotional problems (Mezzich & Raab, 1980). Stress-related symptoms such as tension headaches, migraine headaches, insomnia, generalized anxiety, and lower back pain are commonly treated at behavioral medicine clinics.

One approach to the treatment of stress disorders is biofeedback-assisted relaxation training. This psychophysiological technique has been successfully used in the treatment of chronic pain and stress-related disorders of different types (Diamond & Montrose, 1984; Blanchard et al., 1982; McGrady, Bernal, Fine & Woerner, 1983; Olton & Noonberg, 1980; Budzynski, Stoyva, Adler & Mullaney, 1973). The two pilot studies to be presented illustrate applications in the areas of migraine headaches, tension headaches, and lower back pain. These studies are attempts on the part of the author and others to extend techniques which have been effectively employed with individuals in highly industrialized countries, to low-income Hispanic individuals in the United States and Latin America.

Biofeedback-Assisted Relaxation Training for Hispanics with Migraines

Machado and Machado (1985) applied biofeedback and relaxation treatments in Honduras to patients suffering from chronic migraine headaches. In this study, the participants were nineteen women ages 14 to 56 (M age 33.8) with at least a fifth-grade education and low socioeconomic status (SES). All subjects reported experiencing migraines on an average of twice a week, and were not on prophylactic medication. Participants were randomly assigned to three experimental conditions: a thermal biofeedback group plus modified progressive relaxation (N = 7), a modified progressive relaxation training group (N = 7), and a waiting list control group (N = 5). The dependent measures were self-reported frequency of headaches, index of headaches activity (intensity × duration), medication taken, and disabledness. The physiological measure was the hand temperature measured during each session. The biofeedback plus relaxation treatment consisted of twenty-five-minute sessions once a week for ten weeks. The first five minutes were a baseline period, followed by seven minutes in which the subject was asked to warm her hands with the aid of a feedback signal. Participants then were asked to relax for three minutes without feedback, followed by seven more minutes of feedback, and a final three minutes of relaxation. A thermistor attached to one of the fingers of the nondominant hand was used to record the hand temperature. Four different relaxation taped cassettes were given to the subjects weekly for four weeks, and they were told to practice daily. In addition, all participants kept a headache diary for the duration of the treatment. The modified relaxation group followed the same procedures as above except they received no biofeedback.

Prior to the first session, the subjects were administered the Spanish version of the Crown-Crisp Experimental Index (Crown and Crisp, 1979) and the Epstein-Fenz Anxiety Scale (Fenz, 1967). The Analysis of Variance (ANOVA) on the dependent measures at baseline showed no significant differences.

The results indicated that both treatment groups significantly reduced their index of headache activity, F (2, 28) = 6.36, $p < .05$; headache frequency, F (2, 28) = 9.15, $p < .01$; and medication intake, F (2, 28) = 5.42, $p < 0.5$, when compared with the control group, but not from each other. Only the biofeedback and modified progressive relaxation group significantly reduced the level of symptomatology, F (2, 28) = 7.73, $p < .01$, and disabledness, F (2, 28) = 5.25, $p < .05$.

The Machado and Machado (1985) study is significant because it demonstrates that behavioral techniques that have been used effectively in European and American cultures can be employed successfully in a population that is vastly different. This population was low income, poorly educated, and not psychologically minded. In contrast, traditional psychodynamic psychotherapy, which is the dominant approach in most of Central and South America, has not been shown to be an effective treatment. This study also illustrates that behavioral approaches can be explained and taught to this population in a short period of time. Clearly, this has implications for the application of these techniques with the U.S. Hispanic population. Behavioral approaches are easily administered and cost effective, both important parameters in the current climate of medical cost containment. This study currently is being replicated with a Mexican-American population in the Midwest.

Biofeedback Assisted Relaxation Training for Hispanics with Lower Back Pain

The second study was conducted by Bernal (1986) with Hispanic men and women suffering from lower back pain using relaxation assisted by electromyographic (EMG) biofeedback. In this investigation, nine men and three women suffering from lower back pain of at least one year in duration were given forehead EMG biofeedback along with relaxation exercises. The participants maintained a log of the frequency of pain, an index of pain activity (intensity × duration), and medication intake for two weeks prior to the start of treatment. The subjects also were given a Spanish version of the Psychosocial Pain Profile, and a Spanish version of the Spielberger State Trait Anxiety. Level of depression was assessed from interview data. The participants received ten sessions of EMG biofeedback-assisted relaxation training over a ten-week period. The initial treatment session consisted of a psychophysiological baseline period in which the patient's initial forehead EMG levels were measured for five minutes, and where the subjects attempted to relax on their own for five minutes. This was followed by a twenty-minute relaxation script of modified Spanish autogenic phrases. During this twenty-minute period, EMG levels were monitored, but no feedback given. Sessions two through ten consisted of a five-minute baseline and twenty-five minutes of forehead EMG feedback. The feedback was a tone that varied in pitch proportional to the amount of tension present. All participants were given a tape with the modified autogenic phrases, and instructed to practice twice daily.

The results showed that all the participants significantly reduced their self-reported indices of levels from baseline, and maintained their gains at follow up. The ANOVA performed on the baseline data, frequency of pain, index of pain activity, medication intake, and EMG levels showed no significant difference among the subjects. A repeated measure ANOVA performed on baseline data compared to posttreatment showed significant differences on EMG levels, $F (1, 9) = 5.02$, $p < .05$; frequency of pain, $F (1, 9) = 5.11$, $p < .05$; index of pain activity, $F (1, 9) = 5.10$, $p < .05$; and medication intake, $F (1, 9) = 4.89$, $p < .06$. At follow-up, nine of the twelve patients had continued to practice their relaxation weekly and reported they had maintained their gains. The other three patients were not located at follow up. The psychological measures showed no significant differences between pre- and posttreatment.

Participants were contacted by letter and phone six months after treatment to determine whether their training had been effective. The results indicated that nine of the twelve subjects who had substantially reduced their pain levels from baseline to posttreatment maintained their gains at follow up. This study, while lacking a control group, does show the potential of these psychophysiological techniques in the treatment of Hispanics with stress-related symptoms. More investigations using larger populations and directed at a variety of other symptoms need to be carried out to more fully assess the effectiveness of these techniques with Hispanics.

CONCLUSIONS

This review has attempted to examine some of the issues and problems in the assessment and treatment of stress among Hispanics. It is obvious that there are many gaps in the literature and that much research needs to be done.

There are a variety of conceptual and methodological issues in the assessment of stress and stress-related disorders among Hispanics. The usual approaches of relating life events to stress disorders or symptoms seem to be inadequate for Hispanic populations. Various investigators have sought to conceptualize life events as an undifferentiated, unidimensional construct, failing to take into account mediating variables that may buffer the relationship between life events and stress-related problems.

There does exist a body of literature that has examined the effects of various stressors among Hispanics, including migration, low socioeconomic status, poor jobs, and low education. As noted, several factors may serve to mediate stress, including family and community support networks. Because of the complexity of the different factors involved in the study of stress, there is a need for a coherent model that may direct and focus research in this area. The work of Vega et al. (1984a) and Miranda and Castro (1985) certainly deserve praise for their attempts to develop such a model.

Another problem limiting progress in this area is the lack of valid, reliable psychometric measures in Spanish. Simple translations of existing measures may not be adequate since, as has been shown in the life-events research, there is a difference in those events that are relevant to Hispanics and Anglos.

Finally, there appear to be some promising new approaches implementing behavioral medicine paradigms that may assist in the treatment of stress-related disorders with Hispanics. These techniques are short-term in focus and cost-effective, both important concerns in current medical care.

Directions for Future Research

The stress research paradigm previously described points to several important areas that need to be investigated more fully. One area that needs to be explored in order to more adequately respond to the mental health needs in the Mexican-American population is the psychosocial context of psychological distress symptoms. Most of the literature in this area fails to clarify the relationship between factors and processes that may affect the incidence of psychological problems among Hispanics. For example, we do not know how demographic factors—such as ethnicity, income, and education—and processes—such as immigration and acculturation—relate to produce nonspecific psychological distress. There is a need for consistent theoretical models and accompanying research designs if we are to move beyond epidemiological studies that have only explored variations in symptom levels attributable to gender and socioeconomic status.

The cultural variations in coping behaviors and cognitive processes of different Hispanic subgroups also must be examined, since the factors of poverty, ethnicity, and migration in and of themselves do not produce psychopathology. We do need, however, to more precisely identify which of these factors or combination of factors are associated with stress and risk for mental illness in Hispanics.

In addition, many of the studies cited in this chapter have to be replicated with Hispanic populations. Also, there is a need to develop comparable inventories and scales measuring the type of stressors that affect Hispanics (e.g., immigration, undocumentation, lack of language skills). Instead of using the typical life-events checklist that may not be appropriate for Hispanics, a more appropriate scale may be one conceptually similar to the Hassles and Uplift Scales (Kanner, Coyne, Schaefer & Lazarus, 1981). There are many daily small irritants and pleasant events measured by these scales that when added together are a better predictor of ongoing or future stress symptoms than major life events are. When measuring coping responses, any scale needs to consider: (1) the situational context, (2) the coping response itself, (3) the positive or negative consequences, and (4) the personal demographics of the individual.

There is also a need to study the personal resources of individuals that may serve to buffer stress. Some of the salient resources identified by researchers are self-esteem, self-denigration, and mastery (Pearlin & Schooler, 1978). Identifying these patterns in Hispanics seems especially important.

The social support system that is thought to moderate stressors in the life of the individual needs to be assessed both for size of the network as well as quality. Any scale designed to assess social support should measure both the emotional and informational function of social support. These aspects of social support systems should be measured according to the type of help needed in situations that are culturally relevant to Hispanics.

Finally, more research on the use of behavioral approaches such as biofeedback and relaxation training should be conducted with many different health problems. Biobehavioral approaches may not necessitate as much of a psychological orientation as traditional approaches, and they would be more acceptable to Hispanics who present somatic complaints. Another area of research in these biobehavioral techniques would be to determine if there are any patient-population personality characteristics that can predict success or failure with these methods. The approaches for various types of patients with differing disorders continues to be an important area for future research.

REFERENCES

Andrews, G. A., Tennant, C., Hewson, D. M. & Vaillant, G. E. (1978). Life event stress, social support, coping style and risk of psychological impairment. *Journal of Nervous and Mental Disease, 166,* 307–316.

Aneshensel, C. & Stone, J. (1982). Stress and depression. *Archives of General Psychiatry, 39,* 1392–1396.

Bandura, A. (1982). Self-efficacy mechanism is human agency. *American Psychologist, 37,* 122–148.

Baum, A., Greenberg, N. E. & Singer, J. E. (1982). The use of psychological and neuroendocrinological measurements in the study of stress. *Health Psychology, 1*(3), 217–236.

Bernal, G. A. A. (1986). *EMG biofeedback assisted relaxation training for Hispanics with low back pain.* Unpublished manuscript, Medical College of Ohio, Toledo, Ohio.

Blanchard, E. B., Andrasik, F., Appelbaum, K. A., Evans, D. D., Jurish, S. E., Teders, S. J., Rodichok, L. D. & Barron, K. D. (1985). The efficacy and cost effectiveness of minimal therapist contact, non drug treatments of chronic migraine and tension headache. *Headache, 25,* 214–220.

Blanchard, E. B., Andrasik, F., Neff, D. F., Arena, J. G., Ahles, T. A., Jurish, S. E., Pallmeyer, T. P., Saunders, N. L., Teders, S. J., Barron, K. D. & Rodichok, L. D. (1982). Biofeedback and relaxation training with three kinds of headache: treatment effects and their prediction. *Journal of Clinical and Consulting Psychology, 50,* 562–575.

Brody, E. (1970). Migration and Adaptation: The nature of the problem. In E. Brody (Ed.), *Behavior in New Environments: Adaptation of Migrant Populations.* Beverly Hills, CA: Sage Publications.

Budzynski, T. H., Stoyva, J. M., Adler, C. S. & Mullaney, D. J. (1973). EMG biofeedback and tension headache: A controlled outcome study. *Psychosomatic Medicine, 35,* 484–496.

Caetano, R. (1984). A note on arrest statistics for alcohol related offenses. *The Drinking and Drug Practices Surveyor, 19,* 12–17.

Cobb, S. (1976). Social support as a moderator of life stress. *Psychosomatic Medicine, 38,* 300–314.

Cohen, L. (1979). Culture disease and stress among Latino immigrants. (Research Institute on Immigration and Ethnic Studies). Washington, DC: Smithsonian Institution.

Cohen, R. A., Williamson, D. A., Monguillat, J. E., Hutchinson, P. C., Gottlieb, J. & Waters, W. F. (1983). Psychophysiological response patterns in vascular and muscle contraction headaches. *Journal of Behavioral Medicine, 6*(1), 93–107.

Cornelius, W., Chavez, L. & Jones, O. (1984). *Mexican immigration and access to health services.* (Monograph Series). San Diego: University of California, Center for U.S.-Mexican Studies.

Cox, T. (1979). *Stress.* Baltimore, MD: University Park Press.

Crown, S. & Crisp, A. H. (1979). *Crown-Crisp Experimental Index.* London: Hodder and Staughton.

Day, M., Lentner, M. & Jaquez, S. (1978). Food acceptance patterns of Spanish speaking New Mexicans. *Journal of Nutritional Education, 10,* 121–123.

Diamond, S. & Montrose, D. (1984). The value of biofeedback in the treatment of chronic headache: a four year retrospective study. *Headache, 24,* 5–18.

Dohrenwend, B. P. (1975). Sociocultural and social-psychological factors in the genesis of mental disorders. *Journal of Health and Social Behavior, 16,* 365–392.

Dohrenwend, B. P. & Dohrenwend, B. S. (1969). *Social status and psychological disorder: A causal inquiry.* New York: Wiley Interscience.

Fabrega, H. (1969). Social psychiatric aspects of acculturation and migration. *Comprehensive Psychiatry, 10,* 314–329.

Fairbank, D. & Hough, R. (1981). Cultural differences in the perception of life events. In B. S. Dohrenwend, and B. P. Dohrenwend (Eds.), *Stressful life events and their context,* (pp. 63–84). New York: Product, Neal Watson Academic Publications.

Favazza, H. (1980). Culture change and mental health. *Journal of Operational Psychiatry, 2,*(2), 101–119.

Fenz, W. D. (1967). Specificity and somatic responses to anxiety. *Perceptual and Motor Skills, 24,* 1183–1190.

Garrison, V. (1975). Espiritismo: Implications for provisions of mental health services to Puerto Rican populations. In H. Hodges and C. Hudson (Eds.), *Folktherapy.* Miami: University of Miami Press.

Holmes, T. & Rahe, R. (1967). The social readjustment rating scale. *Journal of Psychosomatic Research, 11,* 213–218.

Holmes, T. H. & Masuda, M. (1974). Life change and illness susceptibility. In B. S. Dohrenwend and B. P. Dohrenwend (Eds.), *Stressful Life Events: Their nature and effects.* New York: Wiley.

Holtzman, W. H., Diaz-Guerrero, R. & Swartz, J. R. (1975). *Personality Development in Two Cultures.* Austin: University of Texas Press.

Hough, R., McGarvey, W., Graham, J. & Timbers, D. (1981). Cultural variations in the modeling of life change-illness relationships. Working paper Life Change and Illness Research Project. Los Angeles: University of California Neuropsychiatric Institute.

James, S. A., Hartnett, S. A. & Kalsbeck, W. D. (1983). John Henryism and blood pressure differences among black men. *Journal of Behavioral Medicine, 6,*(3), 259–278.

Janney, J., Masuda, M. & Holmes, T. (1977). Impact of a natural catastrophe on life events. *Journal of Human Stress, 3,* 22–34.

Kagan, R. R. & Levi, L. (1974). Health and environmental-psychological stimuli: A review. *Social Science and Medicine, 8,* 225–241.

Kanner, A. D., Coyne, J. C., Schaefer, C. & Lazarus, R. S. (1981). Comparison of two modes of stress measurement: Daily hassles and uplifts versus major life events. *Journal of Behavioral Medicine, 4*(1), 1–39.

Kaplan, B., Cassel, J. & Gore, S. (1977). Social support and health. *Medical Care,* *15,* 47–58.

Komaroff, A., Masuda, M. & Holmes, T. (1968). The social readjustment rating scale: A comparative study of Negro, Mexican and White Americans. *Journal of Psychosomatic Research, 12,* 121–128.

Lazarus, R. S. (1968). *Psychological stress and the coping process.* New York: McGraw Hill.

Lefcourt, H. (1976). *Locus of control: Current trends in theory and research.* New York: John Wiley & Sons.

Machado, P. H. & Machado, A. M. (1985, March). *The effectiveness of psychophysiological techniques in the treatment of migraine headaches: A cross cultural study in a Honduran population.* Paper presented at the Annual Biofeedback Society of America, San Francisco, CA.

Magnusson, D. & Statten, H. (1978). A cross-cultural comparison of anxiety responses in an interactional frame of reference. *International Journal of Psychology, 13,* 317–332.

McGrady, A., Bernal, G. A. A., Fine, T. & Woerner, M. (1983). Post-traumatic head and neck pain: A multimodal treatment approach. *Journal of Holistic Medicine, 5*(2).

Mezzich, J. & Raab, E. (1980). Depressive symptomatology across the Americas. *Archives of General Psychiatry, 37*(7), 818–823.

Miranda, M. R. & Castro, F. G. (1985). A conceptual model for clinical research on stress and mental health status: From theory to assessment. In W. A. Vega and M. R. Miranda (Eds.), *Stress and Hispanic mental health research relating to service delivery.* DHHS Pub. No. (ADM) 85–1410 (pp. 174–201). Washington, DC: Government Printing Office.

————. (1977). Culture distance and success in psychotherapy with Spanish speaking clients. In J. L. Martinez, Jr. (Ed.), *Chicano Psychology,* New York: Academic Press, 1977.

Munoz, R. F. (1982). The Spanish speaking consumer and the community mental health center. In E. E. Jones and S. J. Korchin (Eds.), *Minority Mental Health.* New York: Praeger.

Myers, J. K., Lindenthal, J. J. & Pepper, M. P. (1974). Social class life events and psychiatric symptoms: A longitudinal study. In B. S. Dohrenwend and B. P. Dohrenwend (Eds.), *Stressful life events: Their nature and effects.* New York: Wiley.

Olton, D. & Noonberg, A. (1980). *Biofeedback-Clinical Applications in Behavioral Medicine.* Englewood Cliffs, NJ: Prentice Hall.

Pearlin, L. (1983). Role strains and personal stress. In H. Kaplan (Ed.), *Psychosocial Stress* (pp. 3–32). New York: Academic Press.

————. (1975). Sex roles and depression. In N. Datan and L. Ginsberg (Eds.), *Life Span Developmental Psychology: Normative life crisis* (pp. 191–207). New York: Academic Press.

Pearlin, L. & Schooler, C. (1978). The structure of coping. *Journal of Health and Social Behavior, 19,* 2–21.

Price, R. (1981). *Priorities for prevention research: Linking risk factors and intervention research.* Unpublished manuscript, University of Michigan, Ann Arbor.

Rahe, R. H. & Arthur, R. J. (1978). Life change and illness studies. *Journal of Human Stress, 4*, 3–15.

Ramirez, M. & Castaneda, A. (1974). *Cultural democracy: Biocognitive development and education.* New York: Academic Press.

Ramirez, O. & Arce, C. (1981). The contemporary Chicano family: An empirical based review. In A. Baron (Ed.), *Explorations in Chicano Psychology* (pp. 2–27), New York: Praeger.

Roberts, R. & Lee, E. (1980). Health practices among Mexican-Americans: Further evidence from the human laboratory studies. *Preventive Medicine, 9*, 675–688.

Rosemberg, M. (1965). *Society and Adolescent Self-Image.* Princeton University Press.

Rosenberg, E. & Dohrenwend, B. S. (1975). Effects of experience and ethnicity on ratings of life events as stressors. *Journal of Health and Social Behavior, 16*, 127–129.

Roth, J. & Hough, R. (1979). *Anxiety as it is influenced by life change events and internal external locus of control: A multi-cultural approach.* Paper presented at the Southwestern Sociological Association Meeting, Fort Worth, Texas.

Rotter, J. B. (1966). Generalized expectancies for internal versus external control of reinforcement. Psychological Monographs, *80*, (1, Whole No. 609).

Samora, J. (1961). Conceptions of health and disease among Spanish Americans. *American Catholic Review, 22*, 312–323.

Sarason, I., Johnson, J. & Seigel, J. (1978). Assessing the impact of life changes: Development of the life experience survey. *Journal of Consulting and Clinical Psychology, 46*, 932–946.

Schaefer, C., Coyne, J. C. & Lazarus, R. S. (1981). The health and related functions of social support. *Journal of Behavioral Medicine, 4*(4), 381–405.

Schreiber, J. & Homiak, J. (1981). Mexican Americans. In A. Harwood (Ed.), *Ethnicity and Medical Care* (pp. 264–336). Cambridge, MA.

Selye, H. *The stress of life.* New York: McGraw-Hill, 1956.

Shannon, L. & Shannon, M. (1973). *Minority migrants in the urban community: Mexican and Negro adjustment to industrial society.* Beverly Hills, CA: Sage Publications.

Szapocznik, J., Ladner, R. & Scopetta, M. (1979). Youth drug abuse and subjective distress in a Hispanic population. In A. Beschner and L. Friedman (Eds.), *Youth Drug Abuse.* (pp. 493–511). Lexington, MA: Health & Co.

Szapocznik, J., Scopetta, M. & King, O. (1978). Theory and practice in matching treatment to the special characteristics and problems of Cuban immigrants. *Journal of Community Psychology, 6*, 112–122.

Trotter, R. & Chavira, J. (1982). *Curanderismo: The gift of healing.* Athens, GA: University of Georgia Press.

Valle, R. (1980). A natural resource for mental health promotion to Latino/Hispano populations. In R. Valle and W. A. Vega (Eds.), *Hispanic Natural Support Systems: Mental Health Promotion Perspectives.* Sacramento, CA: State Department of Mental Health.

Vega, W. (1980). The Hispanic natural healer, a case study: Implications for prevention. In R. Valle and W. Vega (Eds.), *Hispanic Natural Support Systems* (pp. 65–74). Sacramento, California Department of Mental Health.

Vega, W. A., Hough, R. & Romero, A. (1983). The family life patterns of Mexican-Americans. In G. S. Powell, J. Yamamato, A. Romero and A. Morales (Eds.),

The Psychosocial Development of Minority Group Children (pp. 194–215). New York: Brunner/Mazel.

Vega, W. & Kolody, B. (1985). The meaning of social support and the mediation of stress across cultures. In W. A. Vega and M. R. Miranda (Eds.), *Stress and Hispanic Mental Health Research Relating to Service Delivery* (pp. 48–75). *DHHS Pub. No. (ADM) 85–1410.* Washington DC: Government Printing Office.

Vega, W. A., Warheit, G., Buhl-Auth, J. & Meinhardt, K. (1984). The prevalence of depressive symptoms among Mexican Americans and Anglos. *American Journal of Epidemiology, 120* (4), 592–607.

Vega, W. A., Warheit, G. & Palacio, R. (1985). Psychiatric symptomatology among Mexican American farmworkers. *Social Medicine, 20,* 39–45.

Velez, C. G. (1980). Mexicano/Hispano support systems and confranza: Theoretical issues of cultural adaptation. In R. Valle and W. A. Vega (Eds.), *Hispanic Natural Support Systems: Mental Health Promotion Perspectives.* Sacramento, California State Department of Mental Health.

Warheit, G. (1979). Life events, coping, stress, and depressive symptomatology. *American Journal of Psychiatry, 135,* 459–462.

Weitz, J. (1970). Psychological research needs on the problems of human stress. In J. E. McGrath (Ed.), *Social and psychological factors in stress.* New York: Holt, Rinehart and Winston.

Whitehead, W. E. & Basmajian, L. S. (1982). Behavioral medicine approaches to gastrointestinal disorders. *Journal of Consulting and Clinical Psychology, 50* (6), 972–983.

Ybarra, L. (1982). When wives work: The impact on the Chicano family. *Journal of Marriage and the Family, 2,* 169–177.

9

Counseling Asian-American Parents: A Cultural-Developmental Approach

Felicisima C. Serafica

There now exists a small but steadily increasing body of clinical and research literature on therapeutic interventions for Asian-Americans. Except for a few papers and articles on family therapy (Bucton, 1985; Jung, 1984; Lee, 1982; Wong, 1986), this literature deals mainly with treatment of adult clients who were referred or voluntarily sought help for personal problems (Leong, 1986; Sue, 1988; Toupin, 1984; Yamamoto and Yap, 1984). There is a dearth of articles on counseling Asian-Americans to be effective parents in a multicultural society and/or to deal with specific psychological disorders of infancy, childhood, or adolescence. The aims of this chapter are: (1) to demonstrate a need for mental health services directed specifically to parents in this population; (2) to selectively review Asian-American socialization research; and (3) to propose a cultural-developmental framework for mental health professionals who work with Asian-American parents. The review will focus on: (1) whether the impact of cultural diversity, social change, and race relations on parenting and its outcomes varies with a child's developmental level; and (2) how the data can be used to enhance therapeutic effectiveness. Conclusions and directions for future research will also be presented.

THE NEED FOR SERVICES TO PARENTS

To date, relatively little attention has been paid to the mental health needs of Asian-American parents, possibly for the following reasons. First, Asian-American parents may seem to require little assistance from mental health professionals because mental health service utilization studies typically do not report services to parents in a separate category. Second, Asian-Americans may be more apt to consult medical and/or school personnel regarding child-related concerns (Serafica, 1988). A more accurate assessment of the mental health needs of Asian-American parents and their children might emerge if health and education statistics are used in conjunction with mental health service data. A third reason is that mental health professionals might prefer to use family therapy instead of parent counseling when the identified Asian-American client is a minor. For example, Jung (1984) has argued that since the Chinese cannot perceive the individual aside from his or her family, it is the latter that must be involved in therapy. Therapeutic intervention directed at the individual alone could even exacerbate the problem by further alienating him or her from family members. Jung's arguments are persuasive. When adolescents are involved and the entire family system is dysfunctional, family therapy might indeed be the treatment of choice, not just for Chinese-Americans but for all Asian-American parents.

However, there is also a need for mental health services aimed primarily at Asian-American immigrant parents. This need grows out of the sheer number of Asian-American minors, the context within which Asian-American immigrants must raise their children, and the threats posed by a multicultural society to their credibility and integrity as parents.

Demographic Patterns

School enrollment patterns confirm census data that a large segment of the Asian/Pacific-Islander population consists of minors needing the support of caregivers, usually their parents. The Center for Education Statistics (Stern & Chandler, 1987) reports that Asian/Pacific Islanders are the most rapidly expanding group of minority students. The number of such students enrolled in the nation's public elementary and secondary schools rose from 536,158 in 1976 to 994,108 in 1984, an increment of 85 percent. Figures for more recent years are unavailable because starting in 1988, only transition to and completion of high school are reported by race and ethnicity.

The Context of Parenting

Socioeconomic milieu. Research indicates that while favorable socioeconomic conditions do not guarantee successful parenting, they do facilitate it (Siegal, 1985). Education and income of parents have been found to correlate positively with a number of developmental outcomes (Zigler & Finn-Stevenson, 1987). Asian-Americans intuitively assume this. For many, a primary reason for migrating to the United States is to improve their socioeconomic status and their children's future. They soon discover, however, that any educational advantages they have do not necessarily translate into occupational advantages.

Using 1980 census data, Kan and Liu (1986) showed that most Asian-American groups have high educational level but low occupational status. All Asian groups except the Vietnamese exceeded whites, blacks, and Hispanics in the percent of population with a college education, but the majority of Asians were at the lower end of the managerial, professional, and administrative ranks, and had a higher proportion of self-employed individuals than non-Asian groups. A significant proportion of professional, managerial, and white collar immigrants experience a drop in occupational status into blue collar and service jobs because of language and licensing difficulties (U.S. Department of Health, Education and Welfare, 1974). Immigration brings a higher income and a higher standard of living than was possible in the country of origin but a lower status and sphere of influence. Conceivably, many Asian-American parents may feel dissatisfied, frustrated, and even inadequate while coming to terms with the notion that their qualifications do not win the recognition and rewards given to whites with comparable or even lower qualifications.

For immigrants who are not professionally trained, limited English proficiency and discrimination in small trade, construction, and craft unions leave them little choice but employment in the secondary labor market, that is, the labor-intensive, low-capital service and small manufacturing sectors. Low wages require that both husband and wife work. In these dual worker families (Glenn, 1983), wives and husbands are more or less coequal breadwinners because the pay differential between them is less than in their country of origin, given the downward shift in the husband's occupation. Yet it is still the wives who must juggle full-time work outside the home with child care and housework. This arrangement must create tensions in the marital relationship, requiring redefinition of sex roles. Glenn (1983) found that in these dual worker families, there is a complete segregation of work and family life. Parents' lives are regulated by the disciplines of the job, while children lead relatively unstructured and unsupervised lives, often in the company of peers whose parents also work. Although mothers are usually home by early evening, the fathers' hours may prevent him from seeing the children at all. Together, the parents' fatigue, the long hours of separation, and the lack of common experiences weaken family communication and closeness.

Whatever the difficulties of the Asian-American families described above, they are earning a livelihood that at least enables them to meet their basic needs and more. There are, however, Asian-American families with school-age children who are living below the poverty level. Operationalizing economic milieu as the ratio of family income to the poverty cut-offs used by the federal government, Kan and Liu (1986) reported that among those living below the poverty cut-off point, the Vietnamese have the highest percentage (43%) but the Asian-Indians (10.2%), Chinese (15.7%), and Koreans (12%) also have higher percentages than whites (10%). Only the Filipinos (6.2%) and the Japanese (4.2%) have lower percentages than whites. Immigrants who came after 1975 were more heavily represented below the poverty line than those who came before 1975, except for the Japanese. The nonsignificant difference between pre- and post-1975 percentages for Japanese may be an artifact of their low and highly selective immigration to the United States in recent years.

Family living arrangements. The presence of two parents in the home has a positive effect on the psychological development and adjustment of a child (Steinberg, 1987). Using 1980 census data, Hernandez (1986) described the living arrangements of ethnic minority families and children. In 1980, about 85 percent of Asian-American children lived with two parents, more than white (83%), Hispanic (71%), American Indian (63%) or black (46%). Those Asian children who were not living with two parents (15%) lived with an ever married mother but no father (7%), a never married mother (1%), a father (2%), or with no parent in the home (5%). Presumably, children with no parent in the home were living with mature siblings or other relatives. Of the Asian-American children with one parent, 10.5% lived in a grandparent's house but most (89.5 percent) did not, so for many single parents, the burden of parenting is not reduced by grandparents' help.

Children with special needs. Even parents who are fully prepared to effectively raise their offspring in a multicultural society occasionally need help when they confront unexpected conditions, such as having a child with special needs. Data reported by the Center for Education Statistics (Stern & Chandler, 1987) show that Asian/Pacific Islanders are also represented in all school special education programs. In 1984, they were enrolled in classes for the specific learning disabled (1.6%), educable mentally retarded (0.3%), trainable mentally retarded (0.2%), seriously emotionally disturbed (0.1%), and speech impaired (1.7%). Some Asian-American researchers (e.g., Y. Kim, 1983) contend that the proportions of Asian immigrant children with special educational needs may actually be higher, but they seldom come to the attention of the school-based support team due to referral-inhibiting characteristics of the children, stereotype-inspired expectations of the teachers, inadequate educational policies, and limited availability of bilingual and bicultural staff. The main point is that there are also Asian/Pacific-Islander parents who must meet the special needs of handicapped children. The fact that they are fewer in number than their counterparts in other race/ethnic groups does not make their burden any lighter.

PARENTING IN A MULTICULTURAL SOCIETY

The family is the primary socialization agent, responsible for transmitting societal values and attaining socialization goals. Yet parents typically receive no formal training in socialization. They must rely on their own experience of this process. Hence, parents tend to raise their children according to how they themselves were reared. So deeply engrained is the socialization experience that even those who, as children, vowed to treat their own children differently often find themselves behaving just like their parents, much to their chagrin. Thus, immigration to another country is not likely to automatically alter socialization patterns. Moreover, adherence to tradition serves to allay any lingering separation anxiety or guilt over leaving the country of origin and promotes cognitive consistency regarding the parent's own identity. Consciously or unconsciously, Asian-American parents subscribe to traditional socialization goals and practices. Understanding these is required to help them become effective parents in a multicultural society.

Traditional Socialization Goals

Empirical studies that ask Asian-Americans to specify and/or rank their socialization goals or expectations are few (Del Carmen & Serafica, 1985; B. Kim, 1980; O'Reilly, Ebata, Tokuno & Bryant, 1980). However, contemporary writers (e.g., Suzuki, 1980; Huang, 1981; Wong, 1985) maintain that their major socialization goals still reflect traditional values. These are to instill in the child a sense of collectivity and identification with the family or clan and the ethnic group, dependence on the family, filial piety and obedience, and a sense of responsibility and obligation to the family.

The socialization of affection, aggression, assertion, and achievement are more appropriately viewed as subordinate rather than superordinate goals. Restraining the overt expression of affection and aggression is necessary to maintain group organization, cohesion, and stability. The moderation of assertion facilitates obedience. Achievement serves both the goal of filial piety by bringing honor to the family or clan and its ancestors, and the goal of responsibility and obligation to the family by insuring the prosperity and continuity of the clan.

A variety of childrearing strategies are used to achieve these goals. These include the didactic teaching of basic concepts and precepts, modeling, rewards and punishments, praise, and the use of "shame" and "face" as well as "pride" in ethnic group membership. Underlying the application of these techniques is an assumption that infants and young children require a permissive, indulgent, and nurturant approach while older children and adolescents benefit more from strict discipline.

For more detailed reviews of research on Asian-American socialization goals and techniques, the reader is referred to Harrison, Serafica, and McAdoo (1984) and Serafica (1986).

Parenting amidst Cultural Diversity, Social Change, and Race Relations: A Developmental Analysis

Under ordinary circumstances, parenting can be a stress-inducing process. For the Asian-American immigrant, there are three additional potential stressors: (1) cultural diversity, (2) social change, and (3) race relations (Sue & Chin, 1983). When cultures differ markedly and conformity to one culture brings greater reward, conflict can arise, inducing stress in the individual. The effects of cultural conflict on the child have been discussed in numerous articles (see Powell, Yamamoto, Romero & Morales, 1983), but seldom considered from the parents' perspective. Yet cultural conflict also threatens parental goals and expectations, disrupts the parent-child relationship, and undermines the parent's sense of competence as a parent. Furthermore, the social changes brought about by immigration including lowered occupational status, the necessity for both parents to work long hours in order to earn enough to maintain the higher costs of living in a postindustrial society, and the loss of a familiar social support network are likely to weaken the parents' ability to deal with the effects of cultural conflict. If encounters with racial prejudice and discrimination have already engendered in parents a feeling of inability to control outcomes in the workplace or the community, it can be devastating to have husband-wife and parental roles within the family challenged as well.

However, the impact of cultural diversity, social change, and race relations on the family probably varies with a child's developmental level. The developmental perspective, ignored heretofore in the Asian-American mental health literature, can be useful in identifying potential stress points, planning mental health services, and formulating counseling goals and techniques. An examination of socialization outcomes can reveal when these potential stressors might be perceived as impeding parental goals. To lend clarity to the presentation, the analysis begins with the period of infancy. Actually, however, immigrants seldom arrive in the United States childless or with a newly born infant. Instead, they have offspring of various ages and must contend simultaneously with two or more potential stressors. In this case, a developmental perspective can be even more helpful, revealing the points where interaction between stressor and birth order effects might occur.

Infancy and the early years. Parents with infants and young children may be least likely to experience stress from cultural conflicts because in both cultures, infancy and early childhood are periods when the family is preeminent, closeness and dependence are socially acceptable. If the Asian-American child is more indulged than his Caucasian counterpart in matters of weaning, toilet training, or bedtime (Sollenberger, 1968), this does not present problems. If family circumstances required that the child develop practical autonomy earlier than tradition dictates, Asian-American mothers seem able to accept and foster this without unusual difficulty (Sung, 1979; Young, 1972a).

There are, however, at least four groups of mothers who are especially vulnerable to potential stressors, particularly social change, during the child's early years. In the first group are mothers who already experience emotional disturbance during pregnancy. For example, recent immigrant Chinese obstetrical patients were overrepresented among high scorers on the General Health Questionnaire and among subjects who received a psychiatric diagnosis based on a standard clinical psychiatric assessment and the Diagnostic and Statistical Manual of Mental Disorders or DSM-III (Yeung & Schwartz, 1986). Parenting demands may exacerbate existing psychological distress in these women, particularly if through social change they have lost a social support system but feel uncomfortable about networking with persons outside their ethnic group (Loo, 1982).

Teenage mothers and unmarried mothers comprise the second group. They, respectively, accounted for 5.5 percent and 10.1 percent of live births in the Asian-American population in 1985 (U.S. Bureau of the Census, 1987). The third group consists of women who gave birth to premature and/or low birth weight infants. In 1985, 6.5 percent of births with low birth weights occurred in the Asian/Pacific-Islander population. Last, there is also a small group of mothers whose infants suffer perinatal complications during pregnancy and delivery. Infants born to each of these maternal groups are at risk for development (Clarke-Stewart, 1988) so these Asian-American women and their families might also require support, education, and counseling as they deal with the immediate problems and ponder the long-term implications.

Childhood. The child's entry into school sets the stage for a new potential conflict, one between the goals of the dominant society and Asian-American socialization goals. In addition to social change, cultural diversity and race relations now impinge on parenting.

Insofar as collectivity and ethnic group identification involves acceptance of one's own physical appearance, including the distinctive facial features and physique of one's own ethnic/racial group, its development is at risk. Young Chinese-American children are significantly less likely to identify with children of their own ethnic group (Fox & Jordan, 1973; Springer, 1950). Ou and McAdoo (1980) also found this to be true for boys, but not girls, in their middle class sample. Older (grades four to six) Japanese-American children's ratings of their physical self-concept only are significantly lower than those of their white peers (Pang, Mizokawa, Morishima & Olstad, 1985). Furthermore, item analysis suggested that they were especially sensitive about short stature, flat noses, and physical appearance in general (Pang et al, 1985). With increasing age, negative physical self-evaluations become even more pronounced. Chang (1975) found that as they advanced in grade, Korean-American children rated themselves even lower on the physical appearance subscale of the Piers Harris Self Concept Scale, although they did not differ from a black comparison group on any of the other subscales. These findings suggest that progress toward the Asian-American parents' goal of instilling positive self-concept and ethnic identity is sometimes hindered.

Since no one has ever assessed Asian-American parents' perceptions of their child's self-concept, it is not clear whether they are aware of any low physical self-evaluation. However, about 30 percent of both Korean-American parents and children studied by B. Kim (1980) reported that the child encountered discrimination at school in the form of harassment or name calling, mostly from other children but in two cases, according to parental reports, from adults. To help a child cope with this behavior, Asian-American parents use strategies ranging from passive (e.g., "Take pride in being Japanese") to active (e.g., enrolling the child in karate). Some strategies (B. Kim, 1980) such as telling a child to do better in school may run counter to the peer culture of the dominant society whereas others, like encouraging retaliation, may violate school rules.

Group identification is fostered through the use of a common language so Asian-Americans want their children to be proficient in their native language as well as in English (B. Kim, 1980; S. Kim, 1983). Facility in the native language is acquired when parents speak it in their interactions with each other and use it when reading stories as well as speaking to their children (Kuo, 1974). It is also maintained when the family lives in a neighborhood where other members of the same ethnic group reside (B. Kim, 1980). When these conditions do not prevail, the child's use of the native language decreases as English proficiency increases (B. Kim, 1980). This can result in decreased communication and closeness with parents who have not mastered conversational English, thus setting the stage for low identification with or even alienation from the family and ethnic group during adolescence and adulthood.

Dependence on the family can be threatened by a child's relationships with members of the outgroup. While immigrant parents want their children to get along with peers in school (B. Kim, 1980), they may also exercise constant, strict supervision, carefully screen potential friends, and actively discourage them from socializing outside the family until they are much older (Sung, 1979; Young, 1972b). These behaviors may simply be attempts to avoid fights between children which could impair harmonious relations between parents (Sollenberger, 1968), but they could also be reactions to social change. Parents may deliberately restrict a child's friendships because, embarrassed about their altered socioeconomic circumstances, they feel unable to reciprocate hospitality (B. Kim, 1980). They might also be reluctant to give the child independence before he or she is ready to deal with cultural diversity as represented by neighbors who have a different culture and speak a different language. Whatever the motivation, Asian-American parents strive to keep their children within the confines of the family and dependent upon it for social interaction. However, when economic conditions require both parents to work long hours away from the home, it becomes more difficult to maintain the child's dependence on the family.

The goal of instilling filial piety and obedience might be perceived by Asian-American parents as incompatible with some of the school's objectives and instructional methods. When the assertive, questioning manner encouraged in school is generalized to the home, parents may interpret it as signifying a lack of respect. This is more likely if the communication is in English, which lacks the equivalent forms for expressions of vertical role relationships found in Asian languages such as a Korean (B. Kim, 1980). Child assertiveness, particularly if expressed in a loud voice, might be perceived as showing off. Asian-American parents are more apt than Caucasians, blacks, or Hispanics to notice the use of a loud tone of voice and showing off (Tuddenham, Brooks & Milkovich, 1974). They want their children to become more socially assertive (B. Kim, 1980) because such behavior is adaptive in the dominant society, but many have yet to think about its implications for parent-child interaction, and how they would feel and deal with its manifestations within the family.

During childhood, responsibility and obligation to the family are expected to be fulfilled primarily through academic achievement. By excelling in school, the child brings honor to the family and prepares for future educational and occupational successes that will further enhance the family's social standing and ensure its economic well-being. The importance of academic achievement, seen as made possible by mastery of English, is intensified in many parents by their awareness that they are underemployed or underpaid.

In regard to academic achievement, the goals of Asian-Americans and the dominant society coincide. The academic achievements of Asian-American children are well documented (e.g., Vernon, 1982) but the personal costs have not yet been examined. B. Kim (1980) found that although only 9.5 percent of Korean parents living in Chicago were clearly dissatisfied with their children's school progress, 28.3 percent of the children felt that they were not meeting their parents' expectations in this area. This lack of congruence is not always present but where it is, children are needlessly anxious.

The tendency of Asian-Americans to attribute children's school problems to limited English proficiency (B. Kim, 1980) might make them less sensitive to behavioral indices of specific learning disabilities, mental retardation, or other educationally handicapping conditions. If brought to their attention, they might have great difficulty accepting any of these conditions. Many Asian-American children with special educational needs who require early intervention may not be identified. When Asian Americans do acknowledge a child's learning difficulties, they prefer to handle the problem themselves (B. Kim, 1980) instead of asking the school to provide remedial services.

Adolescence. This is the period when the impact of cultural diversity is most likely to seriously disturb Asian-American parents. All four socialization goals may appear threatened at this time, straining the parent-child relationship.

One source of anxiety among immigrants at this period is whether the adolescent will maintain his or her group identity and retain the parents as models. The extent to which parents will remain powerful models for their children as the latter reach adolescence may depend on the child's developing identity and aspirations, and the extent to which the parent is perceived as similar to what the child is and wants to be (Macoby & Martin, 1983).

The results of studies on the self-concept and ethnic identification of Asian-American adolescents are similar to those for children. Using the Offer Self-Image Questionnaire, Chen and Yang (1986) found that although the self-concept profiles of Chinese-Americans were more similar to those of Caucasian-Americans than Chinese peers, they differed significantly from Caucasians on the Body and Self-Image, Sexual Attitudes, Morals, and Psychopathology scales. The investigators attributed the poorer body image of Chinese-Americans to experiencing racial slurs and prejudice.

Willingness to date members of the outgroup, another sign of acculturation, might be perceived by parents as indicative of low ethnic identification and/or further weakening it. Compared to their male counterparts, Asian-American females engage more in interracial dating. They are more likely to have internalized the dating values of Caucasian adolescents, adjusted to social customs, and been accepted by Caucasian communities (Weiss, 1970). According to Weiss (1970), these results suggest that stereotypically feminine images of the Chinese female in the mass media have promoted their general acceptance as dating partners whereas popular stereotypes of the Chinese male are less complimentary, discouraging them from dating Caucasian-American females while sabotaging their relations with Chinese-American females who subconsciously accept the stereotypes for both sexes.

Although changing preferences for dating partners have been studied, no one has yet systematically assessed parental feelings and reactions to interracial dating. The only available evidence comes from clinical case studies (e.g., Yamamoto, 1968) and, not surprisingly, it reveals parental distress. More likely, interracial dating with the possibility of outmarriage is an area fraught with ambivalence for Asian-American parents. Although it implies acceptance by at least a segment of the dominant society and brings personal safety through assimilation, it could also lead to violations of cultural standards for unmarried female sexual behavior (Abramson & Imai-Marquez, 1982), weaken family cohesiveness, and decrease the commitment to fulfill obligations to one's parents.

Scientific knowledge about what parents can do to promote ethnic identification in adolescents remains scanty. Serving as ethnic role models does not seem sufficient. Okano and Spilka (1971) found in a study of second- and third-generation middle-class Japanese-American high school students and their mothers that although Buddhist mothers, compared to Christian mothers, had a stronger ethnic identification, this difference was not reflected in their offspring. Buddhist adolescents scored higher in both alienation and achievement than Christian adolescents. While strong maternal ethnic identity may foster achievement orientation, it can also give rise to value conflict and feelings of alienation in the adolescent. Value conflict is less likely to occur in a context with a large concentration of same ethnic group members, which has been found conducive to development of ethnic identification in young adults (Young, 1972b).

Generational differences in adherence to the value of dependence upon the family begin to be more obvious during adolescence. McDermott, Char, Robillard, Hsu, Tseng & Ashton (1983) found that Japanese-American parents strongly believed that important family decisions should be discussed, with every family member participating in decisionmaking, and sharing their deepest thoughts with one another. They also thought that family members should prefer to be with each other rather than with outsiders, children should be open and honest with parents, and family members should know how each one feels about things. In contrast, Japanese-American adolescents felt strongly that every member of the family has a right to keep certain thoughts and feelings private, though members should let each other know when they are angry at one another.

The importance attached by Japanese-American adolescents to the expression of anger suggests that parents' attempts to foster dependence upon the family might be impeded by their own socialization of emotional control. Adolescents might feel inhibited about engaging in the amount of self-disclosure sought by their parents if emotional expression, particularly of anger, is unacceptable. Japanese-American parents are significantly less likely than their Caucasian counterparts to believe that family members should openly express their affection for each other or cry openly when sad or upset (McDermott et al., 1983). They are more vague and reticent in expressing individual thoughts and feelings, more restrained and more uncomfortable (Hsu, Tseng, Ashton, McDermott, Jr. & Char, 1985).

During adolescence, it is not unusual for a communication gap to develop between parents and their adolescent offspring. However, according to Han (1985), there is a wider generation gap between Korean adolescents and their mothers than between Caucasian adolescents and their mothers. In Han's study of self-disclosure (1985), Korean adolescents disclosed the most to their same sex friends, while Caucasian adolescents disclosed the most to their mothers. Because acculturation is a slower process for adults than for children, the generation gap in immigrant families is wider than in Caucasians. The faster rate of acculturation in the young, including acquisition of English proficiency, creates a communication gap between them and their immigrant parents that continues beyond adolescence. Jun (1984) found that the greater the English proficiency of Korean immigrant university students, the greater the communication gap between them and their parents.

The concept of filial piety and obedience is also challenged during adolescence. In the McDermott et al. study (1983), mothers and fathers across ethnic groups showed stronger agreement than their adolescents that there should be a clear line of authority within the family, with no one questioning who is in charge. They also held more strongly to the belief that everyone should do the jobs he or she is supposed to do. Finally, they were less likely than their adolescent offspring to believe that adults should admit their mistakes to children.

With increasing age, the views of Asian-American youngsters on obedience begin to diverge from tradition and converge with those of their Caucasian peers. Schwartz (1971) did not find significant group differences in level of compliance between Japanese-Americans and Caucasians in grade six. In grade nine, the Japanese-Americans were significantly more favorable toward family authority and school compliance than the Caucasians. At ages twelve to fourteen years, Chinese-American males respond equally well to authoritarian and democratic leadership styles (Meade, 1985). By grade twelve, however, Japanese-American students are no longer significantly different from Caucasians in their attitude toward family authority, although they are still significantly more favorable toward school compliance (Schwartz, 1971). Cultural diversity effects seem to vary with age, even within adolescence.

Career choice may provide the first real test of socialization for responsibility and obligation to the family. For adolescents, fulfilling this obligation may require satisfying the aspirations of their parents as well as their own. The parents' aspirations typically involve a professional career (B. Kim, 1980), particularly if their own were derailed through immigration. In many families, the aspirations of the adolescent and his or her parents are congruent as suggested by the finding that Japanese-American adolescents have higher career aspirations than their Caucasian peers (Schwartz, 1971). There are, however, exceptions. The dominant society's values support freedom of choice but the adolescent's preferred occupation or career may be viewed by parents as a sign of disobedience, even betrayal. Resolution of this conflict is complicated further if a communication gap between parents and adolescent exists.

Regular employment provides another test. High income levels attributed to Asian-Americans usually represent the combined earnings of multiple breadwinners rather than one or both parents. Children are expected to turn over their earnings to the parents who decide on allocations. Violations of this practice, sanctioned by the individualism of the dominant culture, may be construed as signaling a breakdown in the system of mutual obligations upon which the family's prosperity rests.

Disagreements can be easily contained within the family when the parties are children and adults. With adolescents, the conflict is more apt to be expressed in forms that seriously impair functioning and command attention from individuals outside the home as well as inside. At this juncture, family tensions based on cultural conflict may be expressed through more serious forms of psychosomatic or psychological disorders leading to a referral for professional help.

To summarize, research on Asian-American socialization outcomes prior to adulthood is sparse and fragmented. Available studies provide only indirect tests of cultural diversity effects at most. Studies testing the effects of social change or race relations are lacking but some studies suggest what goals they are likely to affect and when.

Social change resulting in lowered occupational self-esteem and loss of social support may affect parenting as early as infancy. The loss of a long-standing social network and difficulty in forming another in an unfamiliar environment may intensify the normal vicissitudes of pregnancy and caring for an infant. Starting in childhood and continuing into adolescence, changes in occupational status which alter husband-wife roles and family interaction patterns make it more difficult for parents to promote dependence upon the family.

Cultural diversity seems to acquire salience during the childhood years, threatening socialization of piety and obedience. Its salience persists in adolescence when, additionally, it offers alternative views regarding responsibility and obligation to the family. While generational differences appear in both Caucasian and Asian-American groups, suggesting that growing up in a particular sociohistorical era has its own powerful unique effect, they may be felt more keenly in immigrant families where parents must differentiate cultural diversity from cohort effects.

Race relations seems to be implicated in self-concept development from early childhood on, perhaps undermining parental efforts to promote ethnic identification. If ethnic minority membership is not devalued by others, even acculturated members might still identify with their ethnic origins.

Not all of the parenting problems experienced by Asian-American immigrants can be attributed to stresses induced by cultural diversity, social change, or race relations. Sometimes, parental distress is caused by the demands of offspring whose psychological problems are not primarily due to migration and resettlement. The prevalence of such problems remains unknown since epidemiological studies have not yet been conducted. Even comparative studies of mental health problems among Asian-American children and youth are rare. To date, a study conducted more than a decade ago (Tuddenham et al., 1974) remains the main source of information about the prevalence of childhood problem behaviors among Asian-American children ages nine to eleven years, even though it did not have a representative sample. Last, Asian-Americans are not immune to delinquency (Abbott & Abbott, 1968) nor drug addiction (Sata, 1983). Methodologically sound studies of the prevalence of these conditions are needed.

ENHANCING ASIAN-AMERICAN PARENTING: A CULTURAL-DEVELOPMENTAL APPROACH

The preceding review of Asian-American socialization research suggests that parenting can go awry when: (1) the attainment of traditional goals is impeded by external factors such as cultural diversity, social change, or race relations; and/or (2) parents adopt socialization goals of the dominant society that inherently contradict traditional goals they also continue to espouse. Parental distress may be expressed in various ways, including somatization, depression, irritability, and negative parent-child interactions. Health personnel are likely to be consulted regarding somatic complaints and mood changes while school personnel may observe academic and behavioral changes in the child reflecting a

edge; facilitating their selection and implementation of socialization goals and strategies; and helping them to deal with the impact of cultural diversity, social change and race relations.

Phase 3 emphasizes strengthening the parent-child relationship. Whereas Phase 2 focused on cultural aspects of child rearing, this phase addresses more specifically the relationship between parent and child, taking into account the child's developmental level and the cultural context of parent-child interaction. The emphasis is on increasing parental sensitivity to and understanding of the child's behavior, and using these to improve parent-child interaction and communication. In this phase, attention is given to sharpening the parents' observational skills and ability to relate these observations to child behavior, developmental norms, and context. How the parent's new insights can be used to improve parent-child interaction and communication is discussed. Throughout, the relevance of the parent-child relationship to attainment of socialization goals and developmental outcomes is stressed.

In the second part of Phase 3, the emphasis shifts to the parent's own reactions to the child. Having learned how to observe and understand the child's behaviors, the parent will find it easier and less threatening to focus on identifying his or her own interaction and communication patterns, provided these are perceived as relevant to parenting and the parent-child relationship.

Phase 4 is a period of consolidation and integration, with the parent as full partner in the counseling relationship. Parenthood activates and maintains a developmental process in the parent (Benedek, 1959). Within the parent occur physiological and psychological changes parallel to and in transaction with changes in the child and his expanding world which, among immigrants, includes a cultural context new to both. Within a cultural-developmental framework, the changes include: (1) a sense of competence and satisfaction in parenting, and (2) integration into the self-system of the parental role and a bicultural identity that facilitates adaptation of both parent and child to a multicultural society. Increased competence and satisfaction in parenting facilitates the integration of the parental role into the self-concept and personal identity that comprise the self-system.

Since the parent is now functioning adequately, the counselor's role is mainly to provide support when the parent feels impatient over the slowness of change and encouragement during moments of uncertainty. Overall, the counselor's task is to sustain the parent's growth momentum by helping the parents maintain consistency and prepare for the child's next developmental period. As the counselor reviews with the parent the changes that have occurred in the child, the parent, and the parent-child relationship, these changes are related to the parents' own efforts. Through this, the parent is also helped to integrate into his or her own self-concept a more positive definition and evaluation of the self as a competent parent in a multicultural society. Finally, the counselor highlights the sources of the parent's joy and satisfaction in parenting so that these will be accessible to the parent in the future, should difficulties arise again.

Phase 5 is simply a follow-up. At the termination of Phase 4, an agreement is made to meet again or talk over the phone after a specified period to review the functioning of parent and child, reinforce the gains made, discuss any concerns, and reassure the parent that support is available, if needed.

The approach described here can be used with an individual, a dyad, or a group. It can be implemented over a few sessions or a longer period. It can be used as a treatment method or as an approach to prevent mental health problems by facilitating adaptation among immigrant parents.

Counseling Techniques

What has been proposed is a relatively structured, problem-focused approach that involves setting measurable short-term goals to be achieved within a specified time period. The approach calls for a judicious application of educational (or didactic) and counseling techniques. The former would be those required for the effective presentation of information and teaching of new concepts and skills. Counseling techniques can be drawn from different schools of thought, depending upon the counselor's theoretical orientation. Preferably, these techniques should emphasize an active stance in listening and empathic responding, sensitivity to nonverbal and verbal behavior, clarification, restatement, and reflection. In the earlier phases, creative use of crisis intervention techniques, social networking, and concrete, practical suggestions may be necessary. In the later phases, guided problem solving, actively raising questions, and presenting alternative viewpoints or strategies could be used. Throughout, conveying positive regard and support is essential.

It has been said that Asians have a lower tolerance of ambiguity (Leong, 1986) and prefer a directive approach (Sue & Morishima, 1982). On the other hand, Asians also tolerate ambiguity in order to avoid embarassment, shame, hurt, or confrontation. Out of respect for the counselor, they may listen attentively to directions without revealing their reactions. But they may not carry out the directions. Working with Asian-Americans necessitates constant alertness to their use of symbolism and to the hidden meanings in their verbal and nonverbal behavior.

Caution is also warranted in using a behavioral approach. Behavioral techniques such as modeling, coaching, and contingent reinforcement are part of the Asian parenting repertoire, though not labeled as such (Steward & Steward, 1973). Their systematic use can be encouraged in Phase 2, but immigrant parents may find it hard to keep daily detailed recordings of behavior. As with any client, understanding and acceptance of the behavioral approach, motivation, and abilities must be carefully assessed before a formal behavior modification program is introduced.

Evaluation

The proposed approach can be evaluated at two levels: (1) its effectiveness for a particular client, and (2) its relative efficacy compared to other approaches.

Within a cultural-developmental framework, counseling effects can be assessed as: (a) changes in parent knowledge, skills, attitudes, and self-concept; and (b) changes in the child's behavior as evidenced through self-report, teacher-report, and/or behavioral observations. Standardized tests or criterion-referenced measures can be administered before and after counseling. Follow-up assessments can be done to assess temporal stability of outcomes.

Implications for Training

The implementation of a cultural-developmental approach to counseling Asian immigrant parents requires that in addition to receiving the regular graduate training, the counselor becomes thoroughly familiar with theory and research on socialization goals, techniques, and outcomes for both American and Asian societies. This implies that graduate training for mental health service providers, health providers, and educators should include not only courses on minority mental health, but also courses on the development of ethnic minority children and youth since these receive little attention in developmental psychology and child psychopathology courses. A course on childrearing in different countries, although helpful, is not enough. Childrearing in China is not the same as rearing a Chinese-American child in New York City.

Knowledge alone, however, is not sufficient. One also has to conceptualize problems and processes within a cultural-developmental framework. This mode of thinking is facilitated by clinical training within a setting or at least under the supervision of someone who has this perspective. Certain attitudes are also important. These include on one hand a wariness about applying stereotypes and on another, an openness to the positive implications of Asian-American parenting for all families living in a multicultural society.

CONCLUSIONS

1. Census and school enrollment data show that a rapidly growing segment of the Asian-American population is composed of infants, children, and youths needing adequate care and guidance. However, the context within which some Asian-American parents must function is far from ideal.

2. Sociological studies suggest that the inner psychological environment of immigrant parents may not be conducive to calm parenting. They must meet their children's needs while also trying to make the personal and marital adjustments necessitated by socioeconomic changes resulting from migration and resettlement.

3. Psychological studies suggest that attainment of traditional socialization goals may be impeded by social change, cultural diversity, and race relations, depending on the child's developmental level.

4. In the mental health literature, relatively little attention has been given to preparing or assisting Asian-American immigrants for parenting in a multicultural society. Such assistance must draw from both cultural and developmental perspectives.

5. There is a paucity of programmatic research on the mental health needs of Asian-American parents and the psychological development of their offspring. Suggestions for research are presented below.

DIRECTIONS FOR FUTURE RESEARCH

1. Data on the mental health needs of Asian-American parents are badly needed. Ideally, large-scale epidemiological studies should be conducted. For methodological and practical reasons (Liu & Yu, 1986), these are not apt to occur in the near future, but several steps can be taken meanwhile.

2. Mental health service evaluation studies could start reporting services to parents in a separate category.

3. Comparative studies dealing with parental concerns and perceptions, particularly of cultural diversity, social change, and race relations effects on parenting could be conducted.

4. Mental health, medical, and school settings could conduct surveys of parental concerns and needs.

5. Existing health and education data could be analyzed to generate research questions and hypotheses dealing with parental concerns and needs that can be systematically investigated.

6. Programmatic research on Asian-American socialization is also a dire necessity. Elsewhere (Harrison, Serafica & McAdoo, 1984), this writer has suggested some directions. Those suggestions are still relevant. In addition, research on the following are indicated by the analysis of potential stressor effects.

7. Development of Asian-American self-concept and ethnic identity from childhood to adolescence, and the factors that facilitate or impede this process. This ought to include research to identify effective strategies for helping children maintain bicultural identity and self-esteem in an environment that may devalue their ethnicity.

8. The development of same and opposite sex peer relations also deserves study. Available research suggests that the formation of positive relations between Asian-American males and females is at risk as early as adolescence, further exacerbating problems in development of self-concept and self-esteem in males.

9. The effect of cultural diversity on developmental outcomes should be more systematically investigated. Experiments to investigate how children of differ-

ent ages perceive and respond to cultural diversity and make culturally relevant choices are needed.

Finally, research should focus on the positive aspects of Asian-American socialization, not just on the problems, so that they can build on the strengths while modifying or supplementing those which are not conducive to bicultural adaptation. An appropriate mix of Eastern and Western socialization goals and childrearing practices might well be what is needed for effective parenting in a multicultural society.

REFERENCES

Abbott, K. A. & Abbott, E. L. (1968) Juvenile delinquency in San Francisco's Chinese-American community: 1961–1966. *Journal of Sociology, 4,* 45–56.

Abramson, P. & Imai-Marques, J. (1982). The Japanese-American: A cross-cultural, cross-sectional study of sex guilt. *Journal of Research in Personality, 16,* 227–237.

Benedek, T. (1959). Parenthood as a developmental phase. *Journal of the American Psychoanalytic Association, 7,* 389–417.

Bucton, L. (1985, August). Assessment and use of family subsystems in working with Filipinos. Paper presented at the annual meeting of the American Psychological Association, Los Angeles, CA.

Chang, T. S. (1975). The self-concept of children in ethnic groups: Black American and Korean Americans. *Elementary School Journal, 76,* 52–58.

Chen, L. C. & Yang, C. Y. (1986). The self-image of Chinese American adolescents. *P/AAMARC Research Review, 5,* 27–29.

Clarke-Stewart, K. A. (1988). Parents' effects on children's development: A decade of progress. *Journal of Applied Developmental Psychology, 9,* 41–84.

Del Carmen, R. & Serafica, F. C. (1985, April). Locus of control and child rearing in Chinese- and Filipino-Americans. Paper presented at the biennial meeting of the Society for Research in Child Development, Toronto.

Fox, D. & Jordan, V. (1973). Racial preference and identification of black American, Chinese, and White children. *Genetic Psychology Monographs, 68,* 229–286.

Glenn, E. N. (1983). Split household small producer and dual wage earner: An analysis of Chinese-American family strategies. *Journal of Marriage and the Family, 45,* 35–46.

Han, Y. K. (1985). Discriminant analysis of self-disclosing behavior and locus of control among Korean American and Caucasian American adolescents. *P/AAMHRC Research Review, 4,* 20–29.

Harrison, A., Serafica, F. & McAdoo, H. (1984). Ethnic families of color. In R. D. Parke (Ed.), *Review of child development. Vol. 7* (pp. 329–371). Chicago: University of Chicago Press.

Hernandez, D. J. (1986, May). Demographic and socioeconomic circumstances of minority families and children. Paper presented at a conference on "Minority Families and Children" sponsored by the National Institute of Child Health and Human Development, Bethesda, MD.

Hsu, J., Tseng, W., Ashton, G., McDermott, Jr., J. F. & Char, W. (1985). Family interaction patterns among Japanese-American and Caucasian families in Hawaii. *American Journal of Psychiatry, 142*, 577–581.

Huang, L. J. (1981). The Chinese American family. In C. H. Mindel & R. W. Habenstein (Eds.), *Ethnic families in America* (rev. ed.). New York: Elsevier.

Jun, S. (1984). Communication patterns among young Korean immigrants. *International Journal of Intercultural Relations, 8*, 373–389.

Jung, M. (1984). Structural family therapy: Its application to Chinese families. *Family Process, 23*, 365–374.

Kan, S. H. & Liu, W. T. (1986). The educational status of Asian Americans: An update from the 1980 census. *P/AAMHRC Research Review, 5*, 21–24.

Kim, B. C. (1980). *The Korean-American child at school and at home* (Grant No. 90-C-1335 (01). Washington, DC: Administration of Children, Youth, and Families. U.S. Department of Welfare.

Kim, S. P. (1983). Self-concept, English language acquisition, and school adaptation in recently immigrated Asian children. *Journal of Children in Contemporary Society, 15*, 71–79.

Kim, Y. J. (1983). Problems in the delivery of the school based psycho-educational services to the Asian immigrant children. *Journal of Children in Contemporary Society, 15*, 81–89.

Kuo, E. L. Y. (1974). The family and bilingual socialization: A sociolinguistic study of a sample of Chinese children in the United States. *Journal of Social Psychology, 92*, 181–191.

Lee, E. (1982). A social systems approach to assessment and treatment for Chinese American families. In M. McGoldrick, J. K. Pearce & J. Giordano (Eds.), *Ethnicity and family therapy* (pp. 527–551). New York: Guilford Press.

Leong, F. T. L. (1986). Counseling and psychotherapy with Asian-Americans. *Journal of Counseling Psychology, 33*, 196–206.

Liu, W. T. & Yu, E.S.H. (1986). Ethnicity and mental health: An overview. In W. T. Liu (Ed.), The Pacific/Asian American Mental Health Research Center: A decade review (pp. 3–18). Chicago: The Pacific/Asian American Mental Health Research Center, University of Illinois at Chicago.

Loo, C. (1982). Chinatown's wellness: An enclave of problems. *Journal of the Asian American Psychological Association, 7*, 13–18.

Maccoby, E. E. & Martin, J. A. (1983). Socialization in the context of the family: Parent-child. In P. H. Mussen (Ed.), *Handbook of child psychology. Vol. 4.* New York: Wiley.

McDermott, J. F., Char, W. F., Robillard, A. B., Hsu, J., Tseng, W. & Ashton, G. C. (1983). Cultural variations in family attitudes and their implications for therapy. *Journal of the American Academy of Child Psychiatry, 22*, 454–458.

Meade, R. D. (1985). Experimental studies of authoritarian and democratic leadership in four cultures: American Indian, Chinese, and Chinese-American. *High School Journal, 68*, 293–295.

Okano, Y. & Spilka, B. (1971). Ethnic identity, alienation, and achievement orientation in Japanese-American families. *Journal of Cross-Cultural Psychology, 2*, 273–282.

O'Reilly, J. P., Ebata, A. T., Tokuno, K. A. & Bryant, B. K. (1980). Sex and ethnic differences in parental attitudes toward social competence for their children. Unpublished manuscript, University of Hawaii.

Ou, Y. & McAdoo, H. (1980). *Ethnic identity and self-esteem in Chinese children.* Washington, DC: National Institute of Mental Health.

Pang, V. D., Mizokawa, D. T., Morishima, J. K. & Olstad, R. G. (1985). Self-concepts of Japanese-American children. *Journal of Cross-Cultural Psychology, 16,* 99–109.

Powell, G. J., Yamamoto, J., Romero, A. & Morales, A. (Eds.) (1983). *The psychosocial development of minority group children.* New York: Brunner/Mazel.

Sata, L. S. (1983). Mental health issues of Japanese American children. In Powell, G. J., Yamamoto, J., Romero, A. & Morales, A. (Eds.) *The psychosocial development of minority group children* (pp. 363–372). New York: Brunner/Mazel.

Schwartz, A. J. (1971). The culturally advantaged: A study of Japanese-American pupils. *Sociology and Social Research, 55,* 341–353.

Serafica, F. C. (1988). Assessing the mental health needs of Asian/Pacific American children and youth. *Newsletter of the American Psychological Association Division 37, 11,* 3 & 9.

———. (1986, April). Counseling Asian-American Parents: Cultural and Developmental Perspectives. Paper presented at The Ohio State University Minority Mental Health Conference, Columbus, OH.

Siegal, M. (1985). Children, parenthood, and social welfare in the context of developmental psychology. Oxford: Clarendon Press.

Sollenberger, R. T. (1968). Chinese-American child rearing practices and juvenile delinquency. *Journal of Social Psychology, 74,* 13–23.

Sperling, E. (1979). Parent counseling and therapy. In J. D. Noshpitz (Ed.), *Basic handbook of child psychiatry, Vol. III* (pp. 136–148). New York: Basic Books.

Springer, D. (1950). Awareness of racial differences of preschool children in Hawaii. *Genetic Psychology Monographs, 41,* 214–270.

Steinberg, L. (1987). Single parents, stepparents, and the susceptibility of adolescents to peer pressure. *Child Development, 58,* 269–275.

Stern, J. D. & Chandler, M. O. (1987). *The condition of education: Statistical report, Center for Education Statistics.* Washington, DC: U.S. Government Printing Office.

Steward, M. & Steward, D. (1973). The observation of Anglo-, Mexican-, and Chinese-American mothers teaching their children. *Child Development, 44,* 329–337.

Sue, S. (1988). Psychotherapeutic services for ethnic minorities: Two decades of research findings. *American Psychologist, 43,* 301–308.

Sue, S. & Chin, R. (1983). The mental health of Chinese-American children: Stressors and resources. In G. J. Powell, J. Yamamoto, A. Romero & A. Morales (Eds.), *The psychosocial development of minority group children* (pp. 385–400). New York: Brunner/Mazel.

Sue, S. & Morishima, J. K. (1982). The mental health of Asian Americans. San Francisco: Jossey-Bass.

Sung, B. L. (1979). *Transplanted Chinese children.* (Report to the Administration for Children, Youth, and Family, U.S. Department of Health, Education, and Welfare). New York: City University of New York, Department of Asian Studies.

Suzuki, B. H. (1980). The Asian-American family. In M. D. Fantine and R. Cardenas (Eds.), *Parenting in a multicultural society.* New York: Longman.

Toupin, E. S. W. A. (1980). Counseling Asians. *American Journal of Orthopsychiatry,* *50,* 76–86.

Tuddenham, R. D., Brooks, J. & Milkovich, L. (1974). Mothers' reports of behavior of ten-year-olds: Relationships with sex, ethnicity, and mother's education. *Developmental Psychology, 10,* 959–995.

U.S. Bureau of the Census. (1987). *Statistical Abstract of the United States: 1987* (107th Edition). Washington, DC: Government Printing Press.

U.S. Department of Health, Education and Welfare. (1974). A study of selected socioeconomic characteristics of ethnic minorities based on the 1970 census, 161 II: Asian Americans. HEW Publication No. (05) 75–121, Washington, DC: U.S. Department of Health, Education and Welfare.

Vernon, P. E. (1982). *The abilities and achievements of Orientals in North America.* New York: Academic Press.

Weiss, M. S. (1970). Selective acculturation and the dating process: The pattern of Chinese-Caucasian interracial dating. *Journal of Marriage and the Family, 32,* 273–278.

Wong, B. (1985). Family, kinship, and ethnic identity of the Chinese in New York City, with comparative remarks on the Chinese in Lima, Peru and Manila, Philippines. *Journal of Comparative Family Studies, 16,* 231–254.

Wong, H. Z. (1986, April). Clinical assessment of Asian Americans for family therapy. Paper presented at the Ohio State University Minority Mental Health Conference, Columbus, Ohio.

Yamamoto, J. (1968). Japanese American identity. In E. B. Brody (Ed.). *Minority adolescents in the United States* (pp. 133–156). Baltimore, Williams & Wilkins.

Yamamoto, J. & Yap, J. (1984). Group therapy for Asian Americans and Pacific Islanders. *P/AAMHRC Research Review, 3,* 1–3.

Yeung, W. H. & Schwartz, M. A. (1986). Emotional disturbance in Chinese obstetrical patients: A pilot study. *General Hospital Psychiatry, 8,* 258–262.

Young, N. F. (1972a). Independence training from a cross-cultural perspective. *American Anthropologist, 74,* 629–638.

————. (1972b). Changes in values and strategies among Chinese in Hawaii. *Sociology and Social Research, 56,* 228–241.

Zigler, E. F. & Finn-Stevenson, M. (1987). *Children: Development and social issues.* Lexington, MA: D. C. Heath.

Part IV

University, Professional Association, and Government Roles in Promoting Ethnic Minority Mental Health

Introduction

Paul D. Isaac

The training of professionals to conduct research and to provide service addressing mental health needs of the ethnic minority communities is discussed in this section. The first chapter, by Martha E. Bernal, is a useful summary of issues that must be addressed in discussions of minority mental health. Bernal outlines demographic data on minorities and notes their underrepresentation as professionals in psychology. She discusses the implications of this underrepresentation for provision of mental health service and delivery, and for the development of theory and technology appropriate to ethnic minorities. The need to recruit more ethnic minority psychologists is apparent. Bernal assesses the adequacy of current psychology graduate programs and concludes that they are inadequate in their preparation of professionals for research and practice relevant to minority populations. To address this inadequacy, Bernal outlines a conceptual framework for minority mental health training. Mental health professionals must be able to develop intervention strategies that will strengthen the relationships between the ethnic minority groups and the dominant groups of the culture, and that will improve the mental health of individuals from all groups. The implementation of a program addressing the needs of minority mental health requires the presence of faculty knowledgeable in ethnic minority issues who can train graduate students and who have access to community settings which will enable the conduct of relevant research.

The second chapter in this section, by Lillian Comas-Diaz, outlines the history of the APA's involvement with minority issues. She traces this involvement from the establishment of an ad hoc committee on Equality of Opportunity in Psychology in 1963 through the establishment in 1986 of a new APA division, namely Division 45: The Society for the Psychological Study of Ethnic Minority issues, to the formation in 1988 of the American Psychological Society (APS). In the intervening years, APA has been involved in minority issues in a variety of ways with varying levels of commitment. The impact of APA on curricula in training programs through accreditation procedures is not to be minimized. On the state level, committees on ethnic minority affairs are also being established to ensure that state associations address issues relevant to training of professionals ready to deal with problems of minority populations.

The third chapter in this section was written by Delores L. Parron. The 1960s were a time of heightened awareness in our society of issues related to problems of ethnic minority groups. Civil rights legislation affected the entire nation. One outcome of this social movement was the establishment in 1970 of the Center for Minority Group Mental Health Programs within the National Institute of Mental Health. Parron describes the importance of this center for training in research relevant to minorities. Clearly, NIMH and its support of mental health-related research has had a significant impact on the progress of our understanding of the origins and prevention of mental illness in this country.

The three chapters in this section address issues related to professional training and research relevant to ethnic minority mental health. Bernal's chapter provides an overview of what must be accomplished in the training of mental health professionals. Comas-Diaz's chapter provides an outline of actions of a professional organization, the APA, that are relevant to ethnic minority mental health and ethnic minority psychology, and finally, Parron describes the role of the federal government in providing financial aid relevant to research in the area of mental health, especially as it applies to ethnic minority populations.

The demographics of the nation dictate that mental health research and practice must be relevant to ethnic minorities if it is to be relevant to the welfare of society at large. Attention to training of minority and nonminority professionals is essential. Professional organizations and accrediting agencies can use their influence to bring increased attention to minority issues, and government agencies can play an indispensible role in support of relevant research and training programs.

10

Ethnic Minority Mental Health Training: Trends and Issues

Martha E. Bernal

One of the most pressing needs relative to the mental health of ethnic minorities in the United States is the preparation of professionals to serve a multicultural society in teaching, scientific, and service roles. This need has not been adequately addressed by the field of psychology, and there is growing urgency that psychology examine its house, set goals, and move directly to put in place those components of training that are necessary for professional competence in a multicultural society. This opening statement is defended in this chapter through the presentation of demographic data and the subsequent implications of these data for minority mental health. Next, the literature that describes the current status of minority mental health training in psychology will be reviewed. Finally, an integration of some related literature will be presented that forms the basis for a conceptual framework within which to view the training of professionals for work with ethnic minorities.

DEMOGRAPHIC DATA: IMPLICATIONS FOR TRAINING

Ethnic Minority Representation in the U.S. Population

According to the 1980 Census (U.S. Bureau of the Census, 1981), there were 25.5 million blacks, 1.4 million American Indian/Alaskan Natives, 3.5

million Asian/Pacific Islanders, and 6.8 million other ethnic minority group peoples living in the United States. In addition, 14.5 million people of Spanish origin were identified. Adjustment for overlap among the various census categories led to an estimated total of 46.3 million people that belonged to ethnic minority groups. This number represented 20 percent of the total U.S. population of 226.5 million in 1980. More recent data (U.S. Bureau of the Census, 1986) indicates that there were 29.1 million blacks and 5.9 million people of other races, as well as 17.3 million people of Spanish origin in the U.S. data for separate races other than black were not available, and the Spanish origin count overlaps with the race count because people of Spanish origin can belong to any race. Nevertheless, the sum of the ethnic minority population (52.3 million) divided by the total U.S. population of 238.6 million equals an ethnic minority representation of 21.9 percent. Conservative estimates for the year 2000, have the percentage of ethnic minorities in the United States reaching 26.3 percent. This estimate was made by adding the projections of estimates for total race and Spanish origin population by total U.S. population for the year 2000 (U.S. Bureau of the Census, 1986). Thus, one out of four people in this country will be an ethnic minority group member in the near future. In light of this projection about ethnic minorities, it seems particularly relevant to examine the extent to which graduate programs are now, and will continue to be, preparing psychologists who will be working with this population.

Ethnic Minority Representation in Psychology

How is psychology doing in preparing its graduates for work with this population? One way to answer this question is to examine ethnic minority representation in psychology, since such representation probably is an important condition for the incorporation of minority mental health training. In Figure 10.1, data from a number of different sources (Boneau & Cuca, 1974; Howard, Pion, Gottfredson, Flattau, Oskamp, Pfafflin, Bray & Burstein, 1986; Pion, Bramblett & Wicherski, 1987; Pion, Bramblett, Wicherski & Stapp, 1985; Russo, Olmedo, Stapp & Fulcher, 1981; Stang & Peele 1977; Stapp, Tucker & VandenBos, 1985; Suber, 1977, and unpublished APA data) were combined so as to provide estimates of ethnic minority representation in psychology. The surveys from which these data were taken vary in a number of ways: they had different response rates; were conducted by different groups at different time periods; had different degrees of completeness and attention to detail; and, in the case of data on graduate departments, may have combined data for psychology with data for associated fields. Some of the surveys also combined minority faculty figures for Ph.D. and M.A. graduate programs, but no striking differences in data on psychology minority faculty were found between doctoral and master's level programs. In Figure 10.1, these estimates have been plotted over time. In this figure, the past and future growth of the U.S. ethnic minority population up to the year 2000 has been plotted as a standard against which to

Figure 10.1
Ethnic Minority Representation in Psychology Relative to Ethnic Minority Representation in the U.S. Population

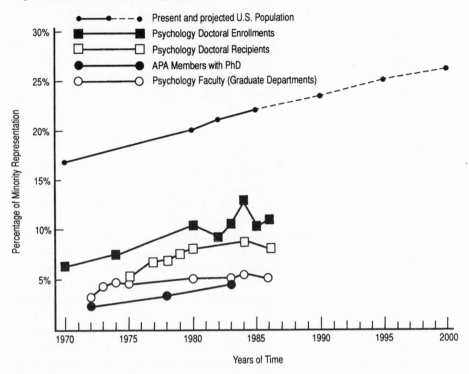

compare present and future ethnic minority human resources in psychology. The figure shows the percentages of ethnic minority psychology doctoral enrollments, doctorate recipients, American Psychological Associations (APA) members with Ph.D.s, and faculty in graduate departments over the years from 1970 to 1986.

The percentage of ethnic minority APA members was no greater than 4 percent up to ten years ago, and no more recent data were available. Estimates of ethnic minority faculty and graduate students have been more frequent because of national statistics and surveys involving educational institutions. Based on the surveys represented in Figure 10.1, levels of ethnic minority faculty have remained relatively stable at 5 percent of the total faculty in graduate training programs. This figure does not show the same growth as in the graduate student enrollment or doctorate recipients, perhaps because, as found by Russo et al. (1981), only 10.5 percent or 37 of the 248 new ethnic minority doctorates in psychology accept positions in universities each year. In combination, these figures indicate a growing disparity between ethnic minority representation in academic and professional psychology and the total ethnic minority population.

Up to 1979, there were consistent increases in ethnic minority psychologists in the educational pipeline fare, but there has been no change in the rate of 8 percent of psychologists completing training since 1980. The proportions of ethnic minority graduate students in doctoral programs over time has grown in the past fifteen years but does not exceed an average of 10.8 percent during the past eight years. The lack of a sharp upward turn in proportions of ethnic minority graduate students indicates that the large and increasing discrepancy between ethnic minority human resources and the proportion of ethnic minorities in the population will continue, and become more severe as the years go on.

Implications of this Discrepancy

There are four major implications of the discrepancy between ethnic minority representation in psychology and in the general population.

1. Ethnic minority groups, who are at high risk for psychological dysfunction because of such factors as discrimination, racism, inadequate education and health care, unemployment, and acculturation stresses, already receive less than adequate mental health services (President's Commission on Mental Health, 1978). Mental health services need to be provided by culturally and linguistically compatible psychologists (Abad, Ramos & Boyce, 1974; Scott & Delgado, 1979; Cuellar, Harris & Naron, 1981). Services based on adaptations of existing psychological intervention theory and technology for use with ethnic minorities are scarce. In the view of the present writer, such services must be growing more scarce due to the decreasing proportions of ethnic minorities in psychology relative to minority population growth, since minority psychologists may be the only ones who are adapting techniques for serving minority groups. This scarcity of culturally sensitive services also is due to the lack of ethnic minority faculty who can prepare trainees to deliver and conduct research on services.

2. A need exists for the development and evaluation of creative innovations in methods for promoting the mental health of ethnic minorities at varying degrees of risk for mental illness. Such innovations are needed because our existing theory and technology were developed for a monocultural Anglo-American society, and there is question about the degree to which this theory and technology are appropriate for ethnic minority populations. Future innovations depend upon research, and on how we train our graduates. This research should be conducted by culturally sensitive psychologists who are knowledgeable about the kinds of questions that need to be asked. The scarcity of culturally sensitive behavioral scientists means that research on innovative minority mental health interventions is not likely to be conducted. Furthermore, the scarcity of culturally sensitive academic faculty restricts the proper training of available human resources. Adding to these problems is the fact that increasing numbers of clinical, counseling, and school psychologists are receiving practi-

tioner degrees and are graduating from educational institutions that are not represented among the top research universities (Howard et al., 1986). In short, fewer numbers of psychologists receive the behavioral science training background necessary to conduct clinical and health services research.

3. An implication of the two points just made is that ethnic minority psychologists must be recruited into psychology in substantially larger numbers than they are now being recruited. Otherwise, the shortage of ethnic minority psychologists will become more and more acute, given the projected increases in the ethnic minority population. Unfortunately, even ethnic minority faculty may be poorly trained for work with ethnic minority populations. Incentives for faculty who are interested in developing these kinds of competencies, and recruitment of faculty who have them, can be important steps toward increasing the numbers of well-trained ethnic minority psychologists capable of working with ethnic minority groups.

4. Because a gradual increase in the numbers of ethnic minority students admitted into graduate training is more likely than the much-needed sharp increase, psychology will need to increase the level of sensitivity of dominant group psychologists to ethnic minority psychology and related topics. Two key problems need to be addressed in order for such training of Anglo-American psychologists to occur: the scarcity of ethnic minority faculty to conduct the training, and the reluctance or indifference of dominant group psychologists to make the necessary career development or retraining efforts. Attention must be paid to methods for increasing the numbers of dominant group psychologists who have the necessary competencies for work with ethnic minorities.

CURRENT STATUS OF ETHNIC MINORITY TRAINING

Minority Mental Health Curricula in Psychology

What kind of training for work with ethnic minorities exists currently in psychology? Four surveys of ethnic minority curricula and training provide some answers to this question. Bernal & Padilla (1982) surveyed 106 APA-accredited clinical psychology programs to assess the kinds of coursework, practica, and research training experiences that existed for work with ethnic minorities. Questionnaires were returned by seventy-six programs, yielding a 71 percent return rate. Directors of clinical training, who were the respondents, were asked to provide a list of courses being taught that had bearing on minorities, whether the courses were required for completion of the Ph.D., and who taught the courses. Table 10.1 presents, by course category, the number of courses offered, the number of programs offering the courses, and the number of programs requiring minority-related courses for the Ph.D. The four course categories were: (1) Minority courses, which included courses entitled minority mental health, minority psychology, issues in minority mental health, development of the minority child, black psychology, psychology of black experi-

Table 10.1
Ethnic Minority Courses and Content Units in Courses in APA-accredited
Clinical Psychology Programs

Course category	Number of courses	Number of programs offering courses	Number of programs requiring courses for Ph.D.
Minority courses	17	12	0
Cross-cultural clinical courses	6	6	1
Sociocultural courses	26	18	6
Cross-cultural research courses	8	8	0
Totals:	57	44	7
Units of minority content in other courses	14	10	5

Note: $N = 76$ respondent clinical psychology programs.
Source: Bernal, M. E., & Padilla, A. M. (1982). Survey of minority curriculum and training in
    Psychology. *American Psychologist, 37,* p. 783. Copyright 1982 by the American Psycho-
    logical Association. Adapted by permission of the publisher.

ence, and psychology of the black child; (2) Cross-cultural clinical courses,
which included multicultural counseling, psychotherapy, or assessment; (3) Sociocultural courses, which included sociocultural or cross-cultural determinants
of human behavior, cross-cultural psychology, psychology of prejudice, and
social issues in psychology; and (4) Cross-cultural research methods.

A total of fifty-seven courses fell within the four categories. Overall, 41
percent of the seventy-six responding programs offered one or more courses
that might contribute to the student's education about minority or other cultures. Furthermore, three-quarters of the courses were taught by sixteen programs, indicating that a small number of programs accounted for most of the
courses. In ten programs, ethnic minority content was integrated as units in
other courses, and five programs integrated minority content into required core

courses. None of these programs required minority or crosscultural clinical courses for completion of the Ph.D. Regular, full-time faculty taught 81 percent of the courses, half the courses were taught once a year, and the other half were taught irregularly.

Other data obtained by Bernal & Padilla (1982) showed that a majority of training programs were aware that their students worked with ethnic minority clients in in-house or community settings, and knew of substantial representation (greater than 10 percent) of ethnic minority groups in their community. However, the fact that only eighteen programs offered any courses dealing with minority mental health (minority courses) or cross-cultural clinical topics, and only one program required such a course for the Ph.D., suggested that students were ill-prepared to work with ethnic minority clients or community groups.

The data on research training revealed that 43 percent of the programs reported at least one faculty member conducting minority-related research, although 50 percent reported no faculty engaged in minority research. Respondents indicated that students who desired to initiate thesis or dissertation research on minority issues would find faculty to chair such research in 54 percent of the programs, but no support at all in 25 percent of the programs. Among programs whose faculty were willing to chair this type of student research, a median of 1.5 such theses or dissertations had been chaired in the previous three years. Thus, this survey, conducted in 1979–1980, demonstrated the apparent indifference of clinical psychology training programs to formal preparation of their students for competence in clinical and scientific work with ethnic minorities.

A similar scarcity of training opportunities for competence in counseling and school psychologists was revealed in a survey of internships conducted in 1981–1982 by Wyatt & Parham (1985). These investigators reported that only seven of the 169 internships surveyed had seminars in which minority issues were discussed. This lack of minority training also surfaced in a broad survey of 398 departments of psychology conducted by the APA (American Psychological Association, 1982). Only 4.3 percent or seventeen of the departments reported that they required courses or practica on the psychological assessment of minorities, while 9.5 percent or thirty-eight of the departments had an elective course or practicum on this topic. Although the teaching of a single course on ethnic minorities is barely minimal preparation, even single courses were scarce in programs participating in this survey.

In a fourth survey, Dunston (1983) assessed the integration and dispersion of ethnic minority content in a modified random sample of APA-approved psychology departments and clinical and counseling predoctoral internship programs. She also attempted to collect information about faculty development efforts to enhance faculty knowledge regarding ethnic minority content. This study had modest response rates of 47 percent for 260 departments and 53 percent for 131 internship programs who received questionnaires by mail, which limited the generalizability of its results. Inclusion of ethnic minority content within curricula or training programs was reported by 66 percent or 80 of the 122 department chair respondents and 64 percent or 44 of the 69 internship director respondents.

Within psychology departments, 48 percent of the courses with ethnic minority content were offered as elective courses, and minority courses were required in only eight departments and six internships. Within internships, minority content was interspersed among courses and practica. The author stated that the variability in the manner and degree of integration of minority content in department curricula, as compared to internship programs, suggested the need to develop linkages between the units in order to ensure continuity of ethnic minority training. No formal mechanism or guidelines for inclusion of ethnic minority content in training was reported by any of the respondents, and small numbers of chairs (14) or directors (18) reported that their programs provided faculty development for inclusion of this content. However, 36 percent of chairs and 52 percent of directors indicated needs for faculty development, resource materials, and guidelines for minority training, and similar proportions of chairs and directors indicated they would allow time for faculty development, especially in summer institutes for department faculty and continuing education for internship faculty.

While more recent survey data on ethnic minority curricula and training in psychology are unavailable for the purpose of assessing progress, there is reason to believe that the degree of attention toward such training has increased. The evidence takes several forms. First, among the resolutions resulting at the National Conference on Graduate Education in Psychology ("Resolutions Approved," 1987) is one entitled, "Issues of Cultural Diversity in Graduate Education in Psychology." This resolution includes a number of recommendations for the APA and for graduate training. For example, the American Psychological Association is encouraged to communicate to training faculty the desirability of emphasizing the multicultural, multinational, and multilingual nature of psychology in formal courses and field experiences. It is recommended that the APA establish a clearinghouse for course outlines and teaching materials; provide workshops for faculty and staff development; publish special issues on cultural diversity; develop an inventory of expert consultants on cultural diversity for use in curriculum development; and create a clearinghouse of scholars from minority and other underrepresented groups to visit graduate departments and schools of psychology as consultants, colloquium speakers, and visiting professors. It urges graduate departments of psychology to address cultural diversity issues; conduct self-study to develop and implement curricula for this area; blend cultural content into the mainstream psychology curricula, especially courses and specialty areas where the influence of culture is most obvious; and develop opportunities and procedures for faculty development. This clearcut mandate regarding the incorporation of cultural diversity as a topic area within the graduate training of psychologists could have significant long-term effects on the field.

A clearinghouse for resource materials, such as those recommended at the above conference, has been one of the charges of APA's Board of Ethnic Minority Affairs to its standing Committee on Ethnic Minority Human Resources Development (CEMHRD). The CEMHRD's goal is to develop resource materials for use by psychologists wishing to teach courses on ethnic minority issues. To gather these materials, this committee solicited syllabi for such courses from individuals and programs listed in *Graduate Study in Psychology,* the *Ethnic Minority Human Resources Directory,* and other sources. Syllabi for more than fifty graduate level courses have been gathered. The CEMHRD is developing prototypic syllabi and bibliographies for ethnic minority content in three areas: developmental, counseling and psychotherapy, and issues of prejudice and racism in society and psychology. When available, these materials will be disseminated through the Office of Ethnic Minority Affairs.

It is worth noting that the courses gathered by the CEMHRD were not concentrated in a few universities, as in the Bernal & Padilla (1982) survey, and that they outnumbered the combined ethnic minority courses and practica for the large number of programs reported in the aforementioned APA survey (American Psychological Association, 1982). Thus, there is additional evidence of increased attention to ethnic minority training in psychology.

Minority Mental Health Graduate and Internship Training Programs

Various graduate programs and predoctoral internship programs now have integrated curricula and experiences designed to prepare psychologists for work with ethnic minority populations, and some of these programs have been funded by the National Institute of Mental Health (NIMH). On the list of eight programs funded in fiscal year 1987 are academic training programs at the California School of Professional Psychology at Los Angeles (CSPP-LA), Colorado State University, Fordham University, Oklahoma State University, Pennsylvania State University, the University of California at Los Angeles (UCLA), the University of Maryland, and Utah State University. The two NIMH-funded internship programs are at New York University Medical Center and the National Asian American Psychology Training Center in San Francisco.

When Bernal and Padilla (1982) conducted their survey of minority curricula in clinical psychology, there probably were no programs that had an organized, systematic curriculum for preparation of psychologists for work with ethnic minority populations. Now there are at least eight academic and two internship programs that have organized programs for training ethnic minorities, and some of these programs also prepare minority and nonminority psychologists for work with ethnic minorities. The range includes "generic" programs that train ethnic minority psychologists within a traditional clinical or counseling program, programs that have a particular orientation or that integrate minority content throughout training of all students, and specialized tracks within programs that prepare ethnic minority students for work with ethnic minorities.

Two important points about these programs is that they serve as existing models of appropriate training and are located in settings (e.g., psychology departments) that can exert leadership in the field. They also represent variations in training models that are applicable in different settings with different trainees and client populations, as well as academic training emphases. Thus, programs seeking to address cultural diversity in their curriculum or graduate student body can find a range of models from which to draw aspects that are implementable in their environments. Six of these programs responded to a request from the present author for information about their training. The following brief descriptions communicate some of the distinctiveness among these programs, all of which state that they follow the scientist-practitioner model.

The CSPP-LA has an ethnic minority mental health specialty track, the goal of which is to train both minority and nonminority students in the understanding of ethnic and cultural issues, the impact of these issues on service planning and delivery. Traditional clinical content and practica are structured within an ethnoculturally relevant framework in various ways, for example, by the addition of units on cultural factors, plus specialty-focused coursework that deals with aspects of assessment and intervention relevant to given cultural groups. Students develop self-awareness about their cultural identity so as to maximize their own resources and ability to work with diverse populations. Basic research courses and practica address research from an ethnic minority perspective, and prepare the student to conduct a dissertation on minority mental health. Two of three required clinical field experiences for trainees supported by the training grant are in settings with ethnic minority clients (Porche-Burke, 1988).

The clinical/counseling training program at Colorado State University is committed to the training primarily of Hispanic students because of the large Hispanic population in the region. However, other ethnic minority students also are trained. The training includes two specialized courses in minority issues, a seminar on minority research, and field practica in agencies serving ethnic minorities and disadvantaged persons. By integrating ethnic minority content and issues into all graduate courses, the program seeks to increase the awareness and knowledge about minority issues of nonminority and minority trainees. There is a strong emphasis on the conduct of research on ethnic minority issues. This program has a long history of ethnic minority student recruitment and success in graduating minority psychologists (Chavez & Deffenbacher, 1986).

At Oklahoma State University, training is not aimed at any specific target group. The aim is to train general clinicians who are members of ethnic minority groups and will work with their own ethnic people. Increasing the number of ethnic minority psychologists in clinical psychology who have an interest in their own culture and will serve as role models is the major goal of the program (Sandvold, K. D., personal communication, May, 1988).

UCLA's minority training is blended into their generic clinical program; there is no separate ethnic minority program. Its aim is to produce well-trained, multiculturally competent minority and nonminority clinicians/scholars. This goal is achieved through various modifications in the traditional program: increasing the cultural diversity of students and faculty and assuring the stable presence of a substantial number of minority students and faculty; changing the ethnocentric biases prevalent in existing clinical models of assessment, diagnosis, treatment, and research; assuring that students see culturally varied clientele in their supervised clinical practica; seeing that issues relative to cross-ethnic, crossclass, and cross-gender psychotherapy and supervision encounters are incorporated in the training; and attending to issues of acculturation relevant to upwardly mobile ethnic minority clients as well as clinicians (Myers, 1987).

The University of Maryland emphasizes the preparation of mental health professionals who conceptualize both health and disorder and the delivery of diagnostic and intervention services within a community psychology perspective. One perspective emphasized is the appreciation of the relevance of ecological and cultural factors to the development, maintenance, and modification of psychological functioning. Its community emphasis sensitizes students to the range of alternatives for diagnosis and interventions, as well as prevention and enhancement of individual functioning through community-level interventions that target social systems and policies. These emphases are realized through courses and experiences, for example, assessment courses include content on assessment of social environments as well as individuals, and practica provide experience in carrying out such assessments in varying environments in order to design interventions (Lorion, 1988).

The predoctoral internship training program at New York University Medical Center may be viewed as a traditional one-year internship that has a Hispanic emphasis and is geared toward both Hispanic and non-Hispanic trainees. The training experiences for Hispanic bilingual/bicultural interns include work with Spanish-speaking, unassimilated patients, while non-Hispanic interns work with Hispanic patients who can communicate in English. Training objectives are the acquisition of advanced clinical skills and integration of these skills with psychological theory and research relevant to Hispanics (Vasquez, 1986).

A different kind of training model is embodied in a program that is not federally funded. It is the Public Service and Minority Cluster of the Clinical Psychology Training Program at the Department of Psychiatry, University of California, San Francisco. This program consists of a one-year general clinical predoctoral internship and a postdoctoral year that adds clinical research to advanced clinical training. The program is based at San Francisco General Hospital which specializes in the treatment of underserved populations. The research programs in which trainees participate are prevention- as well as treatment-oriented, and are designed for trainees who are committed to clinical research on prevention and treatment of depression, substance abuse, and schizophrenia in populations that include ethnic minorities and gays (Munoz, R., personal communication, December, 1988).

Since there is evidence of a spurt in the growth of efforts to prepare psychologists for service and research with ethnic minorities, this may be a good time to sharpen the conceptual groundwork that may guide the development of training efforts. Various sources of information are available for minority mental health curriculum development (e.g., Chunn, Dunston & Ross-Sheriff, 1983; Jones & Korchin, 1982; Ridley, 1985; Rosenfield & Esquivel, 1985; Sue, 1981); however, there is a dearth of such curriculum development material. In describing a conceptual or theoretical framework for curricula, some writers tend to advocate a cross-cultural perspective (e.g., Jones & Korchin, 1982), others emphasize cultural pluralism (e.g., Bernal, Bernal, Martinez, Olmedo & Santisteban, 1982; Kagehiro, Mejia & Garcia, 1985) and still others favor ethnic psychologies (e.g., Jones, 1980). A framework that reflects essential features of ethnic minority groups and that can be generalized across those groups has yet to be developed. To be useful in providing direction for design of training content and experiences, this framework should examine closely the fundamental assumptions made about who should be trained, who will be the recipients of the trained skills and knowledge, what issues are associated with their mental health, and what content and methods need to be incorporated in training in order that trainees can render the most effective service and conduct the most useful research on ethnic minority groups.

A CONCEPTUAL FRAMEWORK FOR MINORITY MENTAL HEALTH TRAINING

In this section, a working conceptual framework for the preparation of psychologists for service and research with ethnic minority populations will be described. In describing the framework, several seemingly elementary but complex questions need to be addressed:

What Is an Ethnic Group?

Definition of ethnic group. To answer the question of what is an ethnic group, as well as some of the following ones, it is useful to refer to John W. Berry's 1984 address to the 7th International Conference of the International Association for Cross-Cultural Psychology. In this address, Berry compared different aspects of cultural psychology with ethnic psychology, including: the types of independent and dependent variables used in the two fields; the general goals of the fields; and the major explanatory constructs in the examination of the relations between independent and dependent variables.

Berry began his analysis by defining a group as an identifiable set of individuals who socially interact. The group maintains itself over time, and has some social structure as well as some system of norms governing the conduct of its members. An ethnic group is defined by two criteria (Berry, 1984): (1) An *objective* criterion of descent from an earlier cultural group in terms of being offspring and derivative. Name and genealogy are objective indicators of people who are biological and cultural offspring. The derivative nature of culture is evidenced in ethnic group behaviors and customs such as food, dress, religion, and language that are not exact replicas of original cultural phenomena. As generations have passed, versions of these customs have been modified over time and space. (2) A *subjective* criterion that is a sense of identity with or attachment to the group. Berry describes this sense of identity as a feeling of an ethnic group's members that they belong to the group, and will strive to maintain the ethnic group and their membership in it. An *ethnic group,* then, may be defined as a group of individuals who interact, maintain themselves, have some social structure and system of governing norms and values, are biological and cultural descendants of a cultural group, and identify as members of the group.

Application of the ethnic group criteria to ethnic groups in the United States probably would result in the finding that some, but not all ethnic individuals fit the criteria of belonging to their ethnic group by reason of descent, or maintaining some derivative ethnic/cultural customs, and of having a subjective sense of ethnic group identity. There is wide variation among individuals who are of ethnic descent in the degree to which they maintain derivative customs and have a subjective sense of ethnic identity. Thus, as Berry points out, all people of ethnic descent are not necessarily members of an ethnic group.

Implications for training. This distinction between being of ethnic descent and being a member of an ethnic group has direct bearing on questions concerning the nature of minority mental health training, because ethnic membership shapes people's values, thoughts, and, perhaps, the effectiveness of different treatment approaches. It seems logical that the characteristics of the group that is the target of training need to be identified in order to assure that it is this group whose mental health is enhanced because of the training. This issue is one with which training programs must grapple.

The reality is that any population described as ethnic is highly likely to vary greatly in terms of the characteristics of individuals. That is, members of the population have varying degrees of strength of ethnic identity, cultural knowledge (including knowledge of their culture's language), preference for ethnic behaviors (including willingness to speak their culture's language) and values. Besides differences among individuals, there are intra-individual differences. Strength and nature of ethnic identity may vary at different periods of an individual's life and in different social contexts. Clearly, planners of training must be well-informed about the complexity of the characteristics of ethnic groups and members of those groups in order to develop training that is directed to that complexity rather than to the popular stereotypes associated with ethnic labels.

Given the variance in ethnic minority populations, some of the questions that should guide planners of training include these suggested ones: Should training be geared for preparation for work with the ethnic group, or with any individuals of the group? What type of training would be needed for proper preparation for service and research? What are the independent variables that are related to high risk in this population? (For example, should the training emphasize ethnic characteristics or low income in relation to mental health and interventions?) Should the program include courses on the group's history and culture, which form a background for the trainee to better understand the client's culture? How should clients for practicum teaching be selected? What cultural and linguistic characteristics would make interventions appropriate for these clients? What should be the nature of research training, and where should it be conducted, using samples from what populations? Which ethnic group mental health questions need to be addressed?

Decisions also need to be made regarding the characteristics of the ethnic trainee group. Which of at least two sets of variables—ethnic membership or socioeconomic background (or both)—should be matched to those of the target ethnic group to be served? In matching for ethnic membership, should trainees merely represent a group of the same ethnic descent, or should they be "real" ethnic group members? What additional cultural and linguistic criteria should be used? Does matching for socioeconomic background, ethnicity, ethnic group identification, language, and so on, matter at all for this training program? Selection criteria that are adopted based on answers to these questions might then be used in recruiting and selecting trainees, in the same manner that criteria such as GRE scores and GPA are used.

Even before discussing the term *ethnic minority*, the preparation of psychologists for work with ethnic groups raises many questions. Lest the conclusion be drawn that this is a case of gilding the lily, the reader is reminded that (1) mainstream psychology is unsophisticated about any except middle-class Anglo-American culture, (2) the history of psychology in this country has been devoted almost exclusively to the development of theory, knowledge, and applications that are appropriate and sensitive to middle class Anglo-American culture; very little of that history concerns any other cultural or social class group, and (3) psychology's training programs implicitly have addressed similar kinds of questions about variations in Anglo culture and social class that are similar to those raised here about ethnic minority groups. The field's heavy emphasis on development of interventions and delivery of service designed for middle-class Anglo clients as targets for training has resulted from identification of and selective attention to people who are most similar and neglect of people most dissimilar to dominant culture group members. Psychology training programs have selected trainees and planned curricula and practica for training in a manner that matches to the characteristics of the Anglo middle-class clients with whom they work. Thus, psychology needs to develop a level and depth of knowledge and expertise with regard to ethnic minorities that is comparable to its knowledge of the cultural group it has been addressing.

What Is an Ethnic Minority Group?

Definition of ethnic minority group. The term *minority* is often used synonymously with *ethnic,* but does not mean the same thing. There are different types of minorities who are not ethnic, such as the handicapped, and there can be ethnic groups who are not minorities. Berry (1984) defines a minority group in terms of three criteria: a minority group is (1) small in number and does not constitute the majority in a society; it may be (2) powerless or subordinate; and it may be (3) the object of discrimination. An ethnic minority group has the added criterion of genetic and cultural group membership. The powerlessness and discrimination experienced by an ethnic minority group depend upon characteristics of other groups with whom the smaller group interacts. These characteristics of other groups include their willingness to share status and resources with the minority group, and on the relations among the groups (Berry, 1984).

Typically, in U.S. society, members of ethnic minority groups who are different in skin color and appearance from the dominant Anglo group experience varying degrees of powerlessness and discrimination, and intergroup conflict with the dominant group. These particular ethnic minority groups are characterized as castelike minorities in Ogbu's (1983) typology of ethnic minority groups, as opposed to autonomous minorities like Polish- or Italian-Americans who occupy minority status by choice, and immigrant minorities like Vietnamese who enter a host society more or less voluntarily, though sometimes as refugees. Autonomous minorities are ordinarily less identifiable unless they choose to be identified, since their appearance does not vary greatly from that of the dominant Anglo society, and their separateness is not based on powerlessness and social degradation. It seems possible that immigrant minorities that fit the ethnic minority categories designated as castelike in this country (e.g., Asian people) may not experience the same degree of powerlessness and prejudice as their U.S.-born counterparts. The present writer's hypothesis about their role in U.S. society is that, since they were born in their own country and have not been raised in a society that relegates them to second-class status, they do not identify as American ethnic minorities and do not subjectively experience racial prejudice in the same way as U.S. minorities. They may, in fact, reject the negative racial and ethnic messages of this society, and view them not as reflective of their own deficiencies but of those of the host culture. It also may be that when immigrant minorities bring with them the expectation of economic success as well as skills and competencies for economic independence, they move into middle-class status more easily than most American minorities. For many U.S. ethnic minorities, the sense of learned hopelessness, limited attainment of skills, and low self-concept that can result from the experiences of poverty and discrimination may be a severe deterrent to the attainment of economic independence.

Implications for training. It is primarily the type of group that Ogbu (1983) calls castelike minorities, then, and some immigrant minority groups, that seem most at risk for mental health problems, because when the dominant society derogates and subordinates these groups economically and politically, there are vast implications for mental health. All of the attendant difficulties of gaining access to adequate health care, education, employment, housing, and life satisfactions, as well as the impact of powerlessness, derogation, and racism on the individual's view of self and own ethnic-group membership, point to the need to move toward the development of the study of the psychology of ethnic minorities.

Ethnic Psychology

Psychology is known as a scholarly and scientifically robust discipline capable of vigorous study of different areas of behavioral science. Intensive pursuit of the development of an ethnic psychology that deals specifically with ethnic minority groups could lead to knowledge that might enhance the mental health of all citizens as well as strengthen our minority mental health training programs by providing answers to the many questions that arise about the content and methods of training.

Recognition of ethnic psychology. Few mainstream psychologists have taken ethnic psychology seriously, and some writers have objected to the need for a "black psychology," or a "Chicano psychology" (e.g., Korchin, 1980). These psychologists might also wish to recall that, in Boring's classical and well-known *History of Experimental Psychology* (1950), sections with such titles as "Austrian Psychology," and "French Psychology," were differentiated from each other. The objection to recognition of an area of study called ethnic psychology seems to be that it is perceived as less than scientifically legitimate. At the same time that this perception may explain such an objection, one should keep in mind the dominant society's ethnocentric position on so many arenas of life, including the study of ethnic psychology.

Distinction between cultural psychology and ethnic psychology. Berry's comparison of cultural and ethnic psychology (1984) defines the two psychologies and conceptualizes some key differences between them. In Berry's view, both cultural and ethnic psychologies involve the scientific study of the systematic relationship between certain independent and dependent variables. The dependent variables of both cultural and ethnic psychologies are the psychological qualities of members of the culture or the ethnic group, respectively. The difference between the two psychologies is in the independent variables which they study. The independent variables of ethnic psychology are: (1) the characteristics of the ethnic group in which the individual develops; (2) the characteristics of other groups of people with whom the individual is in contact; and (3) the characteristics of the interactions among the groups in contact. The characteristics of either cultural or ethnic groups in which individuals develop are expressed in the process whereby individuals learn the traditional content of their culture and assimilate its practices and values; this process is known as *enculturation.* Thus, enculturation affects the psychological qualities of cultural or ethnic group members. Understanding of ethnic psychology, however, also requires the study of the ethnic group in contact and interaction with the dominant host culture which varies in its characteristics (Berry, 1984). In other words, the independent variables that distinguish ethnic psychology from cultural psychology affect the ethnic individual's *acculturation.* Acculturation is a lifelong process of adaptation that ethnic individuals undergo so long as they are in contact with the dominant group. Thus, both enculturation and acculturation are central explanatory constructs in this model of ethnic psychology.

Relation of ethnic psychology to minority mental health. In the lefthand column of Figure 10.2, the aforementioned independent and dependent variables of ethnic psychology are listed. In the center column are shown the two central processes of enculturation and acculturation. Enculturation is determined by independent variable 1, and acculturation by independent variables 2 and 3. In the right-hand column are listed the independent variables which are minority mental health-related examples of each of the independent variables shown in column one. Thus, the adaptational and coping capabilities of the ethnic group, and its cultural values, ethnic role behaviors, and customs, are examples of ethnic group characteristics which determine the types of psychological qualities of mental health (the dependent variables of minority mental health) that the individual develops. These characteristics are expressed through the process of an individual's enculturation. A person whose parents were born in Mexico and whose ethnic socialization included a large extended family with a high degree of ethnic identity and strong adaptational capabilities could show certain psychological qualities of mental health such as strong family values and maintenance of a supportive family system.

Similarly, the attitudes toward other groups, cultural values, and so on, of the dominant group, and the racially discriminatory interactions between the dominant group and ethnic minority group, are two variables that influence the process of the life-long acculturation of the minority person to the dominant society. That is, they are types of characteristics that determine the psychological qualities of mental health of ethnic group individuals because, as part of their adaptation to life, ethnic people must adapt to the dominant society, its culture, institutions, and members. This adaptation or acculturation is heavily influenced by the characteristics of those to whom ethnic minority people must adapt. A feature of this model that is worth noting is that variables expressing themselves through enculturation likely interact with variables expressing themselves through acculturation. That is, the ethnic minority person's ethnic socialization and acculturation together influence the nature of the person's mental health-related psychological qualities. Someone enculturated with strong ethnic and family ties (as in the example above of the person born in Mexico) who is in contact with dominant culture members who express racial discrimination and has negative interactions with them, may be resistant to stresses created by such acculturative experiences. Someone with similar acculturation experi-

Figure 10.2
Ethnic Psychology and Minority Mental Health: Independent and Dependent
Variables and Processes

ETHNIC PSYCHOLOGY		MINORITY MENTAL HEALTH
Independent Variables:	Processes:	Independent Variables:
1. Characteristics of ethnic group in which individual develops.	Enculturation	a. Adaptational and coping capabilities of the ethnic group. b. Cultural values, ethnic role behaviors, and customs.
2. Characteristics of of other groups with which the individual is in contact.	Acculturation	a. Values and attitudes toward other groups. b. Cultural values and social role behaviors. c. Willingness to share resources.
3. Characteristics of the interactions of the groups in contact.	Acculturation	a. Racism, discrimination. b. Adjustment of ethnic group to dominant culture. c. Powerlessness.
Dependent Variables:		Dependent Variables:
Psychological qualities of individuals developing within ethnic group.		Psychological qualities of mental health of individuals developing within ethnic group.

ences, but who has not been enculturated within an ethnic group that has strong ethnic and family ties, may be susceptible to acculturation stresses and show maladaptive psychological qualities.

This conceptualization of minority mental health emphasizes the relevance of ethnic as well as dominant group characteristics. For example, members of the Mexican-American ethnic group are socialized to be cooperative and to place family and group values above individual ones (Knight, Bernal & Carlo, in press). Members of the Anglo-American group are socialized to be competitive and to place emphasis on individuality and self-reliance. The core of the subject matter of minority mental health lies in the interaction of these two groups, with their respective values and characteristics, and with their relative access to power and resources.

This conceptualization of minority mental health also broadens the focus of mental health issues from sole emphasis on the characteristics of the ethnic group to include characteristics of the two groups in relation to each other; the complex pattern of these relationships between groups; and the broader social, economic, and political context that converts attitudes and values into public policy. For example, causes of the high dropout rate among Hispanic-American youths shift from focus on factors of language, ethnic, and socioeconomic background of the youths, that is, characteristics of the Hispanic culture and its enculturation of group members, to the social, political, and intergroup problems that lead to dropout.

Emphasis on the social, political, and intergroups factors that have potential impact on the mental health of ethnic minorities also raises issues concerning the socialization of the professional identity of ethnic minority trainees that result from training experiences. Several writers (e.g., Watts, 1987; White, Parham & Parham, 1980) have emphasized the need to train ethnic minority psychologists in terms of frameworks and perspectives that are required for social change. Watts (1987) has delineated some variables of the construct that he calls a sociopolitical social identity that is desirable in trainees: values regarding the relevance of culture as a guiding value in one's life and work; a theoretical perspective that incorporates contextual theories of human behavior; the view of psychology as having a major role in social change; and career goals that include service and research with ethnic minorities. Research on the relationship between the presence of resources such as ethnic minority faculty and curriculum content in training programs, and the sociopolitical professional identity of black American trainees, has suggested that the presence of such resources is insufficient for the establishment and integration of a sociopolitical identity in trainees (Watts, 1987). Training programs also have to include sociopolitical and other contextually oriented coursework and experiences if trainees are to become socialized as social change agents.

Implications for training. The goals of minority mental health training would be the goals of teaching students about ethnic psychology, and its minority mental health specialty. These goals could be implemented in courses, applied work, and research training. The first two (of the four) goals of training would be to teach students to systematically examine, at both a group and individual level, relationships between: the enculturation of ethnic groups and its impact on psychological qualities of mental health of the ethnic groups; and the acculturation of ethnic groups to the host society, including the characteristics of both groups in relation to each other and their interactions, and dependent variables that reflect the mental health of ethnic groups. The third goal would be to develop interventions for building interactions between ethnic and dominant groups that lead to enhancement of the mental health of both groups. The fourth goal would be to work for social change toward a multiculturally pluralistic society that values and fosters ethnic group differences, provides equal access to societal resources, and eliminates the minority or castelike status (as defined earlier) of ethnic groups.

These goals have social validity but need to be implemented broadly, at various points, levels, and contexts, so that trainees can directly experience them during their training. In the microcosm of training settings, what could trainees learn about intergroup relations and how to improve them? Given some creativity and ingenuity, it seems possible to discover many ways in which to implement these goals. For example, the presence of ethnic minority group faculty and students in training settings would allow the examination of the values and characteristics of members of both ethnic minority and dominant groups and of the interactions between the groups. The purpose of this examination would be to assess, identify, and put into effect changes needed to build a multicultural pluralistic training environment.

The training setting could be used as a field laboratory in which to teach both assessment and intervention skills for building a pluralistic society. Intergroup relations in other parts of the training setting such as clinical or research practica (e.g., schools, hospitals) also could be assessed and analyzed in terms of their potential for creating and maintaining conflict or harmony. Conflicts arising between members of the ethnic minority and members of the dominant culture could be examined with the view that conflicts may be embedded in differences in group characteristics, intergroup process, and acculturation, rather than in personal likes or dislikes. Such examination could be fruitful both as a learning experience and as a means of maintaining intergroup harmony and scholarly productivity.

One of this writer's graduate students (Cota, M. K., personal communication, October, 1988) has offered an example of how the goal of teaching about ethnic psychology and minority mental health has been implemented in her experience. This graduate student is a member of an ethnic identity research team headed by G. P. Knight and M. E. Bernal. She pointed out that, in studying the development and socialization of ethnic identity in ethnic minority children, members of this team have developed an understanding of the complexity and powerful effects of both enculturation and acculturation processes and of their interactive effects on ethnic identity and socialization. It is likely that the opportunity to conduct research on issues of direct relevance to ethnic minorities heightens the salience of ethnic psychology and its key constructs.

Some essential questions concerning the service and research training of psychologists follow from the delineation of minority mental health as a specialty of ethnic psychology. For example, in training psychogists for service, what characteristics of ethnic and dominant group members would be important to emphasize? What aspects of intergroup contact and conflict are relevant to the provision of culturally sensitive services? Adaptation of individual members of ethnic minority groups to the dominant society, the process known as acculturation, would require extended treatment in both coursework and practica. For both the clinician and behavioral scientist, it is relevant to study how individual ethnic minority group members adapt to the majority culture, beginning in early childhood when they enter the society's school systems, and continuing throughout the developmental life span. Along the way, ethnic minorities have to learn to adapt to monoculturally structured schools and other systems that may devalue them. They have to cope with the ethnic identity conflicts that such devaluation produces, in addition to coping with competition for mates, job skills, employment, salaries, and so on. What kinds of individual interventions would strengthen existing ethnic group capabilities for adaptation? What kinds of systemic interventions would change group and institutional practices that impact negatively on people, and promote healthy adaptations to the life-cycle experiences of education, prepare for employment and adult life, parenting? What kind of training results in the development of a sociopolitical professional identity in trainees?

Methodological skills and a strong theoretical base for scientific work whose content has been outlined above are important components of training. Equally important is the presence of faculty who are sufficiently knowledgeable to conduct such research and guide student research, and who have access to community settings in which to conduct the research.

CONCLUSIONS

Examination of the ethnic minority population from 1970 to 1986 and its projected future increases as a standard against which to compare ethnic minority representation in psychology reveals an increasing discrepancy between the current and projected availability of ethnic minority psychologists and the mental health requirements of the rapidly growing ethnic minority population. There are strong and compelling needs for increasing the numbers of both ethnic minority and dominant culture psychologists who are prepared for research and service with this population.

Increasing attention has recently been paid to both of these needs. Programs already exist that serve as models of training for work with ethnic minorities. Programs also exist that have successfully recruited ethnic minority students into graduate study. However, there are few resources for minority mental health curriculum development, and conceptual frameworks for guiding this development are needed.

A conceptual framework that reflects essential features, but not distinctive intra-group characteristics of ethnic minority groups, has been presented. Because this framework does not deal with specific aspects of ethnic groups, such as their unique history of oppression, or cultural characteristics, it can be generalized across those groups. This framework is based on the study of ethnic psychology and its subarea, minority mental health. In this framework, attention is drawn to two major processes that influence the psychological qualities of ethnic minority individuals, enculturation and acculturation, and their relationship to minority mental health. For ethnic minorities, acculturation to the dominant society is an important lifelong adaptation and its nature and course are determined by the characteristics of the dominant society and the nature of interactions between dominant and ethnic minority groups. Fundamental definitions and assumptions about training for work with ethnic minorities are examined, and basic questions and issues are raised about target population as well as trainee characteristics.

It is concluded that psychology's training programs need to develop a level of expertise and depth of knowledge with regard to ethnic minority people and training for work with them that is comparable to its expertise and knowledge about the white middle-class population which it has long sought to understand and serve. Some recommendations for implementation of the conceptual framework for training were made.

RECOMMENDATIONS

Sharp increases in federal, state, and local funds for recruitment, retention, and support of ethnic minority graduate students in psychology are needed, along with various efforts to draw ethnic minority undergraduates into psychology. The training of ethnic minority behavioral scientists capable of conducting clinical and health sciences research and of training other psychologists to conduct this research is absolutely essential in order that advances can occur in the development of innovative minority mental health interventions. Psychology departments and internship programs need to establish avenues and incentives for faculty development, so as to increase the knowledge base of their faculty for minority mental health training. Again, funds for such faculty development are needed.

The fact is, however, that funds for faculty career development are scarce. One source is the National Institute of Mental Health, which has recently initiated an Individual Faculty Scholar Award program that is designed to develop a cadre of academically based teacher/clinicians who are expert in the treatment of major mental health disorders. Applications from ethnic minority faculty are especially encouraged; however, the scholar's training must be in one of the following four priority areas: schizophrenic disorders, mood disorders, severe mental disorders of children and adolescents, and the major mental disorders of the aging. While this program may be a suitable source of training funds for some faculty, the emphasis on the four priority areas limits its appropriateness for others.

Closely related to the ethnic minority human resources need is the method and content of the training of ethnic minority and nonminority psychologists for service and research with ethnic minority populations. Model training programs for this purpose now exist, and it is important that knowledge gained by those who run these programs be disseminated widely within psychology. Workshops, symposia, invited addresses, and paper presentations at meetings and conferences act as vehicles for dissemination, as do journal articles, special journal issues on ethnic minority training, books, and information in APA and ethnic minority association newsletters. Efforts to increase the role of these vehicles in dissemination to both minority and nonminority psychologists should be made.

More effective methods for bringing about the integration of cultural diversity in the curriculum of psychology training programs need to be found. For example, APA accreditation procedures for fulfilling cultural diversity training criteria in the student and faculty representation of programs, as well as in their curricula and practica, need to be strengthened. The presence of ethnic minority psychologists on all site visit teams and the setting of firm and strong standards for change within reviewed programs are two special recommendations.

However, site visitors do not necessarily bring about change; that change needs to come via support from within programs and institutions. Many faculty with a sincere desire to promote cultural diversity within their training programs have tried to do so without having the needed support from colleagues and administrators. This writer recommends that, before embarking on the promotion of a program to promote cultural diversity, the person making this attempt conduct a realistic analysis of the training setting and its surrounding institutional structure to determine what support exists for change. Essential ingredients for such change within training programs are the unequivocal support and direction of the people who administer or direct the training program itself, and of those in power within the larger institutional context in which the program is embedded. Somewhere within the administrative structure surrounding the program there must be support and investment in cultural diversity. Alternately, there may be a core group of faculty who are committed to cultural diversity who can persuade key administrative figures to promote its values. In this case, someone with power and leverage must be persuaded to use it to support those who espouse cultural diversity. Such support can be useful for bringing about increased efforts and activities within training programs that will lead to ethnic minority curriculum changes and increased ethnic minority representation. Some useful mechanisms include incentive structures such as course release time or leaves of absence for promoting faculty career development for both teaching and research purposes.

Careful thought needs to be given the conceptual and theoretical framework within which minority mental health training programs are conceived and developed. Logical development of curricula, including courses, practica, and other training experiences consistent with major needs of ethnic minority groups to be served, is important. Information about the ethnic and minority characteristics and mental health needs of target client populations should be gathered as a basis for building training programs. Linkages between academic and internship training are needed.

The focus of minority mental health issues should be broadened from a sole emphasis on characteristics of ethnic minority groups or on their enculturation to emphasis on the characteristics of both minority and dominant culture groups and the ways in which they interact with each other. The acculturation of ethnic minority individuals and groups to the dominant society, viewed as an interaction between the groups, has powerful mental health implications, and stands out as a process that requires examination and consideration as a central topic in minority mental health training.

Efforts to increase ethnic minority presence in psychology are essential, both in terms of numbers of psychologists and in terms of the theoretical and empirical bases of psychology. The changing demographics of the nation and the world, as well as issues related to the tradition of discrimination, require positive steps to increase the access and contribution of ethnic minority groups to psychology.

REFERENCES

Abad, V., Ramos, J. & Boyce, E. (1974). A model for delivery of mental health services to Spanish-speaking minorities. *American Journal of Orthopsychiatry*, *44*, 584–595.

American Psychological Association. (1982). *Survey of graduate departments of psychology*. Washington, DC: Author.

Bernal, G., Bernal, M. E., Martinez, A. C., Olmedo, E. L. & Santisteban, D. (1982). Hispanic mental curriculum for psychology. In J. Chunn (Ed.), *Mental health curricula and people of color: Strategy and change in the four disciplines* (pp. 65–94). Washington, DC: Howard University Press.

Bernal, M. E. & Padilla, A. M. (1982). Survey of minority curricula and training in clinical psychology. *American Psychologist*, *37*, 780–787.

Berry, J. W. (1984, August). *Cultural psychology and ethnic psychology: A comparative analysis*. Presidential address presented at the 7th International Conference of the International Association of Cross-Cultural Psychology, Acapulco, Mexico.

Boneau, C. A. & Cuca, J. M. (1974). An overview of psychology's human resources: Characteristics and salaries from the 1972 APA Survey. *American Psychologist*, *29*, 821–840.

Boring, E. G. (1950). *A history of experimental psychology* (2nd ed.). New York: Appleton-Century-Crofts, Inc.

Chavez, E. L. & Deffenbacher, J. L. (1986). Training grant application to the National Institute of Mental Health.

Chunn, J. C. II, Dunston, P. J. & Ross-Sheriff, F. (1983). *Mental health and people of color: Curricula development and change*. Washington, DC: Howard University Press.

Cuellar, I., Harris, L. & Naron, N. (1981). Evaluation of a bilingual bicultural treatment program for Mexican-American psychiatric inpatients. In A. Baron (Ed.), *Explorations in Chicano psychology* (pp. 165–186). New York: Praeger Publishers.

Dunston, P. J. (1983). Culturally sensitive and effective psychologists: A challenge for the 1980s. *Journal of Community Psychology*, *11*, 376–382.

Howard, A., Pion, G. M., Gottfredson, G. D., Flattau, P. E., Oskamp, S., Pfafflin,

S. M., Bray, D. W. & Burstein, A. G. (1986). The changing face of American psychology: A report from the Committee on Employment and Human Resources. *American Psychologist, 41,* 1311–1327.

Jones, E. E. & Korchin, S. J. (1982). *Minority mental health.* New York: Praeger Publishers.

Jones, R. L. (Ed.). (1980). *Black psychology* (2nd ed.). New York: Harper & Row Publishers.

Kagehiro, D. K., Mejia, J. A., & Garcia, J. E. (1985). Value of cultural pluralism to the generalizability of psychological theories: A reexamination. *Professional psychology: Research and practice, 16,* 481–494.

Knight, G. P., Bernal, M. E. & Carlo, G. (in press). *Socialization and the development of cooperative, competitive, and individualistic behaviors among Mexican-American children.* In E. Garcia & A. Barona (Eds.), *The Mexican-American child: Language, cognition, and social development.* Tucson: University of Arizona Press.

Korchin, S. J. (1980). Clinical psychology and minority problems. *American Psychologist, 35,* 262–269.

Lorion, R. (1988, June). *Minority mental health predoctoral training models: The University of Maryland.* Paper presented at the National Conference on Clinical Training in Psychology: Improving training and psychological services for ethnic minorities, Los Angeles.

Myers, H. (1987, August). *Minority mental health training at UCLA: Achievements and future projections.* Paper presented in Symposium: Issues in Federal funding of minority training in psychology: What can be done? at the meetings of the American Psychological Association, New York City.

Ogbu, J. (1983). *Crossing cultural boundaries: A comparative perspective in minority education.* Paper presented in Symposium: Race, class, socialization, and the life cycle, in honor of Allison Davis, John Dewey Professor Emeritus, University of Chicago.

Pion, G. M., Bramblett, J. P., Jr. & Wicherski, M. (1987). *Graduate Departments of Psychology, 1986–87: Report of the annual APA/COGDOP Department survey.* Washington, DC: American Psychological Association, Office of Demographic, Employment, and Educational Research.

Pion, G., Bramblett, P., Wicherski, M. & Stapp, J. (1985). *Summary report of the 1984–85 Survey of Graduate Departments of Psychology.* Washington, DC: American Psychological Association.

Porche-Burke, L. (1988, June). *California School of Professional Psychology, Los Angeles Campus Ethnic Minority Mental Health Track.* Paper presented at the National Conference on Clinical Training in Psychology: Improving Training and Psychological Services for Ethnic Minorities, Los Angeles.

President's Commission on Mental Health. (1978). Report of the Task Panel on Special Populations: Minorities, women, physically handicapped. *Task Panel Reports* (Vol. 3). Washington, DC: U.S. Government Printing Office.

"Resolutions approved by the National Conference on Graduate Education in Psychology." (1987). *American Psychologist, 42,* 1070–1085.

Ridley, C. P. (1985). Imperatives for ethnic and cultural relevance in psychology training programs. *Professional Psychology: Research and Practice, 16,* 611–622.

Rosenfield, S. & Esquivel, G. B. (1985). Educating school psychologists to work with bilingual/bicultural populations. *Professional Psychology: Research and Practice, 16*, 199–208.

Russo, N. F., Olmedo, E. L., Stapp, J. & Fulcher, R. (1981). Women and minorities in psychology. *American Psychologist, 36*, 1316–1363.

Scott, J. & Delgado, M. (1979). Planning mental health programs for Hispanic communities. *Social Casework, 60*, 451–455.

Stang, D. & Peele, D. (1977). The status of minorities in psychology. In E. L. Olmedo & S. Lopez (Eds.), *Hispanic mental health professionals.* Los Angeles: Spanish Speaking Mental Health Research Center, University of California, Los Angeles, Monograph No. 5.

Stapp, J., Tucker, A. M. & VandenBos, G. R. (1985). Census of psychological personnel: 1983. *American Psychologist, 40*, 1317–1351.

Suber, C. (1977, January). Minority graduate enrollments—looking up or peaking out. *APA Monitor, 8*, 16.

Sue, D. W. (1981). *Counseling the culturally different: Theory and practice.* New York: John Wiley & Sons.

U.S. Bureau of the Census. (1986). *Current population reports,* Series P-25, No. 995, Projections of the Hispanic population: 1983 to 2080. Washington, DC: U.S. Government Printing office.

U.S. Bureau of the Census. (1981). *1980 census population total for racial and Spanish origin groups in the U.S..* Washington, DC: Author.

Vasquez, C. I. (1986). Progress summary report, Clinical psychology internship, Puerto Rican Hispanic emphasis, 9/3/85-1/20/86, submitted to the National Institute of Mental Health, Grant No. MH18292-02.

Watts, R. J. (1987). Development of professional identity in black clinical psychology students. *Professional Psychology: Research and Practice, 18*, 28–35.

White, J., Parham, T. & Parham, W. (1980). Black psychology: The Afro-American tradition as a unifying force for traditional psychology. In R. Jones (Ed.), *Black psychology* (2nd ed., pp 56–66). New York: Harper & Row Publishers.

Wyatt, G. E. & Parham, W. D. (1985). The inclusion of culturally sensitive course materials in graduate school and training programs. *Psychotherapy: Theory, Research, and Practice, 22*, 461–468.

11

Ethnic Minority Mental Health: Contributions and Future Directions of the American Psychological Association

Lillian Comas-Diaz

Concern about the mental health of ethnic minorities and the education and training of ethnic minorities has recently been prominent in the American Psychological Association (APA). This chapter presents the APA's contributions to ethnic minority mental health, articulating the benefits of organized efforts in exerting an impact on a professional organization. More specifically, the chapter discusses: (1) a strategy whereby ethnic minority mental health can be advanced through influencing an organized professional association; (2) a chronological account documenting the APA's responses and initiatives to ethnic minority concerns, (3) the need, although impressive strides have been made, for the APA to maintain a greater focus in the area of ethnic minority issues, and (4) specific recommendations and ideas for future APA directions in the area of ethnic minority mental health.

HISTORICAL BACKGROUND

The American Psychological Association is a professional organization created with a three-pronged mission—to promote psychology as a science, to promote psychology as a profession, and to promote human welfare. From its founding in 1892, the APA has grown from being a learned society of thirty-one academics to a national organization for academic, applied, and other psychologists, with a membership of more than 95,000. The APA bylaws indicate that its general goal is:

advancing psychology as a science and profession and as a means of promoting human welfare by the encouragement of psychology in all its branches in the broadest and most liberal manner . . . thereby to advance scientific interests and inquiry, and the application of research findings to the promotion of the public welfare. (APA, 1987a, p. 1)

Recognition of ethnic minority issues fits into the association's general goal. There is little doubt that concerns about ethnic minority issues promote human welfare. Moreover, these issues are relevant to substantive and pervasive aspects of psychology as a science and a profession.

The APA, recognizing the importance of the area, has responded to claims for representation and support from ethnic minority psychologists through the establishment of several internal structures. The effectiveness of a focused structural effort is evident in the progress APA has made regarding ethnic minority concerns. A chronological overview of the APA's major contributions to ethnic minority issues is necessary in order to place its responses and initiatives in a framework that helps to identify future directions. The next section will provide the sociohistorical context for the ethnic minority issues in the APA. Table 11.1 presents a chronology of ethnic minority events in the APA.

Before the 1960s, the APA paid no systematic or sustained attention to ethnic minority issues. Consonant with the prevailing sociopolitical climate of the sixties, the APA Board of Directors established an Ad Hoc Committee on Equality of Opportunity in Psychology (CEOP) in 1963. The impetus for the development of the CEOP came from the Council of the Society for the Psychological Study of Social Issues (SPSSI), a division of the APA. SPSSI, in keeping with its long standing concern with equal opportunity for all psychologists, urged the APA to establish such a continuing committee with the association's staff support. Specifically, SPSSI (1963) recommended that CEOP have the major functions of developing procedures, facilities, and methods for: (1) insuring that the opportunities to be trained as a psychologist be available to all; (2) improving the training available to groups who have inadequate training facilities; and (3) extending the employment opportunities of psychologists to groups that have been discriminated against.

After receiving SPSSI's recommendations, the APA Board established the CEOP in order to explore the possible problems encountered in training and employment in psychology as a consequence of race (APA, 1963). CEOP was charged with the following functions:

1. To explore the question of equality of opportunity in employment of black psychologists in professional and academic positions.

2. To monitor the recruitment and selection of students for training in psychology.

Table 11.1

**A Historical Chronology of the American Psychological Association's (APA)
Ethnic Minority Events**

1963   Committee on Equality of Opportunity in Psychology

1969   The Commission on Accelerating Black Participation in Psychology

1970   Office of the Black Students' Psychological Association in APA

1973   Task Group on Professional Training and Minority Groups at the Vail
Conference

1974   Minority Fellowship Program

1978   Expanding the Roles of Culturally Diverse People in the Profession of
Psychology: The Dulles Conference

1979   Office of Ethnic Minority Affairs
Ad Hoc Committee on Ethnic Minority Affairs

1979   Ad Hoc Committee's recommendation to establish a permanent structure
within APA central governance system in the form of a Board of Ethnic
Minority Affairs (BEMA)

1980   Official Bylaws of BEMA approved by the APA Board of Directors, Council
of Representatives, and APA membership

1982   BEMA Task Force on Minority Education and Training

1984   BEMA Task Force on Communications with Minority Constituents

1984   Publication and Communication Board's Ad Hoc Committee on Increasing the
Representation of Underrepresented Groups in the Publication Process

1986   Establishment of the Society for the Psychological Study of Ethnic
Minority Issues (APA Division 45)

1987   BEMA/BSERP Task Force on the Status of Black Men and its Impact on
Families and Communities

1987   BEMA Task Force on the Delivery of Services to Ethnic Minority
Populations

1987   The National Conference on Graduate Education in Psychology
Resolutions on Cultural Diversity: How Do We Enhance Graduate Education
in a Multicultural World?

1988   Underrepresented Groups Project for the APA Journal of Educational
Psychology
Encourages the publication on research addressing issues salient to the
educational psychology of ethnic minority groups

3. To determine steps that may provide training and exchange opportunities for teachers and scholars in black colleges (APA, 1963).

After its inception CEOP expanded its charge and asked APA to endorse the following recommendations.

1. APA should encourage effective measures to acquaint undergraduates in black colleges with the career possibilities for blacks in psychology.
2. APA should adopt appropriate measures to increase the participation of black psychologists in the organization.
3. CEOP should obtain existing statistics for black psychologists and compare them with black populations, in order to ascertain the ratio of black psychologists to black individuals or the extent to which blacks were at a disadvantage in access to education in psychology.

The APA Board of Directors accepted the committee's expanded charge and recommended to the APA Council of Representatives (the governance body that establishes official APA policy) that the CEOP be made a continuing committee under the APA Education and Training Board. The APA Council of Representatives accepted the recommendation that CEOP be made a continuing committee reporting to council through the board of directors, rather than the Education and Training Board (APA, 1971). The committee was charged with the task of "formulating association policy as it affects equality of opportunity in psychology for all" (APA, 1971). Additionally, a specific charge of the committee was to undertake fact-finding studies that would ascertain the extent to which members of minority groups were at a disadvantage in access to psychology undergraduate or graduate education, in employment as psychologists, or in participation in the affairs of the association (APA, 1971).

APA's Response to the "Challenge to Change"

In the late 1960s, the Association of Black Psychologists (ABPsi) began raising issues of concern to black populations. During the 1968 APA Annual Meeting, Charles W. Thomas, representing ABPsi, presented to the Council a challenge regarding the APA's involvement in meeting the needs of black Americans (Blau, 1970). The black psychologists addressed APA in what has become known as the "challenge to change," challenging APA to change its focus in order to include the concerns of black populations. Moreover, R. L. Williams (1970), national chairman of the Association of Black Psychologists, addressed the APA Council stressing the following topics:

1. Statement on Testing—The Association of Black Psychologists supported black parents who opposed having their children tested with psychological tests that were used to mislabel black individuals.

2. Public Policy Statement—the Association of Black Psychologists decided to become active in the development of public policy strategies affecting black populations.

3. Sanctions against Psychology Departments—the Association of Black Psychologists affirmed that psychology departments have systematically excluded black students from their graduate programs.

The Black Students Psychological Association (BSPA) made a presentation at the 1969 annual meeting, articulating similar issues but emphasizing the needs of black students (Blau, 1970). The APA responded to this "challenge of change" by expressing its commitment to working with the BSPA and the Association of Black Psychologists in addressing such concerns (APA, 1970). Funds were allocated to BSPA to explore the implementation of their suggestions. According to Blau (1970) the Commission on Accelerating Black Participation in Psychology (CABPP) was established by APA as a response to the concerns presented by the Association of Black Psychologists and by the BSPA.

In a report published in the *American Psychologist,* Blau (1970), chairman of the CABPP, stated that the commission began its work by addressing barriers such as funding, communication, liaison, leadership, identity, and acceptance. One of its primary goals was the creation of an APA central office and a staff liaison for implementing the BSPA proposal. In 1970, APA opened an office for the Black Students Psychological Association in its headquarters building in Washington, D.C. Blau further stated that the work of the commission, which ended on July 1, 1970, represented the collaboration of the APA central staff office, the board of directors, and about 1,000 members of the association. Notwithstanding the APA's response to the "challenge to change," Blau further asserted that it was a preliminary response only. Moreover, he exhorted that the APA's small beginning made toward "recognizing injustice and inhumanity, rectifying these, and thus truly promoting human welfare, must be continued and made valid by the commitment and involvement of individual members of the Association" (p. 1103).

Historically, another avenue for instituting changes in the discipline of psychology has been national conferences. There have been six major national conferences in psychology. The Conference on Training in Clinical Psychology, held in Boulder, Colorado, in August 1949, was where the framework for most United States' training programs in clinical psychology was developed (Raimy, 1950). The Institute on Education and Training for Psychological Contributions to Mental Health, which took place in August 1955, at Stanford University, focused on mental illness and on the potential roles for psychologists as mental health professionals (Strother, 1956). The Miami Beach Conference on Graduate Education in Psychology, held in 1958, focused on graduate education and training in all fields of psychology (Roe, Gustad, Moore, Ross & Skodak, 1959). The fourth conference, held in Chicago, in 1965, was where the APA appraised psychology's growth over the last twenty years (Hoch, Ross & Winder, 1966). The National Conference on Levels and Patterns of

Professional Training in Psychology (or the Vail Conference), held in Vail, Colorado, in July 1973 (Korman, 1973), was the first national psychology conference at which ethnic minority issues achieved some prominence. Previously, little or no attention was given to ethnic minority concerns. Hence, it will be discussed later. The sixth conference, the National Conference on Graduate Education in Psychology, held at the University of Utah, Salt Lake City, in 1987, also had a significant impact upon ethnic minority issues. This conference will also be discussed in detail in a later section.

The National Conference on Levels and Patterns of
Professional Training in Psychology: The Vail Conference

In July 1973 when the Vail Conference was held, the land was fertile for change, mostly due to the sociopolitical climate of the era. According to Bickman (1987) the Vail Conference took place at a time when American society was immersed in a climate of social unrest resulting from the civil rights movement, the feminist movement, the gay rights movement, the Vietnam War, and the Watergate scandal. He indicated that the conference focused on sociopolitical issues, assessing psychology's responsibility to deal with social issues. Moreover, professional issues were replaced with concerns about the delivery of inexpensive mental health services to poorer and indigent populations. Ethnic minority concerns clearly fit this agenda.

Vail was the first national conference of psychologists to actively seek representation on its steering committee from previously disenfranchised groups. Obviously, having ethnic minority representation influenced the conference's format, content, and selection of specific participants. The absence of ethnic minority participants in previous conferences contributed to the absence of any recommendations specifically geared to the needs of ethnic minorities. The participation of representatives from ethnic minorities on the Vail Conference Steering Committee was further reflected in the establishment of a Task Group on Professional Training and Minority Groups (Korman, 1976).

The Vail Conference viewed as a basic ethical obligation the implementation of affirmative action programs and the identification, recruitment, admission, and graduation of ethnic minority group students. According to Korman (1973), the participants felt that it was important for all students to be prepared to function professionally in a pluralistic society. To this end, it was suggested that: (a) "training experience should occur in a multicultural context both within the university and in fieldwork settings; (b) the content of training must adequately prepare students for their eventual professional roles vis-à-vis a wide diversity of target groups; and (c) students must be helped to maintain a balance between acculturation into a professional and scholarly role, on the one hand, and retention of their group identity and cultural sensitivity, on the other" (Korman, 1973, p. 5).

Because of the dissatisfaction with the scope of the APA's previous response to the concerns of ethnic minorities, the Vail Conference adopted a resolution recommending the following: (1) that a Board of Ethnic Minority Affairs, composed of representatives of ethnic minority groups, be created in the APA and be responsible for examining policies regarding ethnic minority concerns; (2) that this board have prior review functions regarding other organizational units of the APA and that it advise the APA Board of Directors in the general area of ethnic minority affairs; and (3) that an Office of Ethnic Minority Affairs be created, with responsibility for monitoring and evaluating APA projects, programs, and policies, for developing and disseminating information related to minority concerns, and for initiating appropriate relationships with public and private agencies (Korman, 1973).

APA Minority Fellowship Program

The delivery of mental health services to ethnic minorities and the training of ethnic minority mental health professionals constitute an area of concern among several disciplines. In 1969, a group of black psychiatrists, headed by Chester Pierce and James Corner, held a decisive meeting, proposing among other things, that the National Institute of Mental Health (NIMH) develop a distinct organizational unit to promote the development of mental health programs for minority groups. In order to address the need for increasing the number of ethnic minority health professionals, NIMH established the Minority Fellowship Program (MFP) in five disciplines: psychiatry, psychology, social work, sociology, and psychiatric nursing (see chapter by Parron in this volume).

The APA further acknowledged the relevance of ethnic minority education and training by supporting the Minority Fellowship Program. Specifically, the APA, along with the other four professional associations, received a training grant from NIMH to provide fellowship stipends to ethnic minority students eligible for or attending graduate programs leading to the doctorate in psychology. Since 1974, MFP has sought to implement a cost-sharing arrangement with host institutions that includes: (1) payment of tuition; (2) aid in the systematic recruitment of trained, qualified ethnic minority students; (3) living maintenance stipend; and (4) an increase in available information about psychology as a profession to ethnic minority undergraduate students (Jones & Olmedo, 1983). Also since 1974, the program has received support services from the APA. Being administratively housed under the executive office of the association has several major advantages, including financial support and access to personnel resources, in addition to APA governance boards and committees (Taylor, 1977). After the 1987 central office reorganization (discussed in a later section) MFP was placed under the Public Interest Directorate.

The APA Minority Fellowship Program had received funding from the NIMH Center for Minority Group Mental Health Programs in order to provide financial assistance to ethnic minority individuals for up to three years of study. It was believed that these students would subsequently enter professional, research, and administrative areas that would allow them to plan, implement, and evaluate programs for the delivery of services to ethnic minorities. The premise is that ethnic minority persons trained as psychologists are more likely than nonethnic minority persons to pursue professional careers that include treatment of persons from ethnic minority and under-served backgrounds. However, Jones (1985) argues that the training of ethnic minority psychologists is a sociopolitical issue to which most training programs tend to respond in terms of affirmative action. He further states that since NIMH does not have direct control over the content of the training, the institute must assume that having more individuals with credentials will result in improved service delivery. This assumption is at the core of the current minority mental health training. Although MFP has been successful in increasing the number of ethnic minority service providers, the issue of the content and quality of minority mental health curricula remains unaddressed (see chapter by M. Bernal in this volume).

Expanding the Roles of Culturally Diverse People in the Profession of Psychology: The Dulles Conference

In 1977, Dalmas Taylor, then director of the APA's MFP, submitted a proposal to the NIMH Center for Minority Group Mental Health Programs for assistance in organizing a conference of ethnic minority psychologists. The result was a national Conference on Expanding the Roles of Culturally Diverse People in the Profession of Psychology, held at the Marriott Hotel at Dulles Airport in 1978. The Dulles Conference, as it has been renamed, was jointly supported by the NIMH Center for Minority Group Mental Health, the APA Board of Social and Ethical Responsibility, and the APA Board of Directors.

The major purpose of the conference was to "explore specific ways in which ethnic minority psychologists could become more widely involved in a meaningful and effective way in every aspect of the activities of the Association" (Dulles Conference Task Force, 1978, p. 2). A summary report of the conference was presented to the APA Board of Directors (Dulles Conference Task Force, 1978). Included in the summary report were specific proposals for the consideration of the Board as to how these concerns could be reflected in the governance system of APA, in other words, in the board/committee/task force structure. The APA boards, committees, and task forces constitute the governance structure with the major task of developing policy and programs through the Council of Representatives for the association.

Four primary mechanisms or strategies for wider inclusion of ethnic minority psychologists in the APA governance structure were considered: (1) the development of a division within APA; (2) the establishment of a Board/Office; (3) the establishment of a Task Force; and (4) the establishment of a Committee. The conference participants unanimously concluded that a board with a central office structure was the best starting place to implement the structural changes that would serve the common issues of all ethnic minority groups, as well as the specific concerns of individual groups. The participants discussed the prioritization of the strategies in terms of the financial commitment from the APA, the degree of access to central decision making and primary information sources, communication with constituents, and the degree of self-determination.

The Dulles Conference Task Forces' Report (1978) presented those areas where substantial agreement existed. These consisted of: a need for greater monitoring of and influence on APA activities with respect to psychological/educational testing of ethnic minority individuals; and APA accreditation criteria and procedures for psychology training programs, licensure and certification issues for ethnic minorities and individuals working with ethnic minority populations, plus ethnic minority issues in psychology curriculum development. The conference also underlined the need for expanded involvement of ethnic minority persons in the APA central office staff and in the Association's governance structures via boards, committees, and task forces. The Task Force Report stated that the conference participants thought that task forces and committees could be used by the proposed board to develop positions on specific issues, as well as to monitor activities that directly affect ethnic minority persons. It was further recognized that an APA division could be developed at a later time, as a larger structure in which the activities and efforts generated by the board would coalesce. The proposed division could also provide an avenue for the study of ethnic minority issues, thus validating the study of ethnic minority issues as a legitimate field within psychology.

STRUCTURAL CHANGES WITHIN THE APA

The Ad Hoc Committee on Minority Affairs and the Office of Ethnic Minority Affairs

The APA Board of Directors received the report and recommendations stemming from the Dulles Conference. They voted to transmit the Dulles Conference Task Force report (1978) to the APA Council and to recommend to Council the adoption of the recommendations. They also recommended the establishment of an Ad Hoc Committee on Minority Affairs as a prior step to the establishment of a board. A central office staff, with expertise on ethnic minority issues, was hired and assigned to work as a liaison to the Ad Hoc Committee on Minority Affairs. APA authorized the creation of an Office of Minority Affairs with the establishment of an Ad Hoc Committee on Ethnic Minority Affairs.

In January 1, 1979, the Office of Ethnic Minority Affairs was created with the support of appropriate central office staff. The office was charged with coordinating the effective implementation of the recommendations generated at the Dulles Conference. Later, the office's charge was expanded to include the following mission statement goals: (1) to cultivate and advance an increase in the scientific understanding of culture and ethnicity as they relate to psychology; (2) to strive to increase the quality and quantity of education and training opportunities in psychology for ethnic minority persons; (3) to promote the development of culturally sensitive models with the delivery of psychological services; (4) to advocate communication, liaison, and clearinghouse functions among psychologists; and (5) to provide staff support for the governance groups responding to ethnic minority constituents (APA, 1980).

The Ad Hoc Committee on Minority Affairs developed a report and presented it to the board of directors at their June 1979 meeting. This report acknowledged the APA's support of minority psychologists, but noted that "[the APA] has not provided the substantive structural and functional organizational focus necessary to fully address the needs and concerns of minority peoples" (APA Ad Hoc Committee on Minority Affairs, 1979, p. 2). Among the major issues of concern for ethnic minorities presented by the Ad Hoc Committee were: "(a) Psychological/educational testing of ethnic minority individuals; (b) APA accreditation criteria and procedures for psychology training programs; (c) ethnic minority curriculum issues in graduate and professional training; (d) licensure/certification issues; (e) publication/editorial activities of the APA; (f) appropriate representation of ethnic minority psychologists in APA governance structure including council, boards, committees, and central office; (g) legislation in which APA becomes involved; (h) court cases in which the APA becomes involved; and (i) business affairs of the association" (pp. 4–5).

BOARD OF ETHNIC MINORITY AFFAIRS

The Ad Hoc Committee on Minority Affairs recommended to the board of directors the establishment of a standing Board of Ethnic Minority Affairs (BEMA). Specifically, it recommended that an amendment be made to Article 10 of the APA Bylaws. At its meetings of August 31 and September 3, 1979, the Council of Representatives voted to submit the following bylaws amendments to membership for approval:

The Board of Ethnic Minority Affairs shall consist of eleven members of the Association, who shall serve for terms of not less than three years each. It shall have general concern for those aspects of psychology which concern ethnic minorities (American Indian/Alaska Native, Asian/Pacific American, Black and Hispanic). It shall have particular responsibility for the following: (a) Increasing scientific understanding of those aspects of psychology that pertain to culture and ethnicity; (b) increasing the quality and quantity of educational and training opportunities for ethnic minority persons in psychology; (c) promoting the development of culturally sensitive models for the delivery of psychological services; (d) advocating on behalf of ethnic minority psychologists with respect to the formulation of the policies of the Association; (e) maintaining satisfactory relations with other groups of ethnic minority psychologists; (f) maintaining appropriate communication involving ethnic minority affairs with the Association's membership as well as with ethnic minority psychologists and communities at large; (g) maintaining effective liaison with other boards and committees of the Association; and (h) serving as a clearinghouse for the collection and dissemination of information relevant to or pertaining to ethnic minority psychologists and students. It shall have the responsibility for the supervision and coordination of committees it may form or which are assigned to it. Members of the Board shall be selected to represent adequately ethnic minority communities in psychology as well as the range of interests characteristic of psychology in all its aspects. (Article 10, Section 13, APA Bylaws)

The Ad Hoc Committee received as information the outcome of the balloting on the Bylaws amendment proposed by council to the APA membership. It was noted that the amendment to Article 10, adding Section 13, received the necessary two-thirds vote for approval, thus establishing the Board of Ethnic Minority Affairs, known as BEMA (APA, 1980).

BEMA Task Force on Minority Education and Training and BEMA Committee on Ethnic Minority Human Resources Development

As indicated above, one of BEMA's charges pertains to ethnic minority education and training. In order to promote the development of culturally sensitive models for the delivery of psychological services, BEMA established a subcommittee on culturally sensitive materials. In 1982, this subcommittee conducted a survey of APA-identified psychology and counseling internships and graduate school programs to identify who was using training material for psychological services to American Indian/Native Americans, Asian-Americans/Pacific islanders, blacks, and Hispanics. The survey results indicated a very marginal inclusion of culturally sensitive training material, mostly offered at the internship level rather than during classroom training at the graduate level (Wyatt & Parham, 1985).

Along these lines, BEMA worked with MFP on a proposal to the board of directors concerning recommendations for addressing funding issues for ethnic minority training and possible future collaborations between the APA and MFP. The proposal focused on the establishment of a Task Force on Minority Education and Training to function under the aegis of BEMA. Upon presentation of the proposal, the board of directors voted to establish the task force to address the recommendations on education and training from BEMA and to prepare a strategy for dealing with the short-term and long-term implications of the national funding of minority education and training (APA, 1981).

Upon its inception in 1981, the Task Force on Minority Education and Training concerned itself with the incorporation of cultural diversity in the preparation of psychologists who teach, provide service, and conduct research with ethnic minority populations. Thus, it focused on the training of psychologists working with culturally diverse populations, with the underrepresentation of ethnic minority psychologists in the profession, and with the funding of education and training opportunities for minorities in psychology.

Given the magnitude of the task force's charge, BEMA explored the possibility of having the task force replaced by a continuing committee on ethnic minority education and training. Within the APA, the task forces have a short-term duration—they are formed to be specific and as their name suggests, to be task-oriented, achieving their goals within a limited period of time. On the other hand, the APA continuing committees are unrestricted by time.

In 1982, upon BEMA's recommendation, the APA Board voted to expand the charge of the Task Force on Minority Education and Training to include the development of a proposal for a Continuing Committee on Ethnic Minority Education and Training (APA, 1983).

The APA Board of Directors recommended that the new committee, the Committee on Ethnic Minority Human Resources Development (CEMHRD), responding through BEMA, be composed of three members appointed by BEMA, two members appointed by the APA Board of Education and Training, and one member appointed by the MFP. At its February 1985 meeting, the APA Council approved BEMA's proposal for the establishment of CEMHRD (APA, 1985).

The new committee initially identified two major areas of concerns: (1) recruitment and retention of ethnic minority students and faculty; and (2) development of ethnic minority education and training resources. Regarding the first area, MFP continues to work to increase the recruitment of ethnic minority students. However, MFP is able to reach only a few students. Moreover, for a variety of reasons, many ethnic minority graduate students do not complete a graduate psychology program.

Owing to my experience as the former Director of the APA Ethnic Minority Affairs Office and as the Associate Director of the MFP, I was privy to personal communication from ethnic minority students and faculty regarding this issue of noncompletion of a program. My observations indicate that among students, the retention problem seems to be related to variables such as financial constraints, perceived discrimination, and perceived irrelevance of the training programs to the interests of ethnic minority students, among others. According to the data reported in "The Changing Face of American Psychology" (Howard et al., 1986), although doctoral recipients from ethnic minorities doubled from 1975 to 1984, they still represent less than 9 percent of the doctorates awarded in psychology. Minorities remain an underrepresented group. As a response to this issue, CEMHRD is in the process of developing a position paper on recruitment and retention of ethnic minority students and faculty.

Regarding the committee's second area of concern, CEMHRD advocates training in cultural diversity as prerequisite to providing psychological services to ethnic minority populations. In order to accomplish this goal, the committee has presented to the association a position paper, urging that multicultural awareness be added to the criteria used to define the philosophy, goals and requirements, curricula, practica, and composition of training in psychology, just as scientific rigor and clinical expertise currently are used (CEMHRD,

1985). Additionally, the committee is compiling resource materials for use in the teaching of courses on ethnic minority issues. The committee analyzed the syllabi content resulting from a survey on ethnic minority content in graduate psychology curricula (see M. Bernal's chapter in this volume). CEMHRD is attempting to design a model syllabus for teaching ethnicity and culture at the psychology graduate level. This model will be made available through the APA Office of Ethnic Minority Affairs.

In 1986–1987 CEMHRD reorganized itself into four major areas. According to its 1987 Annual Report (Aponte, 1987), CEMHRD added to its two existing subcommittees the following ones: (1) accreditation criteria, procedures, and processes, where the subcommittee will focus on influencing the accreditation of APA psychology programs in order to be sensitive to ethnic minority issues, in addition to establishing the role of ethnic minorities in each of these accreditation components; and (2) ethnic minority data resources, with the task of identifying and compiling relevant data sources within and outside of the APA in order to address education and training needs of ethnic minorities.

BEMA Task Force on Communication with Minority Constituents

BEMA proposed the establishment of a task force that would carry out its mandate to maintain appropriate communication involving ethnic minority affairs with the association's membership as well as with ethnic minority psychologists and communities at large. Given the low ethnic minority representation in APA governance structures, the task force was also charged with facilitating appropriate representation of ethnic minority psychologists in the APA council, boards, committees, and central office.

The proposed task force would have the charge of fostering increased representation of minorities on council, the decision-making structure, by: (1) helping APA divisions/state psychological associations attract and recruit minority members (given that the divisions and state associations have council seats according to vote apportionments, ethnic minority members could be eligible for council seats as their organizations' representatives); (2) helping identify members within divisions/state associations through BEMA's expanding network; (3) helping interested divisions/state associations establish minority-oriented committees; and (4) helping to coordinate efforts of minority psychologists in divisions/state associations to become effectively involved in the governance of these groups (APA, 1983). In 1984, the board of directors approved funds for the establishment of the Task Force on Communication with Minority Constituents.

The task force developed a series of technical assistance packages for achieving its charge. For example, it developed a *Handbook for Increasing Ethnic Minority Participation in APA Divisions, State Psychological Associations, and the Council of Representatives* (APA Board of Ethnic Minority Affairs, 1986).

The number of divisional committees on ethnic minority affairs (CEMAS) increased from 11 in 1983 (Wyatt & Parham, 1985) to twenty-five at the end of my tenure as Director of the Office of Ethnic Minority Affairs in 1986. Similarly, in 1983 there were eleven state association CEMAS (Wyatt & Parham, 1985), while at the end of my tenure as director in 1986 they had increased to twenty-two. With the help of the Office of Ethnic Minority Affairs, the task force also coordinated the development of a coalition of state psychological association and divisional CEMAS. (During the 1988 APA convention, the Office of Ethnic Minority Affairs, in collaboration with the Divisional Office, cosponsored an APA divisions and state associations recruitment fair for ethnic minorities in order to increase ethnic minority membership.) Later on, the work of the task force also served as an impetus for the development of APA Division 45, the Society for the Psychological Study of Ethnic Minority Issues, which will be discussed in greater detail in a later section.

In its December 1987 Annual Report, John Moritsugu (1987), Task Force Chair, presented its accomplishments for the year.

1. Completion and distribution of APA minority recruitment brochures entitled: *APA: A Thrust toward Ethnic Diversity.*

2. Completion of a draft pamphlet on how minority members may be more involved in the APA entitled: *Involvement in APA: A Thrust toward Ethnic Diversity.*

3. Development of an informational packet on establishing Committees on Ethnic Minority Affairs with APA divisions or state associations.

4. Planning and implementation of a panel presentation at the 1987 APA convention: "What Can I Give, What Can I Get?"

5. Development of a mentor program for ethnic minority members.

6. Recommendations to BEMA to identify and to acknowledge ethnic minority APA fellows. The underlying principle of awarding fellows status is to acknowledge APA members who have "unusual and outstanding contributions or performance in the field of psychology" (APA Membership Committee, 1965).

7. Development of public education materials on ethnic minority issues in collaboration with the APA Public Affairs Office.

8. Completion of an Expert Checklist Form for Ethnic Minority Resources (this checklist form provides information regarding ethnic minority psychologists' expertise on areas such as teaching, practice, research, and expert witness).

9. Letters to ethnic minority APA fellows asking them to encourage ethnic minority fellow nominations.

10. Presentations to the State and Divisional Leadership Conferences on Ethnic Minority member recruitment and tracking.

Given the finite nature of task forces in the association, the APA Board reviewed the task force's achievements and decided that its major goals were accomplished. The Task Force on Communication with Minority Constituents was abolished in 1988.

BEMA/BSERP Task Force on Status of Black Men and Its Impact on Families and Communities

At its fall 1986 meeting the APA Board of Social and Ethical Responsibility for Psychology (BSERP) reviewed the activities of the jointly sponsored BEMA/ BSERP Subcommittee on Black Men, and decided that the issues were too large to be handled by a small and limited subcommittee. The subcommittee was initially appointed as a response to the concern engendered by the disproportionate high rate of incarceration, shorter life span due to illness, violence, and drug addiction that plague a large segment of the black male population (APA, 1987b). BSERP was particularly concerned about the lack of black men in psychology graduate programs. It was suggested that a joint BEMA/BSERP Task Force be funded to deal more effectively with the complex issues involved. BSERP and BEMA submitted a proposal to the APA Board of Directors for the establishment of the Task Force on the Status of Black Men and Its Impact on Families and Communities.

The task force was approved by the board at its June 1987 meeting (APA, 1987b). The task force charge outlines several reasons for its salience to the black community, the general public, and psychology. A specific charge is the development of a proposal to obtain funding for a panel of experts who would produce a document on the status of black men in current American society. The document will offer recommendations that will serve as initiatives for research, and inform practice and public policy. The establishment of the Task Force on Status of Black Men and Its Impact on Families and Communities represents another example of the APA's response to the black psychologists' "challenge to change."

BEMA Task Force on the Delivery of Services to Ethnic Minority Populations

In accordance with BEMA's charge of promoting the development of culturally sensitive models for the delivery of psychological services, the board submitted a proposal to the board of directors to fund the creation of a task force on the Delivery of Services to Ethnic Minority Populations. The task force was approved and funded by the Board of Directors (APA, 1987c) at their August 1987 meeting. It was established to address the critical needs for appropriate and adequate mental health service to ethnic minority communities, and to assist in the coordination of APA activities regarding services to ethnic minority populations (APA, 1987c). The work of this task force is considered to be highly relevant to the development of organizational policies affecting ethnic minority mental health. Specific activities of the task force include:

1. Identify special populations and problems within ethnic minority communities;

2. Develop community-specific guidelines for appropriate diagnosis, treatment and follow-up, in conjunction with existing facilities;

3. Review APA ethical guidelines of service providers to ethnic minority populations;

4. Develop models for interagency service agreements to avoid duplication of services and to ensure appropriate treatment for ethnic minority clients;

5. Develop definitions and guidelines for service providers to ethnic minority populations;

6. Identify and explore alternatives and preventive interventions for ethnic minority populations within existing facilities, including traditional healers, indigenous workers, media-based interventions;

7. Address issues of relevance to current service providers to ethnic minority populations (e.g., burnout, community liaison, funding);

8. Develop strategies for public education and information in regard to mental health service resources and mental health issues in general;

9. Develop a model for accrediting and monitoring professionals providing services and training in the area of ethnic minority mental health;

10. Encourage the dissemination of ethnic minority service-related research findings;

11. Develop and update a bibliography of research findings on ethnic minority mental health services;

12. Develop models for linkage between research data and actual services provided;

13. Assess governmental and private sector attitudes and actions affecting ethnic minority mental health provision;

14. Develop liaison with relevant APA governance groups (APA, 1987c).

Based on these specific activities, the task force plans to develop a manuscript offering guidelines for delivering culturally relevant psychological services to ethnic minority populations.

SOCIETY FOR THE PSYCHOLOGICAL STUDY OF ETHNIC MINORITY ISSUES (APA DIVISION 45)

The last Dulles Conference recommendation was realized in 1986 with the establishment of a new APA division, the Society for the Psychological Study of Ethnic Minority Issues (Division 45). The establishment of this division constitutes a significant developmental step in the history of ethnic minority issues at the APA. This accomplishment indicates that the issues and concerns of ethnic minorities achieved a formal place within the professional organization for psychologists. Thus, the establishment of Division 45 marks the beginning of the legitimization of the study of ethnic minority issues as a valid field within the discipline of psychology. The presence of the division facilitates the incorporation of ethnicity and culture into the criteria used to define the training parameters in psychology. Moreover, Division 45 could help to alleviate the problem of underrepresentation of ethnic minority psychologists in the APA decision-making structure by potentially increasing the ethnic minority presence in the APA Council. Furthermore, the division has the potential to attract more ethnic minorities to join the APA, increasing the ethnic minority constituency group, and hence, opening more opportunities for ethnic minority participation in the association's decision-making process.

According to the bylaws of Division 45, the purposes of the organization are:

1. To advance the contributions of psychology as a discipline in the understanding of ethnic minority issues through research, including the development of appropriate research paradigms;
2. to promote the education and training of psychologists in matters of ethnic minority concerns, including the special issues relevant to service delivery with ethnic minority populations;
3. to inform the general public of research, education and training, and service delivery issues, relevant to ethnic minority populations (APA, 1986, p. 1).

Among its initial priorities, Division 45 has identified as a divisional challenge the need to be active in public policy issues affecting ethnic minorities through political advocacy and research. As an illustration, the Division Executive Committee has supported two legislative bills. The first one was the Civil Liberties Act of 1987, aimed at providing redress and restitution to Japanese-Americans who were incarcerated during World War II on the sole basis of ethnicity (Notes from the Society for the Psychological Study of Ethnic Minority Issues, 1987). After the bill successfully passed in Congress, the Division 45 Executive Committee received letters of appreciation from congressional representatives. The second bill supported by the executive committee was legislation that would collect hate crime statistics through the Federal Government (Notes from the Society for the Psychological Study of Ethnic Minority Issues, 1987). This bill represents a response to the increased violence against ethnic minority groups such as Asians, blacks, and Hispanics, and against minority groups such as gays and lesbians. Clearly, Division 45 has begun to fill a void in APA, by providing a "home" for ethnic minority issues and concerns.

FUTURE DIRECTIONS

The Utah Conference: Implications for the Future

In June 1987, the APA sponsored the sixth National Conference on Graduate Education in Psychology. The conference was held at the University of Utah, Salt Lake City, in June 1987, and is therefore, known as the Utah Conference.

Its primary purpose was to review the state of graduate education in psychology and consider recommendations concerning its future. According to Bickman (1987), conference cochairperson, there were a variety of reasons for this national conference, among them a belief that the *zeitgeist* was right for a national conference in all areas of education in psychology. BEMA and other ethnic minority constituents provided input into the planning of the conference, and ethnic minority representation was achieved. Among other concerns, the reduction of ethnic minority representation in the scientific fields, as opposed to the practice fields, was felt to further isolate psychology from society. Thus, one of the conference issues selected by its steering committee for consideration at the conference was *Cultural diversity: How do we enhance graduate education in a multicultural world?* Two major identified areas within this issue included: (1) the nature of inquiry, curriculum design, and course content; and (2) the participation of underrepresented groups in the training enterprise as teachers and as learners (APA, 1987d).

The conference resolutions were published in the *American Psychologist* (APA, 1987d). Some resolutions prescribed specific mechanisms such as publications, faculty development activities, and expert consultants to help achieve the stated goals. Specific resolutions state that:

1. In addition to race and education, education and training programs need to consider diversities of all kinds, such as social class, religion, sexual preference, and so on.

2. The multicultural, multinational, multilingual nature of psychology requires emphasis in many formal courses and field experiences.

3. Departments and schools of psychology should develop an inventory of expert consultants in the relevant areas of diversity for use in curriculum development and student guidance.

4. Graduate departments, schools, and programs should engage in a self-study to develop and implement a curriculum for diversity.

5. Psychology students should be educated in appropriate multicultural diversity, focusing on issues relevant to students' specialization.

6. Graduate programs are encouraged to assist ethnic minorities and other underrepresented groups to obtain their doctoral degrees by developing innovative programs and by financially assisting them to complete their degrees.

7. The APA and departments and schools of psychology should encourage and support the exchange of students and faculty with different countries to promote curriculum development.

8. Individual faculty members should become actively involved in the processes of recruitment and retention of ethnic minorities.

9. Given the extraordinary pressures faced by ethnic-minority faculty members, departments and schools of psychology should develop opportunities and procedures to assist these faculty to satisfy the scholarly and professional criteria for promotion and tenure.

10. The APA should use its advocacy mechanisms to encourage federal, state, and private organizations to facilitate faculty development in areas of cultural diversity.

11. Graduate programs in psychology, in coordination with national, state, and local psychological organizations, should provide continuing education to assist practitioners to provide relevant services to culturally diverse groups.

12. Departments, schools, and programs should assess specific concerns and special needs of students and faculty and consider sensitivity to individual differences in values and life choices.

13. Departments, schools, and programs should increase availability of women faculty as role models.

These resolutions, if implemented and practiced, would facilitate the mainstreaming of ethnic minority issues into psychology. By enhancing graduate education in a multicultural world, the Utah Conference helps to validate and legitimize ethnic minority mental health. Teaching practitioners-in-training the importance of cultural diversity leads to enhancing their skills in delivering mental health services to ethnic minority populations. Likewise, teaching future academicians and researchers the relevance of cultural variables in scholastic pursuits, also enhances the body of knowledge of ethnic minority mental health and psychology in general. The Utah Conference is the second national conference (Vail was the first one) that had ethnic minority issues systematically incorporated into its planning and recommendations. The training of psychologists will reflect the impact of the conference's resolutions on cultural diversity.

Involving Ethnic Minorities in the Publication Process

Another area to which the APA has directed concerted effort and attention is the recommendation of the Ad Hoc Committee on Minority Affairs on increasing publication and editorial activities of ethnic minorities and ethnic minority issues within APA. In 1984 the APA Publication and Communication Board established an Ad Hoc Committee on Increasing the Representation of Underrepresented Groups in the Publication Process. Although the committee's work was completed in 1987, its efforts led to the establishment of the Underrepresented Groups Project (UGP) for the APA *Journal of Educational Psychology*. The UGP encourages the publication of research addressing issues salient to the educational psychology of underrepresented groups (American Indian/Native American, Asian-Americans/Pacific Islanders, blacks, and Hispanics), in addition to developing a mentoring process designed to foster the publication of research on ethnic minority issues (APA, 1987e). Thus, the main responsibility of the newly created position of associate editor, is to foster and facilitate the publication and editorial activities of underrepresented groups in the publication process. The associate editor, who is an ethnic minority person, functions in a mentoring and developmental capacity, and is aided by an advisory group composed of members of underrepresented groups. Although clearly this is a step in the right direction, and one that should be accepted by other APA journals, a more permanent structure is needed to serve as a publication outlet for ethnicity and culture as variables in psychology. Division 45 is currently exploring the development of a divisional journal for the dissemination of psychological knowledge concerning ethnic minorities (Society for the Psychological Study of Ethnic Minority Issues, 1988).

Structural Changes in the APA

It should be noted that the American Psychological Association is in a state of transition. Major structural changes have become imperative. According to the 1987 APA president, Bonnie Strickland (1988), "the rapid growth of the organization and the emergence of psychology as an independent health profession demand an organizational structure for APA that would better serve the diverse interests reflected by the association's membership" (p. 1). Furthermore, the governance structure is cumbersome; forty-five divisions, fifty-three state and provincial associations and over eighty boards and committees develop policies through the Council of Representatives. As an illustration of structural change, in 1987 the APA central office was reorganized into three directorates that correspond to each aspect of the APA's three-pronged mission—to promote psychology as a science and as a profession, and to promote human welfare. These directorates are: Science Directorate, Practice Directorate, and Public Interest Directorate. Figure 11.1 presents the APA's organization chart after the 1987 central office reorganization. The Office of Ethnic Minority Affairs in addition to the Offices of Policy and Advocacy, Ethics, Social and Ethical Responsibility, and Women's Programs were placed under the Public Interest Directory. Figure 11.2 outlines the Public Interest Directory's organizational chart.

The 1988 APA reorganization plan, accepted for membership vote during the February Council of Representatives meeting, stipulated that the association be divided into five semiautonomous societies: science/applied, practice, science/practice, public interest, and state. APA members have the option of joining the societies according to their professional interest (APA, 1988a). Under this plan, the APA would have a smaller legislative body with less policy-making power than the current council and a more corporate board of directors (APA, 1988b).

The implications of the reorganization plan for ethnic minorities were discussed by both opponents and proponents of the plan. Opponents stated that since some boards and committees will be abolished, BEMA among them, many of the gains made by ethnic minorities through BEMA will have to be fought for again (Mays, 1988). On the other hand, ethnic minority supporters of the plan asserted that ethnic minorities will have (1) a key role in forming the Public Interest Society; (2) a stronger voice for ethnic minority issues; (3)

Figure 11.1
Organizational Chart of the American Psychological Association, July 15, 1987

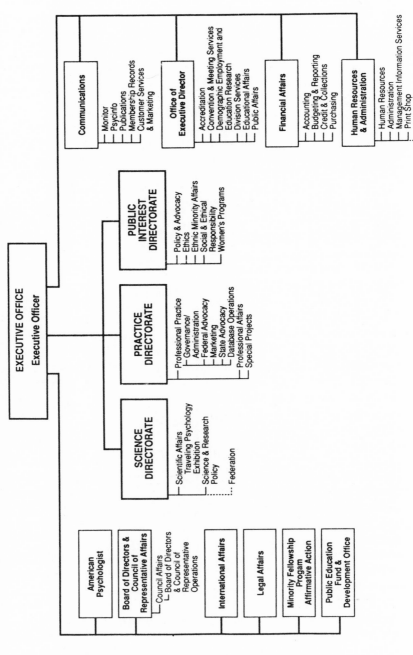

Figure 11.2
Organizational Chart of the Public Interest Directorate, American Psychological Association, July 15, 1987

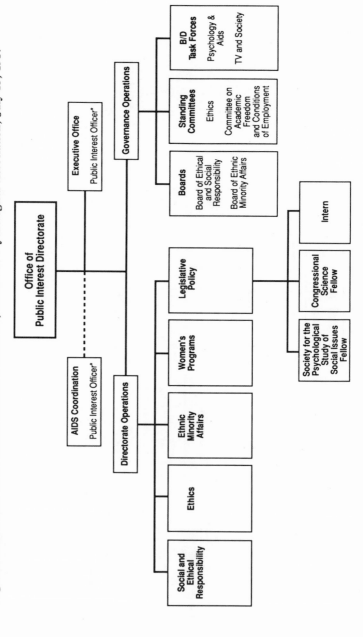

an organized way to influence overall APA policy; and (4) a diversity that will be preserved and enhanced through a bill of rights for members (Reid, 1988).

In July 1988, the membership's vote failed to ratify the 1988 reorganization plan. With the defeat of APA reorganization, the Assembly for Scientific and Applied Psychology (a non-APA psychological organization) voted to become the American Psychological Society (APS). APS is an independent national psychological organization committed to maintaining the scientific base of psychology by: (1) advancing the discipline of psychology; (2) preserving the scientific base of psychology; (3) promoting public understanding of psychological science and its applications; and (4) encouraging the "giving away" of psychology in the public interest (APS, 1988). APS is still in its inception, carving its own niche. It is unclear how the APA will be affected by the formation of this new national psychological association. It is also unclear what the relationship between APS and APA will be. Both of these national psychological organizations are negotiating their mutual relationship. However, what is clear is that the APA still needs to reorganize itself in a different form and/or shape in order to accommodate the growing tensions between practitioners and scientists. Whatever organizational structure ultimately evolves, the future directions and recommendations discussed in this chapter will still be relevant. It is hoped that the association's commitment to cultural pluralism will remain steadfast and the APA will continue to promote ethnic minority mental health. Further, efforts must be undertaken to insure that the APS will also address ethnic minority issues.

CONCLUSIONS

An analysis of the historical chronology of ethnic minority events within the APA reveals a significant expansion of activities in a relatively short period of time. Most of the structural recommendations made at the Dulles Conference have become realities with the establishment of the Office of Ethnic Minority Affairs, its Committee on Ethnic Minority Human Resources, the BEMA/BSERP Task Force on the Status of Black Men and Its Impact on Families, and BEMA Task Force on the Delivery of Services to Ethnic Minority Populations. The establishment of Division 45, the Society for the Psychological Study of Ethnic Minority Issues, appears to have crowned these efforts.

Ethnic minorities have made several gains in their attempts for representation and participation in the APA's affairs. Notwithstanding these accomplishments, the scope and the level of participation of ethnic minorities in the affairs of the association have been limited. A need for a conceptual consideration and a permanent structural focus on ethnic minority issues has been identified by the APA's ethnic minority constituency (APA Ad Hoc Committee on Minority Affairs, 1979). The chronology of ethnic minority events in the APA tells us that it is important to learn "the rules of the game" and play them from the beginning. Although the APA perceives cultural diversity as an organizational value, it is still important to maintain a "watchdog" function for preserving cultural diversity within the APA.

RECOMMENDATIONS

The issue of validating the discipline of ethnic minority psychology or ethnic minority mental health as a bona fide area of expertise is barely at its inception (Comas-Diaz, 1988). While the establishment of MFP, the Office of Ethnic Minority Affairs, BEMA, CEMHRD, and Division 45 are clearly positive organizational changes, the issue of culturally relevant ethnic minority mental health and the enforcement of ethnic minority education and training still remains unaddressed.

Within this context, most of the Dulles Conference recommendations on substantive issues have not been fulfilled. For instance, minimal formal attention has been given to issues of the relationship between APA accreditation and ethnic minority mental health. As an illustration, the APA has revised its criteria for accrediting applied training programs and in doing so, has given a stronger emphasis to cultural diversity. Criterion 2 of the Accreditation Guidelines advocates imparting knowledge of cultural and individual differences to the students, suggesting that this criterion should be reflected throughout the program, and specifically, should be found in skill training (Committee on Accreditation, 1986). However, programs could potentially comply with this criterion by recruiting ethnic minority students, or by offering a course in ethnic minority mental health, regardless of the program's effectiveness in improving students' skills in ethnic minority mental health. There is no formal requirement for demonstrating competence in this specialized area (Jones, 1985). Therefore, cultural diversity is not in itself a required criterion for APA accreditation. Although the APA supports in principle the cultural diversity accreditation criterion, currently it does not offer a mechanism to enforce such a criterion. Clearly, from an ethnic minority mental health perspective, this is an issue that the APA needs to re-evaluate. Although CEMHRD has created a subcommittee on accreditation, more ethnic minority presence and participation in APA could facilitate this process.

Another arena where ethnic minorities could influence the enforcement of ethnic minority training is by participating at their state psychological associations and APA division. On a divisional level, psychologists, and psychologists-in-training could increase their knowledge of how ethnicity and culture interface with specific areas of psychology. At the state level, committees on ethnic minority affairs (CEMAS) could help insure that state psychological associations attend to educational and training, as well as professional and research, issues. The CEMAS constitute an excellent way of sensitizing members to the relationship of topical areas to ethnic minority concerns.

Public policy requires more ethnic minority attention. Similar to the Division 45 strategy of influencing public policy through legislative issues, ethnic minority psychologists could exert an impact on public policy through the presentation of expert testimony. These expert testimonies could include the area of development of competence in ethnic minority mental health. An example of such a need is provided by Wyatt and Parham (1985). They report that the California State Assembly and Senate approved an assembly bill that would have required any person applying for licensure as a psychologist to complete training in ethnic minority mental health. However, the authors further stated that the governor vetoed the bill because of what he reported as the lack of a demonstration of a real public need for the training required by the bill. Political advocacy voicing ethnic minority concerns in legislative issues is needed in order to appropriately affect public policy.

Ethnic minority psychologists could also increase their overall participation in the APA by shaping the decisions that affect ethnic minority psychologists, consumers, and communities. Participation in organized psychology can facilitate psychologists' effectiveness in documenting the mental health needs of ethnic minorities and can facilitate responding to them with scientific research or service delivery programs sensitive to the unique characteristics of these communities. There are two levels that require major attention: the APA internal structure and state psychological national associations. Within the APA internal structure, more effort should be directed at making ethnicity and culture legitimate topics of psychological study. Within this context, the time is ripe for a second "Dulles Conference" focusing on *Expanding the Roles of Cutlurally Diverse People in the Science of Psychology.* The change in the initial title, substitution of the word *profession* by *science,* signifies that the study of ethnic minority issues goes beyond a public interest motivation: it helps to enrich the body of knowledge in the science as well as in the practice of psychology.

APA contributions to the field of ethnic minority mental health point to the benefits of organized efforts to exert an impact on a professional association. Although the process of involvement is at times arduous, the benefits clearly offset the potential shortcomings.

NOTE

The author gratefully acknowledges the contributions to this chapter made by Christine I. Hall. Thanks are also extended to Priscilla M. Trujillo.

REFERENCES

American Psychological Association (1963, December). Proceedings of the APA, *American Psychologist, 18*(12), 769.
———. (1970, May). *APA Board of Directors Meeting Minutes* (p. 6), Washington, DC: Author.
———. (1971, January). Proceedings of the APA, *American Psychologist, 26*(1), p. 30.

———. (1979, June 14). *Report of the Ad Hoc Committee on Minority Affairs.* Washington, DC: Author.

———. (1979, August 31 and September 3). *Council of Representatives Meeting Minutes.* Washington DC: Author.

———. (1980, May 17–18). *APA Committee on Ethnic Minority Affairs Meeting Minutes.* Washington, DC: Author.

———. (1981, November 5–6). *APA Board of Ethnic Minority Affairs Meeting Minutes.* Washington, DC: Author.

———. (1983, May 5–6). *APA Committee on Ethnic Minority Affairs Meeting Minutes.* Washington, DC: Author.

———. (1984, February). *Council of Representatives Meeting Minutes.* Washington, DC: Author.

———. (1986). *Society for the Psychological Study of Ethnic Minority Affairs Bylaws.* Washington, DC: Author.

———. (1987a). *Bylaws of the American Psychological Association* (As amended through August 1987). Washington, DC: Author.

———. (1987b, June). *Minutes of the June 28–30, 1987 Meeting of the APA Board of Directors.* Washington, DC: Author.

———. (1987c, August). *Minutes of the August 26-29, 1987 Meeting of the APA Board of Directors.* Washington, DC: Author.

———. (1987d). Resolutions approved by the national conference on graduate education in Psychology. *American Psychologist, 42*(12), 1070–1084.

———. (1987e). APA journal on underrepresented groups. *American Psychologist, 42*(12), 1135.

———. (1988a, February). *Minutes of the February 1988 Council of Representatives Meeting.* Washington, DC: Author.

———. (1988b, January). *A plan for the reorganization of the American Psychological Association.* Washington, DC: Author.

American Psychological Society. (1988). APS brochure. Department of Psychology, University of Nevada-Reno, Reno, Nevada: Author.

Aponte, J. (1987, December). *Annual Report Committee on Ethnic Minority Human Resources Development.* Washington. DC: American Psychological Association.

Bickman, L. (1987). Graduate education in psychology. *American Psychologist, 42*(12), 1041–1047.

Blau, T. H. (1970, December). APA Commission on Accelerating Black Participation in Psychology. *American Psychologist, 25*(12), 1103–1104.

Board of Ethnic Minority Affairs Task Force on Communication with Minority Constituents (1986). *Handbook for Increasing Ethnic Minority Participation in APA Divisions, State Psychological Associations, and the Council of Representatives.* Washington, DC: American Psychological Association.

Comas-Diaz, L. (1988). State of the Art. In L. Comas-Diaz & E. E. H. Griffith (Eds.). *Clinical guidelines in cross-cultural mental health.* New York: John Wiley & Sons, Publishers.

Committee on Accreditation (1986). *American Psychological Accreditation Manual.* Washington, DC: American Psychological Association.

Committee on Ethnic Minority Human Resources Development (1985). *Issues and concerns regarding the preparation of psychologists for service and research with ethnic minority populations.* Washington, DC. American Psychological Association.

Dulles Conference Task Force (1978). *Expanding the Roles of Culturally Diverse Peoples in the Profession of Psychology.* Washington, DC: American Psychological Association.

Hoch, E. L., Ross, A. O. & Winder, C. L. (Eds.) (1966). *Professional preparation of clinical psychologists.* Washington, DC: American Psychological Association.

Howard, A., Pion, G. M., Gottfredson, G. D., Oskamp, S., Pfafflin, S. M., Bray, D. W. & Burstein, A. G. (1986). The changing face of American psychology. *American Psychologist, 41,* 1311–1327.

Jones, J. (1985). The sociopolitical context of clinical training in psychology: The ethnic minority case. *Psychotherapy, 22(2) S,* 453–456.

Jones, J. & Olmedo, E. (1983). *Minority Fellowship Program Annual Report for 1982–83.* Washington, DC: American Psychological Association.

Korman, M. (1976). Levels and patterns of professional training in psychology. Washington, DC: American Psychological Association.

————. (Ed.) (1973, July 25–30). Levels and patterns of professional training in psychology. Conference Proceedings. Vail, Colorado.

Mays, V. (1988, Spring). *Psychology of Women Newsletter of Division 35, American Psychological Association, 15(2),* 8.

Moritsugu, J. (1987, December). *Annual Report Task Force on Communication with Minority Constituents.* Washington, DC: American Psychological Association.

Raimy, V. (Ed.) (1950). *Training in clinical psychology.* New York: Prentice Hall.

Reid, P. T. (1988, Spring). Ethnic Minorities and APA reorganization: What does it offer? *Psychology of Women Newsletter of Division 35, American Psychological Association, 15(2),* 8.

Roe, A., Gustad, J. W., Moore, B. V., Ross, S. & Skodak, M. (Eds.) (1959). *Graduate education in psychology.* Washington, DC: American Psychological Association.

Society for the Psychological Study of Ethnic Minority Issues (1987, Winter). *Notes from the Society for the Psychological Study of Ethnic Minority Issues, 1(2),* 6 & 10.

————. (1988, January). *Minutes of the January 1988 Meeting of Division 45 Executive Committee.* Washington, DC: American Psychological Association.

Society for the Psychological Study of Social Issues (SPSSI) (1963, November). *New APA Committee—The Committee on Equal Opportunity,* SPSSI Newsletter, p. 8.

Strickland, B. (1988, Spring). APA reorganization. *Psychology of Women Newsletter of Division 35, American Psychological Association, 15(2),* 1, 3.

Strother, C. R. (1956). *Psychology and mental health.* Washington, DC: American Psychological Association.

Taylor, D. (1977, Summer). *Ethnicity and bicultural considerations in Psychology: Meeting the needs of ethnic minorities.* Paper presented at the 1977 Meeting of the American Psychological Association, Washington, DC.

Williams, R. L. (1970). Report to the APA Council of Representatives. *American Psychologist, 25(5),* 27–28.

Wyatt, G. E. & Parham, W. D. (1985). The inclusion of culturally sensitive course materials in graduate school and training programs. *Psychotherapy, 22(2),* 461–468.

12

Federal Initiatives in Support of Mental Health Research on Ethnic Minorities

Delores L. Parron

The 1960s will always be remembered as a time of reckoning for our society. From the Supreme Court and Congress, to private universities and public schools, consciousness was awakened to the existence of persons whose chances in life had been compromised overtly and covertly by discrimination based on race or national origin. The slow process of desegregation had been opening one door at a time until 1968 when racial disturbances touched nearly every large city in the country, including Washington, D.C. In the attempt to understand why these kinds of events occurred in America many scholars finally recognized the destructive effects of prejudice and discrimination at the level of psychological functioning that had been heretofore ignored or denied (Clark, 1965; Grier & Cobbs, 1968; Willie, Kramer & Brown, 1973). Out of these analyses, racism emerged as "both a public health problem, which placed it within the purview of the largest public institutions in this country—government, health and education—and as a mental health problem, which confronts discrimination at its source—the personal and interpersonal beliefs and practices within the larger culture" (Williams, 1975). Questions such as: "Where do we go from here? How do we tackle this very knotty problem?" came with that recognition.

In this chapter, I will describe: (1) the process of building an active portfolio of research on U.S. racial/ethnic minority groups that has been supported by the National Institute of Mental Health (NIMH); (2) programs developed by the

Institute to ensure opportunities for minority students to pursue training for careers in mental health research; and (3) new initiatives promoting research on minorities and encouraging participation of minority investigators in the mental health research enterprise.

NIMH AND RESEARCH ON RACIAL/ETHNIC MINORITIES

In 1970, then Secretary of Health, Education, and Welfare Elliott Richardson announced the establishment of the Center for Minority Group Mental Health Programs within the National Institute of Mental Health (NIMH). The establishment of the NIMH Center is one of the benchmarks in the history of Federal initiatives directed toward minority populations. For the sake of accuracy in historical reporting, it must be pointed out that Secretary Richardson's action was not one that the Federal Government undertook on its own initiative. The Center was the result of two years of formal and informal negotiations between leaders of the Black Psychiatrists of America and the National Institute of Mental Health. Along with other Federal agencies, NIMH was forcefully criticized by black professionals for its failure to accelerate equal employment opportunities and for not including more blacks and other racial/ethnic minorities in decision-making roles (Ochberg & Brown, 1973). From its inception in 1971 until 1985 when it underwent a significant redirection of its program as part of the reorganization of all the NIMH, this Center served as a focal point for all activities within the Institute bearing directly on the mental health needs of minority groups, including programs of research, training, services, and demonstration projects.

NIMH Center for Minority Group Mental Health Programs

Three important accomplishments of the Minority Center should be recognized. First, for about ten years (1971–1981) the Center served the crucial functions of providing funding and an organizational home within the NIMH for studies on the mental health concerns of minorities. Studies on racism and its impact on the mental health of minority persons, the organization and functioning of racial/ethnic minority families, and coping strategies of minority individuals were encouraged and supported. The careers of many young minority investigators were launched and matured under the center's aegis. Second, recognizing the need for systematic efforts to construct reliable data bases on each of the major minority groups—blacks, Asian-American/Pacific Islanders, Hispanics, and American Indians—the Minority Center created the research and development centers program. This program evolved from a series of conferences supported by the NIMH Minority Center during the first two years (1971–1973) of its operation. These meetings provided opportunities for each of the major U.S. minority groups to identify their primary mental health needs and concerns in terms of research, research training, and service personnel development and to recommend mechanisms appropriate to address them. Based on these recommendations six minority research and development centers were established. Two centers focused on blacks (Fanon Research and Development Center at the Drew Post Graduate Medical School, Los Angeles; Institute for Urban Affairs and Research, Howard University, Washington, D.C.); two centers studied Hispanics (Spanish Speaking Mental Health Research and Development Center, University of California, Los Angeles; Hispanic Research and Development Center, Fordham University, New York); one focused on American Indians and Alaska natives (the White Cloud Research and Development Center, Oregon) and one studied Asian/Pacific Americans (the Asian/Pacific-American Mental Health Research and Development Center, University of Illinois, Chicago Circle).

The center approach to research on the special mental health/illness of minorities has proved to be a valuable resource. By supporting a critical mass of researchers in their particular location, these centers: promote collegial exchange and collaboration that can articulate the most promising areas of research on the mental health of the several minority groups; conceptualize research problems in a manner that will generate knowledge applicable to prevention, treatment, and mental health service delivery; adapt or create research methods appropriate for problems under study; provide opportunites for research training, and overall and most important, provide knowledge that will help minorities with their pressing mental health needs.

The third significant accomplishment of the NIMH Minority Center was the initiation in 1973 of the Minority Fellowship Program (MFP), a mechanism for resolving the underrepresentation of minority investigators and clinicians in the mental health field. Awards for administration of the program were made to five professional associations representing the major mental health disciplines: American Nurses' Association, American Psychiatric Association (for advanced clinical training only), American Psychological Association, American Sociological Association, and the Council on Social Work Education. The goal of research training programs at the NIMH is to help educate leaders of the nation's next generation of mental health researchers. In keeping with this goal, the specific purpose of the MFP is to ensure that minority investigators assume a prominent position among these researchers. Each of the associations has designed a program to support the development and training of individuals in doctoral level programs in their particular discipline to enable trainees to undertake active productive careers in scientific investigations related to mental health and mental illness. While it is expected that these future researchers will also become prominent within their professions at large, the MFP is not designed simply to support graduate study for its own sake. Rather, mastery of sound research skills, commitment to future research activity, and promise of future achievement in research endeavors is the desired outcome of successful fellowship training. From 1973 to 1985 the MFP has produced over 254 minority doctorates in the disciplines noted above. In 1987 a MFP in the neurosciences was created. This program is administered by the American Psychological Association and is expected to produce a cadre of minority investigators who will contribute to the rapidly expanding body of research on the brain and mental disorders.

Specialized research training for psychiatrists is especially important to ensure that skilled investigators are available for the future expansion of research on mental disorders and associated fields. The particular demands that are made of psychiatric researchers to become experts in medicine, clinical psychiatry, and scientific research require extensive training to such an extent that competing opportunities, such as entering private practice, become increasingly important as barriers to successful entry into research. These demands are even more serious for specialized areas, such as child psychiatry or geriatric psychiatry, where additional clinical training is usually required in addition to the general psychiatry residency. Such considerations as these have been especially important as barriers for promising minority psychiatrists to undertake research training. In 1989, the NIMH expects to initiate an MFP in psychiatry to assist minority psychiatrists in overcoming barriers and to support their research career development activities.

Moving Research on Ethnic Minorities into the Mainstream of NIMH Activities

During the peak years of its operation, the Minority Center funded virtually all research supported by NIMH of consequence to minorities. But as more well-trained minority investigators entered the field of mental health research and other investigators began to include minority persons in their study samples, other units of NIMH added what could be classified as "minority-relevant" studies to the array of projects they funded. By 1984, 85 percent of the minority-relevant studies were funded by units other than the Minority Center. The leadership of NIMH observed that the mainstreaming of minority research was being accomplished as a part of the naturally occurring process associated with a funding agency whose core activity is shaped by investigator-initiated projects. Since the reorganization of the NIMH in October, 1985, the responsibilities of all three research divisions—Clinical Research, Basic Sciences, and Biometry and Applied Sciences—now include funding research on minorities and research by minority investigators. The mainstreaming of minority research allowed for a refocusing of the activities of the Center for Studies of Minority Group Mental Health that is reflected in its new name—Minority Research Resources Branch.

The activities of the Minority Research Resources Branch concentrate on reducing the well-documented and longstanding shortage of minorities among researchers in the mental health field. Although minorities comprise approximately 19 percent of the U.S. population, blacks, Hispanics, and American Indians were awarded only 8 percent of all doctorates in 1987. More specifically, they received three percent of the doctorates in the biological sciences and 7.5 percent of those in the social sciences. By promoting opportunities for future minority investigators the NIMH research training programs for minority students are pivotal in enhancing the quality and quantity of scientific data regarding minorities. Involvement of minorities as researchers provides the important contribution to the scientific enterprise of perceptions and insights from the perspective of minority group membership that are often quite different from the perceptions of a member of the majority group viewing a minority. This involvement would have significant influence on not only the atmosphere in which research questions are formulated, but also on the conceptual, ethical, and methodological bases of research.

In addition to the Minority Fellowship Program described earlier, the Minority Research Resources Branch has assumed lead responsibility for both the Alcohol, Drug Abuse, and Mental Health Administration (ADAMHA); and the Minority Access to Research Careers (MARC) program; and manages the NIMH Minority Biomedical Research Support (MBRS) program. The MBRS is aimed at assisting institutions with substantial minority enrollment in developing and maintaining the capacity to carry out research. The MARC program is intended to assist institutions with substantial minority enrollment in preparing undergraduate students for graduate study in the alcohol, drug abuse, and mental health fields. MARC Faculty Fellowship awards support minority faculty for advanced training so that they may return to their home institutions to teach and conduct research, and to serve as role models for their students.

Funding for Ethnic Minority-Relevant Research

NIMH expenditures for research that addressed the concerns of minority populations to any degree show a steady increase since 1979 when systematic reporting was initiated. Table 12.1 demonstrates the pattern of growth. While all the five major U.S. ethnic/racial groups are being studied, the majority of studies have been on black Americans. As is generally the case with investigator-initiated research, the Institute's ability to increase its focus on minority populations depends in large part on NIMH's ability to stimulate high quality research proposals in these areas. It also depends on interest among both minority and nonminority investigators in conducting research targeted toward minority mental health concerns.

THE FUTURE OF ETHNIC MINORITY MENTAL HEALTH RESEARCH

Beginning in fiscal year 1986 NIMH selected several research areas as priorities. Selection of these priority areas was based on the scientific opportunities available in them or the need to substantially expand the knowledge base to deal with major problems related to them. These areas include: neurobiology and neurobehavioral sciences, to provide a knowledge base for a better under-

Table 12.1
NIMH Research Grants Relevant to Minorities, 1978–1987

Year	Number of Grants	Total Awards	% of All NIMH Human Subjects Awards
1978	47	$3.2 million	7
1979	142	15.3 million	16
1980	135	16.4 million	16
1981	109	14.0 million	15
1982	104	13.7 million	15
1983	125	17.3 million	22
1984	147	22.5 million	24
1985	144	21.7 million	20
1986	137	24.8 million	22
1987	170	34.0 million	24

standing of mental illness; schizophrenia, a severely debilitating disorder affecting about 2 million Americans; affective disorders, including depressive illness, which are present in 9.4 million Americans during a typical six-month period; Alzheimer's disease, a disorder of unknown cause that affects a small but significant percentage of people, most of them sixty-five or older; anxiety disorders, including phobias, panic attacks, posttraumatic stress, obsessive-compulsive disorder, and others; mental disorders of children, including autism, hyperactivity, and learning disabilities; eating disorders, including obesity, anorexia nervosa, and bulimia; neuropsychiatric and psychological aspects of acquired immune deficiency syndrome (AIDS); basic sciences, including cellular and molecular biology, neurochemistry, neurogenetics, and neurophysiology; research on the delivery of mental health services and special mental health issues involving suicidal youths, minorities, refugees, victims of emergencies and disasters, and the homeless.

To ensure that the needs of minorities are appropriately addressed in the research, knowledge transfer, and national leadership effort of the NIMH and other Institutes of the Alcohol, Drug Abuse, and Mental Health Administration (ADAMHA), the ADAMHA Minority Concerns Strategy was announced in November 1985. The strategy has been built around six goals to be incorporated into the ongoing activities of each of the three institutes that comprise ADAMHA:

1. *Research.* The agency will assure that minority needs are taken into account when it identifies research priorities and agenda. Where feasible and appropriate, given the

nature of the research and available subject populations, projects funded by the agency should be designed to: (a) include minorities in the research sample; and (b) include a plan to analyze the data collected in terms of the effects of conditions/interventions or other variables being studied on the minority groups sampled. As these projects are completed, grantees will be encouraged to publish and report data relevant to minority groups whenever possible. In addition, the agency will develop special research activities focused on minority needs and encourage participation of minority researchers. Special effort will be made to identify and select minorities to serve on agency research review panels and other advisory bodies.

2. *Epidemiology*. Data collection and analysis activities of the agency will include appropriate and adequate sampling of minorities to identify the relative incidence and severity of alcohol, drug, and mental health (ADM) conditions among minority populations. In addition, the dissemination of survey data and treatment analyses should include discussion of important ADM conditions and/or needs of particular relevance to minority populations.

3. *Demonstration Programs*. Demonstration activities undertaken by the agency should focus high priority on the special prevention, intervention, or treatment needs of high-risk minorities. Emphasis should be placed on the development of community initiatives in geographic areas with significant minority populations.

4. *Technical Assistance*. The agency should pay special attention to high-risk minorities in the provision of technical assistance resources to state and local, private, and for-profit service delivery systems.

5. *Knowledge Transfer and Dissemination*. ADAMHA will give high priority to knowledge transfer and dissemination activities that focus on minority needs. Specifically, efforts will be made to design and execute minority-focused publications, media campaigns, and other outreach activities.

6. *Training*. The agency will continue recruitment and training of minority ADM researchers, clinicians, and service providers. Special efforts will be made to attract minority researchers to intramural and extramural research activities of the agency. In this regard, the agency will include in its guidelines for administration of institutional awards provisions related to minority groups currently underrepresented in biomedical and behavioral research and in clinical specialty areas. These provisions will promote broader and more systematic efforts to recruit minority trainees within the context of our traditional commitment to scientific excellence and relevance to the missions of the respective Institute.

The strategy just described represents an open invitation to minority investigators to participate in the research support programs of the NIMH as well as the National Institute on Alcoholism and Alcohol Abuse (NIAAA) and the National Institute on Drug Abuse (NIDA). Even though the NIMH budget has enjoyed modest increases, as have NIAAA and NIDA, the competition for awards continues to be high. Rigorousness, defined in terms of the design of a project and the extent to which results can be quantified and replicated, has become a major criterion. While some believe that the greater emphasis on rigor rules out the likelihood of support for research that cannot be scanned, stained, or centrifuged, this standard of rigorousness, in fact, refers to the way scientists in any discipline frame and analyze questions. It does not relate to the nature or content of the question. Because one cannot predict precisely which disciplines will provide the answers to important questions in the mental health field, NIMH maintains interests across the spectrum of biological, psychological, and social research fields as well as in basic clinical and applied research domains (Frazier & Parron, 1987).

CONCLUSIONS

Over the last forty years, research supported by the NIMH has led to substantial increases in knowledge about the causes, treatment, and prevention of mental illnesses and the factors that help promote mental health of all Americans.

Currently, the NIMH is continuing its commitment to promoting research in those scientific fields that hold potential for moving further toward unraveling the complexities of the burden of illness posed by mental disorders and for identifying promising leads for promotion of mental health. NIMH recognizes that minority researchers are vital to this effort because they constitute a pool of talented scientists yet to be fully utilized in this effort. As we move toward the year 2000, NIMH is committed to mobilizing the best possible intellectual, technical, and moral resources over a wide range of knowledge and perspectives not only to sustain the fine tradition it has established but also to appropriately address the challenges still before us.

REFERENCES

Clark, K. (1965). *Dark Ghetto*. New York: Harper and Row.

Frazier, S. H. & Parron, D. L. (1987). The Federal mental health agenda. In L. J. Duhl, and N. A. Cummings, (Eds.), *The Future of Mental Health Services* (pp. 29–45). New York: Springer Publishing Company.

Grier, W. H. & Cobbs, P. M. (1968). *Black Rage*. New York: Basic Books.

Ochberg, F. & Brown, B. S. (1973). Key issues on developing a national minority mental health program at NIMH. In C. V. Willie, M. Kramer & B. S. Brown (Eds.), *Racism and Mental Health: Essays* (pp. 555–580). Pittsburgh: University of Pittsburgh Press.

Williams, B. S. (1975). Discrimination. In E. J. Lieberman (Ed.), *Mental Health: The Public Health Challenge* (pp. 208–211). Washington, DC.: American Public Health Association, 1975.

Willie, C. V., Kramer, M. & Brown, B. S. (Eds.), *Racism and Mental Health: Essays* (pp. 555–580). Pittsburgh: University of Pittsburgh Press.

Concluding Comments

Andrew I. Schwebel

One of my responsibilities at the conference, "Minority Mental Health: A Multicultural Knowledge Base for Psychological Service Providers," was to deliver closing remarks, building on the presentations and integrating ideas, particularly for the many student-members of the audience. The following pages are based on those closing comments.

TYING THE CHAPTERS TOGETHER

Borrowing a concept from the discipline of physics, I propose that this book, as a whole, offers lessons that go beyond the sum of each of the individual chapters. Let me illustrate this point by discussing several insights I had tying together material "across" the chapters in each section.

World Views, Piaget's Concept of Egocentric Thinking, and Minority Mental Health

Deborah L. Coates, Stephen S. Fugita, and Luis M. Laosa directed our attention to the world views held by members of ethnic minority groups in the United States. You come to see how your world view differs from that of ethnic minority children by reading Coates's account of the phenomenological world of black adolescents and Laosa's description of the sense of loss and abrupt social and cultural discontinuities faced by Hispanic children of documented and undocumented immigrant parents. And, from Fugita's chapter, you come to sense the range of differences in world views among the twenty-nine distinctive groups that fall under the category of Asian/Pacific-Americans.

The topic of world views brings to mind Jean Piaget's concept of "egocentric thinking," (1952; Santrock, 1986), a term he used as follows: "When you function egocentrically, you see the world from your perspective—through your unique lenses. And you assume that everybody else sees, experiences and understands the world in the same way as you do." To illustrate, if a client arrives thirty minutes late and you engage in egocentric thinking, you assume he is late for the same reasons that cause you to be late. But your conclusion might be incorrect, especially if your world view is Euro-American, placing an emphasis and value on time, and your client's is Afro-Centric, valuing what one is doing at the moment, rather than a schedule (Fine, Schwebel & Myers, 1985).

The obvious importance of mental health professionals understanding clients' world views needs no further development here. However, consider a different point, linking egocentric thinking, world views, and public relations aspects of Ethnic Minority Mental Health.

Take Mr. and Mrs. Doe, white voters who experience life through certain lenses and assume that blacks, Hispanics, Asian-Americans, and Native Americans wear the same prescription. Assume that the Does have little meaningful contact with members of ethnic minority groups and little understanding of the barriers and unique challenges faced by members of these groups. If we recognize that the Does have limited information, and if we get past our own egocentric thinking about what other people know, then we immediately see the need for certain action. Specifically, we recognize that part of the process of building support for the field of Ethnic Minority Mental Health involves educating the general public about the need for research in the area and for services guided by that research.

Assessment with Individuals from Ethnic Minorities: Looking beneath the Surface

Ernesto M. Bernal, Lloyd Bond, and Rebecca del Carmen focus attention on questions often taken for granted when making assessments of minority group members' abilities or functioning. Specifically, "what do we want to learn, exactly what do we learn, and what might we be able to learn under optimal testing cumstances?"

Bernal and Bond discuss widely used tests and ask, "What do the results tell us about individuals from certain ethnic minority groups?" Both offer constructive ideas about how psychological and educational testing might be modified in order to be more useful in the assessment of individuals from minority groups (e.g., using Spanish and English when testing a Hispanic child with limited proficiency in English). Both also suggest research ideas and starting points for the development of new types of assessment instruments.

To illustrate what I think is a key point in their chapters, allow me to step back to the 1960s and describe a study I conducted under the supervision of Jerome Kagan, then of the Fels Research Institute. Times were different then, so different that I recruited subjects by going to playgrounds and offering youngsters twenty-five cents to play "games" with me. And nobody called the police or questioned me, even though I worked from picnic benches in an inner-city neighborhood and in one that might well have housed Ozzie and Harriet (complete with fashionably attired housewives applying fresh coats of paint to their white picket fences).

That study of problem-solving behaviors and two others (Schwebel, 1966; Schwebel & Bernstein, 1970; Schwebel & Schwebel, 1974) suggested that children from minority groups, who tended to be cognitively impulsive (responding to questions before devoting sufficient time for thought), make needless errors and score at less than their ability on the school-like tasks. Specifically, subjects were tested on four WISC subtests and two Piaget-reasoning tasks under "free-latency" (they answered questions when they chose to) and under "forced-latency" conditions (they were prohibited from verbalizing answers until several seconds had passed and the experimenter signalled them to proceed). The children generally performed at higher levels—nearer to their true ability—under the latter condition, which was structured to make thinking time available.

Results such as these illustrate the differing kinds of information we can choose to gather in making assessments. Do we want to know how a child typically performs or what he or she is capable of? One tool that would help psychological and educational assessment specialists identify discrepancies between an individual's levels of performance and ability has been described by Feuerstein (1979). He developed "a dynamic approach" to testing, a method he uses to estimate a child's abilities after that child has been taught certain material. Instead of the standard "snapshot" approach to testing, Feuerstein's procedure involves three steps: testing to determine a child's level of functioning, teaching certain knowledge and skills to advance a child's understanding, and retesting to determine how much a child has learned from the tester's educational intervention. Tests such as Feuerstein's could have great value in assessing children from minority groups and identifying which intervention programs would be most likely to foster their fullest development.

Del Carmen alerts us to the fact that we must have a well-conceived plan if we are to effectively assess ethnic minority families. Besides the usual concerns about family structures and roles, communication patterns, and the needs and resources of individual family members, we must attend to a variety of other issues. For instance, in the homes of Asian-American immigrants, special attention must be paid to the impact of migration and discrimination on family

Santrock, J. (1986). *Life-span development.* Dubuque, IA: W. C. Brown.

Schwebel, A. I. (1966). Effects of impulsivity on performance of verbal tasks in middle- and lower-class children. *American Journal of Orthopsychiatry, 36,* 13–21.

Schwebel, A. I. & Bernstein, A. J. (1970). The effects of impulsivity on the performance of lower-class children in four WISC subtests. *American Journal of Orthopsychiatry, 40,* 629–636.

Schwebel, A. I. & Schwebel, C. R. (1974). The relationship between performance on Piagetian tasks and impulsive responding. *Journal of Research in Mathematical Education, 5,* 98–104.

Subject Index

Author Index

About the Editors and Contributors

EDITORS

FELICISIMA C. SERAFICA, Associate Professor in the departments of Psychology and Pediatrics at Ohio State University, received her Ph.D. degree from Clark University. Her specialty fields are clinical child psychology and developmental psychology. She is coauthor of *Psychodynamics in a Philippine Setting* and editor of *Social Development in Context*.

PAUL D. ISAAC, Associate Professor of Psychology and Associate Dean of the Graduate School at Ohio State University, received his Ph.D. degree from the University of Michigan. His specialty field is quantitative psychology. His recent articles deal with recruitment, admission, and retention of ethnic minorities in higher education.

LINDA B. MYERS, Associate Professor in the departments of Black Studies, Psychology, and Psychiatry at Ohio State University, received her Ph.D. degree from the same institution. A clinical psychologist, she is the author of *Moving from the sub-optimal to optimal: Case studies in living* and editor of *Toward an Afrocentric synthesis: Physical science, religion, and psychology*. Recent articles deal with stability in black families and physiological responses to oppression.

RICHARD K. RUSSELL, Associate Professor and current chair of the Affirmative Action Committee in the Department of Psychology at Ohio State University, received his Ph.D. degree from the University of Illinois at Urbana-Champaign. A counseling psychologist, he has edited books and published extensively on the topics of the treatment of anxiety and counseling supervision.

ANDREW I. SCHWEBEL, Professor of Psychology at Ohio State University, received his Ph.D. degree from Yale University. His specialty fields are clinical psychology and community psychology. He is coauthor of several books and monographs, the latest being *Personal Adjustment Text* and *A Guide to a Happier Family*. His research articles include a recent paper on the differing impact of divorce and single parenthood on blacks and whites.

CONTRIBUTORS

GUILLERMO A. ARGUETA-BERNAL, Associate Professor of Psychiatry at the Medical College of Ohio, received his Ph.D. degree from the University of South Carolina. A clinical psychologist, he has published on the topics of the application of biofeedback, behavioral approaches to the treatment of pain, and eating disorders in scientific journals published in the United States and abroad. He has also contributed chapters to several books.

ERNESTO M. BERNAL, Professor and Director of the Division of Research, the Center for Excellence in Education at Northern Arizona University, received his Ph.D. degree from the University of Texas at Austin. His specialty is Educational Psychology. He is the author of numerous articles and papers on psychoeducational assessment of bilingual children and evaluation of educational programs for bilingual/bicultural children, including the gifted.

MARTHA E. BERNAL, Professor of Psychology at Arizona State University, received her Ph.D. degree from Indiana University. A Diplomate of the American Board of Professional Psychology, she gained early prominence as a result of her research on behavioral management of problem behaviors in children. Recent publications dealing with the development of ethnic identity in Hispanic children and minority recruitment, curriculum, and training issues have appeared in scientific journals and books.

LLOYD BOND, Professor of Educational Research at the University of North Carolina, Greensboro, received his Ph.D. degree from Johns Hopkins University. His recent publications deal with admissions testing, effects of special preparation on measures of scholastic ability, and psychological test standards and clinical practice.

REBECCA DEL CARMEN, a postdoctoral fellow at the National Institute of Child Health and Human Development, received her Ph.D. degree from Ohio State University. At present, she is collaborating in a longitudinal study of maternal and infant predictors of attachment. Her most recent publication is a book chapter on mothers' prenatal stress.

LILLIAN COMAS-DIAZ, Executive Director of the Transcultural Mental Health Institute in Washington, D.C., and also Assistant Clinical Professor of Psychiatry and Behavioral Sciences at George Washington University School of Medicine, Washington, D.C., received her Ph.D. degree from the University of Massachusetts. A clinical psychologist, she has published in research journals, edited books on sex roles and treatment of psychological disorders in ethnic minority clients, particularly Hispanic women. She has also coedited two books, *Clinical guidelines in cross-cultural mental health* and *Delivering preventive health care services to Hispanics: A manual for providers.*

DEBORAH L. COATES, Associate Professor of Psychology at the Catholic University of America and Project Director of the Better Babies Project, Inc., in Washington, D.C., received her Ph.D. degree from Columbia University. Her specialty is Developmental Psychology. She has published extensively on social networks of black adolescents, effects of low birthweight on development, and early intervention.

STEPHEN S. FUGITA, formerly Associate Professor of Psychology at the University of Akron and now Acting Director at the Pacific/Asian American Mental Health Research Center, University of Illinois at Chicago, received his Ph.D. degree from the University of California at Riverside. A social psychologist, he is coauthor of two books, *The persistence of community: the Japanese in America* and *The Japanese American Experience.*

JANET E. HELMS, Associate Professor of Psychology at the University of Maryland, received her Ph.D. degree from Iowa State University. Her specialty field is counseling psychology. She has written extensively on racial identity and psychotherapy. Her latest book is *Black and White racial identity: Theory, research and practice.*

LUIS M. LAOSA, Senior Research Scientist at the Educational Testing Service, received his Ph.D. degree from the University of Texas. His specialty is Educational Psychology. He has published numerous research articles and book chapters dealing with the topics of: stress and coping in Hispanic children; family and school influences on human development, particularly of bilingual/bicultural children; performance of Hispanic children on measures of abilities; and the impact of social policy on child development, particularly of children from diverse ethnic, racial, and language groups. He has coedited books, including *Changing families* and *Families as learning environments for children.*

DELORES L. PARRON, Associate Director for Special Populations at the National Institute of Mental Health, received her Ph.D. degree from the Catholic University of America. A social worker by training, she is coeditor of *Health and behavior: Frontiers of research in the biobehavioral sciences.* Recent publications include articles and book chapters on psychological perspectives on health and on the mental health of ethnic minorities and low income groups.